"Israel has been characterized as a society with multiple self-definitions, many different frontiers and borders, and continuing controversies over recognition. Profs Ben-Porat and Turner cycle into these discussions a book that revolves around multiple facets of citizenship. It is a very useful collection of original papers that examine a dozen of the most interesting and complex aspects of Israel today. The book can serve as a fascinating introduction to Israeli society as well as a source of commentary and insight for those already familiar with the cultural complexities of this fascinating country."

Russell A. Stone, Professor Emeritus of Sociology,
American University in Washington, USA.

"Ben-Porat and Turner are offering in this pioneering book an insight into the conflicts embedded in Israel's struggles to define the political meaning of citizenship in a rifted society that is still in search for its collective identity. No future study of citizenship and Israeli society will be complete without a serious reading of this important volume of original scholarship. Highly recommended."

Gad Barzilai, Professor of International Studies,
Law and Political Science, University of Washington, USA.

The Contradictions of Israeli Citizenship

This book provides an integrated analysis of the complex nature of citizenship in Israel. Contributions from leading social and political theorists explore different aspects of citizenship through the demands and struggles of minority groups, to provide a comprehensive picture of the dynamics of Israeli citizenship and the dilemmas that emerge at the collective and individual levels.

Considering the many complex layers of membership in the state of Israel including gender, ethnicity and religion, the book identifies and explores processes of inclusion and exclusion that are general issues in any modern polity with a highly diverse civil society. While the focus is unambiguously on modern Israel, the interpretations of citizenship are relevant to many other modern societies that face similar contradictory tendencies in membership. As such, the book will be of great interest to students and scholars of political science, political sociology and law.

Guy Ben-Porat is Senior Lecturer at the Department of Public Policy and Administration, Ben-Gurion University. He has written widely on Israel and conflict resolution, and his research focuses on conflict resolution, ethnic relations, globalization, public policy and multiculturalism.

Bryan S. Turner is Presidential Professor in the Ph.D. Program in Sociology at the City University of New York's Graduate Center and Professor of Social and Political Thought at the University of Western Sydney, Australia. One of the world's leading sociologists of religion, he has also devoted significant attention to sociological theory, the study of human rights, and the sociology of the body.

Routledge Studies in Middle Eastern Politics

The Contradictions of Israeli Citizenship

Land, religion and state

Edited by Guy Ben-Porat and Bryan S. Turner

Routledge
Taylor & Francis Group

LONDON AND NEW YORK

First published 2011
by Routledge
2 Park Square, Milton Park, Abingdon, Oxon OX14 4RN

Simultaneously published in the USA and Canada
by Routledge
711 Third Avenue, New York, NY 10017

Routledge is an imprint of the Taylor & Francis Group, an informa business

British Library Cataloguing in Publication Data
A catalogue record for this book is available from the British Library

Library of Congress Cataloging in Publication Data
The contradictions of Israeli citizenship : land, religion, and state /
edited by Guy Ben-Porat and Bryan S. Turner.
    p. cm. – (Routledge studies in Middle Eastern politics ; 36)
    Includes bibliographical references and index.
    1. Citizenship–Israel. I. Ben-Porat, Guy. II. Turner, Bryan S.
JQ1830.A92C66 2011
    323.6095694–dc22   2010046460

ISBN 978-0-415-78250-0 (hbk)
ISBN 978-0-203-81718-6 (ebk)

Typeset in New Baskerville
by Pindar NZ, Auckland, NZ

Contents

Figures and tables

Figures

Tables

Contributors

Shmuel Noah Eisenstadt (1923–2010) died on September 2, 2010. Professor Eisenstadt had been appointed to teach at The Hebrew University of Jerusalem in 1959, where he was eventually an emeritus professor from 1990 until his death. His publications and research interests were wide and varied, ranging from the sociology of youth (*From Generation to Generation* [Free Press, 1956]), to the political sociology of empires (*The Political Systems of Empires* [Free Press, 1963]), and to modernization in Japan (*Japanese Civilization: a comparative view* [University of Chicago Press, 1996]). In recent years he became a leading figure in debates about different routes to modernity ("multiple modernities") and different civilizational complexes (developing Karl Jaspers's notion of axial civilizations). Having written his master's thesis under Martin Buber, Eisenstadt's work covered the entire range of the humanities and social sciences. He was the recipient of many prizes and awards (such as the McIver Prize 1964, the Israel Prize 1973, and the Amalfi Prize 2001). He was a member of the American Academy of Arts and Sciences and received an honorary degree from Harvard University. It is with a mixture of pride, pleasure, and sadness that we are able to include his chapter on Israeli society and citizenship in this edited volume.

Ofir Abu is a PhD candidate at the Department of Politics and a Schusterman scholar at the Schusterman Center for Israel Studies at Brandeis University. His dissertation explores the conditions under which ethnic conflicts turn violent, focusing on the Arab–Jewish conflict within Israel. His academic interests lie at the intersection of ethnic politics, collective action, and democracy.

Eyal Ben-Ari is professor of anthropology at The Hebrew University of Jerusalem. His previous publications include *Body Projects in Japanese Childcare: culture, organization and emotions in a preschool* (Curzon, 1997) and *Mastering Soldiers: conflict, emotions, and the enemy in an Israeli army unit* (Berghahn Books, 1998). More recently, he has coedited, with Edna Lomsky-Feder, *The Military and Militarism in Israeli Society* (SUNY Press, 2000), and, with

Timothy Tsu Yun Hui and Jan van Bremen, *Perspectives on Social Memory in Japan* (Global Oriental, 2005).

Guy Ben-Porat is a senior lecturer at the Department of Public Policy and Administration at Ben-Gurion University of the Negev. He is the author of *Global Liberalism, Local Populism: peace and conflict in Israel/Palestine and Northern Ireland* (Syracuse University Press, 2006) and coauthor, with Yagil Levy, of *Israel Since 1980* (Cambridge University Press, 2008).

Evgenia Bystrov is a PhD fellow at Bremen International Graduate School of Social Sciences (BIGSSS), Jacobs University Bremen, and a research associate at Reuven Chaikin Chair in Geostrategy, University of Haifa.

Hanna Herzog is a professor of Sociology and Anthropology, head of the Women and Gender Program at Tel Aviv University. She specializes in political sociology, ethnic relations, and sociology of gender. She is author of *Gendering Politics: women in Israel* (Ann Arbor University of Michigan Press, 1999), coauthor of *Sex, Gender, Politics: women in Israel* (1999), and, with Ann Braude, coeditor of *Gendering Religion and Politics: untangling modernities* (Palgrave Macmillan, 2009).

Amal Jamal is a member of the Political Science Department at Tel Aviv University and the general director of I'lam Media Center for Arab Palestinians in Israel. His research fields include political theory and communication, nationalism and democracy, civil society and social movements. Three of his recent books are *The Arab Public Sphere in Israel: media space and cultural resistance* (Indiana University Press, 2009), *The Palestinian National Movement: politics of contention, 1967–2005* (Indiana University Press, 2005), and *Media Politics and Democracy in Palestine: political culture, pluralism, and the Palestinian authority* (Sussex Academic Press, 2005).

Amit Kama is a senior lecturer at the Department of Communication, Academic College of Emek Yezreel. His research focuses on various minority groups (lesbigays, people with disabilities, and migrant workers) and the construction of their identities vis-à-vis media (re)presentations. He also studies mediated body images. His works include numerous papers and six books.

David Lehmann specializes in the study of Latin America and Israel and of religion and multiculturalism. As well as *Remaking Israeli Judaism: the challenge of Shas* (Oxford University Press, 2006), coauthored with Batia Siebzehner, his publications include *Struggle for the Spirit: religious transformation and popular culture in Brazil and Latin America* (Polity, 1996). He is reader in social science at Cambridge University and in 2009 held a fellowship at the Institute of Advanced Studies at The Hebrew University of Jerusalem.

Yagil Levy is associate professor in the Department of Sociology, Political Science and Communication at The Open University of Israel. His recent books include *Israel's Materialist Militarism* (Rowman & Littlefield/Lexington Books, 2007), *Israel Since 1980* (coauthored with Guy Ben-Porat; Cambridge University Press, 2008), and *Who Governs the Military? Between Control of the Military and Control of Militarism* [in Hebrew] (The Hebrew University Magnes Press, 2010;).

Edna Lomsky-Feder is a professor of sociology at The School of Education at The Hebrew University of Jerusalem. Her research interests include the sociology of education and nationalism, the study of war and the military in Israel from a cultural perspective, and the study of migration and identity. Her previous publications include *As If There was No War: life stories of Israeli men* [in Hebrew] (Magnes Press, 1998); *The Military and Militarism in Israeli Society*, coauthored with Eyal Ben-Ari (SUNY, 2000), and *Visibility in Immigration: body, gaze, representations*, coauthored with Tamar Rapoport (Van Leer Jerusalem Institute and Hakibbutz Hameuchad, 2010).

Yoav Peled is a professor of political science at Tel Aviv University and a lawyer. His latest book is a coedited collection of essays, *Democratic Citizenship and War* (Routledge, 2010).

Michael Philippov is a PhD candidate in the Department of Political Science at The Hebrew University in Jerusalem and researcher at The Israel Democracy Institute in Jerusalem.

Zeev Rosenhek is senior lecturer at the Department of Sociology, Political Science and Communication at The Open University of Israel. His fields of research are state–society relations, the political economy of the welfare state, labour migration, and institutional change. He has published numerous articles on these topics and is the coauthor, with Daniel Maman, of *The Israeli Central Bank: political economy, global logics and local actors* (Routledge, 2011).

Batia Siebzehner is a research fellow at the Truman Institute at the Hebrew University of Jerusalem and a Senior Lecturer at Beit Berl College. She is the author, with D. Lehmann of *Remaking Israeli Jadaism: The Challenge of Shas* (Oxford University Press, 2006), and of a book on the Latin American university in the Age of Enlightenment.

Nurit Stadler is senior lecturer in sociology and anthropology at The Hebrew University of Jerusalem. Her research interests include the sociology of religion, fundamentalism, the Orthodox communities in Israel, and the study of miracles and visions. She is the author of *Yeshiva Fundamentalism* (New York University Press, 2008) and of *Forms of Conversion in the Haredi*

Community in Israel (Hakibbutz Hameuchad and the Van Leer Jerusalam Institute, forthcoming).

Bryan S. Turner is the presidential professor of sociology in the Sociology PhD program at The City University of New York and the director of the Centre for the Study of Contemporary Muslim Societies at the University of Western Sydney. He was the founding editor of the journal *Citizenship Studies.* His recent publications include *Rights and Virtues: political essays on citizenship and social justice* (Bardwell, 2008) and *Vulnerability and Human Rights* (Pennsylvania State University Press, 2006). He edited *The New Blackwell Companion to the Sociology of Religion* (Wiley-Blackwell, 2010), *The Routledge International Handbook of Globalization Studies* (Routledge, 2009), and *The New Blackwell Companion to Social Theory* (Wiley-Blackwell, 2008). His current research is into legal pluralism and religious tribunals.

1 Introduction

Contemporary dilemmas of Israeli citizenship

Guy Ben-Porat and Bryan S. Turner

Citizenship is a legal status conferring privileges of membership in a particular political community and thereby creating processes of social inclusion and exclusion. Inclusion provides members with social status, social rights and the right to take part in collective decision making. As such, citizenship is often a contested ground for individual and group rights, and over the very definition of the political community. Social and political struggles over the boundaries of citizenship and the meaning of citizenship are central to contemporary Israeli politics. These diverse struggles – religious, national, gender, economic and ethnic – are, on the one hand, about equality, recognition and re-defining the collective and, on the other hand, about the practical needs of everyday life. This collected volume engages with contemporary questions about citizenship in Israel as they pertain to particular group demands and to the dynamics of political life in the public arena. Contributors to this volume examine different aspects of citizenship primarily through the needs, demands and struggles of minority groups. In general terms, they provide a comprehensive picture of the dynamics of Israeli citizenship and the dilemmas that emerge at the collective, group and individual levels.

Political struggles in Israel are defined fundamentally by an attempt to reconcile the two conflicting principles of a "Jewish and democratic state." This dual commitment requires a definition of the meaning of democracy and the meaning of a Jewish state – and the quest for some compromise between them. In the past two decades, demographic, social and economic changes have widened the disagreements and intensified the struggles over group rights, collective identity and state institutions. Citizenship has thus become the medium through which many struggles are conducted over the rights, duties and hierarchies of different social groups. In particular, the presence of an Arab minority challenges the overall definition of the Jewish state and questions its ability to be democratic, and furthermore it is evident that the new generation of Arabs is no longer willing to accept its marginal social and political position. At the same time, but for very different reasons, religious and secular Jews are also involved in a contest over the meaning of the Jewish state and the actual role of religion in the public sphere. Old arrangements and conventions no longer retain their authority over the political compromise between these competing groups. To these major fissures in the political fabric, other struggles defined by ethnicity, gender and class have been added; these divisions often intersect with a number of unanswered major political questions. These relatively old debates about membership and identity have been further complicated by mass immigration from the former Soviet Union and by the rapid globalization of Israeli economy and society. These additional ingredients add to the complexity of the debate about ethnicity and the Jewish character of the state and the essential meaning of citizenship and the rights and duties it entails. Citizenship in Israel in sum is a site of contention that illuminates a variety of contemporary struggles between social groups – struggles that in turn raise problems about the legitimacy of the state and its institutions. This volume engages with these questions about citizenship in Israel as they pertain to particular group demands and the dynamic of the political arena. The diverse perspectives which the authors bring to this volume provide a comprehensive account of the dilemmas of Israeli citizenship and explore the complex fabric of political life in terms of various ethnic, cultural and religious differences.

Comparative citizenship studies

Citizenship is essentially a modern concept – the product of revolutionary transformations of society such as the American War of Independence and the French Revolution (Isin and Turner, 2002). Israeli citizenship is a peculiar combination of late nineteenth-century developments in nationalism and Zionism and twentieth-century wars and settlement. Of course, the idea of citizenship was prominent in classical philosophy, for example in Aristotle's account of politics and the city, but the ancient world was a slave economy and participation in the polis was severely limited. We should therefore hesitate to regard Athens as the ancient foundation of participatory citizenship. Women, who constituted the majority of slaves, were excluded from participation in public life in the classical world, because they were thought to be incapable of rational thought and it is more accurate therefore to recognize the severe restrictions on citizenship in classical society than to celebrate the Greek city as the pure foundation of modern democratic politics. We might at the very best call this classical form *political* citizenship, arguing that the revolutionary struggles that produced modernity also produced modern or *social* citizenship. In its contemporary form, citizenship has three important characteristics: it is universalistic, it does not recognize or accept familial and kinship ties as valid conditions of authority and participation in the public arena, and it is closely connected with the rise of the modern state, and hence with effective taxation and military conscription. In addition, this social model is very different, we shall argue, from the individualistic tradition of American liberalism with its emphasis on the private sphere and its reluctance to support any centralized administration or state apparatus to provide collective welfare arrangements for its citizens. The analytical consequence of this model is to suggest that, without a dynamic and flourishing civil society and an affluent middle class, citizenship could not function as the framework of a modern democracy.

Citizenship has been defined as the "right to have rights" and these rights in turn depend on the existence of a political community (Arendt, 1976: 296–7). Thus, membership, rights and participation are three components that make up citizenship, as well as its duties and obligations. T. H. Marshall's classic theory of citizenship (Marshall, 1950) divided citizenship rights into three categories that evolved from the seventeenth century: a civil component for the achievement of individual freedoms, a political component of participation in the exercise of political power and a social component of welfare and security. Citizenship according to this trajectory is about equality based upon collective rights that are institutionalized around habeas corpus, jury system, parliamentary democracy, rule of law and so forth. According to Marshall, citizenship can be regarded as a status that is granted to those who are fully members of a community. Those who possess this status are formally equal with regard to the rights and duties of the community. Similarly, Turner (1986: 135) describes the "movement of citizenship ... from the particular to the universal, since particular definitions of persons for the purpose of exclusion appear increasingly irrational and incongruent with the basis of the modern polity."

Although the modern debate around citizenship in the social sciences starts with the work of the English sociologist Marshall, the limitations of his model are by now only too well understood (Turner, 2009). Marshall focused on class divisions in relation to the growth of social rights and hence ignored both religion and ethnicity as markers of identity. By contrast, much of the debate about modern citizenship has been around the problems of identity in societies that have been transformed by globalization. Obviously the Marshall framework will not work automatically or effectively as the most promising way of conceptualizing citizenship and social rights comparatively (Isin, Nyers, and Turner, 2009). Even as a model of western citizenship, it is confronted by serious conceptual problems. There are, for example, important differences between Britain and America in terms of the rise and nature of citizenship. For example, because the development of modern citizenship presupposes some radical change to society from migration, warfare or revolution, one might assume that the defining issue in American citizenship was the War of Independence and the signing of the Constitution. However, this way of looking at American society neglects the history of slavery and subsequent racial conflict.

To grapple with the American version of citizenship, Judith N. Shklar (1991) coined the phrase "liberalism of fear" (1998) to underscore the long history of racial inequality in America and the deep divisions between the North and South in the history of social rights. She regarded grinding poverty and inequality as key issues to be addressed by citizenship and in her influential *American Citizenship* (1991) she argued that the capacity to earn a living was fundamental to the sense of personal autonomy and responsibility. Earning a living, she argued, distinguished respectable, hard-working but independent citizens from both the landed aristocracy and the property-less slaves. Consequently, the American citizen was associated with an emerging middle class against both a decadent and declining land-owning aristocracy and an exhausted and exploited agrarian class of slaves. Her work has been regarded as the most decisive defense of liberalism in modern political philosophy not as a soft option – everything is permissible, everything is possible – but as a criticism of and defense against what she called "ordinary vices" – indifference, greed, resentment, cruelty and so forth. However, we would qualify this view of Shklar's definition of American citizenship by noting that it defines autonomy by reference to employment and the market, and hence her understanding of liberal citizenship was very different, for example, from the tradition represented by J. S. Mill. Our point here is not to launch into a debate about the character of liberalism, but simply to note that there are important variations within the western tradition.

In order to deal with the very different trajectories that have produced citizenship in the modern world, it is useful to develop a distinction between citizenship as fundamental to a welfare state, and citizenship as the necessary basis of a nation state. Social citizenship is made up of the social rights associated with welfare-state provisions – the right to health care, education, social security and so forth. By contrast, national citizenship involves political membership or a political identity associated with state building, the forging of a nation and typically the suppression of minority cultures and traditions. In the creation of national citizenship, states engaged in the modernization of the military, the development of a universal education system, the construction of a national religion and the imposition of general taxation to create a common national identity often in the face of an inherited social and cultural complexity that resisted national incorporation. Thus, minorities have to be incorporated into the political system, either through coercive integration or more systematic marginalization. Different languages, traditions and religions are characteristically degraded or excluded from the public domain by the state. Perhaps all forms of citizenship require some degree of exclusivity in terms of cultural traits, but national citizenship requires such exclusivity more definitely and, if necessary, violently than either the liberal or social versions of citizenship. State building often required recognition of a dominant religious tradition as defining the national identity or indeed the creation of such a dominant tradition. Two obvious examples are the historical role of the Roman Catholic Church in the Philippines and the place of Buddhism and the monarchy in Thailand. The alternative was to impose a policy of strict secularization in which a nationalist and republican ideology played the role of a civil religion. The classic example would be republican Turkey. While Japanese modernization after the Meiji restoration is probably the most obvious and successful Asian case of authoritarian state building, the creation of a developmental state in South Korea to forge a nation on the back of rapid urbanization and industrialization after the Korean War might be another example (Chang, 2007).We argue that Israel is also in this sense a developmental state with problematic borders, a civil society divided by ethnic and religious differences, and a dominant military stratum given its need for security. In short, Israeli citizenship is essential for state building and has a decidedly exclusionary character.

With regard to these nationalist issues, Michael Mann's account of citizenship with respect for example to the collapsing Austro-Hungarian Empire provides a convincing analysis of continental Europe (Mann 1986 and 1987). National citizenship may have more to do with creating exclusionary boundaries and identities than with building up the legitimacy of claims against the state. Outside continental Europe, the evolution of social citizenship in Britain in the 1950s was less relevant in creating a national identity and forging a nation out of a melting pot of migrant communities than with rebuilding the economy, with urban renewal and with the social issues that followed the social dislocation produced by mass mobilization and industrialized warfare. National citizenship typically requires the exclusion of minority communities, especially in post-imperial or post-colonial contexts, and in emergent nation states with problematic and uncertain borders. Liberal citizenship, as the name implies, involves granting legal and political entitlements rather than building a welfare system or defining a national identity. We might simplify the discussion of these different types of citizenship in the following. Liberalism celebrates individual rights, but says relatively little about corresponding duties and consequently places an emphasis on the private provision of welfare and services through individualized insurance. Social citizenship requires some balance between rights (to welfare) and duties (to the family and the state). These entitlements may be appropriately called "contributory rights." National citizenship has relatively little interest in individual rights and emphasizes duties to the state (especially military duties). These three forms of citizenship – liberal, social and national – are at least worth separating conceptually even where in many empirical cases the forms will become blurred.

These three manifestations of citizenship have at least one thing in common – they presuppose a connection between geographical territory and a political system or a relationship between territoriality and rights or more precisely a relationship between territory and a sovereign state. The relationship with national citizenship is obvious – national identity requires a boundary with recognizable borders that are policed by a nation state, especially where there are hostile or troublesome neighbors. Migrants who are merely denizens are clearly not citizens because the rights and duties of denizenship and citizenship are, at least historically, very different. Ownership of a passport is the hallmark of citizenship, permitting an individual to move in and out of a territory with the support of a state. Perhaps the connection of territory with liberal and social citizenship is less obvious, but both nevertheless define an exclusionary package of rights. In the case of social citizenship, the taxation of citizens within a given territory as the basis of social security claims provides the linkage between residence and rights. This connection between the modern state, sovereignty, territory and rights in many respects represents the core of Max Weber's political sociology in his definition of the territorial sovereignty of the nation state. The relationship of law and territorial sovereignty has become a difficult issue in post-colonial and multicultural societies where claims for separate legal authorities has made legal pluralism appear as one possible solution in dealing with customary or aboriginal claims. It is this relationship which also makes the case of Hong Kong – two systems, one society – unique in modern political history. However, politically divided societies – North and South Korea, East and West Germany, Cyprus and Palestine – are equally problematic and interesting from the point of view of citizenship studies.

One further issue in citizenship studies is the question of secularization; that is, the separation of church and state and the differentiation of the religious and the political spheres. After the Treaty of Westphalia which brought religious wars to an end in seventeenth century Europe, church and state were, in principle, separated and religion became a matter of private conscience. Religious freedom meant freedom as a private practice of religion and the public manifestations of religious practice were largely to be determined by the prince. Lutheranism probably represents the extreme case of such privatization of belief in which the inner sphere of the private individual was utterly separate from the external sphere of state violence. In this Westphalian model of political institutions, it was assumed that secularization was a necessary pre-condition of modernization. However, in recent times, this liberal solution involving a separation of spheres has broken down with the eruption in the 1980s of the Iranian Revolution, the Solidarity movement, the Sandinista revolution and the growth of the radical Christian right in the United States. Sociological attention has consequently shifted to the analysis of the role of religion in the public sphere and José Casanova's *Public Religions in the Modern World* (1994) was important in this evolving criticism of the conventional secularization thesis. His work was in many respects focused on Catholicism in Latin America and on Poland. For obvious reasons, the role of Orthodox Judaism as a "public religion" in Israel provides an equally important case study.

The final weakness in much of the literature on citizenship is that the theory has a strong, if implicit, teleological aspect. This may also be yet another legacy of Marshall for whom the basic rights of the citizen – civil, political and social – emerged in a teleological or evolutionary progression in British history. It is obviously the case that citizenship and social rights can be supported by the policies of the state, but they can equally be violently expunged by military dictatorships and we should therefore remove from our minds any ideal or utopian future where citizenship will be universally and comprehensively recognized by states as the foundation of a viable democracy. This extinction of rights was, to take one prominent example, a traumatic outcome of the dictatorship of the General Pinochet in Chile and in many Latin American societies the growth of what came to be known as "bureaucratic authoritarianism" was the consequence (O'Donnell, Schmitter and Whitehead, 1986). Given the contemporary drift of societies towards greater securitization, it may well be the case that erstwhile liberal democracies take on the hue of authoritarianism. These developments involving a greater emphasis on surveillance and security are likely to result in some degree of the erosion of citizenship (Turner, 2001).

Citizenship, Equality and Political Struggle

Citizenship is associated with privileges of membership in a particular political community and with processes of inclusion and exclusion. Inclusion provides members with status, social rights and the right to take part in collective decision making. As such, citizenship is often a contested ground for individual and group rights over the very definition of the political community. Social, political and culture transformations have placed citizenship at the forefront of the political agenda of many states and societies across the world (Isin and Wood, 1999: 7). Citizenship is not only legal and political membership in a state, but also a set of practices through which individuals and groups articulate their claims for rights (Isin and Wood, 1999: 4), sometimes against the state and its institutions and often in competition with other groups. Consequently, citizenship does not necessarily evolve in a uniform or gradual manner that encompasses all individuals and groups. Rather, different groups can often achieve different sets of rights, often unequally, with the result that citizenship becomes stratified and hierarchical (Shafir and Peled, 2002). While the Marshall model was not particularly sensitive to local traditions, the idea of citizenship has to be contextualized, because it differs significantly from state to state. Citizenship is consequently highly contested (Faulks, 2000: 6). These contestations over citizenship include conflicts around borders and boundaries of the political community, its inclusive and exclusive mechanisms, and the contests over citizenship in terms of the rights included and the demands placed upon citizens by society and state.

Cultural, ethnic and racial divisions within society have an important effect on the construction of citizenship and its practices and those in turn can reinforce existing social and cultural fragmentation (Crawford, 1998). Where existing hierarchies and divisions are challenged, citizenship becomes a site of negotiation, contest and contention where, on the one hand, duties and obligations are defined and, on the other hand, demands for rights and entitlements are presented. Negotiation involves the allocation of resources (and opportunities of political participation) based upon notions of common or imagined solidarity (Turner, 2001). Citizenship, therefore, often delineates a hierarchy between and within social groups in society and consequently structures the opportunities afforded by the state to different people who are included, excluded or marginalized by the very definition of citizenship. Some selective inclusions can be achieved as the state develops new practices of inclusion and co-opts groups that had been previously left out. But, exclusions can be re-inscribed when the state is challenged by internal conflicts or external pressures and chooses to forge social cohesion through the strategy of the exclusion of some group not central to that particular consensus (Marx, 2002). Marginal social groups can all too easily become the scapegoat of more general social and political problems – such as the gypsies of modern Europe.

Because citizenship is a set of processes for the allocation of entitlements, obligations and immunities, these rights and duties are typically acquired as a consequence of social and political struggles. These entitlements are in principle related to the contributions of the individual and the social group to society. Thus, demands for inclusion, or for the extension of entitlements, are often based on services to the state from which entitlements are expected. The relationship between the state and its citizens is characteristically defined by public service such as military service in which citizens are willing to sacrifice their lives (as soldiers) or by their financial contributions in which citizens are willing to sacrifice part of their income (as tax-payers). The simple fact of paying taxes without fraud or corruption is an important aspect of the exercise of citizenship in the everyday world (Steinmo, 1993). Thus, serving in the military and paying taxes are the characteristic "virtues" of the citizen (Turner, 2008). The defense of the territory on which the state exercises its sovereignty by bearing arms is perhaps the ultimate expression of citizenship. Consequently, demands for inclusion, or for the extension of entitlements, are often based on services to the state, bearing the costs of war and the preparations for it in return for civil, social and political rights granted to them by the state. Military service has been especially valued as a service to state and has been central to both state formation and the construction of the identity of the citizen (Burk, 1995; Tilly, 1997, 193–215). This connection between the citizen-warrior and empowerment has often served to underscore the hierarchical and patriarchal nature of citizenship, thereby marginalizing or wholly excluding women, ethnic minorities and the disabled, insofar as they are unable to, or prevented from, contributing to national defense. Conscientious objectors are typically targets of abuse and ridicule, both official and unofficial. By contrast, the war dead are respected through the building of public sites of mourning and the creation of national ceremonies to remember the dead. At the same time, this fact has also underscored the struggles to re-define citizenship and to challenge the hierarchies it entails.

Citizenship, and the struggles involved, can articulate ethnic identity and ethnic political mobilization (Brass, 1985; Rothschild, 1981: 2). Contemporary states, contrary to their self-representation as formed on the basis of cultural homogeneity, must contend with a multicultural, and at times multinational, reality (Connor, 1994; Tully, 2002). Cultural, linguistic, religious and ethnic minorities struggle, not only for equality, but also for recognition and accommodation. These new struggles for identity, often described in terms of a defense of cosmopolitanism and multiculturalism attempt to re-negotiate the status of minority groups and re-define key state institutions, including citizenship. Multicultural realities challenge not only the foundational assumptions of "ethnic states" that provide a national home for a dominant ethnic group "trapped" between commitment to the domin- ant nation and to democracy (Rouhana, 1998), but multiculturalism can also challenge liberal democracies, where dominant majorities are confronted by the new demands of immigrant minorities (Tully, 2002). The presence of aboriginal communities in white-settler societies can also challenge the framework of multicultural politics, when aboriginal groups refuse to be equated with migrants. The question of citizenship is therefore not only one of inclusion, as a question of equal rights, but also one of recognition of special rights and needs. This issue of recognition and inclusion has led in some instances to changes in citizenship regimes and in others to the continued frustration of minorities. Modern cultural politics oscillates dan- gerously between the fear of majorities and the resentment of minorities (Todorov, 2008).

The social aspects of citizenship – the entitlements of the welfare state – have also come under scrutiny. Economic globalization, the rise of neo- liberal ideology and the "financialization of capitalism" have undermined the former consensus over the welfare state and over how public utilities should be funded and delivered. Decisions among the most advanced indus- trial societies to promote the dis-embedded market and to "roll back" the state were influenced and supported by the dissemination of neo-liberal ideas that have made the market economy the optimal solution for social problems. These developments from the 1970s onwards also legitimized policies of "downsizing,", "outsourcing" and "globalizing." In addition, when the allocation of welfare resources was identified with poor ethnic minorities or undesirable "scroungers" their collective provision was further de-legitimized. This roll-back of the state provided opportunities for margin- alized groups to challenge the existing order of a weakened state, but also left significant decisions about social services to the unpredictable outcome of market forces. While the erosion of the welfare state has been attributed to multicultural policies that supposedly eroded solidarity, there was nei- ther theoretical nor empirical substance to validate this claim (Banting and Kymlicka, 2006). This reduction in state functions in favor of the market was combined with a popular policy of cutting personal taxation and selling off public utilities – a set of policies that in theory, and possibly in practice, undermined social citizenship and transformed the relationship between the citizen and the state.

The challenge to the sovereignty of the nation-state that is posed by

globalization, by the growing porosity of state borders and by the partial erosion of state functions has allowed peripheral groups to voice their demands
for equal social rights and for recognition. But these developments are
deeply paradoxical. While political systems may have opened up to more
voices, especially with the growing use of the Internet to create political blogs
for public debate, the ability of modern states to influence and orchestrate
public opinion may be limited, because there has been some diminution of
state authority. In addition, the creation of media-empires and the rise of
communications corporations that have a monopolistic hold over information has often overshadowed information flowing from official government
sources. As a result politics itself may have shifted away from the formal
realm into other modes of organization and influence, at times described as
"sub-politics" (Beck, 1992). Thus, struggles over belonging, rights and duties
extend to new spheres where groups articulate their demands and create a
variety of civil-society associations from voluntary associations, online forums
and lose political networks that provide new opportunities for social participation and active citizenship over issues of human rights. These civil-society
movements can contribute to "social repair" and offer new possibilities for
the revival of democratic politics (Alexander, 2006).

Israeli Citizenship: Rules of the Game

The declaration of independence in May 1948 proclaimed Israel as a Jewish
state but at the same time called upon the "Arab inhabitants" of the state
to become full and equal citizens. These two principles embedded in the
declaration of independence – a Jewish state and a democracy – underscore
many of Israel's ongoing citizenship debates. Essentially, the contradictions between these principles – equality and preference – have profound
implications for the unequal relations between Jews and non-Jews. Israel's
immigration policy, underscored by the law of return, is part of the nation-
building strategy and a means to affect the demographic balance between
Jews and non-Jews occupying the land (Shachar, 1999). Israeli citizenship
rules are both exclusionary in terms of immigration and naturalization, and
hierarchical in regard to differentiated rights among citizens.

For almost fifty years now, since the War of 1967, Israel has occupied the
territories of the West Bank. The failures of the peace process initiated in
1993 have left the Palestinian Authority with only minimal authority and
the Palestinians of the West Bank without the desired sovereignty and citizen rights. Scholars debate whether the War of 1967 was a watershed event
that disrupted the normal process of democratic state building or whether
inequality and discrimination are constitutive of the very foundation of
Israel's social order (Levy and Peled, 1994). Nevertheless, first the future
of the occupied territories became the major divisive issue in Israeli society.
Second, the debate over the territories and the occupation, and the growing
militarization of Israeli society, impacts on every other debate about equality,

rights and duties. But, third, the debate over citizenship remained confined to the populace within the pre-1967 borders. The state of Israel conferred citizenship by residence upon non-Jews that remained in Israel after the establishment of the state in 1948, but excluded citizenship from those who fled or were deported and prevented 1948 refugees from establishing an Israeli citizenship status (Shachar, 1999).

The Israeli citizenship law is neutral and contains provisions of a universal nature regarding the acquisition of citizenship, but also a special law, the Law of Return granting the right of every Jew in the world to acquire citizenship, effectively exempts Jews from the burdens imposed by the citizenship law (Barak-Erez, 2008). The Law grants every Jew the right to immigrate to Israel and become an Israeli citizen thus fulfilling the *raison d'être* of the Jewish state as a safe haven for Jews. While the "organic" Jewish component of the nation is, in theory, open through religious conversion, in practice conversion is difficult and not encouraged. The Law, on the one hand, establishes a formal link between the state of Israel and the community of world Jewry, but, on the other hand, effectively excludes non-Jews from citizenship. While for the majority of Jewish Israelis the Law of Return is part of the Zionist project providing the protection of the Jewish state, for the Arab citizens of Israel its exclusionary character is perceived as discriminatory and unfair.

The category of nationality (*le'om*) was a central part of identity in Israel and did not overlap with citizenship. While nationality applied only to Jews in Israel (and potentially to Jews choosing to immigrate to Israel), citizenship was provided to all residents within the new borders of the state, including the Arab minority. In practice, however, formal citizenship has not amounted to equal status. The Arab citizens of Israel remain a predominantly unassimilated working class that is politically and economically marginalized and they are perceived by the Jewish majority as non-loyal. This question mark surrounding the issue of their loyalty allows the majority to justify the marginality of the Arab minority. In short this labeling of the minority becomes a self-fulfilling process that reinforces their marginality. The social and political preference for Jews over non-Jews is anchored not only in immigration laws but also in the use of state land, access to resources and political influence. Demands for equality in recent years include not only individual-liberal rights but also collective demands for recognition (as a Palestinian minority) and struggles against what is perceived as discriminatory state policies.

Tensions involving the struggles of Arab citizens for equality, on the one hand, and the growing conflicts between Israel and the Palestinians in the territories, on the other hand, have produced the political conditions in which Israeli Jews have sought to re-affirm the Jewish state and further marginalize the minority. In 2003 an amendment to the Citizenship Law states that the Minister of the Interior shall not grant any person of the occupied territories a permit to reside in Israel. The amendment was justified as a provisional security measure but had a significant effect on Israel's Arab population because it prevented the naturalization of Palestinians who had married Arab citizens of Israel (Barak-Erez, 2008). Consequently, Arab and civil rights organizations petitioned against the law they described as an infringement of their basic rights. In the elections of 2009, right-wing parties proposed different laws that would condition citizen privileges with loyalty oaths to a "Jewish and democratic state", directed to further marginalize the Arab minority.

The nationality category separated from that of citizenship is the major instrument of inclusion and exclusion, but the very question of the boundaries of the nation remained in contention. The question "Who is a Jew?," critical for entry under the Law of Return, received different answers from secular and religious (Jewish) Israelis. For secular Jewish Israelis, the boundaries of belonging were either to be determined by self-identification or by a loose ethno-cultural definition that would allow for immigration and naturalization. For religious Jews, conversely, belonging was to be determined by rules of the *Halacha* (Jewish religious law) according to which a Jew means a person who was born of a Jewish mother or has converted to Judaism and is not a member of another religion. In 1970 the right to immigrate under the Law of Return has been extended to include the children and the grandchildren of a Jew, the spouse of a Jew, the spouse of a child of a Jew and the spouse of a grandchild of a Jew. This compromise left open a controversy over the status of immigrants naturalized under the Law of Return, but who were not recognized as Jews by the religious Orthodox rabbinate. This controversy became significant when many immigrants from the former Soviet Union were not recognized as Jews and cannot be married in Israel because only marriages conducted by the religious authority can be registered. Modern Israel is consequently an ethno-national state that is not a secular state and in this respect presents an important contrast to many ethno-national developmental states from Turkey to South Korea that have embraced strict secularization as the basis of the state, thereby relegating religion to the private sphere. In Israel, religion must be constantly represented in the public sphere.

Israel citizenship has not only the ethno-national classifications that exclude non-Jews but also republican classifications that determine hierarchies within the Jewish majority (Shafir and Peled, 2002). This republican citizenship can be traced back to the period before the creation of the state when the civic virtue of pioneering was recognized as the principal measure of all contributions to the collective effort of state building. Statehood in 1948 formalized the institution of citizenship and entailed the incorporation of Arabs and immigrants, though not necessarily on an equal footing. This formal institutionalization of citizenship through the laws of immigration and naturalization was coupled with various informal mechanisms that re-enforced both exclusion and hierarchy in the very structure of Israeli citizenship. While the ethno-national logic of Israeli citizenship has served to separate Jews from non-Jews, the republican logic has added another level of hierarchy determined by contributions to the state. The new ethos of *mamlachtiyut* has "emphasized the shift from sectoral interests to the general interest, from semi-voluntarism to binding obligation, from foreign rule to political sovereignty" (Shafir and Peled, 2002: 18). The state, therefore, has placed high demands on its (Jewish) citizens to maintain the pioneering spirit and serve the collective. Individuals and groups were treated by the state and society in accordance with their contribution to the common good as defined by the original secular Zionist vision of creating active and equal citizens. Ultimately, it was military service that was deemed the highest sacrifice that justifies the highest forms of recognition. Military service, has not only served to exclude Arab citizens from the status and privileges associated with full membership, but has also positioned men, especially of the Ashkenazi veteran elite, in the highest status rank, at the expense of women and marginalized ethnic groups. Republican virtue in fact regarded the real citizen as an heroic male figure or warrior in the new landscape of Israel, deserving its preferential status.

The structure of citizenship established in pre- and early statehood has come under attack and has been challenged since the 1980s by the changing context and the initiatives of different disadvantaged groups. If in the early years of establishing the state, governance was made effective by the combination of a dominant political party, a Jewish commitment to state and nation-building, political agreements and repression, then most of these factors no longer provide a buffer against the demands of marginalized and excluded groups. Citizenship is the medium through which many struggles are conducted in terms of the rights, duties and hierarchies that are contested by different groups. Obviously the presence of the Arab minority challenges the overall definition of the Jewish state and its capacity for democratic politics, especially when the new generation is no longer willing passively to accept its marginal position. Religious and secular Jews are also involved in a contest over the meaning of the Jewish state and the actual role of religion in the public sphere, in a period when the traditional arrangements no longer retain their hold.

To these major schisms, other struggles defined by ethnicity, gender and class are brought into the political arena. First, the mass immigration from the former Soviet Union and the political activity of second-generation Mizrachim (Jewish immigrants from Muslim countries) underscores the rise of ethnicity and struggles for recognition and equality defined in ethnic terms. Second, growing demands for gender equality and gay rights became part of the citizenship debate, challenging both the republican classifications of heroic citizenship and the religious-secular status quo. Third, the growing presence of foreign laborers and their children born and raised in Israel and refugees seeking asylum became part of a heated debate over the ability, desire or duty of Israel to allow them to naturalize. And fourth, globalization, privatization and the neo-liberal turn of Israeli economy and society have raised questions about the social content of citizenship and the contract between the state and its citizens.

The Citizenship Debate

Citizenship in Israelis is a complex and often paradoxical site of social contention; the study of citizenship illuminates a variety of contemporary struggles between social groups and in turn these struggles illustrate a range of problems about the legitimacy of the state and its institutions. The chapters in this volume engage with different aspects of the changing field of Israeli citizenship. The opening article by Shmuel N. Eisenstadt offers a wide-ranging perspective on the changes and transformations of public spheres, civil society and conceptions of citizenship in close connection with the crystallization of new processes of collective identity formation. Macro-social changes that transformed the nature of collective identities in the modern period have had according to Eisenstadt, a significant impact on Israeli society. Specifically, the erosion of the modern structure of the Western state and its related ideologies have raised new issues about the definitions of individual life-patterns and the boundaries of the family and community. These changes opened the way for social movements that either emphasized the construction of new social and cultural spaces and identities and cultural autonomy in general in the direction of post-modernity and multiculturalism, or alternatively promulgated strong anti-modern, anti-Enlightenment and at times strong anti-Western themes.

Situating Israel and the developments of the past three decades in the context of global developments allows us to undertake a comparative-analytical understanding of these social changes. As with other societies, a weakening of the institutional patterns of the hitherto hegemonic nation-state can be recognized in Israel, in terms of a growing process of democratization and an eruption of struggles of social groups to become incorporated into the central framework of state and society. In Israel, the processes were rooted, in Eisenstadt's words, "in the repercussions of the combination of the political-ecological conditions of a small society and the primordial-national and historical revolutionary-ideological orientations of the Zionist movements and of the relations of these Zionist movements to the major themes of Jewish culture." In combination, these processes constitute a continual focus of potential ideological and political contention and generate challenges to the legitimacy of the regime and to constitutional democracy in Israel. The erosion of citizenship, in other words, involves not only the break-up of society into different cultural identities and competing constituencies but the weakening of formal and non-formal institutions.

The military has been a central institution of the republican citizenship structure of Israel in separating Jews from non-Jews and establishing a hierarchy among Jews. Changes in the "Republican Equation" are examined in Yagil Levy's chapter in terms of its impact on citizenship and through the struggles that surround citizenship. Historically, Israel's ability to sustain a situation of armed conflict for a long time was predicated on a republican equation in which the dominant group – the male secular Ashkenazim – exchanged military sacrifice for social dominance. Changes that occurred during the 1970s and 1980s, following the Yom Kipur War, have undermined the status of the military as well as that of the Republican Equation. These changes have encouraged the middle-class Ashkenazim to attempt to reduce the burden of military service through political protest, peace movements or more individual tactics. At the same time, peripheral groups have capitalized on the opportunities that the military offered them in accordance with their capacity to utilize the resources they had at their disposal. Most importantly, social groups, for whom the institutionalized channels of mobility through the military were (or seemed to be) blocked, could now effectively form new channels and thus improve their citizenship status.

The welfare state is perceived as a source of universal citizenship, providing social rights that are designed to reduce inequalities between groups and individuals. Yet, in the Israeli case, Zeev Resenhak argues that the welfare state evolved, together with the building processes of the nation and state, to give different social groups variable degrees of protection from market forces and to offer them differential access to social and economic resources. Thus, instead of serving as an equalizing mechanism that moderates social hierarchy, the welfare state contributed to the reproduction of the ethno-national social order of Israeli society. The dynamics of inclusion and exclusion underlying that hierarchical structure were shaped by two analytically distinct state logics. The first logic derives from the exclusionary foundations of the nation-state and from the specificities of state- and nation-building processes that were grounded in ethno–national principles. The second logic stems from the welfare state's function as a central mechanism of stratification in advanced capitalism. While a neo-liberal discourse and its related policies emerged in the 1980s, their overall impact on the welfare state was limited because electoral politics and the institutional interests of state agencies acted as effective barriers against the attempts significantly to undermine the welfare state. It was the economic crisis that followed the collapse of the Oslo peace process that significantly expanded the structure of opportunities for political actors seeking to promote the neo-liberal project regarding the welfare state. Interestingly, as Rosenhek argues, this trajectory proves that enhanced economic liberalisation can co-exist with the termination or even the reverse of political liberalisation.

These changes in the Israeli state and society have led different peripheral groups to articulate new claims or to re-articulate established ones. Essentially in this political process, the important issue was not just the type of claims being made, but the arenas of struggle in which they were fought over and the resources used by social groups to advance their status in society. First, the Republican Equation that had determined inclusion and status of individuals as measured by their contribution to the collective was challenged by social groups that called into question its value and relevance. Second, some groups have found different ways to articulate their demands for equality and recognition; and third, these struggles were waged not only through political parties in the formal political sphere, but also through civil society and through numerous associations and organizations.

In their chapter, David Lehmann and Batia Siebzehner engage with Shas, a Sephardic-religious party and movement that has been active in both the political sphere and in civil society; the growth of Shas represents one of the important political developments of the past two decades. This party of second-generation Jewish immigrants from Muslim countries, under the spiritual leadership of Rabi Ovadia Yosef, became a significant political power. In a political system that until the early 1990s appeared unreceptive to ethnic or identity-based claims, Shas became an established medium-sized player with significant political influence. The success of Shas is interpreted in the context of Israel as a society of enclaves – political legal, social and territorial. Lehman and Ziebziner describe the strategy of Shas as self-exclusion which is paradoxically effective as a pathway ultimately to political recognition and inclusion. The political appeal of Shas is based on the "triple themes of ethnic renewal, religious renewal and class resentment" and it draws people into its orbit by self-exclusion, bringing them back to religion, and opting out of the secular identity that is shared by most Israelis. Shas leaders follow a corporatist path that demands special treatment, special access to resources and state funding – a strategy used before by other groups in Israel and by the state itself. This path of self-exclusion entails the construction of boundaries between the group and the rest of society, but it is not a strategy that is based on powerlessness. Rather this strategy of social exclusion paradoxically allows for political inclusion thereby permitting Shas to stake a claim to a place inside the state.

Ofir Abu presents a different view on ethnicity in Israel through his study of the Mizrahi Democratic Rainbow, an organization of second- and third-generation Mizrahim. Unlike Shas, the Rainbow expressed a commitment to bring about a radical change by way of pursuing universal values, while promoting the interests of the Mizrahi community by cultivating its collective consciousness. Israel's citizenship structure, Abu demonstrates, has both enabled and constrained Rainbow's activism. While the Rainbow skillfully used different Israeli citizenship discourses – liberalism and republicanism – in order to achieve its aims, its activism was also hampered by these discourses. The Rainbow used the liberal discourse because leading members believed in the notion of liberal equality but also because this discourse was instrumental in its negotiations with the Israeli parliament and Supreme Court. However, as expected, the adoption of the liberal discourse compelled the Rainbow to abandon its plans to advance "Mizrahi goals," in favor of speaking in the name of a "mass movement," in the hope of bringing about a meaningful change within Israeli society. However, its use of the republican discourse, stressing the Zionist virtue of the Mizrahim as a way of garnering public support, undermined its attempt to portray itself as guided by universal values.

The Orthodox religious (*Haredi*) community finds paths to inclusion not only through formal political participation and electoral power, but also through participation in civil society. Electoral politics have been beneficial for ultra-Orthodox parties and their constituencies, especially when their support was necessary for coalition formation. This power, however, backfired in the social arena, where secular resentment of the ultra-Orthodox has risen, especially regarding their exemption from military service. In their chapter Nurit Stadler, Edna Lomsky-Feder and Eyal Ben-Ari examine the ways in which *Haredi* fundamentalists, allegedly perceived as hostile or indifferent to the secular state, participate and contribute to the Israeli collective good through practical strategies that integrate them into mainstream Israeli society, while at the same time maintaining high standards of *Haredi* piety and religiosity.

The *Haredim* reject military service and any attempt to force them to enlist. However, they find alternative channels of participation by either assisting victims of terrorism or in providing aid to the poor and the sick, often occupying the vacuum left by the retrenchment of the welfare state. In doing so, the authors argue that the *Haredim* "challenge the accepted concepts of citizenship, create new practices, and at the same time fuse them with fundamentalist piety and devoted life styles." More specifically the ability of the *Haredim* to combine religious ideals such as "contribution," "participation" and "sacrifice" with similar ideas that are promoted by the discourse of Israeli republican citizenship underscores the presence of new channels of social contribution. For example, their voluntary participation in the treatment of the victims of terrorist violence, which includes the gruesome task of re-gathering human remains and re-constructing the fragmented corpses of the victims of suicide bombing, is a dramatic and visible example of sacrifice and devotion. Similarly, providing medical services for the needy is represented in Jewish concepts that recognize their motivation for serving the general Israeli public. This creative participation represents a new model of citizenry which the authors define as "inclusive fundamentalism," based on a religiously inspired world-view that strives for inclusion in the social sphere.

Women's organizations have also entered the public sphere to challenge exclusion and marginalization. Hanna Herzog argues in her chapter that the intersection between a neo-liberal regime and what she defines as "various 'post' perspectives" that challenge the modern, "classical" social order provided fertile ground for the growth of alternative forms of feminist knowledge and created challenging alliances of women. This political development included the division of the women's movement into many small organizations that simultaneously expanded, diversified their strategies, and developed new options for participation. This restructuring of women's organizations, Herzog argues, resulted not in the de-politicization of the women's movement but in the eruption of new political practices through which the organizations challenged the dominant discourse and offered an alternative counter-culture.

Women's NGOs adopted different perspectives and were aligned with different causes – from questions of ethnic identity to economic inequality and to the peace process – and channeled them toward action and the advancement of concrete, well-defined goals. This "micro-politics" based on women's daily praxis in various social sites creates an alternative network of ideas and underscores a movement that seeks to change the public agenda through daily practices that permeate many different areas of life. This development is not a revolution but rather a process of small-scale micro-political changes that open up new options for women, including their political choices. While women's organizations are less involved in formal politics, they do enter new spheres of activity, and develop alternative venues for social change.

The gender debate as it relates to citizenship appears also in the struggle of gays and lesbians for equal rights in Israel. This struggle of the "lesbigay community", as Amit Kama argues, has been rather successful, and most of their demands for equality have been met and resolved; anti-discrimination laws protect their place at the workplace, same-sex couples and families are recognized to a relatively satisfactory extent, anti-defamation laws safeguard their reputation and status, and their presence in the public sphere and in a variety of institutions is quite ubiquitous. The contemporary situation stands in stark contrast to the past when homosexuality was illegal and Israeli society, by and large, expressed intolerant attitudes toward "sexual deviants." Under these conditions, gay and lesbian identity was not allowed in the open and collective action was not an option. It was not until the 1970s that gay activists began to advocate for their rights in public.

The de-criminalization of homosexuality by changes in the law in 1988 empowered the lesbigay community and encouraged political awareness and activity. These activities included political lobbying with the support of sympathetic parliamentary members, appeals to the courts against discrimination, the work of a wide variety of NGOs and the use of the media to fight against discrimination. The campaign included specific demands to end discrimination in the military against gays and lesbians, and to allow them to share the burden of the military service with the rest of society, in line with the Republican Equation. Lesbians and gays have been negotiating with legal, judicial, and other societal institutions to secure a set of rights and entitlements (such as marriage and adoption) and obligations (for example military service) within the given system. Citizenship, according to Kama, is perceived as the principal solution to allow them to enjoy the full benefits the state allocates to its "loyal" and "respected" citizens. The success of the campaign, he argues, can be explained both by the desire to assimilate rather than challenge the existing order and by the small size and densely networked Israel society of which homosexuals are a part.

While religious Jews, women and the gay and lesbian community can attempt to improve their position in society through the use of the

Republican Equation or through attempts to change that equation, these possibilities are not available to the Palestinian national minority. The peace process between Israel and the Palestinians has raised some hope among the Palestinian citizens of Israel for an improvement in their status. These political aspirations and expectations, as Guy Ben-Porat's chapter demonstrates, were based on a liberal framework of citizenship that would allow for individual equality. But, the peace process, even though couched in liberal economic terms, fostered not a liberal concept of citizenship but rather an ethnic one in which peace was framed as an exchange of territories in order to secure a Jewish state. The slogan used by Israeli politicians, especially in periods in which the peace process lacked support, "we are here, they are there," disclosed the demographic dimension of the peace process, namely a Jewish majority and a marginalized Palestinian minority. This dynamic of exclusion was answered by the demands of the Palestinian citizens not simply for liberal, individual equality but also for group rights and recognition of past and present injustices.

The Arab/Palestinian demand for official recognition as an indigenous people entitled to collective rights that should be translated into self-government, as Amal Jamal demonstrates, extends beyond the constrained formal political arena. Civic associationalism, he argues, forms one of the major modes of minority collective action, seeking to empower society and democratize the state. Thus, Arab civic associations and the ways in which they have become a major vehicle of development, empowerment and democratization in Israel have transformed the social landscape and the political agenda. The inability of Arab political parties to influence the decision-making process in Israeli parliamentary politics has encouraged alternative activities outside the parliamentary framework, for example through social movements, the work of civic associations, and in terms of international lobbying. This wide network of Arab civic associations that operate in different fields forms a "counter-public" where the interests of the Arab community are represented in such areas as land and urban planning, housing, health services, educational infrastructure, legal rights and services, media and communication, and human rights monitoring. However, these collective endeavors do not always succeed because the state often successfully develops ways to overcome civic engagement and thereby to maintain its hegemonic ethnic ideology. Arab civic associations cannot provide their constituency with all the political solutions that are required and they suffer from internal fragmentation, feuds around charismatic personalities and a lack of adequate institutionalization. Arab civic associations managed to change minority-state relations, but have so far failed to democratize the state in the way they had originally planned and anticipated. But, overall, as Jamal argues, their contribution to empowerment and development cannot be ignored.

The struggles for citizenship by women, gays, Arabs and other peripheral groups stand in contrast to the position taken by immigrants from the former

Soviet Union. According to Michael Philippov and Evgenia Bystrov, the "Russians," who migrated to Israel in large numbers after the collapse of the Soviet Union, adopted a "passive citizenship" approach. Russian immigrants, as several authors noted, preferred partial integration and a practical attitude towards the state and the political culture "imported" from the Soviet Union. The result is a mixture of values such as liberal individualism, patriotism and distance from the political sphere. The "Israeli *Homo Sovieticus*," these writers argue, does not believe in his/her ability to influence politics and simultaneously respects the political symbolism in the state. Russian migrant political activity is largely reserved for election periods and often in support of right-wing populist parties. This passivity in everyday political life is inherited from Soviet culture where citizens were inclined to avoid interaction with state authorities and consequently developed no experience of a normative state-citizen relationship within a democratic environment. In Israel, much of this culture has not changed as immigrants can "take revenge" by the use of electoral power while remaining distanced from political life and largely bereft of collective action on behalf of ethnicity.

Yoav Peled's chapter employs the different discourses of citizenship – Republican, liberal and ethno-nationalist – to explain the political shift and the rise of an extreme right-wing party that became a central partner of the 1999 governing coalition. The ethno-republican discourse dominant in the period of pre-statehood not only separated Jews from Arabs but has also introduced a hierarchy among Jews, that was based upon the supposed contribution to the "common good," thereby sustaining the Ashkenazi male elite in a dominant position. Between 1993 and 2000 Peled identifies a continued struggle between the liberal discourse in the economy and the ethno-nationalist discourse in politics, which resulted in declining political stability as illustrated by six national elections and seven Prime Ministers. Since 2001, argues Peled, the liberal discourse became dominant in the economy and the ethno-nationalist one in all other areas of social and political life. This combination of factors translated into a cut in social services provided by the state and an erosion of the political rights of Palestinian citizens. But the growing costs of the occupation of the Palestinian territories, coupled with the devastation wrought by the neo-liberal economic policy, have caused most Israeli Jews to mistrust not only moderate political parties but also the major societal institutions. Under these conditions, the stage was ready for the emergence of an extremist right-wing party.

Citizenship in Israel reflects existing forms of social exclusion and hierarchy. It is a site of group and individual struggles over equality and recognition. These struggles take place over questions of national, ethnic and gender equality, the role of religion in public life, and citizens duties and rights. These political contestations are waged in the context of a dynamic multi-national and a multicultural reality that presents new challenges for the democratic regime and an institutional setting of citizenship that often falls short of meeting these contemporary challenges. In particular the intensification and expansion of demands, which are often contradictory, from the diverse components of Israeli society, that are presented in this volume, are significant evidence of the problematic state of Israel's current citizenship regime. The "revolution of entitlements" to employ an expression from Daniel Bell (1976) presents a critical challenge for Israeli society and to the state which is forced to respond to such a welter of social pressures from civil society in a period of significant external dangers. If expanding citizenship is in some respects the problem, it also, in the long run, has to be the solution.

References

Alexander, Jeffrey (2006) *The Civil Sphere*, New York: Oxford University Press.

Arendt, Hannah (1976) *The Origins of Totalitarianism*, San Diego: A Harvest Book Harcourt Inc.

Banting, K. and Kymlicka, W. (eds) (2006) *Multiculturalism and the Welfare State. Recognition in Contemporary Democracies*, Oxford: Oxford University Press.

Barak-Erez, Daphne (2008) "Israel: Citizenship and immigration law in the vise of security, nationality, and human rights" *International Journal of constitutional Law* 6, 1: 184–192

Beck, Ulrich (1992) *Risk Society. Towards a New Modernity*, London: Sage.

Bell, Daniel (1976) *The Cultural Contradictions of Capitalism*, London: Heinemann.

Benhabib, S. (ed) (1996) *Democracy and Difference: Contesting the Boundaries of the Political*, Princeton: Princeton University Press.

Brass, P. (1985) *Ethnic Groups and the State*, London and Sydney: Croom Helm.

Burk, J. (1995) "Citizenship Status and Military Service: The Quest For Inclusion By Minorities and Conscientious Objectors," *Armed Forces & Society*, 2: 503–29.

Casanova, J. (1994) *Public Religions in the Modern World*, Chicago: University of Chicago Press.

Chang, K-S. (2007) "The End of Developmental Citizenship? Restructuring and Social Displacement in Post-crisis South Korea" *Economic and Political Weekly*, 42(50): 67–72.

Connor, W. (1994) *Ethnonationalism, The Quest for Understanding*, Princeton: Princeton University Press.

Crawford, B. (1998) "The Causes of Cultural Conflict: An Institutional Approach" in B. Crawford, and R. Lipschutz (eds) *The Myth of Ethnic Conflict*, Berkeley: UC Berkeley International and Area Studies Pres.

Faulks, K. (2000) *Citizenship*, London: Routledge

Isin, E. F. and Turner, B. S. (2002) *Handbook of Citizenship Studies*, London: Sage.

Isin, Engin F. and Wood, Patricia K. (1999) *Citizenship and Identity*, London: Sage.

Isin, E. F., Nyers, P. and B. S. Turner (eds) (2009) *Citizenship between Past and Present*, London: Routledge.

Levy, Y. and Y. Peled (1994) "The Utopian Crisis of the Israeli State" in , R. A. Stone and W. P. Zenner, *Critical Essays on Israeli Social Issues and Scholarship, Books on Israel, Vol. 3*, New York: SUNY Press.

Mann, M. (1986) *The Social Sources of Power*, Cambridge: Cambridge University Press.

Mann, M. (1987) 'Ruling class strategies and citizenship', *Sociology* 2: 339–54.

Marshall, T. H. (1950) *Citizenship and Social Class, and Other Essays*, Cambridge: Cambridge University Press.

Marx, A. (2002) "The Nation-State and Its Exclusions", *Political Science Quarterly* 117 (1).

O'Donnell, G., P. C. Schmitter, and L. Whitehead (eds) (1986) *Transitions from Authoritarian Rule: Prospects for Democracy*, Baltimore: Johns Hopkins University Press.

Rothschild, J. (1981) *Ethnopolitics: A Conceptual Framework*, New York: Columbia University Press.

Rouhana, N. (1998) "Israel and its Arab citizens: predicaments in the relationship between ethnic states and ethnonational minorities" *Third World Quarterly*, 19(2): 277–96.

Shachar, A. (1999) "Whose Republic?: Citizenship and Membership in the Israeli Polity" *Georgetown Immigration Law Journal* 13: 233–72.

Shafir, G. and Y. Peled. (2002) *Being Israeli*, Cambridge: Cambridge University Press.

Shklar, J. N. (1991) *American Citizenship: The Quest for Inclusion*, Cambridge, Mass.: Harvard University Press.

Shklar, J. N. (1998) *Political Thought and Political Thinkers*, Chicago: University of Chicago Press.

Steinmo, S. (1993) *Taxation and Democracy: Swedish, British and American Approaches to Financing the Modern State*, New Haven and London: Yale University Press.

Tilly, C. (1997) *Roads from Past to Future* Lanham, Md.: Rowman & Littlefield Publishers.

Todorov, T. (2008) *La Peur des barbares. Au-dela duc choc des civilizations*, Paris: Editions Robert Laffont.

Tully, J. (2002) "Introduction" in A. G. Gagnon and J. Tully (eds) *Multinational Democracies*, Cambridge: Cambridge University Press.

Turner, B. S. (1986) *Citizenship and Capitalism: The Debate over Reformism*, London: Allen & Unwin.

Turner, B. S. (2001) "The Erosion of Citizenship", *British Journal of Sociology* (2)52: 189–209.

Turner, B. S. (2008) *Rights and Virtues: Political Essays on Citizenship and Social Justice*, Oxford: The Bardwell Press.

Turner, B. S. (2009) "T. H. Marshall, social rights and English national identity", *Citizenship Studies* 13(1): 65–73.

2 Collective identities, public spheres, civil society and citizenship in the contemporary era

With some observations on the Israeli scene

Shmuel Noah Eisenstadt

In this discussion, I draw attention to two important aspects of the new international scene that has developed in the contemporary period. First, there has been the undermining of some of the older Western hegemonies and of the modernizing regimes in different non-Western societies. This has often taken place in situations in which the perception of such weakening became relatively obvious among active elites in non-Western countries – as, for instance, after the October War and the oil shortage in the West. A crucial event on the international scene was the demise of the Soviet Union and of the salience of the ideological confrontation between Communism and the West – a demise which was sometimes perhaps paradoxically interpreted as an exhaustion of the Western cultural program of modernity and as signaling the end of history. Concomitantly there took place continuous shifts in the relative hegemony of different centers of modernity – in Europe and the U.S., moving to East Asia and back to the U.S. These transformations in power and influence became continually connected with growing contestations between such centers around their presumed hegemonic standing.

Second, these developments were closely related to internal ideological changes in Western society. We can refer here to the development of what has been called post-modern or post-materialist orientations; and to the concomitant and continual decomposition of the relatively compact image of the civilized man, of lifestyles, of the construction of life worlds, which were connected with the original programs of modernity, and the development of much greater pluralism and heterogeneity with respect to such images and representations. In addition, there have emerged new patterns of differentiation and syncretization between different cultural traditions, which have been so aptly analyzed by Ulf Hannerz. In tandem with these developments, on the structural-institutional level, there also developed an erosion of these relatively rigid, homogeneous definitions of life patterns, and hence also a weakening of the boundaries of family, community, or of spatial and social organization. Occupational, familial, gender and residential roles have become more and more dissociated from *Stände*, class, and party-political frameworks, and tend to crystallize into continuously changing clusters with relatively weak orientations to such broad structural frameworks in general, and to the societal centers in particular.

On the cultural level these developments entailed first, a growing tendency to distinguish between *Zweckrationalität* and *Wertrationalität*, and to the recognition of a great multiplicity of different *Wertrationalitäten*. Cognitive rationality – especially as epitomized in the extreme forms of scientism – has been dethroned from its relatively hegemonic position, along with the idea of the conquest or mastery of the environment – whether of society or of nature.

II

Among the bearers of new political and ideological visions, various new social movements have been of great importance. The first, speaking chronologically, such developments included the new social movements such as the women's movement and the ecological movement that developed in most Western countries. These were all closely related to or rooted in the student and anti-Vietnam war movements of the late sixties and seventies. Instead of a conflictual-ideological focus on the center and its reconstitution or on economic conflicts, which characterized the earlier "classical" social movements of modern and industrial societies, these movements emphasized the construction of new social and cultural spaces and identities which claimed, as against orientations to the center, a growing cultural autonomy for the newly emerging local, regional, and transnational cultural spaces and conceptions of collective identity – in general in the direction of post-modernity and multiculturalism.

The second major type of movements which started to develop, albeit somewhat later, in this period and occupied more and more the center stage on the international scene, were the fundamentalist and communal religious movements which promulgated strong anti-modern, or anti-Enlightenment, ideologies including, in many instances, strong anti-Western themes. Although these movements developed above all in non-Western societies – especially in various Muslim, Hindu and Buddhist societies, they also became visible in Europe and in the U.S. where indeed the first modern fundamentalist (principally Protestant) movements had developed.

Contrary to the basic orientations of the earlier, classical social movements, which focused above all on the constitution and possible transformations of the socio-political center, of the centers of the nation or state, or of the boundaries of major macro-collectivities, these new movements of protest were oriented to what one scholar has defined as the extension of the systemic range of social life and participation, manifest in demands for growing participation in work, different communal orientations, citizen movements, and the like. In Jürgen Habermas' (1981) words these movements moved from focusing on problems of distribution to an emphasis on the "grammar of life." One central aspect of these movements was the growing emphasis, especially among sectors dispossessed by processes of globalization, on the politics of identity; on the constitution of new religious, ethnic and local collectivities promulgating narrow, exclusivist and particularistic themes often formulated in highly aggressive terms (Eisenstadt, 2006).

As a result of these complex processes, in many societies new social sectors have developed – the most important among which were the new types of diasporas and minorities which crystallized in the contemporary world. The Muslim diaspora has of course become the best known among such marginalized communities, especially in Europe and to some extent in the U.S. Parallel developments – yet with significant differences – are to be found among the Chinese and possibly South Korean diasporas in East Asia, in the U.S. and also in Europe. Similar processes have taken place among Jewish communities especially in Europe. The new types of minorities that we refer to here are best illustrated by the Russian ones in some of the former Soviet Republics – especially in the Baltic states and in some of the Asian ones; and for instance the Hungarian ones in the former East European Communist states.

These Russian diasporas should be also compared with the Jews from different former Soviet Republics who came to Israel. Concomitantly, some of the other traditional diasporas – perhaps above all the Jewish ones – have been greatly transformed. On the one hand they have become more – if not always – fully accepted in the countries in which they live, especially in Europe. On the other hand new European Jewish organizations like the European-Jewish Congress have emerged, greatly emphasizing the European-Jewish – as distinct from American or Israeli identities – even if in close relation to them.

III

Within the context of all these processes, there took place the crystallization of new collective identities, all of which went indeed far beyond the classical model of the nation-state. Truly enough, even in the period of the presumed hegemony of the nation-state, there existed, even if often in subdued and disguised ways, a much greater variety and heterogeneity of collective identities that was presumed in the homogenizing strategies of the nation-state. Regional, cultural, religious, linguistic identities and cultural space did not disappear – and they would naturally be stronger in those societies, such as in England, in which multi-faceted patterns of collective identity have prevailed as an historical consequence of its strong secular homogenizing premises. In other societies such as Imperial Germany, they could become foci of political contestation. Closely related to these trends was the continual reconstruction of seemingly non-rational, romantic, esoteric or mystical modes of cultural experience.

But however strong these variegated patterns may have been, there is no doubt that during the heyday of the constitution of nation-states most of these identities – with the partial exception of the religious, especially the Catholic and the Jewish identities – were in a way marginalized from the central public domain. They were relegated to the private domain and at most accepted in a very limited or semi-public way. They did not constitute major components of the central cultural and political program as promulgated by the central socializing agencies of the nation-state – such as the educational system, the army and the different mass-media including newspapers and popular books – in the earlier period of the development of the nation-state. The situation did not change with the development of radio and television later on. Above all, they did not constitute the central definition of formal membership in the nation-state – namely of citizenship and the various entitlements attendant on the acquisition of citizenship. Similarly in this period, the ideological cultural and institutional relations between various immigrant communities and their mother countries were to a large extent indicated by the images of the new nation state and by its model of citizenship that was presumably based on universalistic and homogeneous criteria.

Certainly enough, and contrary to many implicit liberal assumptions, citizenship was never culture-blind or culturally neutral. Citizenship usually entailed participation in a distinct community or nation, and the acceptance of some aspects of its ways of life and collective identities. But such ways of life and identities were usually defined in terms of the homogenizing premises of the nation-state and of the civilizing processes of modernity connected with it. The promulgation of these homogenizing tendencies of the nation-state was closely connected with the ideal human type and the ideal civilized person as the bearers of the civilizing processes and with the master historical and ontological narratives of modernity, that was articulated around the ideas of progress, especially the progress of reason or in the Romantic version of the unfolding of the distinct cultural features of different collectivities.

IV

The collective identities which have been constructed in the contemporary era entailed far-reaching changes in this model of the nation-state. One of the most important developments on the contemporary period has been that hitherto subdued identities moved – albeit naturally in a highly reconstructed way – into the centers of their respective societies, thereby contesting the hegemony of the older homogenizing programs or claiming their own autonomous places in the central symbolic and institutional spaces – be it in educational programs, in public communications and media. In addition, these new identities also make far-reaching claims with respect to the redefinition of citizenship and of the rights and entitlements connected with it.

The common denominator uniting these diverse diasporas and minorities – and closely related to the new visions promulgated by the various new movements – is that they do not see themselves as bound by the strong homogenizing cultural premises of the classical mode of the nation-state and especially by the places allotted to them in the public spheres of such states. It is not that they do not want to be "domiciled" in their respective countries. Indeed part of their struggle is to become so domiciled, but on rather new – as compared to classical models of assimilation – terms. They want to be recognized in the public sphere and in the constitution of civil society in relation to the state as culturally distinct groups, promulgating their collective identities and not accepting their confinement to the private sphere. Thus they do indeed make claims – as illustrated among others for instance in the new debate about *laïcité* in France – for the reconstruction of the symbols of collective identity promulgated in respective states.

Moreover while the identities which they promulgate are often very local and particularistic – in many ways similar to many new ethnic ones – they tend also to be strongly trans-national or trans-state ones. This is very clear in the case of Muslim identities but in different ways this is true also of many other groups including the new Jewish ones especially in Europe. Parallel trans-national identities are promulgated by some of the new minorities. All these developments entail potential changes in the definition of citizenship and struggles and contestations about its nature and function.

V

All these processes and movements attested to a far-reaching shift from viewing the political centers and the nation-state as the basic arenas in which the charismatic dimension of ontological and social visions are implemented. These developments also entailed a very important shift of the utopian orientations that are predominant in these societies from the construction of modern centers to other arenas. All these processes entailed a far-reaching transformation of the classical model of the nation and revolutionary states which were predominant in an earlier period. These processes reduced, despite the continual enhancement of the technocratic, rational and secular policies of the state in various arenas, be it in education or family planning, and the control of the nation-state over its own economic and political affairs. At the same time, the nation states lost some of their (in fact always partial) monopoly of internal and international violence to many local and international groups of separatists or terrorists. Neither the individual activities nor the concerted activities of nation states have proven able to control the continual recurrence of such violence. Above all, the ideological and symbolic centrality of the nation and revolutionary states, of their being perceived as the major bearers of the cultural program of modernity and the basic frameworks of collective identity and as the major regulators of the various secondary identities, was weakened, and correspondingly new political, social and civilizational visions developed.

All these developments generated tendencies towards the redefinition of the boundaries of collectivities and to the development of new nuclei of cultural and social identities which transcend the existing political and cultural boundaries, and of new ways of combining local and minimal transnational orientations. In many of these movements, as for instance among the new diasporas or minorities – the local and the transnational, often with universalistic themes and orientations, were often brought together in new ways. Thus, while many of these new collective identities have emphasized local or particularistic themes against the homogenizing universalistic premises of the nation-states, at the same time many of them promulgated broader trans-national or trans-state identities, and often with universalistic orientations going beyond those of the nation-state. There are many European illustrations of such orientations as well as those rooted in the great religions – Islam, Buddhism, and even different branches of Christianity.

The demands of the new movements went far beyond the original premises of the nation-state and the revolutionary state. They entailed far-reaching changes in the constitution of collective identities and of political arenas and activities. They entailed the transposition of most such hitherto "subdued" identities – albeit naturally in a highly reconstructed way – into the centers of their respective societies and into international arenas, contesting the hegemony of the older homogenizing programs of modernity and claiming their own autonomous places in the central symbolic and institutional spaces of their respective societies – be it in educational programs, in public communications and media. Very often they have also been making far-reaching claims with respect to the redefinition of citizenship and of the rights and entitlements connected with it, all of which went indeed far beyond the classical models of the national and revolutionary states (Eisenstadt, 2006).

VI

These changes developed in a specific historical context, the most important characteristic of which was the combination of first changes in the international systems and shifts of hegemonies within them; second, the development of new processes of globalization; third, processes of internal ideological changes in Western societies; and finally far-reaching processes of democratization, of the growing demands of various social sectors for access into the centers of their respective societies, as well as into international arenas (Eisenstadt, 2006).

With respect to the first issue of changes in international relations, the most important developments in this international arena was firstly the continual weakening and ultimate disintegration of the "Westphalian" international order; second, the disappearance of the bipolar order of the "Cold War"; third, continuous shifts in the relative hegemonic standing of different centers of modernity moving from European and U.S. ones, moving to East Asia and then back to the U.S. – and then possibly again to China and India; fourth, to the concomitant growth of competition or contestation between such centers about their presumed hegemonic standing; fifth, the concomitant intensification of the contestations between different sectors and societies about their place in the international order; and finally the increasing destabilization of many state structures – above all but not only in the different peripheries — all of them contributing greatly to the development of the "New World Disorder" (Jowitt, 1993).

Second, with respect to globalization, new actors became prominent in the international scene – first of all various international agencies – the UN, and its various agencies and also various regional agencies, above all those of the European Union but also other regional frameworks, a plethora of new legal institutions such as the International Court. Concomitantly, these developed multiple new international regulatory arenas and networks – juridical, legal, economic, those of accountants and the like, as well as a plethora of new international NGOs, associations and movements – among which religious, national and transnational associations, acting beyond the scope of any single nation-state and even beyond the more formal international agencies, played an important role. All these agencies focused on the constitution of new institutional spaces; on access to international agencies and arenas and on influencing their policies, and those of the various states.

Many of these agencies and actors, which were very often competing among themselves, sought to influence the promulgation of the new rules of the game in the international arena. Moreover, they propounded new premises of legitimacy – above all those of human rights couched in different distinctively religious persuasions – Christian, Islamic, or Buddhist. These religious discourses that transcend any national boundaries were deployed in calling states to accountability. These developments have been presented by some of these new actors as constituting an international civil society which transcends existing political boundaries. The power of all these agencies was obviously limited and the implementation of their recommendations in any case depended to a large extent on the agreement of and cooperation between the respective states, and above all, but not entirely, on the hegemonic states. Many of the conventional agencies and actors, especially indeed states, continued to play a very important role in the international arenas, and some of them indeed increased their power (Mann, 1997). Yet the new actors became very important.

VII

These changes in the international arenas were closely interwoven with processes of contemporary globalization. The most distinctive characteristic of these processes in comparison with the "earlier" forms of globalization have not just been the extent of the global flow of different, and especially economic, resources. Indeed such economic flows that developed in this period were not necessarily greater in comparison to some of the economic developments of the late nineteenth and early twentieth century. Rather, the specific characteristics of contemporary globalization have been first the predominance of new forms of international capitalism, putting out other "older" production units based to a large extent on Fordist assumptions. Second, and closely connected to this internalization was the shift from industries to the service, financial and professional sectors. Third, there were worldwide processes of migration. Fourth, there were the continual movements of hitherto non-hegemonic, secondary or peripheral societies and social sectors into the centers of the respective national and international systems – often bypassing both the existing national as well as trans-state institutions. Finally, there was the continual growth of discrepancies and inequalities between various central and peripheral sectors within societies and between them.

Of special importance in this context has been the combination of discrepancies between those social sectors which were incorporated into the hegemonic financial and high-tech economic frameworks and those which were left out. Those social sectors that were bypassed became dislocated sectors, suffering decline in their standard of living and giving rise among them to acute feelings of dislocation and of dispossession. Most visible among such dislocated or dispossessed groups were not necessarily – and certainly not only – those from the lowest economic echelons – poor peasants, or urban lumpen-proletariat, important though they were in these situations. Rather, most prominent among such dispossessed sectors were those groups from the middle or lower echelons of the more traditional sectors, hitherto embedded in relatively stable, even if not very affluent, social and economic frameworks or niches and cultural frameworks, which were transposed into mostly lower insecure sectors of the new global economies. In addition there were various highly mobile, "modern" educated groups – professionals, graduates of modern universities and the like who were denied autonomous access to the new political centers or participation in them – very much against the premises thereof. Of special importance in this context was the fact that many of the inequalities, discrepancies and dislocations that developed attendant on these processes of globalization both within different states and between them coalesced with religious, ethnic or cultural divisions – and with that continually growing mutual impingement throughout the world of social sectors of "peripheral" societies and sectors on different centers of globalization.

All these developments were perhaps most clearly visible in the various new diasporas and virtual communities and networks. It was indeed within these virtual communities and networks that there developed extensive and intensified highly transformed "reactions" to the processes of globalization, especially to the hegemonic claims of the different, often competing centers of globalization, attesting, to follow Arjun Appadurai's (2006) felicitous expression, to "the power of small numbers," and constituting one of the most volatile and highly inflammatory components on the global scene; as well as an important factor in the transformation of intercivilizational relations in the contemporary scene, often promulgating visions of clashes of civilizations.

VIII

All the new multiple changes analyzed, especially those attendant on the "re-entry" of religion into both the national and international public spheres culminated in the crystallization of new intercivilizational orientations and relations. While intercivilizational "anti-globalization" or anti-hegemonic tendencies combined with an ambivalent attitude to the cosmopolitan centers of globalization developed in most historical cases of globalization – be it in the Hellenistic, Roman, the Chinese Confucian or Hinduistic, in "classical Islamic," as well as early modern ones – on the contemporary scene they became transformed. First, they became widespread especially by the media throughout the world. Second, they entailed a continual reconstitution in a new global context, of collective identities and contestations between them; third, they became highly politicized, interwoven with fierce contestations between them and the different hegemonic conflict between political and ideological terms; fourth, giving rise to new intercivilizational orientations. The central focus of these orientations were attempts to radically decouple modernity from Westernization, and to take away from the "West," from the original Western "Enlightenment" – and even Romantic programs – the monopoly of modernity; to appropriate modernity and to define it in their own terms or visions. They espoused new "civilizational" visions, highly reformulated images and symbols of civilizational and religious identity – very often formulated in terms of the universalistic premises of their respective religions or civilizations, grounded in their respective Axial religions, and they attempted to transform the global scene in terms of such visions.

What is new in the contemporary era, is first the worldwide reach and diffusion of these themes, and their continual interweaving with fierce political contestations. These discourses moved in the centers of national and international political arenas – and when combined with political, military or economic struggles and conflicts could indeed have become very violent. Second is the fact that in this discourse a very important shift has taken place in the confrontation between the Western and non-Western civilizations or societies. As against the seeming acceptance of these premises combined with the continual reinterpretation thereof that was characteristic of the earlier movements, most of the contemporary fundamentalist and communal religious movements reject these premises. Similarly, many post-modern perceptions, as well as the more general discourse of modernity, promulgated a seeming negation of at least some of these premises, a markedly confrontational attitude to the West, and attempts to appropriate the global system on their own terms couched in modern, but non-Western, often anti-Western, mode.

Third, in many countries there developed also intensive – even if milder – confrontations between the interpretations of multiculturalism by the official representatives of the state who often opened up themselves to the multicultural demand but who were seen by other leaders of such groups as organizing such multiculturalism within the existing premises of the nation-state, as against claims for more authentic, autonomous definitions of the identity of such different groups, by these leaders. The confrontation between these different leaders was very much about who could be, who would be, the gatekeepers of the newly redefined boundaries of the collective identities of the communities, who would be the legitimate promulgator of their symbols, and as to the proper way of representation of these symbols.

In these movements the basic tensions inherent in the constitution of modern states, in the modern political program, especially those between pluralistic and total orientations, between utopian or more open and pragmatic attitudes, and between multifaceted as against closed collective identities, are placed. The mode in which these tensions work out, especially whether they develop in an open pluralistic way as well as the opposite, highly aggressive and totalitarian directions, with growing inter-ethnic or inter-religious conflicts, depends greatly on the extent to which the aggressive and destructive potentialities inherent in these movements will become predominant or tamed and transformed. A central component of this discourse was a highly ambivalent attitude to the West, above all to the U.S., its predominance and hegemony, most fully manifest in the expansion of strong worldwide (including in many European countries) anti-American movements that burgeoned in this period.

These developments signaled far-reaching changes from the earlier reformist and traditional religious movements that developed throughout non-Western societies from the nineteenth century on. Within these movements the anti-global movements' confrontation with the West does not take the form of searching to become incorporated into the modern hegemonic civilization in its terms, but rather to appropriate the new international global scene and modernity for themselves, in terms of their traditions. These visions become connected with increasing contestations, very often couched in "civilizational" terms which often endow them with highly ideological and "absolutizing" dimensions, in many societies, in local and global scenes and arenas alike, between on the one hand the original Western conceptions of modernity as embodied in the modern nation-state or revolutionary state and promulgated by the different centers of Western hegemony, and on the other hand the newly emerging local, regional, and above all transnational civilization.

At the same time, however, these vistas grounded in these traditions and have been continually reconstituted under the impact of "modern" programs. Indeed these discourses and the discussions around them resemble in many ways the discourse of modernity as it developed from its very beginning in the very centers of the modernities in Europe, including far-reaching criticisms of the predominant Enlightenment program of modernity which has developed in the framework of this discourse. Thus, for instance, many of the criticisms of the Enlightenment project as made by Qutub, possibly the most eminent fundamentalist theologian, are in many ways very similar and often also related to the major religious and "secular" critics of Enlightenment from its very beginning, starting with de Maistre, the romantics; also many of the populists (Slavophiles and the like) in Central and Eastern Europe and above all, but not only in, Russia, and in general those who, in Charles Taylor's words, have emphasized the expressivist dimension of human experience, then moving, of course, through Nietzsche up to Heidegger (Taylor, 2008).

Such attempts at the reformulation of civilizational premises have been taking place not only in these movements, but also in new institutional formations such as the European Union, in different local and regional frameworks, as well as in the various attempts by the different "peripheries" – as for instance in the discourse on Asian values, to contest the Western, especially American, hegemony, as well as to forge their own constitutive modernities. The debates and confrontations in which these movements or actors engage and confront each other may be formulated in "civilizational" terms, but these very terms – indeed the very term "civilization" as constructed in such a discourse – are already couched in the language of modernity, in total, essentialist, and absolutist terms derived from the basic premises of the discourse of modernity, even if it can often draw on older religious traditions. When such clashes or contestations are combined with political, military or economic struggles and conflicts they can indeed become very violent. They may give rise, in contrast with the symmetric wars between nation-states in the framework of the Westfalian order, to what G. Münkler (2003) has defined as non-symmetric wars between them, which became a continual component of the international order. Of special importance was the multiplication, extension, and intensification of aggressive terrorist movements and intercivilizational contestations and encounters, which became a seemingly permanent component of the new international intercivilizational scene.

Changes in Israeli Scene

IX

From about the mid-seventies there developed in Israel many processes which have effected some far-reaching changes in the overall formations of the political system of the constitution of collective identities, very much in general directions that have been taking place throughout the world and which were briefly analyzed above.

Truly enough, the basic constitutional format of parliamentary regimes based on universal legal rights which crystallized with the establishment of the State of Israel in 1948 did not change. This political framework was in principle rooted in the basic premise of the modern nation-state – entailing basic equality of all citizens and establishing social cultural-politic homogeneity – the core of which was in Israel the Zionist vision and the conception of the state as a Jewish one, but granting full equality to all its citizens. Truly enough, the semi-consociational and sectorial arrangements which characterize this format have continually been changing in an incremental way – but the basic overall framework or format seems to remain intact.

This format started to change under the impact of the Six Day and Yom Kippur wars, the exhaustion of the labor-Zionist hegemonic mold, the concomitant far-reaching increase in heterogeneity and pluralism of Israeli society, and with the movement of many sectors hitherto secondary or marginal into the center, culminating in the 1977 election when Labor lost its hegemonic position it enjoyed even from before the establishment of the State.

X

Many of these processes of change that developed in this period in Israeli society can be identified – as we have attempted to do in the first part of this chapter – in their general outlines in many modern societies, attendant on weakening of the hitherto hegemonic modern nation-state institutional patterns; on the growing process of democratization; and struggles of social sectors to become incorporated into the central frameworks of their respective societies. But the concrete ways in which these tendencies develop varied between different societies according to their specific historical context. In Israeli society these processes were rooted in the repercussions of the combination of the political-ecological conditions of a small society and the primordial-national and historical revolutionary-ideological orientations of the Zionist movements and of the relations of these Zionist movements to the major themes of Jewish culture. This combination created a situation in which problems related to the constitution of symbols and boundaries of the emerging collectivity have constituted a continual focus of potential ideological and political contention. The potential for such struggle – especially with respect to its relationship to the Jewish historical and religious heritage and the relative importance of the different historical, religious, territorial components of that heritage, as well as with respect to the place of the Zionist settlement and the State of Israel in the Middle East – existed from the very beginning of the Zionist movement, but it was indeed in this period with the disintegration of the hitherto homogeneous Labor mold and under the impact of the processes analyzed above that they again come to the fore, giving rise to the far-reaching changes in the Israeli constitutional system and into the entire ambience of Israeli society generating challenges to the legitimacy of the regime and to constitutional democracy in Israel.

All the developments which developed from about the seventies on and analyzed above impinged on all sectors of Israeli society and public life and its major institutional frameworks, giving rise to the struggles and contestations about the reconstruction of the premises, symbolic and institutional boundaries of Israeli society, and the premises of political regime. A central aspect of these developments was contestations about the patterns of legitimacy thereof. These contestations developed in two directions: One was the strengthening of the primordial-particularistic religious or national components thereof, the other a stronger emphasis on the civil components, often couched in legal or universalistic terms, of Israeli collective identity, with growing emphasis on adherence to human rights as the basis of the legitimacy of the Israeli political system. At the same time developed within some "Leftist" intellectual groups the discourse about post-Zionism which often entailed also questioning of the legitimacy of the Zionist enterprise, became a very central and continual focus of public, intellectual and academic discourse – closely interwoven with political contestations.

XI

Contestations about the symbolic and institutional contours and boundaries of the state of Israel were closely related to the struggles attendant on the growing democratization and opening up of the public spheres, and manifest in their growing active participation in all political and public arenas for incorporation of these hitherto secondary or marginal sectors – such as the Oriental, civil-bourgeoisie, religious and Arab sectors, and later of the new immigration from the former Soviet Union – into the central framework of Israeli society. These contestations moved in several directions. The most important such directions which developed among all the sectors, but with varying concrete constellations, were demands for incorporation of the symbols of these sectors and themes promulgated by them into the central symbolic repertoire or repertoires of Israeli society; the construction of new social and public spaces, of life worlds with some distinctive sectorial (political, religious, ethnic) flavors; demands for allocation of resources, often in terms of corrective affirmative action – all of which moved in the direction of growing heterogeneity and pluralism of major aspects of Israeli society, and all of which entailed continual challenges to the hitherto existing hegemonies and institutional and ideological premises, and were often presented and perceived as such.

A distinct pattern of construction of cultural spaces and growing permeation into the central framework and different sectors of Israeli society developed among the Arabs in Israel. There developed in most sectors of Israeli society a growing sensitivity to the specific problems of the Arab population, first of all to their demands for greater allocation of public funds for Arab municipalities, local councils and school systems, so as to mitigate against the discrimination which they suffered as compared to the Jewish sectors; to struggle against discriminatory attitudes against Arabs in many sectors of Israeli society. While there was relatively little readiness to accept the demands of some of these groups for changing the symbols of the Jewishness of the State of Israel, the problem became quite central to Israeli political discourse.

XII

Concomitantly, there developed a far-reaching transformation of the Israeli political system, above all of Israeli constitutional parliamentary democracy. The most important of these changes were first, the weakening of representative institutions and of political parties and the seeming growing concentration of power of the executive; second was the increase in the power of the courts and of controlling institutions like the State Comptroller and a strong tendency to the "legalization" of many social arenas and of the courts becoming, in fact, in some of these cases, arenas of political contestation; third, these developments entailed "legalization" of many spheres of life, making the court, especially the Supreme Court, into a very important actor in the political arena; fourth, was the growth and diversification of extra-parliamentary activities; fifth, was a concomitant growth in the power of the media in the political arena and growing tendencies to populist politics.

The growing politicization of the Supreme Court developed in two ways. One was a far-reaching change in the standing of various petitioners with respect to the rather unique Israeli institution of the *High Court of Justice* (albeit with strong roots in the British common law tradition of *order nisi*) – the appeal for *orders nisi* to the High Court of Justice; the second was a growing tendency to promulgate judicial review, seemingly rooted in a series of basic laws, of legislation by the Knesset. The crucial steps with respect to the problem of the standing of different groups in *Bagatz* appeals was the acceptance by the Court of the groups of interested citizens who were not just directly interested parties – not citizens or groups who saw themselves as influenced by the actions of authorities – but rather citizens with a general concern in these matters.

The strong activist tendencies of the courts became a very central focus of political contestation. They were often conceived by many sectors of Israeli society as attempts to change by judicial action the basic components of Israeli collective identity. While its most vehement opponents came from the religious sectors who challenged the supremacy of the Supreme Court in matters religious, yet strong opposition to the tendencies developed from within the epicenters of the legal and judicial professions.

The common denominator of all these changes, leading to far-reaching changes in the structure of the political institutions, was the almost total disintegration of the various consociational arrangements which were characteristic of the original institutional formation. Concomitantly, the

combined effect of the tendencies to the increase of powers of the executive and the extension of the role of the courts and the continual feedback
between them tended to weaken the representative institutions, the Knesset
and the political parties. The combination of all these processes was closely
connected with growing articulation in the central arenas of public discourse
and of political struggle in Israel, of several problems bearing on the central premises of institutional format and of Israeli collective identity, easily
generating – especially when combined with movement of many sectors and
their convergence on the center – relatively intensive cleavages and conflicts.

   The most important among these problems were those connected with
the possible contradictions between the Jewish and democratic components
of the Jewish-democratic state; the closely related problem about the exact
nature and definition of the Jewish components of the State; of the relations between the primordial or cultural and civil, and between the Israeli
and the Jewish components in the construction of Israeli identity; and with
the conceptions thereof among many sectors of Israeli society; and with the
continual reconstitution of different collectivities within Israeli society, and
the designation of the gatekeepers thereof; with discussions about the relative standing of the legal institutions in public life and in the construction of
Israeli collective identity. While the problem of the nature of the settlement
with the Palestinians and Arabs continued to be the single central point of
contestation in Israeli society, these new problems became more and more
salient and central in the public discourse, becoming foci of often intensive
contestations.

XIII

All these processes entailed rather paradoxical, contradictory tendencies
from the point of view of the changes, transformations and challenges to
the Israeli constitutional democratic system. On the one hand, the continuous opening of political life in Israel combined with a growing critical
attitude to the political institutions and leaders and growing demands for
their accountability, reinforced the democratic, potentially consensual,
tendencies. The continual power-sharing between different sectors of the
society which has hitherto to no small extent assured the continuity of the
Israeli constitutional-democratic system continued also in this period – in
some ways becoming even more extended. On the other hand, these very
processes gave rise to the development of strong conflictual tendencies –
manifest in growing divisiveness between major sectors of Israeli society,
as well as in the erosion or weakening of many, especially but not only the
political institutions and norms governing them and public life in general.

   There were many such signs of the possibilities of de-legitimization, of
potential threat to this system – the low level of public discourse, including
in the Knesset, the verbal abuse and violence oriented expressly at Rabin and
the Government, and the discussions in some rabbinical circles about the

possibility of declaring Rabin or the Government as illegitimate in Halakhic terms. All these developments activated, even if not only from some sectors of the extreme religious groups, the tendency to principled political anarchism – principled because rooted in the belief in direct access of members of the community to God, a tendency which constituted a continual component in the Jewish political tradition and became manifest in different sectors of Israel in different periods. Such tendencies to principled political anarchism indeed started to simmer already with the establishment of the State of Israel. In the early period of the State they were found above all in the margins of leftist groups, gained strength, bursting out with a vengeance forcibly in the period after the Six Day War – above all among some sectors connected with the *Gush Emunim* which constituted the spearhead of the settlement in the West Bank and Gaza. While large sectors among these groups moved into the center of Israeli society and were very influential in shaping the policies of the respective governments, some of these sectors went well beyond the center. Within some sectors, there developed strong characteristics of many modern fundamentalist movements – promulgating a very specific total, uncompromising and highly political interpretation of tradition. These divisive potentialities, the tendencies to the de-legitimization of the constitutional framework, culminated in the assassination by a rightist-religious extremist of Prime Minister Rabin on November 4, 1995.

Moreover, the increase of the power-sharing tendencies also contributed to the weakening of many aspects of the major public institutions such as political parties, of the legislature, and the erosion or weakening of many of the aspects of political discourse and process and of the normative frameworks of the public arena. All these developments generated the weakening of trust of the public in many of these institutions, with the partial – and somewhat decreasing – exception of the Supreme Court. Moreover, many polls indicated a rather partial acceptance of democracy among large sectors of the population, and often very vocal, even – at least verbal – violence, and strong, even if subterranean, tendencies to de-legitimization of the constitutional system – which constitute new challenges for it.

All these contradictory tendencies became apparent in the last decade of the twentieth century and the first one of the twenty-first one – from the second Lebanon war up to the elections of February 2009, coming immediately after the military operation in the Gaza area – all of them attesting to the exhaustion of the older institutional and ideological models, and with the development of many contradictory orientations. First, there took place earlier a very strong shift in the economic policy in a neo-liberal direction which while being initially positive for economic development, at the same time was connected with far-reaching social dislocations, discrepancies between different social sectors, which especially affected many of the more marginal lower- and middle-class groups as well as the many foreign workers which became – under the impact of globalization – part of the Israeli scene. These tendencies became intensified as a result of the world crisis of 2008–9, with increasing unemployment in some high-tech groups. At the same time, there developed growing erosion or malfunctioning of many institutional formations, and a growth of corruption. At the same time the 2009 elections indicated both a clear shift in the direction of religious and political struggles, but, at the same time, the fragility of the political frameworks.

References

Appadurai, A. (2006). *Fear of Small Numbers: An Essay on the Geography of Anger.* Durham: Duke University Press.

Eisenstadt, S. N. (2006). "The New Setting – Changes in the Modes of the Models of the Nation and Revolutionary State", in , S. N. Eisenstadt, *The Great Revolutions and the Civilizations of Modernity*, Leiden/ Boston: Brill, pp. 185–220.

Habermas, J. (1981). "New Social Movements." *Telos*, 49.

Jowitt, K. (1993). *New World Disorder: The Leninist Extinction.* Berkeley: University of California Press.

Mann, M. (1997). "Has Globalization Ended the Rise and Rise of the Nation State?", *Review of International Political Economy*, 4 (3): 472–96.

Münkler, H. (2003). *Über den Krieg: Stationen der Kriegsgeschichte in Spiegel ihrer theoretischen Reflexion.* Weilerwist: Velbrück.

Taylor, C. (2008). *The Secular Age.* Cambridge: Harvard University Press.

3 Military hierarchies and collective action

Yagil Levy

Introduction

Historically, Israel's ability to sustain a situation of armed conflict for a long time and with a relatively large degree of internal autonomy was predicated on the *republican equation*. In this equation, the dominant group – the male, secular Ashkenazim –exchanged military sacrifice for social dominance. Nonetheless, the 1973 Yom Kippur War and later events brought about the violation of this equation, as the military burden grew asymmetrically in relation to the shrinking rewards reaped from military participation. Ashkenazi groups therefore worked to reconstitute the equation by means of collective action. More importantly, however, by leveraging this change, other groups, who had long been marginalized by the military or asymmetrically rewarded for their military contribution, were able to enter the political scene, challenge the hegemonic military symbols, and significantly upgrade their social status in Israeli society.

Chief among these segments of society were women, who had been marginalized in the military and in a manner that impacted on their semi-peripheral social status, as well as Ashkenazi religious groups, who had been somewhat marginalized, and Mizrahi groups (immigrants from Muslim countries), who occupied the lowest rung on the Israeli Jewish social ladder. The Mizrahi groups played a major role in eradicating the long rule of the Ashkenazi-based Labor Party by joining the *Likud Party* and later the *Shas Party*, while religious Ashkenazim engineered the settlement project that made the Israeli occupation of the West Bank difficult to reverse. This article is aimed at linking the pattern of collective action to the groups' status in the military.

Students of Israeli politics and society have traced the emergence of most of the patterns of the above-mentioned collective action to the outcomes of the Yom Kippur War (1973). This failed war, in which Israel was surprised by an Egyptian-Syrian attack, weakened the omnipotent image of the Israel Defense Forces (IDF) and that of the Ashkenazi elites that had been identified with the army. The war also activated various groups belonging to the Ashkenazi middle class who had been politically marginalized in this "elite society." Joining these groups were Mizrahi Jews and Ashkenazi religious groups who had been socially, culturally, and politically marginalized. These changes led to the weakening of the (until then) dominant Labor Party's ability to mobilize these groups, especially the Mizrahim (Grinberg 1993; Shapiro 1984). Equally important were the effects of social changes wrought by the 1967 Six-Day War, central to which was the revival of ethno-religious sentiments due to the occupation of perceived holy places, such as the Old City of Jerusalem and Hebron, which gave legitimization to these groups' public voice (Kimmerling 1985; Shafir and Peled 2002). At the same time, the war contributed to the mobility of blue-collar Mizrahim because of the influx of the Palestinian labor force from the Occupied Territories. Given this new-found social mobility, many Mizrahim felt dependent on the ruling party to a lesser degree (see Shalev 1992: 268–75, 286–90).

Nevertheless, while these explanations suffice for understanding the emergence of collective action, scholars have not yet traced the differences between patterns of collective action among the groups. While the secular middle-class Ashkenazim opted for protest action, religious Ashkenazim embarked on the settlement project mainly through *Gush Emunim*, the Mizrahi groups opted for political action by joining ethno-national parties, such as the *Likud Party* and religious parties, such as the *Shas Party*, and women embarked on parliamentary and legal action. Why did each group adopt the approach that it did? That is the puzzle with which this article is concerned.

It is argued that the status of each group in the military, which itself underwent an erosion in its social status, played a major part in shaping the nature, scope and strategy of each group's collective actions. The groups capitalized on the opportunities that the military offered them in accordance with their capacity to utilize the resources they had at their disposal.

The first section of this paper deals with the theoretical concept of the republican equation and is followed by the second section, which applies this concept to the Israeli experience with a special focus on the violation of this equation since the 1970s. The third section describes how the groups involved reacted to this violation and how their reactions shaped the character of collective action.

The Republican Equation

Historically, the nation state was founded on the republican order that established a reciprocal relationship between the state and its citizens, according to which citizens were willing to sacrifice their lives (as soldiers) and wealth (as tax-payers) for bearing the costs of war and the preparations for it in return for civil, social and political rights granted to them by the state.

Seeing military sacrifice as the supreme civic obligation underlined the republican tradition that ascribed great value to active participation in democratic politics in order to promote the "common good" (Oldfield 1990). This exchange of sacrifice for rewards constituted the mutually generating mechanism between war and state formation, as reflected in Tilly's war-makes-state argument (Tilly 1992). In turn, the war-incited state formation laid the foundation for Western democracies and the creation of the welfare state. By definition, therefore, modern military service fulfilled a historical role in defining the boundaries of citizenship by equating it with bearing arms (Burk 1995; Tilly 1997: 193–215). However, this approach also created a social hierarchy based on one's status in the military, which marginalized women and ethnic minorities backed by differential citizenship discourse.

This pattern of exchange is ruptured when the republican equation is violated, as when the gains made in the military are socially devalued relative to the level of sacrifice. First, leading groups may come to believe that the security provided by the state is too materially or morally expensive, and as such is disproportional to the purported threats. For example, since the Cold War drew to a close during the 1970s, economic and physical security has continued to be valued positively but their relative priority has become lower than in the past (Inglehart 1977).

Second, leading groups may (implicitly or explicitly) claim breach of contract following the erosion of the republican criterion for the distribution of social goods and the justification for social dominance – with military sacrifice at the center. Erosion of this sort was experienced by upper-middle class groups in the United States and Western Europe from the 1950s onwards. Whereas the equation of soldiering with citizenship traditionally generated social mobility, as soon as groups attained a status of their own that was no longer conditional on military sacrifice, while the level of sacrifice remained stable, the groups lost much of their interest in serving in the army (Burk 1995). With the Cold War and nuclear disarmament, moreover, the traditional role of the citizen-soldier gave way to a new pattern of warfare based on professional soldiers. The result was the erosion of the citizen-soldier as a social role (Turner 2001). In turn, selectivity in recruitment devalued symbolic rewards reaped from the military, mainly because the equation of the army with the nation became obsolete. Thus, those who were still burdened were further encouraged to claim breach of contract.

As much as the republican equation is a subjective construct that relies on the subtle dissemination of perspectives as universal and natural – in this case, the soldiering-citizenship link that became a hegemonic concept in many countries deprived of ongoing bargaining – the violation of it is subjectively constructed as well. It becomes a subject for negotiation over the terms of the contract that originated in the groups' perception of their rewards versus sacrifice. A breach of contract may create a political opportunity structure for collective action, alongside other reactions such as apathy and "exit" (Hirschman 1970), which amounts to avoiding military service through bargaining power.

In this case, collective action may have been aimed at reconstituting the republican equation by either decreasing the burden or increasing the return, in a manner that may hinder the state's ability to manage its military policies. At the same time, social groups that hold minor positions in the army or are excluded from military service may struggle to gain access, or improve the existing access, to positions of power within the military. For these groups, the undermining of the general contract or, conversely, its reconstitution, creates an opportunity to improve their position (see Krebs 2005). It follows that the republican equation does not necessarily act as a causal factor in the development of the various forms of collective action. Rather, the equation is among the factors that foster or inhibit a political opportunity structure (in the terms of Tarrow 1994) that the actors can leverage by creating the contextual template for action or inaction.

This argument does not claim that the republican equation is limited to a bargain or contract in which self-interest (either that of the individual or the group) is the main motivating factor. Values matter for three reasons. First, when the contract is undermined, groups are more open to considering alternative options that may have strong moral components. Second, value-driven actors may be equipped with more tools to act when the contract is undermined and thus raise new opportunities and legitimize their value-based demands. Third, the reward side of the equation embraces values such as ideological fulfillment or the pursuit of a "common good," a central component of republicanism.

Collective action is mainly patterned by the resources the groups seize, the political and cultural traditions that set the limits of legitimate action, the structure of power in society that affects the degree to which collective action will be supported or suppressed by adversary groups, and the form of the collective bargaining system (see mainly Tilly 1978). Israel provides a suitable case study of this process.

Israel's Republican Equation and its Violation

Jewish Israeli society has assimilated the republican principle of the citizen-soldier as a core value deeply ingrained through compulsory service in the IDF for all Jewish men and women. Male Ashkenazi, secular, middle-class Jews formed the core of this service, as the group that founded the army, staffed its upper echelons and was identified with its achievements. Due to the republican ethos that defined Israeli society's devotion to the military effort as a supreme social value under the guise of the statist ideology – *Mamlachtiyut* (*statism*) – military service became a decisive standard by which rights were awarded to individuals and groups that were portrayed as acting in the service of the state (Shafir and Peled 2002). Accordingly, male Ashkenazi warriors, identified with the glorification of the military, succeeded in translating their dominance in the military into what was regarded as legitimate social dominance, through which they were granted preferential social status relative to the groups that were relegated to peripheral status in the military, primarily the Mizrahim (Levy 2003: 33–81).

Ashkenazi groups also preferentially enjoyed additional material fruits of war, such as the availability of a cheap Palestinian labor force, Palestinian property, and the growth of the military-industrial complex, all of which served as engines of economic growth. As long as it advanced its social status, the secular Ashkenazi group supported the militaristic ideology (ibid).

Militarism was entwined with political apathy. Since the founding of the Jewish colonial project in Palestine, the Ashkenazi groups effectively managed elitist politics in the sense that major decisions were made in the upper echelons of the political level and took the form of relations of exchange at the interparty level. The media and interest groups, not to mention the citizenry at large, played a minor role in shaping politics. The Ashkenazi-based Labor Party (*Mapai*, which later became *Ha'avoda* Party) established itself as the dominant party and held this position for about 50 years. Militarized socialization contributed to this type of political apathy, especially among the younger generation, which is expected to serve as an agent of change (Shapiro 1984).

At the lower level of the social hierarchy, Mizrahi immigrants who streamed to Israel during the early 1950s from Arab countries suffered from inequities perpetrated by the state. A large proportion of this stratum was settled by the state in the country's hinterlands, along its new borders and on the outskirts of the large cities where they lived in overcrowded conditions and in sub-standard housing, employed as cheap labor and receiving a ramshackle infrastructure of social services. For the most part, they replaced Ashkenazi workers, who gradually improved their lot by exploiting the Mizrahim as a cheap labor force (Bernstein and Swirski 1982).

Social marginality translated into marginality in the army and vice versa. Secular Ashkenazi males replicated their dominant status in civilian life by dominating the military hierarchy. Given its form as a modern Western army, the IDF rewarded the education, values, and skills that Ashkenazim brought with them, attributes that were less compatible with the background of Mizrahi recruits. While Ashkenazim were identified with the new status symbols of the warrior, Mizrahim were relegated to the margins of the army, holding the less prestigious combatant and blue-collar positions (Smooha 1984).

Most important was the role the IDF played in legitimizing social inequalities. Warrior-based symbols wrapped in the republican ethos of *Mamlachtiyut* imbued the Mizrahim with the idea that their social position depended solely on their contribution to the state. Accordingly, they were expected to enter society through "contributory" social activity. However, until the Mizrahim could affirm their contribution, they had to accept their inferiority vis-à-vis the Ashkenazim, whose contribution (certainly in historical terms) was portrayed as greater than theirs. Thus, the more a group is portrayed as shouldering the glamorous burden of national redemption, the less other groups are able to blame it for having achieved social dominance, especially when the former group's achievements become the criterion for determining the status of individuals or groups in the social hierarchy. Conditions were thereby created for legitimizing this social dominance by ruling out, at least for the short term, social protests by Mizrahim against the very arrangements that reproduced this social inequality. Inequality in the military was thus instilled into societal relations (Levy, 2003: 33–82). Furthermore, because Mizrahi immigrants believed the official ideology that military service constituted an entry ticket to the society, their very induction, rather than their status in the organization, became a symbolic resource in itself, and as such brought about a distinction between them and the Palestinian citizens of Israel.

Religious recruits were also excluded from significant positions within the IDF because of their fears about coming into close contact with secular conscripts in mixed combat units, an anxiety that led many of them into auxiliary roles and away from the possibility of a military career (see Cohen 2004). Here again, marginality in the army was reflected in social marginality, as religious Ashkenazim exchanged their loyalty to the ruling secular elites for minor political partnerships and arrangements that preserved the status of religious observance in the secularized public sphere. As with their Mizrahi peers, the hegemonic power of the *Mamlachtiyut* culturally blocked any attempt to challenge the dominance of the secular Ashkenazi stratum that had been identified as the builders of the state.

Historically, the IDF is the only Western army that drafts women by law as part of an egalitarian ethos. Nonetheless, women have been relegated to the sidelines and have served mainly in auxiliary roles because of their alleged unfitness for combat. By linking masculinity with military service, the demeaned position of women in the army was transferred from the military to the civilian sphere. Male-based soldiering dominates the public sphere while the family embodies the private-domestic sphere – domain of women – with maternity being considered as woman's primary contribution to the "common good" (Berkovitch, 1997; Herzog, 2004). This status was reflected in low representation in the upper echelons of the civil service, wage differentials, the Jewish law that governs family laws and treats women as a subordinate class of person, and more (Shafir and Peled 2002: 96–109).

With the exception of certain groups, such as the Druze, Israeli-Palestinian citizens were completely excluded from military service. Confiscation of lands and property along with exclusionary policies that distanced this group from the primary labor market in the state's first years entrenched the group's low social status in Israeli society. Exclusion from military service reinforced the marginalization of the Palestinians because individuals classified as ex-soldiers were offered preferential access to various civilian jobs and state allowances.

This pattern of exchange was ruptured when the republican contract was violated. The Yom Kippur War served as the initial trigger but was followed by the upheaval of 1977 (in which the *Likud Party* ousted the Labor Party from power after almost 50 years of dominance), the First Lebanon War and Israel's becoming a market society. Initially, the weakness demonstrated by the army in the 1973 war, amplified by the failures in the First Lebanon War (1982–85) contributed to the erosion of its prestige and thus denied the Ashkenazim much of their symbolic power as seemingly omnipotent warriors. Unlike in previous wars, no Ashkenazi heroes arose from the 1973 War, whereas the few heroes who did emerge were Mizrahi. Moreover, unlike previous wars, which had led to an expansion of the Israeli economy, the Yom Kippur War brought a financial crisis, thus reducing the material rewards the Ashkenazi secular middle class received for bearing its burden. Furthermore, the real cost of security actually increased. The need to rehabilitate the army after the war added to the public's fiscal burden by increasing external and internal government debts and elevated the investment in security to a peak of about 30% of the GDP in 1974–76 from around 20% during the period prior to the war. Similarly, the burden of military service became even more onerous because the human resources of both the regular and reserve soldiers were utilized more frequently and more heavily (Barnett 1992: 185–209).

In addition, the motivation to make such a military sacrifice had also declined due to the growing materialist, consumerist ethos among the middle class. This ethos was itself a consequence of the economic fruits of the 1967 Six Day War, together with the rise of economic globalization, mainly from the mid-1980s, which gradually took hold of Israeli society and transformed it into a market society. The ethos of the market economy eroded the army's role in defining the social hierarchy. The value of one's contribution to the state through military service was no longer necessarily the criterion that would determine the distribution of social goods and thus justify the social domination of a particular group. Instead, individual achievement replaced the test of statism (see Ram 2007).

Furthermore, the 1977 upheaval created the sense among members of the middle class that the state had been "taken away" from them, that is from the Ashkenazi-based Labor, and given to the Mizrahi-based *Likud*. Groups that did not serve in the army, or who made a lesser contribution – such as the ultra-Orthodox Jews, Palestinian citizens, and women – were now even able to reap some rewards, not based on the test of military service but rather based on their own political power, wrapped in the liberal discourse of citizenship. Nothing was more symbolic of this change than the government's decision (in the early 1990s) to drop the requirement for military service as a basic condition for employment in the public sector as well as to extend the payment of child benefits to everyone, regardless of their service in the military (see Aronoff, 1999, 44). Whereas the Ashkenazim retained their social dominance, it came at a higher price, while in a market society, their social status relied less and less on their military sacrifice. In short, the state was demanding a higher payment for reduced returns, thereby violating the terms of the republican contract. Such violation breeds collective action.

Multiple Patterns of Collective Action

With the undermining of the republican contract, Israel's political culture experienced a dramatic change by the expansion of the scope of political participation. Various groups engaged in collective action. In each case, the form of that action was related to the group's status within the IDF. Table 3.1 sums up the argument, to be subsequently detailed.

The Protest of the Ashkenazim

Ashkenazi-based groups were the first to protest following the "blunder" of the Yom Kippur War, protests that were spearheaded by ex-reservists demanding the resignation of the government and an inquiry into the events that had led to the failure. Following this protest, the government established a judicial commission of inquiry to investigate the military's performance in the war. The commission's findings led to the dismissal of several generals, followed by the resignation of Prime Minister Golda Meir and Defense Minister Moshe Dayan (1974), signifying the unprecedented impact of political protest on the oversight of the military.

The second wave of protests came at the end of the 1970s following the upheaval of 1977, and the beginning of the 1980s, after the First Lebanon War. *Peace Now* was the most notable organization in this regard. A mass movement of young, mainly Ashkenazi ex-servicepersons, led by officers in the reserves, *Peace Now* called on Menachem Begin's government (the first to be led by the *Likud* Party) to exhaust all political opportunities for peace against the background of what had been viewed as Israel's reluctance to accommodate Egyptian President Sadat's peace moves. This was the first time a mass movement was organized outside a political party, and it was natural that it should be led by the social stratum that had experienced an imbalance between its military contribution and its socio-political status, which had been on the wane ever since the Mizrahi-based *Likud* Party had come to power (see Feige 1998 and others below). Interestingly, *Peace Now* had a predecessor – *Another Zionism* – that was organized following the 1977 elections but failed (Reshef 1996: 15–16). The ideological goals of *Another Zionism* had to wait for fulfillment until a broader constituency embraced openness to its challenging ideas.

During the war in Lebanon (1982), several new protest movements sprang up to oppose the transformation of the war in Lebanon from a quick operation to the attempt to shape a "new order," culminating in the siege of Beirut. *Yesh Gvul* ("There's a Limit," where "gvul" also means "border") organized reserve soldiers who, for the first time, selectively refused to carry out military missions first in Lebanon and later in the Occupied Territories because of the IDF's allegedly aggressive behavior. Nothing can testify more eloquently to the violated equation than the emergence of conscientious objection so powerful that it could overcome the republican rhetoric that set cultural

Table 3.1 Patterns of Collective Action

The feature/group	Women groups	Gush Emunim	Shas Party	Likud-based activity	Black Panthers	Peace and protest movements
Social base	secular middle-class women	national religious youngsters	peripheral Mizrahim	less upwardly mobile Mizrahim	peripheral Mizrahim	Middle-class Ashkenazim
Military and social status	semi-peripheral	semi-peripheral	peripheral	peripheral	peripheral	dominant
Main social resource	parliamentary lobbying and legal resources	social networks, political channels	social networks	masses translated into party resources	local community networks	social networks, organizations, money
Focus of collective action	social rights	alternative track for social mobility	alternative track for social mobility	social and political rights and cultural recognition	reducing social inequalities in access to the draft	reduced duty
Accepting/rejecting the army's role in shaping the social hierarchy	partly accepting	rejecting	rejecting	accepting	accepting	accepting
Accepting/rejecting the criteria for role allocation in the army	rejecting	accepting	accepting	accepting	rejecting	accepting
Accepting/rejecting the mode of rewarding military sacrifice	accepting	accepting	accepting	rejecting	accepting	rejecting
The main achievement	partial social mobility irrespective of mobility in the military	challenging the state's rational-secular authority	new pattern of citizenship	access to state resources and cultural recognition	access to the draft and a temporary change in the public agenda	political monitoring of the military, policies of de-escalation, reduction in military duties

barriers to collective action which challenged the very underpinnings of the totality of conscription. Yet, because of those barriers, *Yesh Gvul* was inclined to use communitarian discourse and employ national symbols without questioning the state's authority to conscript its youth (Lainer-Vos 2006: 286–87).

Yesh Gvul, Peace Now and other organizations practically demanded an alternative to the accepted military ethos (see Helman 1999). Central to this discourse was the definition of the First Lebanon War as a "war of choice," distinguished from the ostensibly "war of no choice" of the past, thus inculcating the idea that there was an alternative to bellicosity. Due in large part to these protests, the IDF partly and unilaterally withdrew from Lebanon in 1985.

The partial success of these two waves of protest was embodied in the increased allocation of political rights to the Ashkenazi middle class in the form of its ability to influence military policy, an ability it had previously been denied. As a dominant group that had exhausted its ability to reap more significant benefits from military service, it was natural that Ashkenazim would focus on the other side of the equation, namely reducing the military burden, by seeking to limit the autonomy of the army.

For these groups, the most important resource for collective action was the social networks created between the reservists. Social ties among reserve combatants, who meet for about one month every year during their service, can be translated into collective action. Along with networking, the groups took advantage of their other resources – organizational skills, money, motivation, and free time – to indirectly bargain with the state over the character of their missions.

After exhausting its ability to broaden its political rights to supervise the army and military policy, this stratum made relatively fewer demands for more rights from the state than other groups and naturally focused instead on reducing the security burden. Accordingly, along with protest activities, secular Ashkenazim tried to exert pressure to reduce military sacrifice or increase the rewards for it by turning to more individual tactics.

One way of achieving this goal was by a reduction in motivation for combat duty. This trend was apparent in the slow and continual decline in the general willingness to enlist, particularly for combat units, and the significant increase in the number of young recruits dropping out before and during their service on the grounds of apparent mental ill-health (for various aspects see Mayseless 1993; Nevo and Shor 2002: 9–35). Those who preferred to serve bargained with the military, in personal or via their social networks, over the terms of their service to determine their individual role in the army or made missions conditional on economic remuneration or political consent in the form of selective and 'grey' refusal. This pattern embodies a retreat from *obligatory militarism*, which sees compulsory military service as an unconditional contribution to the state, and the adoption of *contractual militarism*; that is, making service conditional on its meeting the individual's ambitions and interests (Levy et al. 2007). As a dominant group, the Ashkenazim could rely on individual and network resources to achieve their aims through bargaining, and therefore did not have to resort as often to collective action.

With the downturn in the image of the omnipotent male Ashkenazi warrior, other groups, who had been marginalized in the IDF, or asymmetrically rewarded for their military contribution, were also able to enter the political scene and challenge, directly and indirectly, the hegemonic military symbols. Furthermore, as the army came to need new reserves of manpower, because of its post-1973 massive build-up that encountered a reduced motivation among the secular Ashkenazi middle class to serve, the bargaining power of other groups increased, offering them the opportunity to rebalance the equation by focusing on the rights' allocation side of this equation. (Levy 2003: 236–63).

The Mizrahi and Religious Challenges

The Ashkenazi hegemony faced three challenges (see also Levy 2003: 121–33):

Challenge A: The struggle for accessibility: Acceptance of the principle that the army defines the social hierarchy while challenging the criteria for role allocation within the IDF

In the early 1970s, prior to the outbreak of the Yom Kippur War, the *Black Panthers*, a movement of young men of North African extraction, demanded that the army draft groups of socially disadvantaged Mizrahim that it hitherto had screened out because of their lack of education. In this way, the *Panthers* acknowledged that the supreme test of full acceptance into Israeli society was admittance into the military (Etzioni- Halevy 1975: 505). This was the first time that a protest movement had specifically linked social rewards with military service. By and large, the army met these demands, as its universalist image of the "people's army" together with the politicians' interests in co-opting the protest, forced the army to even recruit people whose perceived abilities did not match the IDF's needs. Nonetheless, the organizational resources of the *Panthers* were limited and relied on community networks (as a Jerusalem-based group). So, as the 1973 War put military needs at the forefront again, at least temporarily, the group was silenced.

Challenge B: The struggle for rights: Acceptance of the principle that the army defines the social hierarchy and acceptance of the criteria for role allocation in the military while challenging the allocation of the rewards that are derived from military service

This challenge sprung from the increasing consciousness among Mizrahim that the republican equation did not work for them. In other words, they were not rewarded for their military sacrifice as well as their Ashkenazi peers had been. This consciousness dealing with the linkage between army service and the allocation of resources was heightened by the 1973 War and the subsequent wars in which many soldiers from Mizrahi communities participated and died in significant numbers, when the ranks were gradually opened for them. Mizrahim then began to ask themselves why the interethnic equality that prevailed on the battlefield was not replicated in civil society. As a Mizrahi activist claimed:

> It was precisely in the Lebanon War that a gross disparity revealed itself between the equality in victims and comradeship in battle, and the inequality in the society between the Mizrahi class and the Ashkenazi class (Idan 1983: 41).

To some degree, these expectations for increased rewards gave rise to the construction of a hawkish identity and stimulated the massive flocking of Mizrahim from the Labor to the right-wing *Likud* Party. Unlike Labor, the *Likud* offered the Mizrahim a different vision of Israeli society based on the ethno-national ethos.

Ethno-nationalism had strengthened in response to the 1967 Six Day War's aftermath in which the encounter between the Israeli Jewish community and historically venerated sites, such as the Old City of Jerusalem and Hebron, was renewed. For religious and rightist groups, the occupation was a stimulus to reasserting their identification with Jewish tradition. Traditional Judaism, which resonated with many in the Israeli Jewish community, became a crucial factor in redefining the boundaries of Israeli society.

Thus, as opposed to the republican ethos, the ethno-national ethos saw the state as an extension and as the embodiment of the Jewish community, not as an instrumental entity separated from it. True, from the beginning, Israeli citizenship had a strong primordial element inasmuch as the republican criteria institutionalized the marginal status of Palestinian citizens. What is new here is the expectation among the bearers of the ethno-national discourse of citizenship that the republican criteria would no longer justify rights' allocation but rather the primordial affinity will justify citizenship.

Therefore, citizenship was not viewed as based on individual rights or duties deriving from the individual formally belonging to the state. Instead, status was expected to be attained merely by belonging to the Jewish collective, and was no longer seen as dependent on historical or contemporary contributions – military or otherwise – as associated with Ashkenazi dominance and legitimized by the statist, republican discourse. This new discourse thus laid the foundations for the erosion of the symbols of the Ashkenazi elites, especially the *kibbutz* (the collective agricultural community). At the same time, the ethno-national discourse sharpened the distinction between Jews and Arabs, casting the groups as group-based primordial identities. This distinction created a hierarchy defined by ascriptive belonging. An aggressive stance toward the Arabs, rooted in a theocratic or nationalist rationale, was the outcome.

The ethno-national discourse was a magnet for less mobile Mizrahi groups, who themselves had been marginalized and thereby alienated by the ethos of *Mamlachtiyut*. Ethno-nationalism offered them a meaningful partnership in shaping the "common good" of the Jewish-Israeli community. Unlike the secular ethos of Israeliness, this discourse gave the Mizrahim a sense of belonging to the society as equal partners without blurring their ethnic distinctiveness and without making their membership conditional on a contribution to the state – primarily through military service – as entailed by the *Mamlachtiyut* (see Shafir and Peled 2002: 87–94). Here again, ideological grievances could emerge and be transformed into strategic action under conditions of a structural change that created opportunity for marginalized groups.

Politically, the *Likud* hammered home the point that the country's national-military achievements could not have been attained without the Mizrahim, while, at the same time, the new discourse revalidated the value of military service by re-contextualizing its worth in defending the Jewish community. Prime Minister Menachem Begin, the party's leader, concentrated on that theme in his speeches at mass outdoor rallies in the 1981 election campaign, which became an inter-ethnic struggle. With his rhetorical skills, Begin gave the Mizrahim, who flocked to his rallies from development towns and disadvantaged urban neighborhoods, the feeling that they themselves had participated in the army's heroic exploits (Gertz 1983). Begin could thus highlight the joint contribution of both ethnic communities to the national struggle and deflect the ridicule heaped on him by a popular entertainer working for the Labor Party during the campaign, who charged that Labor (Ashkenazi) supporters had served in front-line combat units, while the Mizrahim had been posted to rear-guard service units. Thus, the *Likud*'s hawkish political identity defended the Mizrahim's battlefield gains and counteracted what had been portrayed as the Ashkenazi left's attempt to devalue these gains by criticizing the IDF and advocating the end of the Arab-Israeli conflict. Strategically, rather than the co-opting of existing networks, the *Likud* mobilized unorganized Mizrahim and translated their masses into political power.

In sum, while the *Black Panthers*' demand to be recruited reflected their internalization of the republican equation, this later wave of Mizrahi protest demanded recognition for their military contribution in defiance of the Ashkenazi failure to do so. The Mizrahi protest also served as a springboard for more substantial political involvement, which ultimately led to the ousting of the Ashkenazi-based Labor Party from power. With their new-found political clout, Mizrahi groups could gradually gain access to the state's power resources as well as public acknowledgment of the achievements of Mizrahi combatants.

Challenge C: The struggle for an alternative equation – Challenging the principle that the army defines the social hierarchy while internalizing the criteria for role allocation in the army and the social rewards that derive from such participation

Groups who had been disappointed by their inability to gain the recognition embodied in the previous challenge, especially their inability to attain positions associated with some degree of status in the army, adopted other forms of protest. Two major organizations associated with this form of protest are the *Shas Party* and *Gush Emunim.*

Shas, a Mizrahi ultra-Orthodox movement set up in the 1980s by a young yeshiva student, attracted the less upwardly mobile Mizrahi segments that were disappointed with the neo-liberal social policies of the *Likud*-led governments. Given that social mobility in civilian tracks was blocked and these youngsters had limited opportunities in the army, especially as the military itself lost much of its status following the Lebanon War of 1982, these Mizrahi elements sought social status divorced from the military. For such disadvantaged Mizrahi youngsters, military service would have meant either dropping out or a marginal position in the blue-collar segment of the military.

Shas did impressively well in the elections of 1984, becoming a part of most of the governing coalitions. Armed with the power of this success, *Shas* demanded that yeshiva students' exemption from military service be increased; however, not at the expense of the privileges awarded to ex-servicepersons. This demand was an alternative to the centrality of the army and the Gordian knot that had been tied between soldiering and citizenship.

A few hundred youngsters were exempted in the early years of the state, as part of a gesture made by Ben-Gurion to the ultra-Orthodox rabbinate during the early 1950s to assist in rebuilding the Orthodox yeshivas after the devastation of the Holocaust. In the 1990s this number climbed to around 10% of potential recruits. It was mostly *Shas* that contributed to the institutionalization of the military exemption given to yeshiva students under the slogan of *"Torato Omanuto"* ("the study of Torah is his livelihood"). Furthermore, unlike the Ashkenazi ultra-Orthodox parties, *Shas* refused to bow down to hegemonic secular militarism, instead unhesitatingly presenting the route of studying Torah as no less worthy, if not more so, than the military one.

Shas thus constructed an alternative pattern of rewards for an increasingly ultra-Orthodox population in the form of huge funding for state-subsidized Mizrahi yeshivas. This route offered greater material and symbolic rewards than did military participation (on *Shas* see Peled 2001).

For the first time in the country's history, this *Shas*-based Mizrahi reaction marked a shift to the construction, by political means, of a unique ethnic identity distinct from the rest of society. This action effectively signaled the collapse of the successful Ashkenazi *Mamlachtiyut*-based strategy to present Mizrahi political organizations as illegitimate because of their ethnic composition. More importantly, *Shas'* action reflected the formation of a new concept of citizenship that challenged the republican hegemonic concept.

What these three forms of protest by Mizrahim – *the Black Panthers, Likud* and *Shas* – had in common was the absence of any criticism of the army for its part in creating social inequality, a tendency that had its roots in the deep-seated legitimacy of the IDF's ethos of egalitarianism. Thus, Mizrahi social protest was channeled into indirect strategies, even after many Mizrahim had become aware of the illusory nature of the ethos. Equally significant, by either opting to work within the confines of the republic equation (under the direct auspices of the state) or outside of it (but with dependency on state funds for *Shas'* yeshivas), the state channeled the Mizrahim's protest into the military and cultural sphere, rather than into the social sphere, lest it have an immediate impact on the reproduction of social inequalities.

A parallel challenge with similar characteristics was also made by the religious Zionist movement in the form of *Gush Emunim* ("Bloc of the Faithful"). Ideologically, the organization of *Gush Emunim* was related to the renewal of the discourse concerning the state's borders following the 1967 War. This debate was fueled by the 1973 War which, as noted above, highlighted ethno-national patterns in politics. Sociologically speaking, *Gush Emunim* was a group of young religious people, largely from the Ashkenazi middle class, identifiable by their "knitted skullcaps." They were graduates of religious high schools and yeshivas, and had served in the army, many as junior officers.

The appearance of the *Gush* reflected a rebellion on the part of the younger generation of the national-religious sector against their parents' generation (who worked within the framework of the National Religious Party), and whom they accused of a timid approach to politics, of being dragged along by the Labor Party, and of making pragmatic comprises in the "rearguard battle" over the religious character of Israeli society. This was an uprising of the young religious Ashkenazi middle class protesting against their marginal, cultural and political status as well as their exclusion from equal participation with the secular Ashkenazi stratum in shaping the "common good" of the Zionist project. Their activities demonstrated their disappointment not only with the weakness of their parents' generation but also with their semi-peripheral status in the army, where they played only a secondary role, partly due to their rabbis' concerns about the army's secularizing influence and with the secular nature of the organization. With the refutation of the myth of the Ashkenazi warrior's military omnipotence following the failure of the Yom Kippur War, the *Gush* formulated an alternative to the symbols of army service by advancing the idea of settlement in the territories.

The *Gush* believed in the idea of the "Greater Land of Israel," i.e. Israel spreading from the Jordan River to the Mediterranean. *Gush Emunim* acted on this belief by initiating protest activities against political concessions, but its main agenda was the establishment of (often illegal) Jewish settlements in populated areas of the West Bank. This project contradicted the government's policies and sometimes led to violent clashes with the army, which tried to block the *Gush*. By imposing a historical, metaphysical mission on the state, one which ignored rationally calculated diplomatic moves, this group stood against the statist rationale. Moreover, the *Gush* even disputed the secular militarist approach, by putting forward religious criteria (such as the sanctity of the land) for deploying military force over and above the standard secular criteria that were based on considerations such as the balance of forces. Thus, *Gush Emunim* was quite willing to confront head-on one of the state's most lofty symbols and the embodiment of secular militarism, namely, the IDF itself.

Central to its activities was the movement's capacity to draw organizationally from the National Religious Party by utilizing the yeshiva-based social networks as well as to urge the party to take advantage of its membership in the government coalition to advance the *Gush*'s demands (Lustick 1993: 42–71).

In other words, the *Gush* opted for collective action that challenged military service rather than struggling over its group's status in the IDF which, up to that point, had blocked or alienated religious youth. The group developed an accessible track instead of competing with inferior tools.

Over time, *Gush Emunim* was co-opted by the state's policies to fund and build settlements. *Gush Emunim*'s status as a neo-pioneer vanished. And when *Gush Emunim* set up institutions to manage the settlement projects, it became a bureaucracy that was dependent on the state's favors and thus functioned as an interest group. Yet, the movement left its political mark by redrawing the boundaries of settlement in the West Bank, making the occupation of these territories difficult to reverse, and instilling theological ideas in the political discourse.

During the 1980s, these religious youngsters, many of whom had not been involved in settlement activity, strengthened their hold on the combat units from which they had been culturally excluded in the past. Their ability to attain these positions came only when the army's need to overcome its manpower shortage drove it to encourage their enlistment. In other words, these religious youngsters returned to the first mode of challenge: they internalized the principle that despite the erosion in the army's status, it could still play a significant role in defining the social hierarchy by restoring its national mission. Religious youngsters therefore leveraged the weakening of the IDF to improve their status within the hierarchy by endeavoring to make this hierarchy relevant again.

From the reactions of *Gush Emunim* and *Shas*, it would appear that the ethno-national ethos itself developed as an expression of the erosion of the army's status. Groups legitimized an alternative ethos, in the shape of an alternative route that represented a counter-reaction to the decline in the worth of military service. The decline in the army's status spurred them on, either because the barriers preventing activities that would undermine the foundations of traditional militarism had fallen, or because of the reduced attractiveness of an organization on the wane that drove the construction of alternative routes.

Women's Organizations

Women's organizations challenged the male dominance in the public sphere, mainly from the 1980s, when women's issues became a legitimate part of the political agenda and the traditional women's organizations adopted a more feminist tone (Shafir and Peled 2002: 107–08). To a large extent, the feminist agenda has leveraged the "constitutional revolution" of the 1990s, namely the enacting of three basic laws that enhanced civil rights and the court system's role in enforcing them. Nonetheless, inequality in the military did not stand at the center of the feminist agenda and did not inspire women to organize, part of the cultural barrier to challenge the IDF's practices.

A watershed for the feminist movement was Alice Miller's petition to the High Court of Justice in 1995. The court accepted Miller's complaint about the rejection of her application to the pilots' training course, and these courses were consequently opened up to women. Miller's struggle was backed by, as much as triggered, women's organizations and female members of the *Knesset* (Israeli Parliament) who, for the first time, put military service on their agenda.

Consequently, in 2000, the *Security Service Law* was amended to state that equality would be maintained throughout the military. In practice, many combat roles were opened up to women, who could volunteer for them (unlike men, who were obligated to serve in most of them). In 2003, it was decided that women volunteering for such positions would have to serve for 36 months, like their male counterparts, instead of the 24 months generally required of female soldiers. Consequently, the percentage of open jobs for women rose from 56% in the 1980s to 88% in 2005. Barriers were reduced but have not completely disappeared, as the remaining 12%, which they cannot join, are mostly combat roles (Chief of Staff's Advisor on Women's Issues 2005).

Apart from the "constitutional revolution," this struggle was enhanced by the decline in the IDF's social status because of two factors. First, military failures created the opportunity to challenge the male-warrior. Second, shortage of human power that resulted from the reduced motivation among the secular Ashkenazi middle class opened a new place for women (see Sasson-Levy 2007).

Struggles to increase access to combat roles were promoted by liberal feminist activists, among them women politicians, NGOs (*Israel Women's Network*, *Naamat* – Movement of Working Women and Volunteers, *Wizo* and others) and the Chief of Staff's Advisor on Women's Issues, a brigadier-general whose mission is to advance gender equality in the ranks. Liberal feminist activists believed that equal service was instrumental in eliminating cultural-social barriers in the civil sphere, equalizing gender rights, and facilitating democratic principles (Chazan 2005; Raday 2002). In other words, military service was seen in republican terms of leveraging access to power resources in the civil sphere, or at least, eliminating barriers to such resources. This agenda was shared by the Chief of Staff's Advisor on Women's Issues, who claimed:

> The main idea is to take their [women's] basic potential – their motiva-tion and experience, and work together with them ... We will work on 'feminine strength' so that they can use this great resource when they go on to find their way after their service (cited in Eliyahu 2008).

In short, the focus was not on the military alone but on the potential to transfer gender equality from the ranks into the civilian sphere. Israeli liberal feminism reflected what Feinman (2000) described as "feminist egalitarian militarists," namely, the demand to allow women access to all areas of com-bat in the expectation that equality of service with men would promote full citizenship. Liberal feminists sought to dismantle the masculine symbols that have barred the full integration of women into the army, symbols reflecting the idea that women have inferior ability. Central to those symbols is the prevalent myth that war is manly (Stiehm 1989).

Women's organizations thus set their agenda somewhat between Challenge A and C (as was launched by Mizrahi and the other religious groups). They sought to challenge the criteria for role allocation within the IDF but at the same time also turned to partly challenge the principle that the army defines the social hierarchy by demanding rights irrespective of their military contri-bution. This conclusion is drawn from the appearance of the civilian-feminist agenda prior to the military-feminist one. Still, the liberal, mainstream groups refrained from severing the republican ties binding soldiering to citizenship, an agenda that was raised by the more radical, albeit marginal, feminist wing; liberal feminists only sought to release these ties. To their end, these organizations could act primarily in the legal and the public arenas by invoking normative principles of gender equality that had been backed by the "constitutional revolution" rather than embarking on street protests.

Women's status in the military affected the choice of this pattern of col-lective action. Women could exploit the overall liberal agenda and the new military-related opportunities opened to them during the 1990s to demand equal access to combat roles in an effort to leverage this access to social mobility. At the same time, the huge gap between equal access, in cultural rather than only formal terms, drove the organizations to focus much of their attention on the civilian agenda by seeking to loosen the traditional republican ties.

Evidently, women even refrained from exploiting the full potential of integration into the combat units. Middle-class women possibly internalized the failure to enjoy equal opportunities in an organization that remains a masculine stronghold (Chief of Staff's Advisor on Women's Issues 2005). And even when women were successful in advancing their status within the military, the IDF's declining status and the value of the resources attained within it, along with the empowerment of liberal values in the civil society that facilitates the civilian promotion of women irrespective of their military service, all make the IDF less instrumental as a significant site for gender equality (see Levy 2007). On the contrary, military service actually impedes the integration of skilled women into the competitive labor market (Jerby, 1996: 74, 102–03). Indeed, whereas women were successful in occupying some senior positions in the IDF, the more noticeable figures among women occupied high positions in the State Attorney's Office, politics, media and business, areas in which they served as forerunners.

Israeli Palestinian citizens, the most peripheral group in Israeli society, have not taken part in these waves of protest. They could not demand a place in the republican equation because internal and external barriers prevented them from integrating into an army fighting their own nation. Likewise, breaking the current equation and constructing a new one is a more feasible strategy for ethno-nationalist Jewish groups, as ethno-nationalism may serve as a legitimate alternative to "secular" militarism. Palestinian citizens lack similar resources. Their limited attempts to improve their social status have rested on the liberal discourse of civil rights and their minor political power (see Shafir and Peled 2002).

Conclusions

The 1973 War, together with subsequent events, led to a violation of the republican equation that sparked collective action by dominant and peripheral groups alike. While the aftermaths of the war dovetailed with the social and cultural changes that Israeli society experienced following the Six Day War nicely explain the very emergence of collective action, this article has endeavored to trace the differences between patterns of collective action among various groups. The article maintains that the status of each group in the military played an important role in patterning the mode of collective action.

Drawing on Tilly (1978), the route chosen by each group reflected its resources, the political and cultural traditions that set the limits of legitimate action, and the structure of power in society. This combination created the conditions in which value-driven actors could mobilize support effortlessly within the potential constituencies.

Therefore, social status in itself cannot explain the route of collective action unless it is correlated with the resources offered in the military arena, particularly during the 1970s and 1980s, when military service was still crucial for determining social status. For example, Mizrahim were in a socially peripheral position in both the 1970s and the 1980s, but their changing attitude towards military service reflected the dynamics of the IDF's status, and thus the opportunities it offered to the groups. Recognition of these changes affected their pattern of collective action.

As the analysis indicates, groups framed their goals according to their social status in correspondence with their military one. As a dominant group, the middle class Ashkenazim reacted to the imbalance between military burden and social rewards, leveraging their military dominance to advance the right to monitor the IDF politically as a means of reducing their military burden. Individual tactics in the form of *contractual militarism* complemented these efforts. Social rights were less relevant. While this group was focused on the burden side of the equation, peripheral, religious groups and women were centered on the rewards side of the same equation, in some cases demanding access to those rewards (*Black Panthers*, the *Likud*-based action and women) and in other cases, creating a new equation exogenic to the military (*Shas* and *Gush Emunim* and partly women). For these groups, the Ashkenazim's action, together with the attenuated status of the military, catapulted their entrance into the political scene.

For each group, the potential opportunities offered by the IDF determined the focus of collective action: access to military roles (*Panthers* and women), leveraging the draft for civil gains (middle-class Ashkenazim and serving Mizrahim) or alternatively, creating an exogenous hierarchy from the expectation that the IDF would offer limited opportunities.

Each group utilized the resources it had at its disposal. While the Ashkenazim, both secular and religious, took advantage of the military-based and yeshiva-based social networks to bypass the party system, other groups built on community-based networks through which they could act politically, either through the existing party establishments, mainly the *Likud*, or by creating a new framework (*Shas*). Women, on their part, leveraged the "constitutional revolution" to act in the parliamentary and legal arenas.

Most importantly, the scope of collective action stemmed from the barriers set by the dominant political culture. Ashkenazim, the *Black Panthers*, *Likud* activists and women's organizations, all internalized the republican rhetoric that had set cultural barriers, and therefore demanded rights in exchange for social sacrifice or access to sacrifice that could be leveraged for social rewards. Even the *Shas* and *Gush Emunim* activists overcame these barriers by drawing on ethno-nationalist rhetoric and the portrayal of their mission as advancing the national interests through alternative means supported by theological rationales. This being the case, these groups could avoid the (then) impossible challenge of confronting the military hierarchy and bypassed the need to expose the IDF's hidden biases toward its secular Ashkenazi founders.

Finally, with the erosion of the IDF's social status, the republican equation lost much of its value for the serving groups, dominant and peripheral alike, as military assets were less convertible into social assets. Thus, the more the group internalized the republican rhetoric and abided by its rules, the more its achievements were limited. On the contrary, *Shas* and *Gush Emunim* have successfully left their imprint on Israel's political culture due to their effort to break away from the hegemonic framework by establishing an alternative route for voice and mobility (as only during the late 1980s would religious youngsters turn to improve their status within the military hierarchy). In other words, the groups for which the institutionalized channels of mobility through the military were (or seemed to be) blocked could effectively form new channels and thus improved their status more effectively than those who chose to work from within. Women were among the first to acknowledge this disparity, and therefore moved their struggle from the military, in which they were successful in lifting some barriers to service, to civilian sites.

In sum, the group's location within the military hierarchy (or exogenously to it) determined the chosen pattern of collective action taken to realize previously or concurrently constructed ideas and values. Thus, the notion of the republican equation helps us understand that by differentially classifying social groups, military service not only determines uniform eligibility for citizenship, but also its status. The resources that groups can accumulate through their military service and the capacity to translate them into collective action, materially and culturally, determine the success of the groups' collective actions.

References

Aronoff, M. J. (1999) 'Wars as Catalysts of Political and Cultural Change,' in E. Lomsky-Feder and E. Ben-Ari (eds.), *The Military and Militarism in Israeli Society*, Albany, NY: SUNY Press.

Barnett, M. N. (1992) *Confronting the Costs of War: Military Power, State, and Society in Egypt and Israel*, Princeton, NJ: Princeton University Press.

Berkovitch, N. (1997) 'Motherhood as a National Mission: The Construction of Womanhood in the Legal Discourse in Israel,' *Women's Studies International Forum* 20: 605–19.

Bernstein, D. and Swirski, S. (1982) 'The Rapid Economic Development of Israel and the Emergence of the Ethnic Division of Labour', *British Journal of Sociology*, 33: 64–85.

Burk, J. (1995) 'Citizenship Status and Military Service: The Quest For Inclusion By Minorities and Conscientious Objectors,' *Armed Forces & Society* 2: 503–29.

Chazan, N. (2005) What Resulted from the Parliamentary Struggle for Gender Equality in the Military? A Lecture at the Women's Parliament Session, May (Hebrew).

Chief of Staff's Advisor on Women's Issues (2005). *Trends in Women's Military Service* (Hebrew). www.aka.idf.il/SIP_STORAGE/files/8/57978.pdf.2005

Cohen, S. A. (2004) 'Dilemmas of Military Service in Israel: The Religious Dimension,' *The Torah u-Madda Journal* 12: 1–23.

Eliyahu, S. (2008) Renewing a Bond – WIZO and Female Combat soldiers, *IDF Site*, 18 January.

Etzioni-Halevy, E. (1975) 'Protest Politics in the Israeli Democracy,' *Political Science Quarterly* 90: 497–520.

Feige, M. (1998) 'Peace Now and the Legitimation Crisis of "Civil Militarism",' *Israel Studies* 3: 85–111.

Feinman, I. R. (2000) *Citizenship Rites: Feminist Soldiers and Feminist Antimilitarists*, New York: New York University Press.

Gertz, N. (1983) 'Few Against Many: The Rhetoric and Structure of Begin's Electoral Speeches,' *Siman Kria* 16–17: 106–26 (Hebrew).

Grinberg, L. (1993) *The Histadrut Above All*, Jerusalem: Nevo Publishing House (Hebrew).

Helman, S. (1999) 'From Soldiering and Motherhood to Citizenship: A Study of Four Israeli Peace Protest Movements,' *Social Politics* 6: 292–313.

Herzog, H. (2004) 'Family-Military Relations in Israel as a Genderizing Social Mechanism,' *Armed Forces & Society* 31: 5–30.

Hirschman, A. O. (1970) *Exit, Voice, and Loyalty: Responses to Decline in Firms, Organizations, and States.* Cambridge, Mass.: Harvard University Press.

Idan, A. (1983) 'On War and Equality,' *Apirion* 1: 41 (Hebrew).

Inglehart, R. (1977) *The Silent Revolution: Changing Values and Political Styles Among Western Publics*, Princeton, NJ: Princeton University Press.

Jerby, I. (1996) *The Double Price: Women Status and the Military Service in Israel*, Tel-Aviv: Ramot Publishers (Hebrew).

Kimmerling, B. (1985) 'The Reopening of the Frontiers, 1967–1982,' in Ernest Krausz (ed.), *Studies of Israeli Society, Vol. 3: Politics and Society in Israel*, Brunswick, NJ: Transaction Books.

Krebs, R. R. (2005) 'One Nation Under Arms? Military Participation Policy and the Politics of Identity,' *Security Studies* 14: 529–64.

Lainer-Vos, D. (2006) 'Social Movements and Citizenship: Conscientious Objection in France, the United States and Israel,' *Mobilization* 11: 277–95.

Levy, Y. (2003) *The Other Army of Israel: Materialist Militarism in Israel*, Tel-Aviv: Yedioth Achronot Books (Hebrew).

Levy, Y. (2007) *Israel's Materialist Militarism*, Madison, MD: Rowman & Littlefield/ Lexington Books.

Levy, Y., Lomsky-Feder, E. and Harel N. (2007) 'From "Obligatory Militarism" to "Contractual Militarism": Competing Models of Citizenship,' *Israel Studies* 12: 127–48.

Lustick, I. S. (1993) *Unsettled States, Disputed Lands: Britain and Ireland, France and Algeria, Israel and the West Bank-Gaza*, Ithaca, NJ: Cornell University Press.

Mayseless, O. (1993) 'Attitudes Toward Military Service Among Israeli Youth,' in Daniella Ashkenazy (ed.) *The Military in the Service of Society and Democracy*, Westport, CT: Greenwood Press.

Nevo, B. and Shor, Y. (2002) *The Contract Between The IDF And Israeli Society: Compulsory Service*, Jerusalem: The Israel Democracy Institute (Hebrew).

Oldfield, A. (1990) *Citizenship and Community: Civic Republicanism and the Modern World*, London: Routledge.

Peled, Y. (ed.) (2001) *Shas: The Challenge of Israeliness*, Tel-Aviv: Yedioth Achronot Books (Hebrew).

Raday, F. (2002) 'The Military: Feminism and Citizenship,' in Daphne Barak-Erez (ed.), *Military, Society and Law*, Tel-Aviv: Ramot Publishers (Hebrew).

Ram, U. (2007) *The Globalization of Israel: Mcworld in Tel Aviv, Jihad in Jerusalem*, New York: Routledge.

Reshef, T. (1996) *Peace Now*, Tel-Aviv: Keter (Hebrew).

Sasson-Levy, O. (2007). 'Contradictory Consequences of Mandatory Conscription: The Case of Women Secretaries in the Israeli Military,' *Gender & Society* 21: 481–507.

Shafir, G. and Peled, Y. (2002) *Being Israeli: The Dynamics of Multiple Citizenshim*, Cambridge: Cambridge University Press.

Shalev, M. (1992) *Labor and the Political Economy in Israel*, Oxford: Oxford University Press.

Shapiro, Y. (1984) *An Elite Without Successors: Generations of Political Leaders in Israel*, Tel Aviv: Sifriat Hapoalim (Hebrew).

Smooha, S. (1984) 'Ethnicity and the Military in Israel: Theses for Discussion and Research,' *Medina, Mimshal Viyahsim Benleumiyim* 22: 5–32 (Hebrew).

Stiehm, J. H. (1989) *Arms and the Enlisted Woman*, Philadelphia: Temple University Press.

Tarrow, S. (1994) *Power in Movement: Social Movements, Collective Action and Politics*, New York: Cambridge University Press.

Tilly, C. (1978) *From Mobilization to Revolution*, Reading, MA: Addison-Wesley.

Tilly, C. (1992) *Coercion, Capital, and European States, AD 990–1992*, Cambridge, Mass.: Basil Blackwell.

Tilly, C. (1997) *Roads from Past to Future*, Lanham, Md.: Rowman & Littlefield Publishers.

Turner, B. S. (2001) 'The Erosion of Citizenship,' *British Journal of Sociology* 52: 189–209.

4 Dynamics of inclusion and exclusion in the Israeli welfare state

State-building and political economy[1]

Zeev Rosenhek

The welfare state represents a key institutional field where differential categories of membership in the political community are constituted and actualized. This is due to the close connection, both historical and analytical, between the formation and strengthening of the nation-state, and the institutionalization of the category of citizenship and the notion of social rights included in it. The welfare state embodies in the clearest and most material way the coupling between identity and rights – the two fundamental elements underlying the concept of citizenship (Soysal 1994). Moreover, as a main distributive mechanism in advanced capitalism, the welfare state is a crucial factor in shaping and reproducing the structure of inequality in society. Hence, it functions as a central nexus connecting the constitution of differential categories of membership with processes of resource distribution that determine the position of various groups in the socio-economic hierarchy.

The aim of this paper is to examine the historical dynamic of exclusion and inclusion processes of different social groups in the Israeli welfare state. Despite the long period during which the Zionist labour movement controlled Israel's politics (first via the political institutions of the pre-statehood Jewish community, and after 1948 through the control of the state institutions), and notwithstanding the existence of a centralised and powerful workers' organization, the Israeli welfare state did not develop along lines complying with the social democratic model of social policy (Shalev 1992). Unlike that model, the Israeli welfare state is typified by low levels of benefits, a relatively extensive use of selective programmes based on means tests and, principally, by the operation of formal and informal exclusionary practices towards subordinate social groups. The Israeli welfare state grants different populations differential degrees of protection from market forces and access to social and economic resources, in accordance with ethnic and national origin, and citizenship status. Therefore, instead of serving as an equalizing mechanism that moderates social hierarchy, as posited by welfare state ideology, the Israeli welfare state has functioned as a factor that not only reflects but also contributes to the institutionalisation and reproduction of the ethnic-national social order of Israeli society – that comprises Ashkenazi (of European origin) Jews, Mizrachi (of Moslem countries' origin) Jews, Palestinian citizens of the state, Palestinians from the Occupied Territories, and migrant workers (Shafir and Peled 2002).

As I show below, those dynamics of inclusion and exclusion are linked to the exclusionary foundations of the nation-state, particularly when as in Israel it is defined in ethnonational terms. They are also connected to the ideological and institutional affinity that crystallized between the welfare state's actions and tasks of state-building in Israel. And moreover, they are linked to the inner logic of the welfare state as a stratification order, that not only moderates the inequality created in the capitalist economic arena, as the classical understanding of the welfare state maintains, but also creates a dimension of inequality according to the differential degree of protection from market forces that it provides to different social groups.

The analysis is presented according to the historic trajectory of the institutional and political dynamic of the Israeli welfare state, from the establishment of the state up to the developments that got underway in recent years following the renewal of the violent conflict with the Palestinians in 2000. This way of presentation derives from the analytical perspective that underlies the analysis, which maintains that inclusionary and exclusionary practices and processes are affected by the specific modes of operation of the welfare state's inner logic at different periods under varying broad political-economic conditions. A historical presentation makes it possible to reveal and analyse the dialectic relations in place between inclusion processes of certain social groups, and exclusion processes of others, and thus illustrates my argument concerning the link between them and the logic of the welfare state as a stratification order.

Dynamics of inclusion and exclusion and the political economy of the welfare state

The welfare state is among the principal foundations of the sociopolitical order that characterizes advanced capitalism (Offe 1984; Therborn 1989). Its impact is felt in significant aspects of social life, such as processes determining the life chances of individuals and groups, and the relationship between the state and its citizens. The main principle underpinning the welfare state is the active and direct involvement by the focus of political authority – that is, the state – in processes of economic resource distribution and their partial removal from the market arena. As a result, the actions of the welfare state play a central role in structuring both the life of individuals and families at the micro level, and the political economy at the macro level. The welfare state is therefore not only an intervening mechanism that may moderate the structure of inequality in society; it also serves as a stratification regime that constitutes and arranges particular systems of social and political relationships (Esping-Andersen 1990).

Following the pioneering work of T. H. Marshall (1950) on the connection between the evolutionary extension of citizenship and the normative and political institutionalisation of the notion of social rights, the welfare state has become an important research site for examining the inclusionary and exclusionary processes of particular social groups and the construction of social hierarchies. Growing attention is being paid to the status of subordinate groups – such as women, ethnic minorities, and migrants – in welfare states. Many studies have engaged with the exclusion and inclusion of those groups in the welfare state, the ideological, institutional and structural factors that engendered them, and the impact of inclusionary and exclusionary dynamics on patterns of their political and economic incorporation (e.g. O'Connor 1996; Quadagno 1994; Rosenhek 1999; Sainsbury 1999; 2006). Those studies contribute both to understanding the political economy of the welfare state, and to exploring broader processes of constituting distinct categories of membership in the political community. The importance of the welfare state as a site for examining those issues lies in its being a central institutional field that draws together discursive categories of belonging, state-managed processes of resource distribution, and the shaping of advanced capitalist political economy.

If, as Marshall claims, the emergence of the welfare state is closely related to the expansion of citizenship, we must then bear in mind that some social groups – such as marginal populations, women, and ethnic minorities – were only partially included in the category. Despite the inclusionary principles inherent in the concept of citizenship, politically and socially subordinate groups were and are excluded from it (Turner 1993). Even in cases where rights are formally formulated as applying to the whole population of citizens or residents, there is no certainty that subordinate groups will enjoy the structure of opportunities that would allow them to realise those rights. With regard to the welfare state, limited access to rights creates a situation where excluded groups are less protected from market forces than the rest of the population. Hence the significance of the welfare state as a stratificatory order stems not only from the fact that in principle it weakens the connection between citizens' life chances and their market position, but also from its differential actions towards different social groups. That variation – a tangible manifestation of exclusionary patterns – creates a hierarchical structure where different groups are differentially dependent on and vulnerable to market forces and other risks. The excluded groups' greater vulnerability to the market intensifies and reproduces their subordinate status in the labour market, as well as within the social structure in general.

It is important to notice that from a political economy perspective, exclusionary practices do not derive only from the exclusionary principles underlying the nation-state, or from other exclusionary ideologies. They are attached to the very inner logic of the welfare state, and to the ways it operates as a central component in the political economy of advanced capitalist societies. As argued by John Goldthorpe (1984), the development of a political economy in which the state protects the workers and thus constrains the 'free operation' of market forces, was accompanied by the emergence of economic sectors where those forces can act more freely. Thus those peripheral sectors act as a mechanism that balances 'rigidities' existing in the core sectors of the labour market; rigidities created, among other factors, by the decommodification effects of the welfare state (Peck 1989). The activities of peripheral sectors depend on the constitution of workers whose vulnerability to market forces channels them into these least desirable positions in the labour market. It transpires that by granting differential protection from market forces, the welfare state not only impacts on the life chances of different groups in terms of their ability to access goods and services; it also shapes their opportunity structure in terms of their incorporation into different segments of the labour market. In other words, excluding subordinate social groups from the welfare state is a mechanism for constituting them as a flexible and unprotected workforce that is channelled towards the secondary labour market (see Freeman 1986).

Thus the process of broadening the welfare state, which brings with it the stronger social protection that it provides to parts of the population, creates the conditions that encourage the constitution of groups that – because of their exclusion from the welfare state's field of operation – remain dependent on and exposed to market forces. It transpires that underlying the political economy of the welfare state there is a strong link between two ostensibly contradictory trends – the inclusion and exclusion of social groups. We should therefore view the phenomenon of exclusion not as a deviance from the welfare state's principles caused by exclusionary ideologies that are 'exogenous' to the welfare state, such as ethnic nationalism, but as a substantive component of its inner logic.

Following this line of analysis, in the next sections I examine the historical dynamic of inclusionary and exclusionary processes in the Israeli welfare state, underscoring the interaction between its functioning as an instrument for promoting state-building tasks and its inner logic as a stratification order.

The institutionalization of a segmented welfare state

During the pre-statehood era emerged among the dominant Zionist institutions, especially those belonging to the Labour Movement, a policy paradigm that viewed welfare policy as a key tool to promote Zionist tasks of state-building. Two policy goals were prominent: supplying the Zionist settlers' basic needs to encourage them to remain in the country and boost their loyalty to the dominant political institutions, and managing the conflict with the local Arab population (see Rosenhek 1998). Despite the far-reaching political, social, and demographic changes that occurred in 1948–49, the main institutional and ideological principles of that welfare policy paradigm kept characterizing the Israeli welfare state after the establishment of the state. Like the Zionist institutions before 1948, the Israeli state continued to use social policy as an instrument for promoting Zionist goals, thus granting legitimacy to its efforts in that arena. This continuity within the framework of the new political and social setting created with statehood, led to the institutionalization of a welfare state segmented along ethnonational lines. Veteran Jews (of Ashkenazi origin), new immigrants (particularly Mizrachi Jews), and Palestinian citizens, received differential levels of protection from market forces and varying access to public resources, according to their positioning in the political community. Veteran Jews and new immigrants were dealt with by separate institutional mechanisms that provided different levels of benefits and services, and acted in compliance with different institutional principles; whereas Palestinian citizens were almost completely excluded from the welfare state's sphere of activity. The dynamic of inclusion and exclusion of different populations, and its stratification outcomes, clearly reflected the stratified character of citizenship in Israel – embodied in the hierarchic distinction between republican, ethnonational, and liberal citizenship (Shafir and Peled 2002).

In all areas of social policy, the patterns that crystallized were of institutional distinctions and an unequal allocation of resources, directly or indirectly. For example, a large part of the veteran Jewish population, who were employed in the primary labour market, enjoyed Histadrut occupational pension plans that were based on the principle of income-substitution and granted relatively large pensions, assisted by generous state subsidies. In contrast, the rest of the population, principally the new immigrants and Palestinian citizens – who were employed in the secondary labour market – were entitled solely to universal old-age benefits that were granted by the National Insurance Institute (NII) from 1953. These allowances were and still are awarded on the principle of basic subsistence and are therefore extremely low.

A clear manifestation of the welfare state's segmented nature in the first two decades following statehood is visible in the mode of operation of the institutional mechanisms dealing with immigrants in the 1950s and 1960s. They were assisted mainly by local welfare bureaux that granted them extremely modest economic aid. Moreover, this social assistance mechanism, intended to assure a minimal standard of living for the needy population, operated in accordance with typical principles of residual welfare policy. It acted without a legal framework for defining citizens' entitlements and in compliance with rigid selectivity rules of means tests; aid-seekers were stigmatized as a dependent and 'non-productive' population; no formal and universal criteria were in place for determining entitlement and the benefit level; and there were salient differences in the scope of support between the local welfare bureaux at different localities (Doron and Kramer 1991; Klein 1959). This system operated principally among the immigrant population, while in Arab communities it had almost no presence at all or if so, it provided a far lower amount of aid.

Housing is a central policy domain where hierarchic distinctions created by the welfare state took shape, and where one can identify their link to the process of state-building and its stratification implications. Because of the massive scale of immigration, housing became a major field of operation for the Israeli welfare state (Roter and Shamai 1990). In the 1950s and 1960s, two very distinct tiers of housing policy were in place. The first consisted of the construction and allocation of public housing for Jewish immigrants who had arrived after 1948; the second consisted of housing programmes targeting the veteran Jewish population, many of which were implemented by the Histadrut with the help of generous state subsidies. In compliance with the Zionist principles that guided housing policy, Palestinian citizens were totally excluded from this sphere of action.

Throughout the whole period, housing policy goals were formulated and phrased in Zionist vocabulary connected to state-building and to the management of the national conflict: principally 'immigration absorption' and 'population dispersal' (Zaslavsky 1954); two goals that were defined as intertwined. David Tenne, Director-General of the Ministry of Housing at that time, noted that 'the central mission [of housing] is therefore a combined one – housing immigrants as part of their social and economic absorption, while settling and populating sparsely populated regions' (1962: 439). According to those goals, most of the public housing allocated to new immigrants was built in peripheral regions 'sparsely populated' by Jews.

It is important to stress that the significance of the apparently neutral concept 'population dispersal' is strongly connected to the territorial dimension of the national conflict and state-building, and to the relationship between the Israeli state and its Arab-Palestinian minority. Following on from the territorial policy of the Zionist institutions before 1948, the strategy of dispersing the population was aimed at boosting Jewish presence in regions where it was sparse in comparison to the Arab presence. Enhancing the Jewish presence and changing the demographic balance between the two populations – that is, Judaizing the territory – were considered key means for enacting the state's sovereignty and consolidating its control over the territory and over the Palestinian citizens (Newman 1989; Yiftachel 2006). The fundamental role of the state's geopolitical interests in determining housing policy found explicit expression in a range of official documents; for example a report by the inter-ministerial committee for population dispersal from 1964, classified as 'confidential', forcefully states:

Dispersing the population, or increasing the share of the Jewish population residing in the Southern and Northern regions and in Jerusalem, in comparison with those residing in the coastal area, is first and foremost the reflection of a social-Zionist goal: settling the wilderness. Another consideration is the political one, which negates leaving 'open areas' that might 'invite' severance from Israel, particularly in view of the refugee problem that is still unsolved. A similar reason requires the Jewish population to be augmented and become the established majority in the Arab towns of Nazareth and Tarshiha-Ma'alot.[2]

The immigrants' total dependence on the public housing system and their political weakness made them ideal instruments for achieving the state's geopolitical goals. Decision-makers were well aware of the possibilities inherent in that structural weakness, an awareness reflected in a statement by the Ministry of Housing Director-General:

> Changes in the demographic map of the country were principally enabled by the directed geographic dispersal of the vast majority of the immigrants, in the framework of planned absorption – which could only be done to a limited extent among the veteran population, which is well-rooted in its places of residence (Tenne 1962: 446).

As Tenne's words imply, veteran Jewish citizens would not consent easily to state regulation in this matter, so that they could not serve as an instrument to advance the state's geopolitical goals.

This does not mean though that the state refrained from allocating them housing resources. Over the 1950s and 1960s, several public housing programmes were implemented for the long-established Jewish population: *Shikun Vatikim* (Veterans Housing), *Shikun Amami* (Popular Housing), *Hisachon Le-Binyan* (Savings for Housing), and special housing programmes for particular categories of state employees – army and police officers, and civil servants. Some of the programmes were implemented by the Histadrut for its members with generous financial assistance of the government, and others were run directly by state agencies. In all of them, housing costs were heavily subsidized by the state (Drabkin-Darin 1959).

Public housing programmes for the immigrant population were very different from those targeting the veteran Jewish population in every respect. As noted, most housing for immigrants was built in peripheral regions of the country. In contrast, public construction for veteran citizens was performed principally in the large towns and established colonies (*moshavot*) in the central area. Furthermore, substantive gaps were discernible in terms of the apartments' size and other indicators of housing quality (Barzilai 1969). Obviously, these differences in housing resources have had important and long-standing stratificatory effects, and their impact is still felt today in the socio-economic hierarchy between Ashkenazi and Mizrachi Jews. The gaps in the economic and social value of the housing impacted on both populations' life chances in other spheres, such as employment opportunities and access to social services. Beyond that, the main stratifying implications of that policy were inherent in the different home-ownership arrangements. In programmes designated for the veteran population, the allocation of housing resources by the state was legally and ideologically defined as a purchase granting property rights. In contrast, most housing for new immigrants was allocated on the basis of long-term leasehold. As a result, housing for that population could not serve as a basis for accumulating capital and transferring it to the next generation, as was the case for a large part of the veteran population that benefited from the other housing programmes. As Lewin-Epstein and Semyonov (2000) have pointed out, inequality in patterns of housing resources ownership resulting from the mode of operation of the welfare state was a major factor in forming and reproducing the ethno-class hierarchy in Israel.

Another welfare policy domain where a complex dynamic of inclusion and exclusion of different populations is revealed is the child-allowance programme. In September 1959, the first child-allowance programme ('Allowances for Large Families') came into force, in which the NII paid a monthly allowance to families from the fourth child onwards, until age 14. Political considerations of the dominant Mapai (Labour) party played a key role during the programme's drafting. When he presented the programme to Mapai's Inner Secretariat, Minister of Labour Mordechai Namir stressed that its target population was Mizrachi Jewish families. The plan's explicit goal was to neutralise potential threats to Mapai's political status stemming from that population's economic and social distress. Namir declared:

> Nests of fascism and communism can be prevented by the most inexpensive method of insurance: the workers will pay pennies to identify with those who are menial labourers, and those menial labourers live in temporary camps [for immigrants], and those menial labourers living in temporary camps have families of nine or ten people, and everything overlaps. All those families live on 80 liras per month and they vote for Herut or Maki.[3]

Before the programme could be approved the government had to overcome the political forces that opposed it. Perhaps surprisingly, the Histadrut was the chief source of objections. It opposed the original programme which stipulated that financing of the allowances would be shared equally between the state, employers, and the employees through their social security payments. The Histadrut's leaders were concerned that its established members (mainly Ashkenazis) who because of their demographic profile would not receive those benefits, would have to finance them by larger payments to the NII.[4] To overcome their objections, the programme's supporters – headed by Mapai leaders – had to convince the Histadrut that the programme's cost would be negligible, and that financing it would not require a significant increase in the sums paid by employees. The arguments that Namir used to convince the Histadrut's leaders are particularly illustrative for discussing inclusionary and exclusionary processes. Namir asserted that: 'This is a matter of 50,000 families and 80,000 children, from the fourth child on and they do not include Arabs. Special arrangements will be made so that the programme does not include the Arabs, and it [the allowance programme] will cost very little.'[5]

Namir's proposal for the use of practices aimed at excluding Arab families from entitlement to the benefits was not implemented, and at this early stage of the child-allowance programme's development, no 'special arrangements' excluding the Arab population were made. A compromise was ultimately reached with the Histadrut that lowered the allowances to an extent that made it possible to exempt the employees from financing part of the programme. Yet, the proposal raised by the Minister in charge of welfare policy reveals Palestinian citizens' vulnerable status in the Israeli welfare state. The proposal also discloses the link between inclusionary processes and the expansion of the welfare state on the one hand, and processes excluding subordinate populations on the other. Palestinian citizens were defined as candidates for having their rights negated in order to reduce the cost of the programme which, in turn, was aimed at improving the social and economic conditions of the Mizrachi population with the goal of ensuring its loyalty to the regime and the legitimacy of the political order. At that stage, as noted, that potential vulnerability was not realized and Arab families were officially included in the programme. In the coming section we will see that this vulnerability became particularly relevant and was actualized during the process of broadening the child-allowance programme, and the Israeli welfare state more generally, in the 1970s.

The short and limited Golden Age of the Israeli welfare state

The decade of the 1970s represents the golden age of the Israeli welfare state (Doron and Kramer 1991), though a quite short and limited one. At that period, the coverage of statutory social security programmes was widened and their benefits were increased, and new social security programmes were launched. A particularly important manifestation of this trend was the establishment of the unemployment insurance programme in 1973, after decades of strong opposition to such a programme from the Zionist labour movement (Gal 1997). Another new programme, that came into force in 1980, was the income support benefit. It resulted in the formalization and universalization of assistance to needy populations. Unlike the relief system that had operated until then, the new programme – administered by the NII – defined on a legal basis the right to economic assistance, and stipulated official and uniform criteria for entitlement to the benefit and its amount. The process of broadening and institutionalization of the welfare state in Israel in the 1970s is reflected in the significant increase in state expenses on social services and social security programmes, from 13.2 per cent of the GNP in 1970 to 20.1 per cent in 1980 (Kop, Blankett and Sharon 1986: 90).

An important result of the universalization of welfare policy was a significant reduction in the institutional distinction between systems whose activities targeted the veteran Jewish population, and those dealing with the immigrants from the 1950s and 1960s. That is, regarding the Jewish population there was a considerable diminution in the segmentation of the Israeli welfare state. At that period, moreover, the state broadened and deepened the protection against market forces that it granted to its Jewish citizens. A relatively wider range of services and goods were removed from the market arena and distributed to citizens according to the notion of social rights that are anchored ideologically in the institution of citizenship.

This process was generated and shaped by the combination of several factors. First, the broadening of social security programmes was a reaction by the state apparatus and the ruling party to signs of political and social ferment among the second generation of the 1950s and 1960s immigrants that emerged after the 1967 war, and manifested in the Black Panthers movement (Hofnong 2006). Second, the specific character of the welfare state expansion was strongly influenced by the balance of power between various state agencies. A fundamental component in the process was the strengthening of the NII and the ideology of universalist social policy that it carried and sought to advance. In the 1960s the NII began a gradual process of professionalization and institutional strengthening within the state apparatus that matured in the 1970s. It was thus able to promote policy initiatives that matched its ideology and institutional interests; particularly the extension of statutory universal programmes of social security that were under its jurisdiction, as compared with the selective assistance programmes that were under the authority of the Ministry of Social Assistance.

As noted above, the expansion trend in welfare policy was partial and entailed mainly the growing inclusion of Mizrachi Jews, and it was accompanied in important cases by the implementation of formal exclusionary practices directed at limiting Palestinian citizens' access to resources allocated by the state. A significant manifestation of the link between the growth of the welfare state on the one hand, and the formalization of Palestinian citizens' exclusion on the other, is the developments occurred in the child-allowance programme. In the 1970s, the programme was broadened substantially, both in terms of benefits level and of the number of children for whom allowances were paid. With this development, this programme became a key component of the social security system in Israel, and an important tool for redistribution. It functioned as a major mechanism of income support for large families and managed to significantly reduce the number of families, mostly Jewish, below the poverty line (Achdut and Carmi 1981).

During the late 1960s, the socio-economic condition of disadvantaged populations, particularly that of large families of Mizrachi origin, entered into the political agenda. Consequently, and in reaction to several signs of social ferment, political elites and the state bureaucracy started to debate different methods of improving the condition of that population, attempting to neutralize a possible threat to the political and social order (Doron and Kramer 1991). The approach that crystallized among social policy-makers was to use an existing tool – child allowances – for achieving those goals. When it was decided to increase the child allowances substantially, the question arose of transferring economic resources to the Arab population, among which there was a great number of large families. As I noted previously, from the initial stages of the child-allowance programme the issue had been in the background; some expressed their disappointment at the time with the decision to formulate it in universal terms and include the Arab population in it, as this contradicted the demographic interests of the state.[6] At that stage, however, the benefit was small and the issue was of marginal importance, but with the decision to expand the programme it became more crucial and moved higher on the decision-makers' agenda. The state had to cope with the tension between the political interest in significantly increasing the allowances, and the political interest in preventing economic resources from being allocated to Palestinian citizens. A central facet of that tension originated from what is termed in Zionist discourse as 'the demographic problem'; that is, the ratio between the number of Jewish and Palestinian citizens.

Under the policy paradigm that defines social policy as an instrument for promoting Zionist goals of nation- and state-building, increasing the child allowance was viewed as a tool for encouraging the Jewish birth-rate and 'improving' the demographic balance. Within this political context, the purpose of excluding Arab families and to channel larger benefits to the Jewish population alone came to be considered of critical importance. For instance, an internal NII document explicitly mentions the intention of excluding Palestinian citizens. Increasing the amount of the child benefits was intended 'to protect families' standard of living against a severe drop as a result of having children'. Nevertheless, 'the protection of the family's well-being at that level will be determined principally for the Jewish population; and a lower level will be set for the non-Jewish population …'.[7]

Different options were formulated in order to reduce Arab families' rights, without the move affecting Israel's self-definition as a democratic state that supposedly promises equal rights to all its citizens. Ultimately an 'expert committee' established by the government decided to condition the entitlement to larger benefits on one member of the family having served in the army. As is known, the vast majority of Palestinian citizens are not drafted into the army by governmental decision. As noted by the committee, the significant advantage of this exclusionary practice was that the distinction between Jewish and Arab families was based on an ostensibly universal criterion – military service – that would be politically acceptable both at home and abroad.[8] It enabled exclusion to be institutionalised within a statutory universal programme that was under the responsibility of the NII.

The formalization of exclusion in the child-allowance programme was enacted by the introduction of a new benefit programme that was anchored in the Demobilised Soldiers (Return to Work) Law. Under an amendment to the law, passed by the Knesset in July 1970, a programme called Child Allowances for Army Veterans granted special benefits to the children of families with record of military service.[9] From September 1970 significant benefits were paid for the fourth child and onwards, and in November 1974 the entitlement was broadened to cover the third child as well. The family member whose army service entitled the family to a special benefit was defined as: (a) the father or mother of the children; (b) the brother or sister of the children; and (c) the grandfather or grandmother of the children. That broad definition of a family of army veterans clearly demonstrates the state's intention to include in the programme as many Jewish families as possible. Under the original plan, however, a not inconsiderable number of Jewish families remained outside the circle of entitlement to increased benefits: recent immigrants; ultra-orthodox population that are exempted from military service; and people exempted from military service for health or social reasons. To include these groups, an arrangement was established under which the NII would pay an increased allowance to the new immigrant population, with Jewish Agency funding; ultra-orthodox yeshiva students would receive an increased allowance from the Religious Affairs Ministry budget; and the NII would pay an increased allowance funded by the Finance Ministry's budget to those who were exempt from service for health or social reasons and received assistance from the Ministry of Social Assistance.[10] As a result, virtually all Jewish families were entitled to the additional benefits, whether they served in the army or not. Due to several measures taken during the 1970s, the level of the additional child benefits from which Palestinian citizens were excluded increased, and so the gap between the universal child allowances and those that reached only the Jewish families. As a result, whereas for Jewish large families, mainly of Mizrachi origins, child allowances had significant redistributive effects as a tool for reducing poverty, for Palestinian families these impacts were negligible (see Rosenhek 1999).

That dialectic between inclusionary and exclusionary processes characterized the housing sphere too. The most important change that occurred in Israel's housing policy in the 1970s was the decrease in direct state involvement in the construction and allocation of public housing, and a transition to programmes of subsidized mortgages to increase the ability of entitled populations – especially young couples – for participating in the private housing market as consumers. Programmes of subsidised mortgages and grants were created in response to political and economic processes that became noticeable after the 1967 war. On one hand, there was a notable shortfall of housing due to declining construction during the 1965–66 recession. On the other hand, because of the accelerating economic growth that characterised the Israeli economy after the war, there was a strong demand in the housing market – a situation that led to steep rises in housing prices (Hirsh and Paitelson 1972: 3). As part of the broad process of attempts to neutralise social unrest by broadening the welfare state, new assistance programmes for housing were drafted and the coverage of existing programmes was broadened. Steps were also taken towards formalizing criteria for defining different groups' entitlement to the subsidized financing. Similar to events in other social policy areas, those changes ostensibly reflect a process of growing universalization in housing policy throughout the 1970s; but the trend covered mainly Jewish citizens, while Palestinian citizens were excluded from most programmes of housing assistance or entitled to significantly lower levels of aid.

As in the case of child-allowances, the major exclusionary practice was based on the politically convenient rule of conditioning of the entitlements to military service. A second practice that blocked Palestinian citizens' access to the assistance programmes was that receiving a subsidized mortgage was contingent on the housing unit being located in specific towns. Until 1977 no Arab locality appeared on the list of towns approved by the Ministry of Housing. This conditionality blocked access to the benefits by Palestinian citizens who did comply with the criterion of military or other form of security service – such as the Druze, the Circassians, some of the Bedouin, and others who served in the police force or the prison service. By 1977, 16,394 subsidized loans had been approved in the programme of housing assistance for young couples and of these, only 34 had been granted to Arabs (Lithwick 1980: 137).

According to the policy paradigm that defined the welfare state as an instrument for advancing state-building, at that period, too, the objective of dispersing the Jewish population still influenced housing policy. Several procedures were employed to encourage the purchase of homes in peripheral regions, defined as 'development regions': larger mortgages, better repayment terms, and standing loans that became a grant if the occupants remained at least five years in the development region (Lerman 1976). In compliance with the goal of 'improving' the demographic balance in peripheral regions, all the benefits listed above targeted obviously the Jewish population alone, and no Arab locality was included on the list of development regions.

Besides the considerable exclusion of Palestinian citizens from the trend of expansion of the Israeli welfare state, another extremely significant dimension of its segmentation which developed in the 1970s resulted from the inflow of large numbers of Palestinian labourers from the Occupied Territories into the Israeli secondary labour market, after the 1967 war. On the basis of their political status of non-citizens under occupation, those workers were almost completely excluded from the Israeli welfare state and its social security programmes, being constituted as an extremely flexible and unprotected labour force (Rosenhek 2003). The access of employers in the secondary labour market to this unprotected labour force reduced the 'rigidities' in the labour market induced by the broadening of the welfare state that granted Israeli workers, especially Jews, better protection from market forces than in the past.

The partial character of the golden age of the Israeli welfare state reflects the dialectic connection between the dynamics of inclusion and exclusion that were shaped by interactions between the welfare state's role as an instrument for state- and nation-building and its inner logic as a stratification order. The broadening and institutionalization of the welfare state in the 1970s meant principally a considerable trend of inclusion of the Mizrachi population, and the granting to it of a greater degree of protection against the market. Their inclusion was a condition for preserving the state's ability to mobilize the Jewish population for collective goals – particularly for managing the conflict with the Arab countries and the Palestinians through military means. Alongside that trend, formalization of several exclusionary practices towards Palestinian citizens got underway, and as a result they were left less protected from the market and other risks than their Jewish counterparts. Through this exclusionary pattern, they – and even more patently the Palestinian non-citizens from the Occupied Territories – were constituted by the state as unprotected labour channelized to the secondary labour market.

The 'Crisis of the Welfare State' and the neoliberal project

The period of expansion of the welfare state in Israel ended in the 1980s. Like in many other countries, the Israeli welfare state underwent changes over the next two decades that are often seen in the public arena as indicating a deep crisis. This is a period characterized by falling real value of benefits, tightening of entitlement criteria for various programmes, reduced payments to social security by employers, increasing use of selectivity principles of means tests, and privatisation of certain social services (Doron 2000; Gal 1994a). Attendant on those policy changes was the strengthening of the neoliberal ideology that defines the welfare state as a major obstacle to economic growth, and the institutional reinforcement of state agencies which are carriers of that ideology – first and foremost the central bank and the Ministry of Finance. In most cases, their attacks on the welfare state are formulated in seemingly undisputed and objective terms, such as efficiency, competitiveness, the need for a more flexible labour market, and economic imperatives dictated by globalisation. Within this politics of economic liberalization, the rhetorical use of an assumed inevitable connection between the global economy's functional requirements and the need for reducing the welfare state, serves as a particularly powerful source of legitimacy to neoliberal policies and institutional arrangements (see Maman and Rosenhek 2008).

Those changes in the politics of the welfare state are undoubtedly part of the broader transformation of Israel's political economy, that entails the liberalization of financial and of other markets, deregulation of the labour market, privatization of state- and Histadrut-owned companies, reduced government spending, and ever-growing integration in the global economy. These developments are linked to changes occurring in the class structure of Israel, particularly in the strengthening of a new upper-middle class whose direct dependence on the state is far less pronounced than before. This class is now closer to the global economy and exposed to neoliberal ideological models that praise individualism, privatization, deregulation, and the reduction of the welfare state. As a result, its members are less willing to mobilize on behalf of collectivist goals of state-building (Shafir and Peled 2002). All those structural, institutional, and ideological changes are immensely important for the politics of the welfare state. The consequence of changes in the class structure and in the balance of power within the state apparatus has been the strengthening of political actors with clear interests in the retrenchment of the welfare state and in reducing the socio-economic protection it affords the population.

As Michael Shalev (2000) has demonstrated, however, the liberalisation of Israel's political economy has been more ambiguous and characterised by contradictory trends than might be concluded from the neoliberal rhetoric of most powerful political actors. The contradictions and the complexities of the process are clearly visible in the mixed patterns of continuity and change in the welfare state. The trend of retrenchment in the welfare state, at least up to 2002, was in fact far less decisive than could have been inferred from the hegemonic status of neoliberal rhetoric in the public arena. On one hand, it is clear that the political context where social policy is formulated and implemented has changed, and that ideological trends viewing the welfare state as an obstacle to economic efficiency have gained prominence in the political arena. But on the other hand, as I show below, it was only after 2000 – with the worldwide slowdown and the economic crisis caused by the failure of the Oslo process and the renewed violent conflict with the Palestinians – that the structure of opportunities of political actors advancing the neoliberal agenda and seeking to significantly curtail the welfare state became sufficiently broad to generate drastic changes in Israel's social policy.

The complex trends that characterised the Israeli welfare state since the 1980s are reflected in data on state spending in the social sphere. National Insurance payments have increased, from 5.05 per cent of the GDP in 1980 to 6.54 per cent in 1990 and to 7.69 per cent in 1999 (Bank of Israel 2000: 332). At the same time, in contrast to events during the 1970s, most of the rise in spending did not originate from broadening existing social security programmes, or implementing new ones. On the contrary, it is almost entirely explained by processes 'external' to the welfare state: an ageing population, higher unemployment levels, and mass immigration from the CIS. Contradictory trends are discernible in state spending on social services (education, health, housing, and personal services). In the first half of the 1980s, there was a significant drop in the real value of that spending, while in the second half it remained at a constant level. By contrast, spending in the first half of the 1990s increased rapidly: between 1989 and 1996 the average rate of annual growth in real terms was 10.1 per cent (Weinblatt et al. 2000). A major, if not exclusive, cause for the changing trend was the mass immigration from the CIS. It transpires therefore that the Zionist nature of Israel's welfare state – that is, its definition as an instrument for promoting tasks of nation- and state-building like 'immigration absorption' – still played a central role in its dynamic.

We can also discern contradictory trends in the welfare state's operating principles. Despite the trend for tightening of entitlement criteria, some changes did occur towards expanding the welfare state. For example, during the 1980s and the early 1990s selectivity principles were introduced to the child allowance programme, but in 1993 the government decided to revoke them. In the same year, the conditioning of increased child-allowances on military service that was directed at excluding Palestinian citizens was can-celled. For the first time since 1970, the child allowance programme became a truly de facto universal programme; Palestinian citizens now became entitled to the same benefits as Jewish citizens received. The revocation of a prominent expression of the partial exclusion of Palestinian citizens resulted from particular circumstances in parliamentary politics during the years of the Rabin government. Arab parties conditioned their necessary support for the ruling coalition, though without joining it, on equal child-allowances for Arab families (Rosenhek and Shalev 2000).

Furthermore, several new programmes were introduced to the Israeli welfare system over the last two decades of the twentieth century. In 1986 a long-term-care insurance programme was established, which provided par-tial funding of long-term nursing care by the NII (Ajzenstadt and Rosenhek 2000). Another important development in the social security system, prin-cipally pertaining to the gendered character of the welfare state, was the passing of the Single-Parent Family Law in 1992. The law awarded those families a higher income-support allowance that was later raised again in the framework of two laws passed in 1994 and 1995. Due to those changes, the incidence of poverty among single-parent families after transfer payments fell from 40.7 per cent in 1994 to 25.7 per cent in 1995 (Swirski et al. 2003: 12). In general, notwithstanding the dominant neoliberal rhetoric, until 2001 the system of payment transfers managed to continue functioning as a major mechanism for resource redistribution and for reducing the incid-ence of poverty. For example, in 2000 transfer and tax payments reduced the number of families below the poverty-line by 45.3 per cent (National Insurance Institute 2001: 14).

The most significant change that has occurred in the last decades in the institutional configuration of the Israeli welfare state is undoubtedly the legislation of the State Health Insurance Law in 1994, which legally anchors for the first time citizens' rights to health services. Its main principles are the following: universal coverage of all residents of the state (migrant workers are not legally classified as residents, so they are excluded from the programme); the formal definition by the state of a general and uni-form 'basket' of services; setting insurance fees as a proportion of salary; and cancelling the automatic link between membership in the Histadrut's

'General HMO' and membership in the Histadrut (Zalmanovitch 1997). Developments in the field of health services reflect the contradictory trends typifying the welfare state in Israel. On the one hand, the new insurance pro- gramme embodies the formal recognition by the state of fundamental social rights and the promise of universal access of (almost) the entire population to health services, yet on the other hand, there are recurrent attempts by the state to recommodify health services, limiting the basket of services and setting additional payment for receiving them (Filc 2004).

During the 1990s a new population joined Israeli society, that of migrant workers, and it posed the Israeli welfare state, and Israeli society in general, an unprecedented challenge. Since they are not citizens and lacked the legal status of residents, similar to the case of Palestinian workers from the Occupied Territories, the migrant workers – both documented and undocu- mented ones – are excluded almost completely from the Israeli welfare state. In this way the state constitutes them as a flexible and unprotected labour force, designated for the secondary labour market. Replacing Palestinian workers whose employment in Israel was based on daily commuting, with migrant workers who not only work in Israel but reside there too, created a new situation in terms of the inclusionary and exclusionary dynamics in Israel's welfare state. The presence of migrant workers and their potential for putting down roots contradict the exclusionary ethnonational founda- tions of Israel's migration regime, which in principle does not recognise the possibility of non-Jewish immigration. The migrant workers' exclusion from the welfare state stems therefore not only from the interest of constituting an unprotected workforce, but also from the wider political significance that could arise from recognizing the migrant workers' social rights in terms of their status in the political community. Hence, the major consideration underlying its exclusionary policy is the state's concern that should it grant the migrant workers social rights, this might imply that it recognises them as legitimate members of Israeli society. At the same time, certain state agen- cies, particularly at the local level, have implemented practices of partial inclusion in compliance with their specific institutional interests and profes- sional logics (Rosenhek 2000).

As noted, since the 1980s there has been a fundamental change in the political status of the welfare state. As unemployment increased, the unem- ployment insurance programme has become a central issue in the politics of the welfare state; and against the backdrop of the almost hegemonic neoliberal rhetoric of liberalisation, fiscal austerity, decreased state involve- ment, and labour market's deregulation, it has become a prominent and popular target for attacks by the welfare state's opponents (Gal 1994b). The Bank of Israel and the Ministry of Finance have played a major role in the process, claiming that unemployment insurance is among the major factors contributing to the rise in unemployment, because its generous rules allow the unemployed to turn down job-offers, reducing their incentive to work and creating rigidities in the labour market. As early as 1982, the Bank of

Israel argued that additional increases in the real value of unemployment payments should be avoided to prevent the 'negative effects of unemployment insurance' (1982: 69). In the years that followed, as unemployment levels increased and the issue rose higher on the public agenda, the Bank of Israel's criticism of unemployment insurance became more stringent. For example, the Bank's report for 1992 states that 'among the principal causes [of growing unemployment] we can indicate the development of unemployment insurance systems that have lowered the pressure on workers to return to the labour market' (Bank of Israel 1993: 149). The professional echelon of the Ministry of Finance also actively participated in attacking unemployment insurance. A document drafted by the Budgets Division at the Ministry emphasized the allegedly negative impact of the social security system on incentives to work. Particularly significant is the stance presented in the document regarding the negative impact of unemployment insurance on wage levels and labour costs. The argument is that by offering an alternative source of income for unemployed people, unemployment insurance reduces the possibility of using unemployment to curb wage levels (Shaviv 1999). This demonstrates that the considerations of the Ministry of Finance went well beyond concern over the budgetary costs of the unemployment benefits. They were part of a much broader agenda concerning the political economy of labour market regulation, and particularly the general implications of the unemployment insurance programme on the degree of protection against market forces that Israel's citizens enjoy.

Despite those assaults on the unemployment insurance programme and on the welfare state in general, by 2002 material changes in policy were relatively few and did not result in drastic retrenchment. As in other welfare states (Pierson 1995; Starke 2006), factors related to electoral politics and to institutional interests of state agencies also acted in Israel as highly effective barriers to the attempts to significantly narrow the welfare state (Rosenhek 2004).

Since the renewal of the violent conflict with the Palestinians in 2000, however, there has been a substantive change in the politics of the welfare state. Neoliberal rhetoric, which seeks to downsize the welfare state in the name of economic rationality and integration into the global economy, had already achieved hegemonic status in the public discourse years before. Yet, only the economic crisis that followed the collapse of the Oslo process significantly broadened the structure of opportunities for political actors seeking to promote the neoliberal project regarding the welfare state.

In conditions of economic recession, and through the political construction of an emergency situation threatening to bring down the economy completely, those actors managed to carry out plans for severely constricting the welfare state that had been blocked or moderated during the 1990s via the parliamentary process. Finance Ministry programmes that had been shelved in previous years or blocked at early stages of the decision-making process, were now advanced and implemented. Consequently, since

2002 there has been a significant decrease in real, and even nominal, values of most allowances paid by the NII – particularly income-supplement allowances, unemployment allowances, single-parent family allowances, and child allowances – and entitlement criteria have become far more restrictive. As a result, while in 2002 the transfer payments system reduced the incidence of poverty among families by 46.6 per cent, in 2005 it did so only by 38.7 per cent (National Insurance Institute 2006: 12).

The advancement of the neoliberal project of curtailing the welfare state is paradoxical in the context of the renewed violent conflict with the Palestinians. In their analysis of the political dynamics of citizenship in Israel, Gershon Shafir and Yoav Peled (2002) posited that the liberalization process of the political economy in Israel, including the retrenchment of the welfare state, is tightly connected to processes of political liberalization and the decolonization of the Occupied Territories. According to this argument, the transition from a mobilised society to a liberal one, in which the Oslo process had a major role, weakened the welfare state's political status because it was always considered a key element of the institutional configuration aimed at creating and preserving high mobilization levels within the Jewish population for the collective goals of state- and nation-building, particularly concerning war-making. But paradoxically, the gravest reduction in social security benefits and social services occurred when political liberalization and decolonization processes halted and the return to the mobilized-society pattern intensified. If renewed violent conflict was a lever for the advancement of the neoliberal agenda, then apparently the Gordian knot between the Israeli welfare state and its roles as an instrument for state- and nation-building in the context of a mobilized, collectivist society has finally unravelled. The severing of ties between economic liberalization, and political liberalization and decolonization raises an important question about the theoretical and empirical affinities between the two processes. The analysis offered by Shafir and Peled (2002) might imply that those affinities are deterministic. In contrast, developments in the Israeli welfare state since 2002, as well as in other aspects of the political economy, indicate that enhanced economic liberalization can co-exist with a halt, and even reverse, of political liberalization. The question is whether the contradiction between the neoliberal project – which constrains the welfare state and enhances ethnic–class polarization within the Jewish population – and the continuing occupation and conflict with the Palestinians, which requires a society mobilized for collectivist goals – can persist over time? While there is no clear answer to this question at the present time, it appears that this contradiction, and its significance for the formulation of citizenship and social rights, will be a major motif in the politics of Israel's welfare state in coming years.

Conclusions

An essential characteristic of the Israeli welfare state is the hierarchic distinction between different social groups in terms of their access to resources. As a result of dynamics of inclusion and exclusion manifested at the institutional and policy levels, Ashkenazi Jews, Mizrachi Jews, Palestinian citizens, Palestinians under occupation, and labour migrants were differently positioned in the welfare state's field of operation. Hence the welfare state in Israel not only reflects but also helps to produce and reproduce a stratified structure, where different populations are entitled to differential degrees of protection from market forces and other socio-economic risks. The dynamics of inclusion and exclusion underlying that hierarchic structure were shaped by two analytically distinct state logics. The first logic derives from the exclusionary foundations of the nation-state and from the specificities of state- and nation-building processes in Israel in the context of a colonial project grounded on ethnonational principles. The second logic stems from the welfare state's functioning as a central stratifying mechanism in advanced capitalism, that impacts not only on the life chances of individuals and groups but also on the political economy in general, and on the structure and dynamic of the labour market in particular.

As I have shown in this analysis, since the pre-statehood period and until today, the political dynamic of the Israeli welfare state has been closely connected to state- and nation-building processes. According to the policy paradigm that became institutionalized, the welfare state functioned first and foremost as a tool to promote Zionist goals – such as territorial control; political, social, and economic incorporation of the Jewish migrants; and creating socio-economic conditions that enhanced the state's ability to mobilize the Jewish population. This pivotal role was reflected both at the ideological and institutional levels, as well as at the level of policy formulation and implementation. In view of that affinity, the welfare state emerged as a central institutional field where the ethnonational hierarchic configuration of Israeli citizenship was constituted and reproduced.

However, the dynamics of inclusion and exclusion in the welfare state do not reflect only discursive categories of differential incorporation in the political community, or simply the exclusionary foundations of the nation-state. These dynamics are also connected to the inner logic of the welfare state as a stratificatory order. As a central distributive mechanism in advanced capitalism, the welfare state does not only moderate some inequalities deriving from the labour market functioning; it also creates a particular dimension of inequality according to the degree of protection against market forces that it provides different groups. In turn, this dimension of inequality serves as a central factor that influences patterns of incorporation of different groups in the labour market. As such, welfare policy can function as a central factor in constituting subordinate social groups as an unprotected and flexible labour force, designated to enter the secondary labour market. Those implications are manifested in the Israeli case in the connection between the status in the welfare state of Mizrachi Jews, Palestinian citizens, Palestinians from the Occupied Territories, and migrant workers, and the patterns of their incorporation into the labour market at different periods. Accordingly, the dynamics of inclusion and exclusion of those groups derived not only from factors 'exogenous' to the welfare state, such as exclusionary ideologies towards minorities, but also from the political economy of the welfare state as a stratification order and a major mechanism for political regulation of the labour market. This analytical perspective reveals, therefore, one fundamental facet of the connection between differential inclusion of social groups into the institution of citizenship and the production and reproduction of socio-economic hierarchies.

Notes

1 This is an updated and elaborated version of the article published in Hebrew in *Generations, Locations, Identities: Contemporary Perspectives on Society and Culture in Israel*, edited by Hanna Herzog, Tal Kochavi, and Shimshon Selniker (2007) Jerusalem: The Van-Leer Jerusalem Institute and Hakibbutz Hameuchad Publishing House, pp. 317–49.
2 'First Report of the Inter-Ministerial Committee for Population Dispersal, submitted to the Ministers Committee for Population Dispersal in March 1964', p. 41. It is noteworthy that this report is stated to be grounded 'on the arguments of an IDF representative and the Advisor on Arab Affairs at the Prime Minister's Bureau' (p. 48) – underscoring the centrality of the issue of territorial control of the Arab population in the decision-making process.
3 Minutes of a meeting of Mapai's Inner Secretariat with the Wages Committee, 31 October 1958, Labour Party Archives, file 24, division 2. Herut was a right-wing political party, predecessor of Likud, and Maki is the acronym for the Israeli Communist Party.
4 At a meeting on 21 September 1958, the Histadrut's Central Committee resolved to oppose the draft programme, as long as its funding would require raising the National Insurance fees that its members paid. At that meeting, to bolster the objections, it was claimed that around 80 per cent of those entitled to the benefits will be Mizrachis, and only 20 per cent would be Ashkenazis (Histadrut's Central Committee, Labour Archives).
5 Minutes of the meeting of Mapai's Inner Secretariat with the Wages Committee, 31 October 1958, Labour Party Archives, file 24, division 2.
6 For instance, in a letter dated 24 November 1968 to Zina Herman, Director of the Centre for Demographic Problems, Yitzhak Kanev – who is considered the architect of the Israeli welfare state – wrote: 'We should have thought how to amend the law and to transfer payments for large families to the Jewish Agency or to the government's Absorption Department which deals only with *olim* [Jewish immigrants]. These payments encourage birth rates among the minorities, more than among us, and it creates a vicious circle in our demographic situation' (NII Archives, 2, 49/263).
7 'Family Allowances for Children', 1 April 1970, NII Archives, 1, 599/84.
8 Report of the 'Committee on the matter of increasing allowances for families with children', 12 April 1970, NII Archives, 1, 599/84.
9 The Demobilised Soldiers (Return to Work) Law, Amendment 4, 22 July 1970.
10 Summary of a meeting with the participation of the Minister of Labour,

representatives of the National Insurance Institute, and representatives of the Ministry of Finance, 28 January 1972, NII Archives, 2, 263/49.

References

Achdut, L. and Carmi, M. (1981) *Twenty Five Years of the National Insurance Institute*, Jerusalem: National Insurance Institute (in Hebrew).

Ajzenstadt, M. and Rosenhek, Z. (2000) "Privatization and New Modes of State Intervention: The Long-Term Care Program in Israel", *Journal of Social Policy*, 29: 247–62.

Bank of Israel (1982) *Bank of Israel Report, 1981*, Jerusalem: Bank of Israel (in Hebrew).

— (1993) *Bank of Israel Report, 1992*, Jerusalem: Bank of Israel (in Hebrew).

— (2000) *Bank of Israel Report, 1999*, Jerusalem: Bank of Israel (in Hebrew).

Barzilai, Y. (1969) *The Development of Housing Standards in Israel in Comparison to the General Improvement in Life Standards*, Jerusalem: Ministry of Construction and Housing (in Hebrew).

Doron, A. (2000) "Targeting Social Security Payments: The Case of Child Allowances in Israel", *Chevra V'revacha*, 20: 5–24 (in Hebrew).

Doron, A. and Kramer, R. (1991) *The Welfare State in Israel – the Evolution of Social Security Policy and Practice*, Boulder: Westview Press.

Drabkin-Darin, H. (1959) *Public Housing – An Overview of Public Housing in Israel during the Decade 1948–1958*, Tel-Aviv: Gadish (in Hebrew).

Esping-Andersen, G. (1990) *The Three Worlds of Welfare Capitalism*, Cambridge: Polity Press.

Filc, D. (2004) "Post-Fordism's Contradictory Trends: The Case of the Israeli Health Care System", *Journal of Social Policy*, 33: 417–36.

Freeman, G. (1986) "Migration and the Political Economy of the Welfare State", *The Annals of the American Academy of Political and Social Sciences*, 485: 51–63.

Gal, J. (1994a) "Commodification and Privatization of the Welfare State – Implications for Israel", *Chevra V'revacha*, 15: 7–24 (in Hebrew).

— (1994b) "The Development of Unemployment Insurance in Israel", *Social Security*, Special English edition, 3: 117–36.

— (1997) "Unemployment Insurance, Trade Unions and the Strange Case of the Israeli Labour Movement", *International Review of Social History*, 42: 357–96.

Goldthorpe, J. (1984) "The End of Convergence: Corporatism and Dualistic Tendencies in Modern Western Societies", in J. Goldthorpe (ed.) *Order and Conflict in Contemporary Capitalism*, Oxford: Oxford University Press, pp. 315–43.

Hirsh, A., and Paitelson, I. (1972) *An Outline for Assistance Housing Policy for Young Couples*, Jerusalem: Ministry of Housing (in Hebrew).

Hofnong, M. (2006) *Protest and Butter: The Black Panthers Demonstrations and Allocations for Social Needs*, Jerusalem: Nevo Publishers (in Hebrew).

Klein, P. (1959) *The Ministry of Social Welfare in Israel: Proposals on Program and Administration Prepared for the Government of Israel*, New York: United Nations Program for Technical Assistance.

Kop, Y., Blankett, J. and Sharon, D. (1986) "Government Expenditures on Social Services", in Y. Kop (ed.) *Changing Social Policy – Israel, 1985–86*, Jerusalem: The Center for Social Policy Studies in Israel, pp. 1–107.

Lerman, R. (1976) *A Critical Overview of Israeli Housing Policy*, Jerusalem: Brookdale Institute.

Lewin-Epstein, N. and Semyonov, M. (2000) "Migration, Ethnicity, and Inequality: Homeownership in Israel", *Social Problems*, 47: 425–44.

Lithwick, I. (1980) *Macro and Micro Housing Programs in Israel*, Jerusalem: Brookdale Institute.

Maman, D, and Rosenhek, Z. (2008) "Making the Global Present: The Bank of Israel and the Politics of Inevitability of Neoliberalism", *Israeli Sociology*, 10: 107–31 (in Hebrew).

Marshall, T. H. (1950) "Citizenship and Social Class" in T. H. Marshall, *Citizenship and Social Class and other Essays*, Cambridge: Cambridge University Press, pp. 1–85.

National Insurance Institute (2001) *Trends in Poverty and Inequality in Income Distribution*, 2000, Jerusalem: National Insurance Institute.

— (2006) *Poverty and Inequality in Income Distribution, 2005*, Jerusalem: National Insurance Institute.

Newman, D. (1989) "Civilian and Military Presence as Strategies of Territorial Control: The Arab-Israel Conflict", *Political Geography Quarterly*, 8: 215–27.

O'Connor, J. (1996) "From Women in the Welfare State to Gendering Welfare State Regimes", *Current Sociology*, 44: 1–124.

Offe, C. (1984) *Contradictions of the Welfare State*, Cambridge: The MIT Press.

Peck, J. (1989) "Labour Market Segmentation Theory", *Labour and Industry*, 2: 119–44.

Pierson, P. (1995) *Dismantling the Welfare State? – Reagan, Thatcher, and the Politics of Retrenchment*, Cambridge: Cambridge University Press.

Quadagno, J. (1994) *The Color of Welfare*, New York: Oxford University Press.

Rosenhek, Z. (1998) "Policy Paradigms and the Dynamics of the Welfare State: The Israeli Welfare State and the Zionist Colonial Project", *International Journal of Sociology and Social Policy*, 18: 157–202.

— (1999) "The Exclusionary Logic of the Welfare State: Palestinian Citizens in the Israeli Welfare State", *International Sociology*, 14: 195–215.

— (2000) "Migration Regimes, Intra-State Conflicts and the Politics of Exclusion and Inclusion: Migrant Workers in the Israeli Welfare State", *Social Problems*, 47: 49–67.

— (2003) "The Political Dynamics of a Segmented Labour Market: Palestinian Citizens, Palestinians from the Occupied Territories and Migrant Workers in Israel", *Acta Sociologica*, 46: 151–69.

— (2004) "Globalization, Domestic Politics and the Restructuring of the Welfare State: The Unemployment Insurance Program in Israel", in E. Benvenisti and G. Nolte (eds), *The Welfare State, Globalization, and International Law*, Berlin: Springer, pp. 79–101.

Rosenhek, Z. and Shalev, M. (2000) "The Contradictions of Palestinian Citizenship in Israel: Inclusion and Exclusion in the Israeli Welfare State", in N. Butenschon, U. Davis and M. Hassassian (eds), *Citizenship and the State in the Middle East: Approaches and Applications*, Syracuse: Syracuse University Press, pp. 288–315.

Roter, R. and Shamai, N. (1990) "Housing Policy", in M. Sanbar (ed.) *Economic and Social Policy in Israel – The First Generation*, Lanham: University Press of America, pp. 171–84.

Sainsbury, D. (1999) "Gender, Policy Regimes, and Politics", in D. Sainsbury (ed.), *Gender and Welfare State Regimes*, Oxford: Oxford University Press, pp. 245–75.

— (2006) "Immigrants' Social Rights in Comparative Perspective: Welfare Regimes,

Forms in Immigration and Immigration Policy Regimes", *Journal of European Social Policy*, 16: 229–44.

Shafir, G. and Peled, Y. (2002) *Being Israeli – The Dynamics of Multiple Citizenship*, Cambridge: Cambridge University Press.

Shalev, M. (1992) *Labour and the Political Economy in Israel*, Oxford: Oxford University Press.

— (2000) "Liberalization and the Transformation of the Political Economy" in G. Shafir and Y. Peled (eds) *The New Israel – Peacemaking and Liberalization*, Boulder: Westview Press, pp. 129–59.

Shaviv, M. (1999) *From Ensuring Income to Ensuring Employment*, Jerusalem: Budget Department, Ministry of Finance (in Hebrew).

Soysal, Y. (1994) *Limits of Citizenship – Migrants and Postnational Membership in Europe*, Chicago: University of Chicago Press.

Starke, P. (2006) "The Politics of Welfare State Retrenchment: A Literature Review", *Social Policy and Administration*, 40: 104–20.

Swirski, S., Kraus, V., Konor-Attias, E. and Herbst, A. (2003) *Solo Mothers in Israel*, Tel-Aviv: Adva Center.

Tenne, D. (1962) "Housing in Israel's Development", in I. Ronen (ed.) *The Economy of Israel –Theory and Practice*, Tel-Aviv: Dvir, pp. 439–48 (in Hebrew).

Therborn, G. (1989) "States, Populations and Productivity: Towards a Theory of Welfare States", in P. Lassman (ed.) *Politics and Social Theory*, London: Routledge, pp. 62–84.

Turner, B. (1993) "Contemporary Problems in the Theory of Citizenship", in B. Turner (ed.) *Citizenship and Social Theory*, London: SAGE Publications, pp. 1–18.

Weinblatt, J., Blankett, J., Blass, N., Nachshon-Sharon, D., Katan, Y. and Shirom, A. (2000) "Social Services and their Development", in Y. Kop (ed.) *Israel's Social Services, 1999–2000*, Jerusalem: The Center for Social Policy Studies in Israel, pp. 17–152.

Yiftachel, O. (2006) *Ethnocracy – Land and Identity Politics in Israel/Palestine*, Philadelphia: University of Pennsylvania Press.

Zalmanovitch, Z. (1997) "Some Antecedents to Healthcare Reform: Israel and the United States", *Policy and Politics*, 25: 251–68.

Zaslavsky, D. (1954) *Immigrant Housing in Israel: Building, Planning and Development, 1950–1953*, Tel-Aviv: Am-Oved (in Hebrew).

5 Corporatism and multiculturalism as responses to ethnic claims and socio-economic inequality

The case of Shas[1]

David Lehmann and Batia Siebzehner

In April 2009, Shas, a party and movement identified ethnically with Israeli Jews of Middle Eastern and North African origin but religiously with observance in accordance with Ashkenazi ultra-Orthodoxy, took its place in the newly formed Netanyahu government with four cabinet seats – more than it had ever had before. Shas has managed to combine strong religion, ethnic identity and features of modernity, in a political system which, until the early 1990s, appeared unreceptive to ethnic or identity-based claims arising from the many Jewish diasporas which 'landed' back in the Middle East. It has become an established player possessing a fairly secure tenancy on a quota of cabinet seats. This paper provides an interpretation of the movement and party's rise by starting from two aspects of Israeli citizenship: the corporatist character of the country's political system and the web of ethnic, religious and institutional enclaves which, grid-like, but also in something of a crazy quilt, demarcate its social structure. It is through these affiliations and mechanisms of access that Israelis claim to belong to one or another, or a combination, of their country's innumerable sub-cultures. These are classified *inter alia* by national or ethnic (including Arab) origin, by religious observance, by political allegiance, and by place of residence. But this is only the framework: the paper illustrates the dynamics of political inclusion by showing how a strategy of social self-exclusion, surrounding its membership and their institutions with material and symbolic frontiers in a manner characteristic of contemporary fundamentalist and evangelical movements, can enable a movement to stake a claim to a place inside the state. In the course of the argument some approximations are made with multiculturalism, for the Israeli response to ethnic and religious pressure is a good example of the ways in which corporatism offers a framework for multicultural accommodations.

Israeli Politics and Ethnicity

The Israel polity presents, as is well known, all manner of conundrums and puzzles for theories of citizenship. One prominent political scientist, writing about the country's party system, described it as 'a most baffling case—and this quite apart from the fact that it is a microcosm of all the conceivable complexities' (Sartori 1976). The founding of the state itself was legitimated in international law by virtue of UN resolutions, but without the war which accompanied it and which led to the forced exile of a large number of what would have been an Arab majority population, the Jewish character of the state, also validated by the UN, could hardly have been established. The resulting tension between ethnicity and democracy remains, of course, unresolved to this day. This victory did not, however, mean that the Jewish population would be homogeneous ethnically or even religiously: despite, but also because of, their Jewishness, the diversity of their provenance made of Israel a multi-ethnic, multicultural and class-divided society in a way no one at that time imagined and indeed few outside Israel imagine even today.

Despite this heterogeneity, from its origins in the pre-state institutions before 1948 until well into the 1980s and even later, Israel's politics saw off all attempts to mobilize Jewish ethnic identity in the political arena: even Arab identity was expressed through the (Jewish-led) Communist Party until Palestinization brought its mutation into Balad (Louër 2007). Although there were numerous ethnic lists in successive elections going back as far as the pre-state *Yishuv* institutions in 1920, these were almost invariably the vehicles of particular politicians' transitory interests and of the corresponding patronage of the largest parties (Herzog 1986) and never exceeded 5 per cent of the vote. As far as religious controversy was concerned, the ultra-Orthodox parties – with some 5 per cent of the vote – eschewed almost entirely the holding of Ministerial office due to their principled objection to the idea of a secular Jewish state, confining themselves to the narrow sphere of budgetary wrangling and endless arguments over the official enforcement of religious observance.

The propagators of the Zionist utopia, in the ideologically formative pre-state period, had barely acknowledged the existence of millions of North African, Middle Eastern and Central Asian Jews (let alone those in South India and Ethiopia) – while religious traditionalism was respected only as a relic of a world which most of them had abandoned when they left Poland and Russia in the early twentieth century, destined to gradually disappear under the influence of modernity and secularization. Even the long-established, deeply observant Ashkenazi Jewish community in Palestine – who were very hostile to Zionism – were ignored. But by now Israel has been touched by identity politics and the country's culture and politics have been reshaped by waves of immigration from different parts of the world and some resulting waves of political mobilization: from Yemen before 1950, the Middle East and North Africa in the 1950s and 1960s, the USSR in the

1970s, from Ethiopia in the 1980s, and again from the former USSR and from Ethiopia in the 1990s and from North and South America throughout the period since 1960. Shas showed one way by realigning the politics of religion and ethnicity and took its place as the voice of the religious and ethnic revival of Middle Eastern and North African Jews (Sephardim[2]), thus enlarging the existing modes of representation, even though only a minority of the Sephardi electorate vote Shas. And later the extreme right-wing politician Lieberman founded Yisrael Beiteinu (Israel, our Home), a party appealing mainly to the Russian electorate, espousing hostility and distrust towards the Arab minority (20 per cent of the population) and the Palestinians – as well as a less explicitly articulated but evident dislike of the ultra-Orthodox[3] and their encroachment on the secular public sphere. In retrospect one might say that ethnicity-based mobilizations were inevitable – they just took time to mature.

Sephardim in Israel are the Jews originating in the Middle East and North Africa, the largest single contingent in Morocco. The Statistical Yearbook 1999 (Table 12.15) shows consistent under-representation of persons whose father was born in Asia and Africa (the nearest approximation in census categories) among academics, professionals and managers, and over-representation among unskilled workers. Among students and applicants to universities they were also under-represented (though once admitted they performed as well as other groups). In the absence of direct indicators, we can gauge the position of Sephardim from indicators of Israel's development towns, to which they were so frequently sent on arrival in the 1950s and 1960s. These are located in peripheral areas, and are a classic example of modern urban developments becoming concentrations of poverty. Seventy-five per cent of their population was Sephardi in the 1980s, accounting for one-quarter to one-third of the country's Sephardi Jews. In 1987 these localities stood 'below 70 per cent of the entire population' on a socio-economic index calculated by the Central Bureau of Statistics. In 1983 College graduates were only 10 per cent of their population, compared to the national average of 14 per cent, and 63 per cent were without high-school diplomas compared with the national average of 56 per cent; they accounted for 40 per cent of the country's unemployed in 1987, and in 1989 their rate of unemployment was double the national average (Shafir and Peled 2002: 81).[4] Shas spokesmen say they also suffer from the classic problems of family disintegration and drug abuse which characterize urban decay, and that their party's emphasis on the restoration of parental authority and on disciplined behaviour is welcomed in these places.[5]

Despite being spared almost all the genocide wreaked by the Nazis, North African Jewish immigrants to Israel suffered greater institutional destruction than their Eastern European cousins, having been unable to re-establish their institutions in Israel. This was probably because those institutions in the countries of origin had been under the personal authority of Jewish notables and had not supported a robust civic culture, and also because the North

African Jewish elite tended to emigrate to France and the Americas (Adler and Inbar 1977; Shokeid 1995), while most of those who went to Israel were from the poorer and less educated strata who, for example, spoke no French and had little familiarity with the Zionist idea of a Jewish state, or indeed with the very idea of a modern society and state. Once in Israel they were confronted by an immigrant absorption apparatus which paid little respect to their way of life and by a fiercely competitive society ruled by a determinedly modernist bureaucracy. For decades, until the rise of Shas, yeshivas were not transplanted from Morocco or even from the jewel of Jewish North Africa, the island of Jerba (Deshen 1982), and until today the Sephardi religious elite prefer to send their sons to the prestigious Ashkenazi yeshivas.[6]

A Society of Enclaves

The success of Shas has to be interpreted in the context of Israel as a society of enclaves – political, legal, social and territorial.

The State inherited from the Ottoman Empire via the British Mandate, arrangements for separate judicial arrangements regarding personal status law for Jews, Christians and Muslims, which for practical purposes has meant that in Israel a state-funded Chief Rabbinate – divided between Sephardi and Ashkenazi – with its court and its bureaucracy, decides on who can marry whom, and who qualifies as a Jew[7], and certifies the ritual acceptability (*kashrut*) of food in the name of the state. Muslim and Christian courts likewise deal with marriage, divorce, and other family law issues. In addition, the division of the education system according to religious criteria (secular, national religious[8], ultra-Orthodox) was inherited from the pre-State period (the *Yishuv*) when non-state Jewish institutions ran their own schools. These separate arrangements have been preserved in parallel to the patronage power of political parties in the state, also inherited from the pre-State period when the various Zionist parties – left, right, centre, religious and secular and various permutations of these – in accordance with the enclave principle, managed their own kibbutz settlements, cooperatives, medical services, football teams and much else besides. No wonder then that already in the 1980s a standard text on Israeli politics spoke of how 'social enclaves tend to form around movements which act as secondary centers that mobilize and allocate resources and commitments, receiving continuity through socialization and indoctrination' (Horowitz and Lissak 1987: 28). The enclave principle also extends into the character of neighbourhoods and of course to the settlements in the West Bank. The word denotes visible or palpable boundaries backed by a degree of institutionalization, and also the superimposition of several different boundaries – for example territory, race, marriage restrictions, language, dress codes.

This enclave concept can be analytically formulated in terms of frontiers, following Barth (Barth 1969). Barth insisted on the institutional character of boundaries, and argued against the notion that they are rooted either in tradition, or in colour or race, or in any of the differences which they claim to be built on, arguing instead what has now become conventional wisdom, namely that they are constructed and preserved through political processes – though not for that are they any the less real.

Frontiers embody rules, though the rules do not usually forbid frontier-crossing – rather they specify, implicitly or explicitly, the conditions under which borders can be crossed: rules, for example, governing intermarriage, commercial arrangements, or political affiliation. We speak here of a very long axis: there are porous frontiers, contested frontiers, walled and barbed-wire frontiers and so on.

In Israel, as in many other places, the frontiers of ethnicity and inherited tradition of religious observance have for several decades been reconfigured by movements of religious renewal which often defy ready-made assumptions about introversion, about the rejection of modernity, about other-worldliness, about social cohesiveness. That is to say: the observation of tight internal control and uniform habits of dress and time allocation which purposively express rejection of consumerism, of the commodification of the body, of the permissive society, among many other things, may lead observers to assume that a group is therefore shutting itself behind high and thick walls and is incapable of engaging with the institutions of modernity. They frequently combine a strong emphasis on internal discipline and separation from the 'world of darkness' with keen involvement in politics, with street-based and media-borne campaigns of evangelization. Indeed one might be forgiven for thinking that the greater a movement's investment in 'outreach' (as proselytizing among secularized Jews is called in the jargon) the more numerous, thick and superimposed are its boundaries. Yet the frontiers are penetrating ever further into spheres which have previously been the preserve of the secular. Nurit Stadler's account of recent developments in Israeli fundamentalist culture describes numerous ways in which its members have become involved in civil society beyond their frontiers, through large-scale charitable work and prominent involvement in body rescue and emergency medical attention after terrorist attacks at first and then after all sorts of other emergencies. All this without renouncing their frontiers or weakening them (Stadler 2009: 135 ff.). In Israel's society of enclaves, the Shas leadership also has managed frontiers with some dexterity. From the religious point of view they built a fairly tight constituency adopting most of the haredi (ultra-Orthodox) lifestyle, and imparting its observance in their schools, but from the ethnic point of view they have played a soft, non-exclusionary game in contrast to the Ashkenazi *haredim*[9], and in politics they have campaigned in the wider society in a manner previously unheard of in ultra-Orthodox politics. They have also mixed and matched frontiers by adopting many aspects of Ashkenazi ultra-Orthodox lifestyle (large families for example), while deftly preserving key differences to mark themselves out. These latter include an injunction on their women to wear hairnets rather than wigs, cleaner groomed beards, very distinctive Arab-style melodies at prayer, and much besides.

The frontier is politically very useful, and it is a central thesis of this paper that while acting as a self-excluding mechanism, it also helps the gatekeepers, in this case Shas, to exert political influence. In Jerusalem, where *haredim* remain (still) a minority of the population, Ashkenazi Haredi parties recently held the mayoralty, not least because they usually produce a turnout vastly in excess of that of the other parties.[10] Among the reasons for this is the management of a system of religious observance which penetrates all the interstices of the lives of individuals and of the collectivity, as well as the leadership's control over patronage derived from the state or from private donors, like subsistence allowances for yeshiva students and older full-time Talmud learners, or over housing committees which ensure the religious homogeneity of Haredi housing projects, in such a way that they are sometimes divided between different haredi groups and sects, as well as separating haredim from the secular world – witness examples in the town of Bet Shemesh and the Jerusalem suburb Ramat Shlomo (on occupied territory). In Jerusalem in 1995 and 1996, for example, 29.9 per cent of the Jewish population lived in areas where the religious parties received more than 70 per cent of the vote, and a further 10.5 per cent in areas where those parties gathered 40–69.9 per cent. Those two types of area also exhibited a substantially higher total fertility rate[11] than the rest of the city's Jewish areas: 6.37 and 4.44 respectively, against a total for the Jewish areas of 3.78 (and an overall national rate of 2.75) (della Pergola 2001). [12]

We observe here the efforts of a leadership to consolidate and thicken frontiers which would otherwise be multiple and criss-crossing, intensifying the mutual reinforcement of some frontiers and removing others. (For example, blurring and eventually eliminating frontiers among Middle Eastern and North African Jewish traditions, such as the Iraqi and the Moroccan, to name but two.) Thus ultra-Orthodox housing developments in Israel are formed by new developments (not unusually on Occupied Territory) in which religious officials can veto purchases of dwellings, where consumer cooperatives sell to members at advantageous prices, where very large numbers of children per family create a particular sort of atmosphere, where even a moderately secular lifestyle (men with uncovered heads, women in short sleeves or uncovered hair) is very costly, if not impossible in practice. These observations reflect identifiable strategies and the mobilization of identifiable resources to manage frontiers and create incentives and disincentives to retain those who live and work within their enclaves. But they are not confined, or not any longer, to the religious. Secular Jews – who also have their own name in Israeli jargon as *hilonim* – have, perhaps belatedly, also begun to develop strategies to defend their space. This came to the fore in a recent court case in Jerusalem brought to prevent a private home being used surreptitiously as a synagogue. The city council's attorney brought a case in response to complaints from local residents about the wrongful use of a residential building for the holding of religious services. The secular residents' spokesman, a Peruvian-born politician who cuts a distinctive figure with his abundant grey beard and pony-tail, said: 'It is obvious that the Haredim want to move into Kiryat Hayovel as they did into Ramat Eshkol … It is a well-planned process. Today there is a not a single secular person in Ramat Eshkol' (*Haaretz*, 1 April 2009).

Political strategy apart, we must add a further observation about the proliferation of religious markers and fields in Israeli life, and the progressive extension of the religious domain in education, in public space and in the calendar, in retail trade, in dress codes and more besides.[13] There is surely an element of spontaneity, in the sense of accretionary adoption of practices, as they spread, epidemiologically, through the country's space. The polarisation of secular Tel-Aviv and religious Jerusalem is accentuated as those who can afford to in the more secular middle classes move out of Jerusalem, and this is reflected, of course, in house prices, which tend to fall with the haredization of neighbourhoods, except those inhabited by the more prosperous. The haredi dress code itself is dismembered and recombined by various collective imaginaries in a multiplicity of uniform codes denoting religious, national and New Age affiliations and combinations thereof. Some women in a faction of the National Religious currents wear long colourful skirts and sandals with a headdress and blouse of white muslin reminiscent of nineteenth-century portraits of Old Testament matriarchs. The wearing of a modest head covering in the form of a peaked hat topped with a button, a rounded beret embroidered in Oriental mode or a tightly bound headscarf, is spreading far beyond the ultra-Orthodox. These are all variations on the theme of head covering and go together, especially in Jerusalem, with widespread use of calf-length skirts. The grammar of fashion is intricate: long pencil-like skirts signal a nod to modesty, but also a clear distancing from the wide, thigh-length skirts and thick stockings of haredi women themselves.

Ethnic signals, or signage, for their part, are articulated subtly, almost unspokenly: when activists look like Sephardim and the neighbourhoods they operate in are heavily Sephardi, there is no need to evoke openly or frequently their ethnic belonging: it goes without saying. The Sephardi liturgical text is little different from that of the Ashkenazim, but there is plenty of scope to mark out their difference in melodies, and in specific customs (*minhagim*): women are enjoined to wear hairnets, not wigs or headscarves, and skirts reaching their feet rather than their calves; men trim their beards, wear a slightly different (Borsalino) design of hat and even seem to carry themselves differently from the hurried, nervous gait of Ashkenazi yeshiva students who have rarely done military service, unlike Shas followers who are so often returnees (*hozrei bet'shuva*) from a secular lifestyle. They have taken the *haredi* religious archetype and 'tweaked' it in a manner which is instantly recognizable as different yet, in the kinship sense, related. This phenomenon of 'rubbing off', of gaining recognition by allusion as much as by direct strident invocation, is repeated with Shas's aura of ethnic belonging which has attracted some 250,000 votes from an overwhelmingly Sephardi constituency who, although not for the most part highly observant, are nevertheless respectful of tradition.

Stated simplistically, the Jews of North African descent in particular, having avoided or escaped the opening up to a modernity in which religion and non-religion (the secular) could occupy separate spheres – having been spared the fierce tensions between traditionalists and modernists which the Enlightenment brought upon the Jewish populations and institutions of Poland and Russia – retained a respect and an affection at least for the religious rituals. Indeed, Shas activists make much of this contrast. Their softer tradition-orientation has opened North African Jews to persuasion by Shas activists that it was time to take the fulfilment of Torah's commandments and the authority of the Rabbis who interpret them more seriously, both in Israel and elsewhere (in France, in Canada). The paradox of course is that Shas, whose founders and leaders are trained in the rigorous disciplines of the Lithuanian[14] yeshivas, was to bring precisely this very Ashkenazi division into the Sephardi world, since t'shuva could only mean the adoption of a way of life marked by a separation of the observant from the rest. Furthermore, although Shas, as we have said, tweaked the haredi archetype, the result was nothing like the traditional lifestyle of the countries of origin. But that does not matter: the principle of drawing boundaries is to be distinguished from their content, as Barth taught. In this example, side by side with markers that by their content denote Sephardi heritage, Shas has adopted many Ashkenazi practices that mark out its adherents as ultra-Orthodox – a category which has no history in pre-modern extra-European Jewish culture – and yet also, on account of crucial details, also marks them out from the Ashkenazim.

These apparently detailed observations are precisely not details: they are at the heart of the choreography of the Israeli public space, and, being quasi-subconscious, unarticulated, they dispel the impression that boundaries are purely political constructions. The tyranny of these small but fundamental differences never passes unnoticed, and the examples we mention are but a small part of the whole. How they develop and propagate remains mysterious, a subject probably for cognitive science, like religious behaviour (Lehmann 2005), but that is for others to explore.

Barth's analysis is particularly useful today because it offers an alternative to the vagueness, the psychoanalytic connotations, and indeed the essentialism of the word 'identity'. It provides a neutral formula which denotes neither exclusion nor inclusion, neither discrimination nor favouritism, which obliges us to remember that the effect of these and other boundaries on individuals' lives can range from constraint to empowerment. It also enables us to take into account the knowledge that individuals operate in multiple spheres, in many of which their capabilities and entitlements are defined by a frontier – for example a person's race (or combination of racial characteristics and background), professional status, place of residence, sexuality, religious affiliation(s). And as the list shows, frontiers are usually intangible and often symbolic – they may be expressed in clothes, accent, jargon, ritual and so on.

In Israel's society of enclaves the Shas style, or its sensibility, exemplifies the meaning of the notion of negotiating frontiers: from the religious point of view it tends towards the thickening of frontiers, accentuating the symbolic, physical and temporal divisions between the religious and secular. In this it resembles the Ashkenazi ultra-Orthodox. But unlike the Ashkenazi ultra-Orthodox, Shas followers and activists deploy ethnic signs and symbols in a manner which cuts across the orthodox-secular divide, and also send out signals of solidarity with the poor – for which read very often the Sephardim – which softens their boundaries. It also of course serves as an electoral strategy. Somehow, Shasniks, as they are known, manage to emphasize their separation from secular society while drawing close to their Sephardi constituency, religious and secular.

Corporatism

The next point to understand in linking the enclave system with the social self-exclusion of religious revival and the political inclusion of the revivalist movements and their followers, is that, of course, leaders themselves also have interests distinct from, though usually overlapping with, those of the groups in whose names they speak, and that brings us to a consideration of corporatism, a concept which, in some of its acceptances, fits certain aspects of Israeli politics well. Philippe Schmitter (Schmitter 1974) classically described corporatism as a set of arrangements in which the state recognizes or licences 'a limited number of singular, compulsory, noncompetitive, hierarchically ordered and functionally differentiated categories' and grants them 'representational monopoly ... in exchange for observing certain controls on their selection of leaders and articulation of demands and supports' (pp. 93–4). Twelve years later, however, he recognized the dangers of colonization of the state by private interest groups or vice versa (Streeck and Schmitter 1985).

This is a useful schema, but corporatism is also a potentially unstable system in which there is a constant struggle for prerogative on the part of agents within the state and within associations, in their attempts to steal a march on each other by gaining control of the rules of the game, that is of regulating institutions as well as chunks of the government's budget. Associations are entitled to take part in state decision-making on resource allocation, but the decisions are biased in favour of the political or commercial interests of the office-holders in unions and associations.

In our consideration of Israel we use this concept of corporatism to explore the pattern of inclusion pursued by Shas in particular, and to show how it is compatible with, if not an incentive to, the religiously-driven strategies of self-exclusion followed by Shas, by the haredim generally and by settlers (though we do not discuss these). In Israel like in many of those countries, but for the most part unlike Western Europe, it is possible for non-state entities, ranging from trade unions to political parties via religious institutions, business groups, state corporations, or state employee associations, to colonize institutions of the state even on a long-term basis, encroaching on the control exercised over them by central government. Examples are the educational networks operated by Shas and other haredi interests, the old Histadrut – trade union movement – before the privatization of the industries it controlled, and the settler councils which seem to be able to flout or circumvent formal government regulations and create state-funded institutional spaces of their own (Sprinzak 1991; Aran 1994; Sprinzak 1999).

Enclaves are variously religious, political and economic: the ultra-Orthodox haredim were, on the founding of the state, granted state-funded educational autonomy and legal prerogatives over personal status law for all Jews, rendering mixed marriage and civil marriage impossible within the state. The trade union movement operated cooperatives and industries as well as representing workers and wielding much political influence until crisis and liberalization started a long process of subsidy withdrawals and privatization in the 1980s. The kibbutz movement was also something of a law unto itself: kibbutzim regulated and limited entry, and had their own economic practices outside the market economy, and their own educational arrangements – all funded by the state until the same crisis of the 1980s. Educational enclaves provide a separate education system for Arabs and four main educational systems for Jews of different religious affiliation – including, as we shall see, the 'Shas' network known as 'The wellspring of Torah education' (*HaMa'ayan Hachinuch Hatorani*). Territorial enclaves are embodied, among others, in the de facto segregation of Arabs in municipalities where hardly any Jews live (though legally it is not prohibited), by homogeneous Jewish ultra-Orthodox neighbourhoods, by West Bank settlements ranging from fully fledged towns to a string of legal and quasi-legal settlements and illegal unplanned outposts, and by the exclusion of Arabs from buying houses in communities established on Jewish Agency land. Finally, Ministers run their Ministries like private fiefdoms, or party fiefdoms, to the extent that we have in recent years thrice seen Foreign Ministers who, despite open disagreement with the foreign policy of the government, successfully hold on to their posts[15] and hundreds of thousands of settlers who have obtained state funding over long periods through whatever Ministry their political patrons have occupied – notably through Sharon when he was at Agriculture (1977–1981). These enclaves can operate because they enjoy official approval or mere indulgence and direct or indirect economic support from the state, combined with mobilization from 'below'. The original development of the settlers' movement (Sprinzak 1991) and our case, the Shas movement, illustrate well this very Israeli combination of determined grassroots pressure and governmental indulgence.[16]

So where excluded groups, or groups whose leaders claim a history of exclusion, are concerned, corporatism offers precedents for special treatment, special access and the institutionalization and state funding of self-governing quasi-autonomous entities, while enclaves have become so normal in Israeli society that leaders can establish social and symbolic barriers around their group without provoking much surprise. It also offers an arrangement in which leaders of groups enjoying corporatist access can act as privileged intermediaries or gatekeepers in the distribution of the fruits of that access.

These circumstances have come to favour a strategy whereby self-exclusion can be of particular use as a path to political recognition and inclusion. Self-exclusion here means setting up and thickening social and symbolic barriers between the group and the rest of society, through a process of mobilization and under a determined leadership, to be distinguished from exclusion in the sense of powerlessness and material deprivation.

It is not intended here to give the impression that people in pivotal positions in these corporatist arrangements are all venal or out of control. But Shas has tended to concentrate power in a personalistic way: it is visible in the party's lack of formal rules of membership and internal election, in the cult of personality surrounding its supreme leader Ovadia Yosef, and in the scandals about appointments and contracts, notably over their school transport arrangements during the Barak government in the late 1990s and early 2000s, and the corruption charges which led to the imprisonment of their charismatic leader Arieh Deri in 1999.

Shas: a conversion-led movement

We bring evangelical and fundamentalist movements together under the combined category of conversion-led movements because proselytizing, conversion and quantitative expansion are their *raison d'être*, and this more analytical term enables us to include movements of reconversion, which exhibit very similar social and psychological features. Usually conversion is thought of as a move from one religious affiliation, or none, to another, but the phenomenon of reconversion, observed notably among Jews and Muslims, in which an individual returns, or 'reverts', to a stringent or intensely observant version of his or her own religious heritage, is not significantly different: it too involves the rejection of a previous dissolute or meaningless way of life and the espousal of a new one, joining new social networks and severing ties with their old friends and sometimes also their workplaces and even their families. The Pentecostal variant is now amply described in an abundant literature (Martin 1990; Lehmann 1996; Haar 1998; Corten 1999; Martin 2001); the Muslim variant is covered in a general sort of way in Cesari (1981; 2004), Kepel (1987) and Roy (2004; 2008) and in greater detail by Metcalf (1996) but still cries out for more ethnography; the Jewish variant is well described in Friedman's writings on the Lubavitch sect (Friedman 1994; Heilman and Friedman 2010), those of Aviad (1983) and Danzger (1989) and more recently Marta Topel on São

Paulo (Topel 2008). Conversion movements mobilize a myriad of modes of communication, notably cable TV, and also operating, for example, through self-improvement or confidence-building courses such as the 'Alpha course' in the UK, and in Israel an organization called *Arachim* ('values') which runs weekend seminars and short courses aimed at drawing people back to strict observance. Having burnt their bridges, converts become dependent on the new group and its leadership, and the demands placed on them by the organization or movement (Iannacone 1997) facilitate the construction of enclave-style social and symbolic frontiers which operate as mechanisms of social self-exclusion. The leadership is empowered by its control over converts to negotiate with politicians hungry for votes and can thereby gain benefits for followers, and is itself then seen as a tempting source of votes and alliances by other political groups.

In Judaism the movement of reconversion or return, known as *t'shuva* (variously translated as repentance, return and 'an answer') has become an established feature of religious and community life, pioneered by the Lubavitch sect in the postwar period and later taken up by others. Campaigns are conducted among Jews from a secularized background and some are drawn to the life of strict observance, changing job, changing their circles of friends, and changing the entire rhythm of their lives. This is not a campaign to make a person a little more observant, by for example joining a Liberal synagogue: the life offered is that of the ultra-Orthodox. The campaigners do not in fact regard Reform or Liberal Judaism as Jewish at all.

In the case of Shas the movement has acquired a particularly strong impact because it has been focused on an entire community – the Sephardim in Israel, and later outside Israel as well. So the proportionate effect has been far greater than the more dispersed effects of other campaigns. Shas's binding of their religious call with an ethnic call and a demand to be included in the political elite also distinguished it from t'shuva campaigns elsewhere, but nevertheless the dynamic of conversion reinforces the frontier-building characteristic of haredi Jewish culture and of corporatist politics, helped by the penumbra of ethnic identification, leading to strong ties of bonding – of mutual interaction and dependency – among followers. In these circumstances the incentives and the pressures to vote and to vote together are very great, reinforced by the classic formula of a core of totally committed cadres supported by successive rings of activists and participants, and at the outer edge those who simply vote for the party.

Development of Shas

Shas started out in the early 1980s as a party fighting local elections within the ultra-Orthodox community. Its leaders were rebelling against the patronizing treatment and discrimination they faced as Sephardim in the institutions of study (*yeshivas*), which are at the heart of that very Ashkenazi world. Whereas high-achieving Ashkenazi students could expect to gain teaching positions, to marry a girl from a prestigious family, and eventually even to be head of a yeshiva, even the best students, if they were Sephardi, were excluded from these prizes. In addition, distinguished institutions imposed – as they still do – a *numerus clausus* on Sephardi admissions, and the ones which had to specialize in taking Sephardi students were starved of funds and attention. These grievances internal to the Ashkenazi system lay behind the formation of Shas, but its activists discovered that they had success among secularized Sephardim as well, a receptiveness to a classic revivalist message of strict religion heralding a world free from drugs, sexual licence and disrespect for parents, with the added element of ethnic revival, under the motto 'Restoring the crown to its ancient glory', written around a drawing of a palm tree and an oasis reminiscent of the lost world of Jews in Arab lands. For example, Rabbi Reuven Elbaz, who became a prominent figure associated with Shas in the 1990s, had begun like an evangelical preacher, trawling the billiard halls of Jerusalem, persuading young men to take up a religious lifestyle, and founding the first of his Or HaChayyim ('Light of Life') network of yeshivas – religious study centres – for returnee men, in 1968. Aviad describes him invading low-income neighbourhoods with his team, broadcasting loud religious music and preaching 'hellfire and brimstone': 'you were animals and you want to become like the animals of Rehavia' – Rehavia being a prosperous, predominantly secular, neighbourhood (Aviad 1983: 42). Today, we were told by a pupil, he has 200 branches dotted around the country and a towering, albeit unfinished, headquarters in the heart of Jerusalem's central haredi neighbourhood of Bukharim. Or HaChayyim's specialization in bringing young men back from the criminal world was seen as his main *raison d'être* by Danzger already in the 1970s, who also mentions that he was entrusted by the authorities with people on parole (Danzger 1989: 114). Thirty years later Elbaz remains particularly proud of the young men he says he has reformed, bringing them back to religion and persuading them to abandon a life of criminality, as he explained in an interview in late 2009.[17] His yeshivas are all funded by the state on the basis of student numbers, and the full-time students receive an allowance of up to $300 per month in accordance with the agreements reached with Agudat Yisrael – the representatives of the Haredi world – in 1947. At the time of the foundation of the state, politicians believed that they were preserving ultra-Orthodoxy and full-time Rabbinic study as relics of the past, not as what would become the fastest-growing segment of Judaism.

After surprisingly gaining seats in the 1983 Jerusalem municipal elections, Shas moved onto the national stage in 1984 and won four Knesset seats at its first appearance. After 1990, under the then-benign, distant patronage of Ovadia Yosef, a former Sephardi Chief Rabbi, and the dynamic leadership of the very young Arieh Deri, it negotiated the establishment of its school network funded by the state on a similar basis as the existing Ashkenazi ultra-Orthodox network, but with more favourable conditions in recognition of the low incomes of their clientele: these include extended school hours, school buses, and hot lunches. Shas continued in the coalition with two interruptions until the present day, and in the 2003 and 2005 elections seems to have reached its stability level of 11 out of 120 Knesset members. The party has also fought hard to obtain extra child allowances for large families, who of course are heavily represented among the ultra-Orthodox. These allowances had been raised and lowered and abolished for various numbers of children over the years, and in 2000 the 'Alpert' Law on Large Families was passed, providing for enhanced allowances for the fifth child and upwards at a cost of NIS600m (slightly less than USD$150m in 2009). The secular public regarded these measures as encouragements and subsidies to the ultra-Orthodox and the whole entitlement was slashed in 2004 (by Netanyahu, as Finance Minister) but it was partially restored under Olmert in 2008 and restored even further by the selfsame Netanyahu in the negotiations for the 2009 coalition government. Unsurprisingly, Shas is the object of sometimes bitter hostility among secular Israelis, but its leaders have been little affected by this, save that they can use it to enhance the image of their party as victim of secular discrimination.

Shas's campaigning method – used also by other Israeli organizations, notably the West Bank settlers but also the founders of the state itself – creates quasi-institutional 'facts on the ground' which become jumping-off points for political pressure. Unpaid activists may go into a neighbourhood and start free kindergartens or some other type of religious-educational ventures in a building site caravan or an air-raid shelter (both pervasive features of the country's urban landscape) and later press local government for financial support. This fits also with the view we frequently heard in interviews with Shas sympathizers that it is the one party which maintains a continuous and active local presence, with activists propagating the message of religious revival, echoing the resentment of potential supporters against the sophisticated, globalized irreligious elites who rule over the country's institutions and media.

Shas's schools and yeshivas network enables the movement to man its boundaries with numerous gatekeepers and to compete for resources with a reliable core electorate. It also provides a space in which to continue the campaign for t'shuva, for example among the parents of their pupils. The network is an institutional fiefdom where its cadres (often teachers of course, and teachers whose enthusiasm far surpasses that of their secular counterparts) can operate almost out of the sight of secular Israel: its pupils numbered between 20,000 and 30,000 children in 2002, according to data obtained at that time from the Department for 'Recognized Non-official Education' which is responsible for haredi education in the Ministry of Education. Figures for 2008 show scarcely any increase, which leads us to believe that there have been difficulties in obtaining reliable statistics on Shas schools. In addition Shas has a separate network of associations, discussion groups, and adult and religious education activities under the confusingly similar name of *El HaMa'ayan* ('towards the wellspring'), which are nominally apolitical so that they can be subsidized by the state, although their style, content, and clientele leave no doubt as to their political complexion. The autonomy of the Shas education system, and of the haredi education system generally was reinforced by the appointment of a member of the messianic nationalist Tkuma faction of the ex-National Union Party as Vice-Minister of Education in the 2009 Netanyahu government.

During our fieldwork, social workers and political activists in modern ultra-Orthodox neighbourhoods explained to us that municipal Rabbis (all of whom are salaried state employees responsible for marriage, *kashrut* certification and the like) appointed directly or indirectly by the Shas spiritual and charismatic leader Rabbi Ovadia Yosef are active organizers in their neighbourhoods. Their role involved everything from obtaining a mortgage to marshalling an audience for the satellite transmission of Yosef's weekly Saturday night homilies. Shas municipal councillors, who maintained their representation even after the party declined from its high score of 17 Knesset seats in 1999, have influence in allocating housing for groups with differing religious affiliations, and who thus follow different rules concerning access to electronic media, male–female interactions and the like. So the self-exclusion is helped by the corporatist habits of Israeli politics – in this case party control over allocation of land or housing. The party is able to raise scholarships for its cadres to follow university-level, or at least university-style, courses which bring them the qualifications needed to occupy senior civil service positions, and now one of Yosef's daughters has founded what is known as a 'Shas College' to enable haredi cadres and especially women to follow a university-level course under the auspices of Bar-Ilan University and others, without involvement in the normally secular world of Higher Education.[18] The College has already produced 350 women graduates and a further 250 men and women are expected to graduate on what seems to be a second premises in Jerusalem in 2010. Here again we see, as in Stadler's study of Ashkenazi haredim, how the movement does not only retreat behind thick walls: frontiers are also pushed into hostile or secular spheres where new dimensions of religiosity are developed.

A New Dimension to Israeli Jewish Citizenship

With the rise of Shas, Israel has extended arrangements which previously operated in the Jewish religious sphere – and which certainly have a multi-cultural flavour – to the ethnic sphere, at least *de facto*. Although a flourishing Ashkenazi system of religious schooling existed since long before the establishment of the state, and continues to be funded (but not controlled) by it, Shas persuaded the state to create what is in effect a special, strictly Orthodox educational network for children of North African and Middle Eastern parentage even though the ethnic qualification is not anywhere officially recognized. Since the founding of the Israeli state in 1948, the idea of a unified Jewish nation had made no allowance for ethnic differences among immigrants, least of all for the potential misfit of Jews from the Middle East: the only ethnically based special provision – of education, in areas with predominantly Arab population – was of a discriminatory kind, a low-level citizenship for the Arab population. The existence of parallel Ashkenazi and Sephardi Chief Rabbinates are based on different traditions of worship and religious observance, in which ethnic identity is an appendage. The political class, in their efforts to create unity and equality of treatment among Jewish citizens – took the implicit view that diversity was a matter for the population themselves to preserve, in their religious rites and in popular religious celebrations. It did not actively seek to suppress diversity, but neither did it ever seriously consider the notion of a politics of identity as a device to achieve inclusion. If affirmative action (not the same thing as multiculturalism) existed, it was for the Arab population, to enable them to be admitted to universities. Among the Jewish population, poverty and exclusion – the issues which often underlie claims for ethnic recognition – were treated as matters for social policy. Even when, as in the 1970s, differences of origin were recognized as causes of differential educational achievement, and catch-up programmes were devised for the social and economic disadvantaged, mostly of Sephardi origin, this was in no way intended to be an identity-specific education or a basis for any kind of identity politics. Indeed, such measures were based on the assumption that Israel was destined to be a Western country with a Western culture.

Note, however, that ethnic identity is no more a matter of straightforward labelling here than anywhere else. The ethnic belonging is implicit – coded but uncodified – and the educational institutions can only condition entry on religious observance. In Shas's schools the pupils are overwhelmingly Sephardi and, together with their parents, subject to rigorous criteria of correct religious behaviour. The Sephardi character and Shas allegiance of the schools is manifested in dress, physical appearance, melodies, the liturgical use of Sephardi Hebrew pronunciation, ubiquitous pictures of Ovadia Yosef – but hardly in the substance of the curriculum, which is heavily religious and ultra-Orthodox, and has little distinctively Sephardi content. For example, we found no references to the 1500 years or more of history of Jews in Arabic-speaking societies. In contrast with Ashkenazi haredi institutions, which have a position of prestige to defend and also are fortunate to face excess demand from their own constituency, especially at the highly regarded Beit Yakov girls' schools, and the 'top' yeshivas, Shas teachers were eager to express pride in their openness, and saw in their few non-Sephardi pupils a recognition of the quality of the service they offer. Their interest, as 'underdogs', is in not having a *numerus clausus*.

Enclaves like these may not fit some contemporary definitions of the notoriously fluid concept of multiculturalism, but by establishing a set of institutional arrangements in response to the needs or traditions of different groups – defined in these cases religiously and to some extent even ideologically – the state has set a precedent for something like the group-differentiated rights which are Kymlicka's defining feature of multicultural citizenship (Kymlicka 1995). The arrangements in Israel exhibit the flexibility – which some would call arbitrariness – of multicultural arrangements, in contrast to Kymlicka's attempt to construct a consistent architecture. The separate arrangements for the *haredi* community laid down in 1947–48 were in effect multicultural, as were the arrangements for the Arab population, discriminatory though they were. This is not an overarching or consistent multiculturalism – if such a thing could ever exist. Nor does Shas demand a comprehensive welfare system, despite its leaders' insistence on the socio-economic exclusion of its constituency. On the contrary, as is so often the case in corporatist and multicultural contexts, Shas prefers special treatment for sub-groups and discretionary allowances for identifiable groups. On the other hand, the country does not have a declared overall multicultural policy. If the Israeli political elite were using ethnic particularism to attack socio-economic exclusion, then they might also pay attention to the Ethiopian population, who now number about 90,000, are a visible presence, and clearly suffer serious social marginalization as well as repression of their culture (Herzog 1995; Weil 1997), yet have not benefited from any special institutional provision.

Nor can Israel's recent immigrant Russian population be thought of as demanding or receiving multicultural treatment. Yisrael Beiteinu, the political party of Avigdor Lieberman, is a distinctively Russian voice, but it does not promote a distinctive heritage or even collective interest, save in the matter of marriage – since the Rabbinate makes many difficulties for the Russians who cannot prove their Jewish descent to the satisfaction of the Rabbinical Court. Its main feature is Lieberman's irredentist and expansionist rhetoric, and his heavily accented Hebrew which leaves his birthplace in no doubt. Israelis of recent Russian origin are physically distinctive and recognizable for appearance, accent and even dress to some extent, and have an active intelligentsia – as seen in Russian bookshops, newspapers and theatre – and an active business community – ranging from small Russian shops to the very prosperous Israel-Moscow business axis. There are an unknown number of after-school classes established by groups of Russians on their own account to provide enhanced science and Russian language education – not just Russian culture. But they do not demand special subsidies, exemptions or privileges from the state.

Israel, then, has de facto multicultural practice but not general multicultural citizenship architecture. On the one occasion when Shas did use explicit multicultural arguments in a judicial context, it lost. This was when the party had to defend itself against accusations of improper practices during the 1999 election campaign. Another party had complained about the distribution of amulets by Shas campaigners, and the response from Shas's leader Arieh Deri was, as Barzilai has explained, classically multicultural: he defended the practice in terms of the cultural practices peculiar to his constituency, thus acknowledging that Shas voters were different from others, and deserved different consideration, because they were almost all Sephardim. A distinguished anthropologist was called to testify on the basis of his knowledge of the political mores of North African society and the Electoral Court took the view that such practices did indeed amount to vote-buying (Barzilai 2003). By then of course the election was long over.

Multiculturalism as a Variant of Corporatism

Shas reminds us of a core ambiguity, even hypocrisy, in the concept of multiculturalism as bandied about in public debate in the UK and France for example, because in practice multicultural arrangements assume the continued existence of a dominant or hegemonic set of practices, symbols, and affiliations usually associated with a dominant elite or class. These are not – despite the implicit equality of consideration implied by the term – on an equal footing with the traditions favoured or promoted by multiculturalism, but rather are set outside, beyond and over and above a multicultural arrangement in virtue of the elite's social capital (in Bourdieu's concept). To illustrate the point, we may note the argument sometimes deployed by Israeli political scientists who see the sponsorship of a separate Shas school network by the state as a way of avoiding the massive expense and upheaval which would be required to bring the entire Sephardi population into the once-dominant mainstream with better education and employment opportunities (Peled 2001). Is it not a classic tactic of co-option or inclusionary corporatism (Stepan 1978) to confer the power of patronage on a minority elite and leave them to manage their followers? The Israeli state, especially the Labour Party (Mapai) did the same with the Arab population until any pretence of common interests became untenable, driving even conservatively inclined Arab leaders towards Palestinization (Louër 2007). Now the relationship is in an authoritarian mould, but still corporatist.

The Shas leadership made no secret of the issue of exclusion yet it seems to be satisfied with the provision of an enclave, which places it in positions of power and may signify recognition, but not universalistic welfare policy or state or judicial action against discrimination suffered by Sephardim either in society as a whole or in the haredi world itself – and this despite the resentment against precisely that discrimination which has been a Shas keynote from its very beginning. To admit the intervention of the secular state in the internal affairs of the haredi world, even if to relieve these discriminations, is unthinkable for Shas leaders and cadres. Despite their candid statements to us, Shas activists and leaders usually shy away from speaking publicly about the contradiction between that bitter experience and their continuing desperation to get their children into elite Ashkenazi schools and yeshivas.

The stresses and strains appear from time in complex ways. In 2009–10 in an ultra-Orthodox West Bank settlement, Immanuel, the Ashkenazim excluded Sephardi children from the Bet Yakov ultra-Orthodox girls' school.[19] The conflict went all the way to the country's Supreme Court, which ruled that the action was illegal, and the Minister of Education also condemned it. But the Shas leadership was very hesitant on the subject: it seems to have preferred to avoid offending Ashkenazi ultra-Orthodoxy even in this situation.

Israel in Comparative Perspective

Until the advent of multiculturalism it was taken for granted that the modern citizen was a universal individual whose rights and obligations derived only from his or her personhood and location in a territory governed by a state. Bryan Turner's major article of 1990 (Turner 1990) reaffirmed widely recognized ideas from Parsons and originally Max Weber about 'the constitution of an abstract political subject no longer formally confined by the particularities of birth, ethnicity or gender'. Max Weber, in 'The Occidental City' (Weber 1978 vol. II, pp. 1236–51) over and over again goes back to the idea of free individuals whose membership and entitlements as citizens is accorded to them as individuals and not by virtue of clan, tribal or ethnic belonging. Even when Christian belonging was required in medieval associations of municipal government, this was in Weber's words 'by its nature a religious association of individual believers not a ritual association of clans' (p. 1247). Other recent contributions have been similarly focused on the importance of individual as distinct from group belonging in forming the basis of political participation: O'Donnell's entire elaboration of a set of criteria for assessing the quality of democracy (O'Donnell et al. 2004) starts out from the idea that the legal definition of an agent lies at the basis of the political right to participation. It is the presumption of agency, which constitutes each individual as a person in law, and a bearer of rights.[20]

In Israel the Supreme Court may follow the corresponding liberal universalist concept of individual citizenship, but it seems to act in a condition of permanent contradiction to the ethnic features which are absolutely central to the constitution of the state. There can be few countries where the branches of the state – the executive and the judiciary – incarnate at the same time, and so eloquently, opposed conceptions of what it is to be a citizen. Of course, the executive and the different currents of opinion in the Parliament do not elaborate their ideas with the same sophistication as the Supreme Court judges, but the contradictions are still self-evident.

Conclusion

This paper has explored the mechanics through which, in Israel, groups and their leaders enhance their claims and achieve social inclusion through a corporatist path which is in some cases – notably that of Shas – tinged with ethnic particularism. Israel is not alone in having a political system which encourages such orientations; even though many arguments can be produced to show that in principle a universalist social-democratic welfare policy would provide a more just and more effective solution for all those covered by the claim. But the principle of universal entitlement does not always find enough favour in a democracy. Although the Shas leaders are not neglectful of the socio-economic interests of Middle Eastern and North African Jews as a whole, their prime commitment is to their followers' religious identity and to potential recruits to the life of ultra-Orthodox Judaism, who fuelled their campaigning in the boom years of growth and were prepared to make the sacrifice of self-exclusion.

Proportional representation in general seems to favour the corporatist approach to social policy, and Israel's extreme form of PR is something of an exceptional case. The pattern of corporatist inclusion is then enhanced by Israel's version of religiously motivated social closure and by the multicultural-style policies which have been applied in education. The resulting self-exclusion, as we have called it, has multiple causes, but also turns out to have very interesting political potential. It is hard and perhaps unnecessary for us to decide whether the claim for recognition expressed in self-exclusion is a motive, an outcome, or a pretext, but we have tried to show that it can help the leadership to achieve their purposes, namely access to office, to resources and to recognition.

Notes

1 This paper is derived from our 'Self-exclusion as path to political inclusion: the case of Shas', *Citizenship Studies*, 12 (3), 2008. The authors thank Henry Wasserman, Sergio della Pergola, Mario Sznajder and Menachem Friedman for their help. David Lehmann acknowledges the generosity of the Institute of Advanced Study of the Hebrew University in providing a Fellowship during which the paper was completed. It is based on extensive fieldwork carried out between 1999 and 2006 during which we visited yeshivas and synagogues, interviewed Shas activists, took part in women's discussion groups and courses for returnees to religious observance (*ba'alei t'shuva*), spoke to neighbourhood Rabbis – in short we undertook a multi-levelled approach in participant observation by following up one contact to another in a lengthy networking exercise which took us near to the summit of the Shas hierarchy and 'down' to the poorer districts of Jerusalem and Petach Tikva. Funding for the research was provided by the Leverhulme Trust and builds on our *Remaking Israeli Judaism* (2006).

2 This word means, strictly, Spanish, in reference to the Jews who were expelled from Spain and spread across the Northern Mediterranean where they lived for centuries as far as Istanbul and Salonika. The Jews of the Middle East and North Africa are often called 'Mizrachim' (Easterners) but the followers of the ethnic-religious renewal embodied by Shas prefer to be called Sephardim, thus distancing themselves from the connotations of an inferior social status which 'Mizrachim' still carries.

3 Lieberman advocates civil marriage and the separation of religion and state – which make him anathema to the ultra-Orthodox, although they nevertheless sit at the same Cabinet table.

4 Recent research has also documented exclusion from promotion in the Army in the early years of the state. An article in *Haaretz* (22 September 2010) based on

a doctoral thesis by the former head of research for the chief of staff's adviser on gender issues in the IDF (Zeev Lerer: "Quality Groups: A Social History of Classification in the IDF": no date is given) states that whereas 'native-born soldiers inducted into the army between 1959 and 1961 had an 8.5 percent chance of becoming an officer; soldiers born in Europe or America had a 5.4 percent chance. Only 1.4 percent of soldiers born in other Middle Eastern countries became officers, and the figure for other groups of Mizrachi soldiers was 0.5 percent ... The gaps lessened following the Yom Kippur War ... after the 1973 war, officers of Mizrachi ancestry rose from 20 percent to 33 percent of the total, and the percentage of Ashkenazi officers dropped from 75 percent to 66 percent.'

5 In Shas schools we visited we were told that children behaving badly can be excluded and also that religious observance in the home was also monitored.

6 Migrants from North Africa are often called Mizrachim (Easterners) but those who have become more religious, and perhaps others, have come to prefer the term Sephardim ('Spaniards') which has now come to designate all the Jews from the world outside Europe – except for Yemenis, Indians and Ethiopians. The word Sephardi does not have the connotation of inferiority that tends to be attached to 'Mizrachi' among the mass of the population.

7 In this it is selectively flexible – notably in the case of hundreds of thousands of Russian immigrants whose status as Jews, if it were subjected to the rigorous scrutiny applied for example to people converted outside Israel by non-Orthodox Rabbis, would cause serious difficulties.

8 National Religious schools were at first established in recognition of the existence of a religious wing to Zionism at the founding of the state and before. Their curriculum is more religious than that of state secular schools, and their pupils tend to achieve less and to come from poorer backgrounds. They are run by the Ministry of Education, unlike the schools of the ultra-Orthodox and Shas which are funded by the Ministry but managed independently.

9 Literally, those who live in fear of God. Haredim, here, are almost all Ashkenazi Jews, heirs to the Russian-Polish tradition; later that changes as we shall see.

10 Due to internal differences, this pattern was less in evidence during the 2009 Jerusalem municipal elections.

11 Defined as the number of children a woman would have if she was subject to prevailing fertility rates at all ages in a given year, and if she survives to the age of 49 – i.e. through her child-bearing years.

12 It must be added firstly, that these polarizations are likely to be more pronounced in Jerusalem than in other cities, and also that much more detailed geographical and demographic documentation, as well as charting of patterns of social interaction, would be needed to fully document the enclave model. The idea of an ethnocracy developed by Yiftachel has affinities with the enclave idea, but of course it deals only with the most excluded, namely Israel's Arab citizens: O. Yiftachel (1998).

13 Passover preparations, which once might have occupied a single day for clearing households of bread and other food with fermented ingredients, now involves exchanges of presents on a Christmas-like scale and certification by Rabbinic authorities of fake transactions whereby certified non-Jews notionally buy the prohibited items and sell them back after the festival. The Purim festival now brings a day's *de facto* public holiday even though tradition does not prohibit work on that day, plus dressing up in the same habit used for Christmas in Britain and the US (red outfits, white pompoms, etc.) while in haredi neighbourhoods, following a carnavalesque tradition of 'the world turned upside down', children dress up in exotic military uniforms, and yeshiva students mock their teachers (within limits ...).

14 So called because they follow the study methods of the yeshivas in what was once the large state of Lithuania, and in the tradition of the Vilna Gaon, the sage who so fiercely opposed the Chassidim in the late eighteenth century (Hundert, 2004, p. 175).

15 Silvan Shalom was against Sharon's disengagement, from Gaza and Tzipi Livni was apparently against the 2006 Lebanon War and later, in April 2007, called on Prime Minister Olmert to resign, but without doing so herself. In September 2007 she remained in place and indeed seemed back on good terms with her Prime Minister! In 2010 and 2011 the Foreign Minister in the Netanyahu government, Avigdor Lieberman, similarly challenged the Prime Minister on various issues of policy and patronage.

16 The high level of mobilization and associationism in Israel is illustrated by the country's extraordinary density of NGOs, which in one survey places it fifth out of 22 countries: there are 22,000 formally registered NGOs, plus perhaps another 8,000 unregistered, and some 1,500 are created every year – while no doubt others close down (Anheier and Salamon 1998).

17 We have not sought access to documentary evidence of such claims. This statement is based on a conversation with Elbaz in December 2009.

18 Its founding has been filmed in a 2009 documentary by Yohai Hakak and Ron Ofer entitled *Haredot* (English title: 'The Rabbi's Daughter and the Midwife'). See the article by Tamar Rotem in *Ha'aretz*, 25 December 2008 and see Oren Majar: 'Israel's hi-tech future: haredi women', *Haaretz*, 8 September 2010.

19 Or Kashti: 'Haredi school network fined for dscriminating against Sephardim', *Haaretz*, 8 April 2010.

20 This formula is translated from the Spanish original (O'Donnell et al. 2003, pp. 59–60).

References

Adler, C. and M. Inbar (1977). *Ethnic integration in Israel: A comparative case study of Moroccan brothers who settled in France and Israel.* New Brunswick, Transaction Books.

Anheier, H. and L. Salamon (1998). "Social origins of civil society: Explaining the nonprofit sector crossnationally." *Voluntas* 9(3): 213–248.

Aran, G. (1994). "Jewish Zionist Fundamentalism: The Bloc of the Faithful in Israel (Gush Emunim)" in M. Marty and R. S. Appleby, *Fundamentalisms Observed.* Chicago, Chicago University Press.

Aviad, J. (1983). *Return to Judaism: Religious renewal in Israel.* Chicago, Chicago University Press.

Barth, F. (1969). *Ethnic groups and boundaries: the social organization of culture difference.* Boston, Little, Brown and Company.

Barzilai, G. (2003). *Communities and law: Politics and cultures of legal identities.* Ann Arbour, University of Michigan Press.

Cesari, J. (1981). *Etre musulman en France: Associations, militants et mosquées.* Paris/Aix-en-Provence, Karthala/IREMAM.

—. (2004). *When Islam and democracy meet: Muslims in Europe and the United States.* New York, Palgrave Macmillan.

Corten, A. (1999). *Pentecostalism in Brazil.* Basingstoke, Macmillan.

Danzger, M. H. (1989). *Returning to tradition: the contemporary revival of Orthodox Judaism.* New York, Yale University Press.

della Pergola, S. (2001). "Jerusalem's population, 1995–2020: Demography, multiculturalism and urban policies." *European Journal of Population* 17(2): 165–99.

Deshen, S. (1982). "The social structure of southern Tunisian Jewry in the early twentieth century" in S. Deshen and W. Zenner (eds), *Jewish Societies in the Middle East: community, culture and authority*. Washington DC, University Press of America.

Friedman, M. (1994). "Habad as messianic fundamentalism: From local particularism to universal Jewish mission" in M. Marty and R. S. Appleby, *Accounting for Fundamentalisms: The dynamic character of movements*. Chicago, Chicago University Press.

Heilman, S. C. and M. Friedman (2010). *The Rebbe: The life and afterlife of Menachem Mendel Schneerson*. Princeton, N.J.; Oxford, Princeton University Press.

Herzog, H. (1986). "Political factionalism: The case of ethnic lists in Israel." *Western Political Quarterly* 39(2): 285–303.

—. (1995). "Penetrating the system: The politics of collective identities" in A. Arian and M. Shamir, *The Elections in Israel – 1992*. Albany, State University of New York Press: 81–102.

Horowitz, D. and M. Lissak (1987). *Trouble in Utopia: The overburdened polity in Israel*. Albany, SUNY Press.

Hundert, G. D. (2004). *Jews in Poland-Lithuania in the Eighteenth Century. A Genealogy of Modernity*. Berkeley: University of California Press.

Iannacone, L. (1997). "Introduction to the economics of religion." *Journal of Economic Literature* 36(3): 1465–95.

Kepel, G. (1987). *Les banlieues de l'Islam: Naissance d'une religion en France*. Paris, Seuil.

Kymlicka, W. (1995). *Multicultural citizenship: A liberal theory of minority rights*. Oxford; New York, Clarendon Press.

Lehmann, D. (1996). *Struggle for the spirit: Religious transformation and popular culture in Brazil and Latin America*. Oxford, Polity Press.

—. (2005). "The cognitive approach to understanding religion." *Archives des Sciences Sociales des Religions* (131–32): 199–213.

Louër, L. (2007). *To be an Arab in Israel*. New York, Columbia University Press.

Martin, D. (1990). *Tongues of Fire: The Pentecostal revolution in Latin America*. Oxford, Blackwells.

—. (2001). *Pentecostalism: The world their parish*. Oxford, Blackwells.

Metcalf, B. (1996). "New Medinas: The Tablighi Jama'at in America and Europe" in B. Metcalf, *Making Muslim space in North America and Europe*. Berkeley, University of California Press: pp. xix, 264.

O'Donnell, G. A., J. Vargas Cullel, and O. M. Iazzetta (2004). *The quality of democracy: Theory and applications*. Notre Dame, University of Notre Dame Press.

Peled, Y., Ed. (2001). *Shas: The challenge of Israeliness* (Hebrew). Tel-Aviv, Yediot Aharonot.

Roy, O. (2004). *Globalised Islam: The search for a new Ummah*. London, Hurst.

—. (2008). *La sainte ignorance: Le temps de la religion sans culture*. Paris, Seuil.

Sartori, G. (1976). *Parties and party systems: A framework of analysis*. Cambridge, Cambridge University Press.

Schmitter, P. (1974). "Still the century of corporatism?" *Review of Politics* 36(1): 85–131.

Shafir, G. and Y. Peled (2002). *Being Israeli: The dynamics of multiple citizenship*. Cambridge, Cambridge University Press.

Shokeid, M. (1995). The religiosity of Middle Eastern Jews. *Israeli Judaism*. S. Deshen, Charles Liebmann and Moshe Shokeid. London, Transaction Publishers.

Sprinzak, E. (1991). *The Ascendance of Israel's Radical Right*. Oxford, OUP.

—. (1999). *Brother against brother: Violence and extremism in Israeli politics from Altalena to the Rabin assassination.* New York, The Free Press.

Stadler, N. (2009). *Yeshiva Fundamentalism: Piety, gender, and resistance in the ultra-Orthodox world.* New York, New York University Press.

Streeck, W. and P. Schmitter (1985). "Community, market, state – and associations? The prospective contribution of interest governance to social order." *European Sociological Review* 1(2): 119–38.

Topel, M. (2008). *Jerusalem and São Paulo: The new Jewish Orthodoxy in focus.* Lanham MD, University Press of America.

Turner, B. (1990). "Outline of a general theory of citizenship." *Sociology* 24: 189–217.

Weber, M. (1978). *Economy and Society: An outline of interpretive sociology, edited by Guenther Roth and Claus Wittich.* Berkeley, University of California Press.

Weil, S. (1997). *Ethiopian Jews in the Limelight.* Jerusalem, NCJW Research Institute for Innovation in Education, Hebrew University (Hebrew).

Yiftachel, O. (1998). "Democracy or ethnocracy? territory and settler politics in Israel/Palestine." *Middle East Report* (207): 8–13.

6 Citizenship, identity, and ethnic mobilization in Israel

The Mizrahi Democratic Rainbow – between universalism and particularism

Ofir Abu[1]

Introduction

The Mizrahi Democratic Rainbow[2] (hereinafter, the Rainbow) is an organization of second- and third-generation Mizrahim.[3] Established in March 1997 in a conference attended by more than 300 people, who came from all parts of the country and from the entire political spectrum, the Rainbow was based from the outset on two primary principles, which can be described as "universalism" and "particularism."

> The Mizrahi Democratic Rainbow [in Hebrew, Hakeshet Hademokratit Hamizrahit] is an apolitical, non-parliamentary social movement whose goal is to affect the current public agenda with the aim of bringing a radical change into Israeli society as a whole and to its institutions. *The organization is Mizrahi … in its goals, universal in its beliefs and open to all those who identify with its values. This group strives to become a mass movement* and to bring about a meaningful change within Israeli society by implementing values of democracy, human rights, social justice, equality, and multiculturalism (www.ha-keshet.org.il/files/about.html, my emphasis).[4]

The identity of the Rainbow, as manifested in this quote, exhibits a seeming contradiction. On the one hand, the Rainbow expresses commitment to universal beliefs but, on the other hand, declares its intention to become a mass Mizrahi movement and to promote Mizrahi goals. What kind of social movement organization is the Rainbow? Is the Rainbow a Mizrahi/particularist or an Israeli/universalist movement? Is it a Mizrahi/particularist or a Zionist/Jewish movement? Or is it an Israeli/universalist or a Zionist/Jewish movement? Lastly, is the Rainbow a mass Mizrahi movement or a small lobby group?

Based on documents, statements, and commentaries by observers from within and without the organization, I provide both description and analysis of the way the Rainbow dealt with the 'universalism/particularism' dilemma. As we shall see, the Rainbow advocated a perspective that views particular grievances as giving rise to a struggle whose outcomes are essentially universal. However, this progressive standpoint failed to gain ground among the Israeli public. The Rainbow was able to win public support for its activism primarily by using the particular contribution of the Mizrahim to the Zionist project. The Rainbow was able to accomplish this by exploiting the human resources within the organization, but it did not become a mass Mizrahi movement. As will be shown in the paper, the dilemma between universalism and particularism was clearly manifested in the Land and Housing campaign, the most successful campaign in the history of the Rainbow.[5]

This article's main assumption is that structures enable, but can also constrain, agency. In the course of this paper, we would unravel the interplay between structure and agency (Archer 2003) by showing how Rainbow members skillfully used the opportunities offered to them by Israel's citizenship structure in order to achieve their goals, but how their activism was hampered by this structure.

The rest of the paper is divided into three sections. The first section provides background on the Mizrahi movement for equality through discussion of the Mizrahim's subordinate position within the Israeli citizenship structure in terms of culture, socioeconomic status, and politics. The second section examines the most successful campaign in the history of the Rainbow: the Land and Housing campaign. This section is divided into two sub-sections: the first sub-section presents the factual background for the Land and Housing campaign. The second part analyzes how the universalism/particularism dilemma affected the Rainbow's activism in this campaign. The last section summarizes the main argument of the paper.

Mizrahim in Israel's Citizenship Structure[6]

Cultural Subordination

The Zionist movement was a European movement in its goals and orientation. Inspired by the Enlightenment and other nationalist movements, it shared the Orientalist worldview of the European colonial movements and considered its national project an outpost of Western civilization in the Levantine East (Shafir and Peled 2002: 75). This Orientalist worldview did not only shape the attitude of the Zionist movement toward the Palestinian-Arabs, but also helped to form the way Mizrahi immigrants had been treated by the Zionist and Israeli establishment (Shohat 1988). Since the First and Second Aliyot (immigration waves), when Zionist leaders first made a distinction between Ashkenazim as "idealistic workers" and Mizrahim (mostly Yemenite Jews) as "natural workers" (Shafir 1990), Zionism's attitude towards Mizrahim has always been ambiguous. On the one hand, the

Mizrahim were allowed to participate in the national project not because of their ideological belief in Zionism, but because of their primordial roots as Jews. On the other hand, since they were perceived as non-modern, their contribution to the national project was defined as merely quantitative, as opposed to the qualitative contribution of the Ashkenazim (Shafir and Peled 2002: 76). Thus, their contribution to the Zionist effort was perceived as inferior to that of the Ashkenazim.

Despite relentless denials by both Ashkenazim and Mizrahim, Jewish Orientalism continues to hold ground in Israel until this very day. The Mizrahim have been depicted in Israeli popular culture (e.g. movies, plays, novels, children's books and movies, songs, etc.) as irremediably primitive, violent, lazy, loud and ill-mannered (see Shohat 1989, Urian 2001, Regev and Seroussi 2004: 213–35). While the representation of the Mizrahim in the popular culture has been biased and negative, school history books have rarely included the history of the Jews in Arab and Muslim countries. In the mid-1990s, an education scholar found out that in a specific history book, only nine out of 400 pages (about 2.5 percent) were devoted to the history of Jews from North-African and Middle Eastern countries (Ben-Amos 1995).

This sub-section sets the cultural background for the Mizrahi movement for equality in Israel. In the tradition of the new social movements, Mizrahi social movement organizations promoted the notion that cultural subordination cannot be detached from other forms of "oppression" (see Young 1990: 39–65). Thus, the Mizrahi movement has always believed that the cultural subordination of the Mizrahim is intimately connected to their marginalized position in the socioeconomic ladder in Israel. To the latter factor we now turn.

Socioeconomic Marginalization

Since their arrival to the new state, the Mizrahim have had limited access to state institutions, in particular housing and education. While providing housing to all immigrants, the Israeli state often used this service to achieve state goals, such as "population dispersion" (see Yiftachel 2006: 214–17). Consequently, many Mizrahi immigrants suffered from spatial, hence also social and economic, marginalization. Similarly, the education of the Mizrahim was also used to achieve state ends, such as national assimilation and creating a mass of skilled blue-collar workers desperately needed for the industrialization of the fledgling state. As a result, many Mizrahi immigrants (and their descendants) have achieved lower educational attainments, which have left them vulnerable to the negative repercussions of Israel's economic liberalization and more reliant on the state's welfare services, although these have been shrinking in recent years.

Despite general growth in life quality in Israel, the socioeconomic gaps between Mizrahim and Ashkenazim continue to persist and, in some respects, even to widen. Several studies have shown that although educational and income gaps between first-generation Mizrahim and first-generation Ashkenazim have decreased over the years, occupational gaps between second-generation Mizrahim and Ashkenazim have increased (Cohen and Haberfeld 1998: 515). In 1995, for example, 20 percent of Ashkenazi males had an academic occupation compared to only 6 percent of Mizrahi males. This fact had an impact on the lower chances of first-generation Mizrahim (20.6 percent) to have a liberal profession (a doctor, a lawyer, an engineer, a consultant, an executive, etc.), while those of first-generation Ashkenazim (38.6) were almost two times better. This gap is even larger in the second generation – 21.1 for Mizrahim and 50.1 for Ashkenazim (Cohen 1998).

Status and income gaps between Ashkenazim and Mizrahim also continue to persist and even widen. Seventy-two percent of second-generation Ashkenazim worked in white-collar occupations in 1995 compared to only 46 percent of second-generation Mizrahim. Similarly, 28 percent of second-generation Ashkenazim were blue-collar workers compared to 54 percent of second-generation Mizrahim. Unemployment among second-generation Ashkenazim in 1993 was 4.9 percent, and among Mizrahim 13.9 percent. Among wage-earners, the gap has been widening: an Israeli-born Mizrahi wage-earner earned 79 percent of the income of an Ashkenazi wage-earner in 1975, 70 percent in 1982, and 68 percent in 1992 (Cohen and Haberfeld 1998: 515). In 1975, for example, the income of an Israel-born Mizrahi employee with a college degree was equal to that of a similarly qualified Ashkenazi, in 1995 the former's income was only 78 percent of the latter's (Cohen 1998: 124).

Another factor that contributes to the widening of gaps between second-generation Mizrahim and Ashkenazim is the fact that first-generation Ashkenazim can bequeath more to their children than can first-generation Mizrahim (Semyonov and Lewin-Epstein 2004). This factor has particular effect over disparities between the groups in ownership of housing (Lewin-Epstein and Semyonov 2004). Scholars have found that the probability of Ashkenazim owning housing is two times better than that of Mizrahim, who arrived in Israel before 1952 (Lewin-Epstein et al. 1997: 1452). As for the housing prices, Elmelech and Lewin-Epstein found that the value of the housing owned by second-generation Ashkenazim is 65 percent higher than the value of the housing owned by their Mizrahi peers (Elmelech and Lewin-Epstein 1998).

Education is a prominent factor in determining the socioeconomic gaps between Mizrahim and Ashkenazim (Cohen and Haberfeld 2004). The best indicator of educational achievement in Israel over the years has probably been the ability to gain the state matriculation certificate (in Hebrew, teudat bagrut), a high-school diploma that is necessary (although no longer sufficient) for admission to higher education institutions. Comparing the numbers of students of different ethnic backgrounds eligible for this certificate gives us a good indication of Mizrahim's position in Israeli citizenship structure. The proportion of Mizrahi 18-year-olds holding the certificate in

1995 was 28 percent, up from 17 percent in 1987, while among Ashkenazi 18-year-olds it was 38.7 percent in 1995, up from 31.6 in 1987. Of the 1986–7 cohort of matriculation certificate earners, 45 percent of Ashkenazim, compared to only 30 percent of Mizrahim, had gone on to post-secondary education by 1995 (Swirski 2000). These figures refer to students who are second-generation, in some cases third-generation, Mizrahim. They reflect, therefore, the workings of the Israeli educational system.

By the mid-1990s, the socioeconomic discrepancies between Mizrahim and Ashkenazim not only have not yet been closed, as expected by academics and government officials alike, but they actually have been maintained and even deepened. Throughout the years, numerous Mizrahi activists have been a part of a collective struggle for equality between Mizrahim and Ashkenazim. Most of them have fallen to a systematic process of political de-legitimization. We now turn to the description of this process.

Political De-Legitimization

The State of Israel granted full political civil rights to all Mizrahi immigrants. However, attempts to promote distinct Mizrahi interests and identities were curtailed and de-legitimized. Politically, the Mizrahim have been channeled into the left–right division and, in recent years, especially since the emergence of Shas, into the religious–secular divide. As a result, the Mizrahi vote has rarely assumed a distinct voice. Moreover, Mizrahi mobilization has consistently been stigmatized as "ethnic," hence sectarian, so as to imply that it pursues narrow Mizrahi interests, rather than broader Zionist or Israeli goals (Herzog 1985: 51, 58). This has been an important factor in shaping the Mizrahi collective mobilization for equality.

In contrast to class-based expectations, Mizrahi mobilization did not join forces with the Palestinian-Arab citizens. The Mizrahim – located between the Ashkenazim on the top and the Arab citizens on the bottom – have sought to ally themselves with the Jewish state and with the Ashkenazim who control it, rather than with the Arab citizens, with whom they share cultural subordination and socioeconomic marginalization (Shafir and Peled, 2002: 88). As a result,

> [M]*izrahi* protest has rarely taken an unambiguously conflictual stand in relation to the Zionist ideology. It has assumed, rather, the form of integral Jewish nationalism and, in the case of *Shas*, of politicized Jewish religiosity. In both cases, the *mizrahim*'s oppositional consciousness has espoused the integrative aspects of the dominant ideology, while negating its (intra-Jewish) discriminatory elements (Peled 1998: 707, original emphasis).

Similarly to the cultural attitude towards them, the political attitude towards Mizrahi mobilization has also been ambiguous. As long as

Ashkenazi-dominated political parties and interests (from the left or the right) were able to harness the Mizrahi vote to their own advantage, they accepted it willingly. For example, until 1973, more than 50 percent of the Mizrahim voted for the dominant center-left party, Mapai (or Labor). After 1973, more than 50 percent of the Mizrahim voted for the right-wing party, Likud. In 1977, for example, the Mizrahim gave Likud 32 out of its 43 seats in the Knesset, and in the 1981 elections, 75 percent of the Mizrahim voted for Likud (Chetrit 2003: 198; see also Peres and Shemer 1984).

However, when the Mizrahim established independent political parties and movements, they were chastised as sectarian, separatist, and as undermining Jewish unity. On July 9, 1959, feelings of subordination and marginalization among North-African immigrants led to the Wadi Salib uprising, the first large-scale mobilization effort by Mizrahim in Israel. The leaders of the uprising were accused of weakening Israel's internal unity at a time of numerous security threats from the surrounding Arab world (this was not the last time security considerations were exploited in order to quell Mizrahi protest). Operating in the early 1970s, the Israeli Black Panthers also suffered from harsh de-legitimization: they were portrayed in the media as violent criminals, drug dealers, and radical leftists (primarily because they were among the first Israelis who met Yasser Arafat and other PLO leaders and acknowledged the relationship between social equality and peace with the Palestinians).[7]

In sum, when pursuing collective Mizrahi goals, Mizrahi social movement organizations and political parties have had to battle de-legitimization. The fear of de-legitimization caused Mizrahi protest groups to divert their activism from the streets to lobbying the parliament and the courts. The Rainbow was one of the spearheads of this trend in the Mizrahi movement for equality and social justice. The Rainbow's Land and Housing campaign, to which we will shortly turn, illustrates this trend very well.

This section has provided background on the subordinate status of the Mizrahim in Israel's citizenship structure, which resulted in the emergence of the social movement for equality between Mizrahim and Ashkenazim in Israel. The Rainbow, as the most recent link in the chain of Mizrahi social movement organizations, was highly influenced by Israel's citizenship structure. Shafir and Peled (2002) argue that Israel's citizenship structure has always been characterized by competitive relations between the liberal and the ethno-national discourses. The liberal citizenship discourse highlights the principle of equality – regardless of nationality, ethnicity, gender, or religion – while the ethno-national discourse gives preference to one ethno-national group over others. The tensions between these two principles in Israel's citizenship structure have been alleviated due to the existence of the republican civic discourse, which holds that a citizen's civic virtue depends on his/her contribution to the societal common good. In the Zionist ideology, the republican civic discourse is manifested in the contribution of every Jew to attaining and maintaining the Zionist project, i.e. the State of Israel.

Similar to the Zionist movement, the Rainbow faced contradiction between its commitment to universal values and its aspiration to promote the particular interests of its kin group. The Rainbow also used the republican principle to ameliorate the tensions between liberal universalism and ethnic particularism. Just as the Zionist movement (and, later on, the State of Israel) was able to ease the tensions between democratic governance on one side and Jewish particularism on the other by bringing into play the republican principle, this principle allowed the Rainbow to make demands on behalf of the Mizrahim (ethnic particularism) by invoking their contribution to the Zionist project (Jewish nationalism). Apparently, the logic of ethno-republicanism is shared by both movements,[8] although the ethnic component is different, with Jews as the reference group of Zionism and Mizrahim (an ethnic group within the Jews) as the reference group of the Rainbow. This logic of ethno-republicanism hampered the universal ethos of the Rainbow, excluding the Palestinian-Arab citizens of Israel from any meaningful participation in the Israeli public debate. The next section analyzes these dynamics in the Rainbow's Land and Housing campaign.

Before moving on to the analysis of the Land and Housing campaign, let me just note briefly on the main rival of the Rainbow in the Mizrahi movement for equality between Mizrahim and Ashkenazim in Israeli society: Shas, the Sephardic ultra-Orthodox party. While sharing the same goal, Shas differed from the Rainbow in that it relied on the ethno-national citizenship discourse, rather than the ethno-republican discourse, in its political and social activism. The goal of Shas has always been to equalize the playing field between Mizrahim and Ashkenazim based on their ethno-national roots, wherein there is no apparent difference between Mizrahim and Ashkenazim. For Shas, as long as the contribution to the Zionist common good, rather than ethno-religious affiliation, determines one's civic virtue, Mizrahim and Ashkenazim would never be equal in Israeli society. In short, Shas has tried to "redefine" Jewish nationalism to make it more inclusive and hospitable for Mizrahim (Peled 1998).

The Mizrahi Democratic Rainbow's Land and Housing Campaign

Background

Privatization of Land

Israel's land policy was designed to prevent one main threat: transfer of Jewish land to hands of non-Jews (especially Palestinian-Arabs) (Yonah 2005: 181). From the outset, the state of Israel enacted an array of formal and informal procedures in order to ensure the possession of land resources solely by Jewish people. The aim of these measures was to block the return of the Palestinian refugees that fled (or were forced to flee) from Palestine between 1947 and 1949. Moreover, these legal acts facilitated the settlement of Jewish immigrants coming to Israel during the 1950s (Yiftachel and Kedar 2003: 29). Although the main goal of Israel's land regime was to prevent Arabs from acquiring land, this land regime created hierarchy among groups within Jewish society as well, notably between Mizrahi and Ashkenazi Jews. This hierarchy was manifested in unequal distribution of land. The distribution undoubtedly reflected the favoritism of the Ashkenazim over the Mizrahim. Legal categorizations embodied this favoritism in differential allocations of land to Mizrahim and Ashkenazim.

The Jewish ownership of Israel's lands institutionalized completely with the enactment of the Basic Law: Israel Lands (1960) (www.knesset.gov.il/laws/special/eng/basic13_eng.htm), which transferred the management of Israel's lands to the Israel Land Administration (ILA) (www.mmi.gov.il/Envelope/indexeng.asp?page=/static/eng/f_general.html). The ILA is the statutory executive which secures, manages, and develops Israel's land reserves.[9] The first clause of the Basic Law says: "The ownership of Israel lands, being the lands in Israel of the State, the Development Authority or the Keren Kayemet Le-Israel, *shall not be transferred either by sale or in any other manner*" (www.knesset.gov.il/ laws/special/eng/basic13_eng.htm, my emphasis). However, clause 4 in the Covenant between the State of Israel and the JNF (1960) maintains that "lands shall be administered in accordance with the Law, that is to say, on the principle that land is not sold, but only given on lease" (www.kkl.org.il/kkl/english/main_subject/about_kkl/a_ amana.htm). The ILA stipulates that, "'Ownership' of real estate in Israel usually means leasing rights from the ILA for 49 or 98 years" (www.mmi.gov.il/Envelope/indexeng.asp?page=/static/ eng/f_general. html). Clause 10a of the ILA's decision from May 17, 1965, determined that whenever the council considers a change in the status of a land from agricultural to urban (which allows the construction of shopping malls and/or residence complexes), the lease agreement would immediately expire and the land would return to the ILA possession (www.mmi. gov.il/Moatza Web/InterHachById.asp?HachId=1).[10] As soon as the Council completes this process, the former holder of the land would receive reparations for the investments and the expropriation of his entitlement to hold the land in a rate that would be decided by the Council. Clause B of the resolution from November 11, 1986 (which updated the resolution from May 17, 1965) maintains that if the status of the land has been changed, the lessee would receive reparations without regard to the value of the land after the status change (www.mmi.gov.il/ MoatzaWeb /InterHachById.asp?HachId=343).

All these regulations were either suspended or removed when the process of privatization of Israel's lands began in the early 1990s. In 1992, the ILA passed several significant resolutions aimed at changing all the regulations detailed above in order to strengthen the rights of the farmers, who mainly hold agricultural lands. What was common to all these resolutions was that the farmers would not only have the option to change the land status, but also receive ownership rights on a substantial share of the land in its new status. These resolutions were supposed to give a substantial benefit to the farmers (the majority of whom are Ashkenazi Jews), as the value of the land would have been much higher than the compensation to which they were entitled before these new resolutions had passed. Not only this, but these recent resolutions delivered control over a considerable part of Israel's land reserves to less than 3 percent of the Israeli population (Yiftachel and Kedar 2003: 37–38).

The Rainbow submitted a petition to the High Court of Justice[11] (hereinafter, HCJ) on January 10, 2000, asking it to abolish the new ILA's resolutions (www.ha-keshet.org.il/articles/lands/horaat/atirat2_haforum.htm). The Rainbow maintained that these resolutions allow a small portion of the Israeli population to obtain far-reaching benefits on lands, over which Israeli society has (or at least should have) an equal claim. Furthermore, this unequal allocation of land would leave large groups, who desperately need land and housing solutions, outside the circle of the beneficiaries. On August 29, 2002, the HCJ ruled in favor of the Rainbow's petition and ordered the ILA to cancel the new regulations (HCJ 244/00).

Privatization of Public Housing

In 1997, the government initiated a privatization plan for public housing. There are almost 120,000 apartments under the ownership of the state, and different public housing companies manage them. These companies sublet these apartments to people who have an entitlement for public housing at a subsidized monthly fee.[12] With the passing of the tenants, the apartments return to the public housing companies to sublet them to others who are entitled to public housing. It is noteworthy that the majority of those who reside in the public housing projects are Mizrahi Jews living in development towns or in large cities' working-class neighborhoods.

The privatization of public housing included only the management and maintenance of the housing (Yonah 2005: 188). The Israeli government used to initiate public housing sale campaigns from time to time at subsidized prices. However, these campaigns usually consisted of very low market-value housing, while the government refused to acknowledge the property rights of the tenants over their housing. This latter fact stood in stark contrast to the state's willingness to acknowledge the farmers' land rights. This difference is even starker when comparing the real estate value of the public housing to that of the lands and private houses the farmers possess. According to Globes, the most influential business newspaper in Israel, the value of a public housing apartment in Israel's periphery is equivalent to around 75,000 dollars while the value of agricultural land (after changing its status to urban land) could skyrocket to approximately two million dollars (Avidan 1998).

On October 17, 1998, the Knesset enacted the Public Housing Law (Purchase Rights), offered and composed by the Rainbow, despite the fierce objection of Binyamin Netanyahu's government (Yonah 2005: 189). The purpose of the law was to allow public housing tenants to purchase their apartments at a subsidized price. The law maintained that the longer the period of the tenancy, the higher the subsidy. For instance, tenants who lived in an apartment for more than 25 years would be entitled, according to the law, to a subsidized rate of 85 percent of the apartment real-estate value. However, Netanyahu's government avoided implementing this law by first "freezing" the law until the year 2001 within the framework of the Economic Arrangements Law. In the meantime, the government initiated a campaign to sell public housing apartments to tenants, where the selling terms were far less favorable than what the Public Housing Law had offered. In 1999, the Labor Party, headed by Ehud Barak, won the elections partly based on its commitment to execute the Public Housing Law. However, Barak's government also avoided implementing the law and actually postponed its implementation until January 2002. When January 2002 arrived, Ariel Sharon, who by then was the prime minister, postponed the implementation again until 2005. In short, the law has not been implemented until this very day (Gan-Mor 2008: 12 n. 28).

The Universalism/Particularism Dilemma in the Rainbow's Land and Housing Campaign: Between Theory and Praxis

The universalism/particularism dilemma occupied a major place both in the theoretical and the practical aspects of the Rainbow's activism. Questions such as "whose interests do we represent?" and "what kind of demands should we put forward?" were influenced much by this acute dilemma. On the one hand, the Rainbow set out in this campaign to represent not only Mizrahi grievances, but rather all those who would potentially be disadvantaged as a result of the privatization processes in land and housing. However, as mentioned above, the Rainbow was not only committed to "universal beliefs," but also to pursuing "Mizrahi goals." This meant that the Rainbow sought to secure the interests of the Mizrahim in those privatization processes.

   The Rainbow dealt with the universalism/particularism dilemma in two ways: in theory, the Rainbow advocated a philosophical position in which the motivation for the struggle for equality is indeed particular, but the goals of the struggle are universal. In praxis, however, the transformation from the particular to the universal was not as smooth as it seemed in theory. When the Rainbow had to market its Land and Housing campaign to the Israeli public, it discovered that a "transmission gear" was required to complete the transformation from the particular to the universal. This "transmission gear" was embodied, for the Rainbow, in the Zionist virtue of the Mizrahim. The Rainbow had been able to justify its demands in this activist campaign with the contribution of the Mizrahim to the Zionist national project. The next two sections analyze these dynamics.

Theory

In theory at least, the Rainbow seemed to find a way to overcome the universalism/particularism dilemma. For the Rainbow, the Mizrahi experience provides the impetus for social activism, whose goal is to bring about a change in Israeli society as a whole. This position is based on the experience of feminist and "race" movements, whose motivation is particular (discrimination based on gender or race), but their goal is to create more equal and more just societies. By eliminating oppression directed at particular groups, these movements believe the world can become a better place to live in (see Young 1990).

For some Rainbow members, this point of view was reflected in the Land and Housing campaign. Yossi Loss, one of the Rainbow's senior members, crisply articulated this position:

> The Rainbow needs to find ways to express its positions in a *universalistic manner.* The guidelines must be equality of opportunity and distributive justice. Thus, the starting-point of the Land and Housing campaign was located in a specific experience – real needs and daily reality – of Mizrahim. The guiding principles suggested persistently by the Rainbow did not affect Mizrahim alone, but were rather concerned with the benefit of all Israel's citizens who could not afford purchasing land or decent housing for themselves and their families. *The Rainbow articulated the objectives of this campaign in a way that would reflect not only the injustices toward Mizrahim in land and housing allocation, but also the inequality between the farmers 'minority' and the rest of Israel's citizens* (2002, my emphases).

In the same vein, Yossi Yonah and Yehouda Shenhav, both university professors and among the founders of the Rainbow, assert in their book *What Is Multiculturalism* that,

> The Rainbow's campaigns for recognition of the public housing tenants' property right on their apartments, [and] against the 'agrarian revolution' that threatened to transfer Israel's land reserves to the hands of the farmers' offspring and business entrepreneurs ... provide another example for an activism that has indeed a *particularistic starting-point,* but ends up promoting *universal values.* This campaign started with the promotion of the Mizrahim's socioeconomic interests, but they corresponded with other groups' interests and even promoted them as well (2005: 30, my emphases).

Similarly to Loss, Yonah and Shenhav claim that the activism of the Rainbow was based on universal values of equality and justice:

> The universal values of distributive justice guide multicultural struggles for recognition and redistribution. It must also aim to create ties among all groups that are exposed to cultural and socioeconomic oppression. Thus, although the Rainbow is a Mizrahi movement, what guides its activism is the aspiration to act according to these universal values. Those were the guiding lines, for instance, in the Rainbow's Land [and Housing] campaign … (ibid: 170).

Loss, Yonah and Shenhav believe, then, that the fact that the Rainbow is a Mizrahi organization does not rule out the possibility of promoting interests shared by non-Mizrahi groups. This rhetoric exemplifies the Rainbow's commitment to universal values of equality and social justice. But was this rhetoric able to withstand its ground in the public sphere as well? Was the Rainbow really able to maintain its universal ethos in the Land and Housing campaign? We now move on to analyze the way the Rainbow dealt with the universalism/particularism dilemma in praxis.

Praxis

The ideas of equality and social justice for all in Israeli society guided the activism of the Rainbow in the Land and Housing campaign. Both the petition to the HCJ and the Public Housing bill emphasized liberal values of equality and distributive justice. In the petition, for example, the Rainbow did not seek to represent the interests of the Mizrahim alone, but rather the general interest of Israeli society. As Moshe Karif, one of the Rainbow's founders, suggested, "We do not only represent Mizrahi'im [sic]. We represent universal justice" (Gibson 2002). As noted above, the Rainbow argued in the petition that the ILA's new resolutions diminish the possibility of large segments in Israeli society to lead viable lives. These resolutions, the petition further asserted, compromised the equality among individuals and groups in Israel. The petition also included a quantitative analysis of land allocation in Israel that showed clear and constant disparities between different groups in Israeli society, namely between Ashkenazim and Mizrahim and between Jews and Arabs (to whom the state has allocated only around ¼ percent of its land until this very day). In addition, the Rainbow argued, the generosity of the state as manifested in the policy towards the farmers was not consistent with the way other sectors in Israeli society have been treated in terms of land allocation.

The Public Housing bill was articulated in the same manner. Ideas of human dignity and equality were apparent in the bill as well. The fundamental assumption upon which the bill was founded was "the basic human right of people to have proper housing" (Karif 2005: 464). The Rainbow also made a clear connection between the housing issue and the land issue. Thus, the bill suggested that the revenues that the state would gain from selling agricultural lands after status change to urban lands should sponsor the implementation of the Public Housing Law. This notion was guided by the ambition of the Rainbow's members to rectify past injustices suffered by the Mizrahi population, who is a majority among the population of public housing tenants (see www.ha-keshet.org.il/english/land_struggles.htm).

However, the Rainbow's members' beliefs in universal values were not the only reason the Land petition and the Public Housing bill were articulated the way they were. A strong assumption of this paper is that in order to understand "agency," one must take into account the "structure" as well (see Archer 2003). Although it might be true that the Rainbow members genuinely believe in the equal worth of all Israeli citizens, we must also look into the structural conditions facing the Rainbow's activism in order to get a more comprehensive picture.

In its activism, the Rainbow faced both a cultural and an institutional structure. The institutional structure was composed of the two state institutions approached by the Rainbow in the Land and Housing campaign. In this campaign, the Rainbow dealt primarily with the HCJ and the Knesset, both of which adhere (at least rhetorically) to the universal value of equality. As Shafir and Peled argue, the equality principle has become a fundamental norm in Israeli political culture since the 1980s (2002: 218–29). The Rainbow members were well aware of this fact (three law professors – Dr. Yossi Dahan, Dr. Sandi Kedar, and Dr. Gad Barzilai – were involved in preparing the petition to the HCJ), and this fact helps us to understand why the Land petition and the Public Housing bill were articulated in a universalistic idiom. The Rainbow activists knew that they do not have enough political leverage to pressure the Knesset to enact the Public Housing bill into a law. The articulation of the bill in terms of equality, rather than the narrow grievances of a specific group, enabled broad support in the Knesset for the enactment of the law.

Similarly, the Rainbow could not base its demands in the housing issue on the collective rights of the Mizrahim. It is noteworthy that although it is agreed among many scholars that the Israeli HCJ upholds liberal values and ideas, it nonetheless has a conservative view of them. The court rarely takes collective rights under consideration, such as the right for collective culture, the right for communal education, etc. There is no recognition of collective minority rights in Israel (except for religious rights to the different denominations and the semi-autonomous status granted to the ultra-orthodox community). As a result, the HCJ does not acknowledge collective rights and has been reluctant to accept petitions that uphold such rights.[13]

Thus, we can understand why the Rainbow chose to frame its demands in line with the norm of equality so dear to the HCJ as well as to the Knesset. I do not suggest by any means that the Rainbow members made a cynical use in the principle of equality just in order to advance their claims to the HCJ and the Knesset. I do argue, however, that they were competent enough to acknowledge that if they would frame their appeals to these institutions by using the equality norm, they would be more likely to succeed in their quest. I will deal with the issue of the skills the Rainbow members used in this campaign later in the paper.

The Rainbow also faced a cultural structure, embodied primarily in the de-legitimization of every Mizrahi mobilization effort by the Ashkenazi establishment. The Ashkenazi group represents the normative Israeli society. Moreover, Ashkenazi elites have always claimed to represent the common good, while castigating every Mizrahi social movement organization or party for representing narrow sectarian interests. The articulation of the Land petition and the Public Housing bill in universalistic terms allowed the Rainbow to dodge the argument that the Rainbow pursues only Mizrahi goals. In this case, the Rainbow used universalistic discourse wittingly to avoid a structural predicament for any Mizrahi mobilization effort. Not only that, but the Rainbow also sought to make a clean break from previous Mizrahi social movement organizations, which were accused of acting unlawfully for confronting the state's coercive forces. The Rainbow did not want to be "burned" by Ashkenazi de-legitimization in this respect,[14] so it adopted a different strategy than clashing with the police in the streets.

Instead of becoming a "mass movement" as intended, the Rainbow members decided to lobby state institutions peacefully and respectfully. In fact, the Rainbow developed into a "small and smart" organization. Yossi Yonah explained this logic:

> We're a top-down, not a bottom-up, organization … We never will attract the masses, and that's OK. We will use our skills, even if the people we serve don't even know us or our names and even if they aren't grateful. That's OK. I accept their lack of gratitude with love. We do what we believe is right and moral, but we don't [sic] intend to impose our views on anyone (Gibson 2002).

The Rainbow arrived at the conclusion that the only way for the organization to bring about social change was to utilize the human resources it possessed in lobbying the courts and the parliament and handling the media. As Vicki Shiran, a veteran of the Mizrahi movement and one of the founders of the Rainbow, put it, "We have other skills [than previous Mizrahi activists]. Because we speak the language of the elites, we can penetrate into elite institutions, like the media and the courts" (ibid).

The Rainbow became, in effect, a legal and parliamentary lobby (or advocacy group). In the housing issue, a small number of law specialists from the Rainbow (and other civic organizations) articulated the Public Housing bill before submitting it (through MK Ran Cohen from the left-wing party, Meretz) to the Knesset. In the land issue, the Rainbow used a litigation route by issuing a petition to the HCJ in order to stop (or at least stall) the implementation of the ILA's resolutions with regards to the privatization of public lands. In the meantime, Moshe Karif was working closely with different media outlets (but especially with the daily Israeli newspaper, *Globes*) to bring these issues onto the public agenda.[15] Thanks to Karif's intensive and thorough work, the Land and Housing campaign received a fair amount of exposure in the media during the years 2000–2003 (see the appendix). Moreover, the strategy of the Rainbow created a significant change in the way Mizrahi mobilization efforts were now perceived by the Ashkenazi elites. This is how the daily *Haaretz*, the mouthpiece of the Ashkenazi elites, described the Rainbow's activism in the enactment of the Public Housing Law in the Knesset:

> The Public Housing Law would always be remembered as a rare success for the 1950s immigrants and their offspring. For the first time in their lives, they are a part of the democratic legislative process, which is supposed to defend their rights, without burning even one tire. In opposition to the Wadi Salib riots and the violent demonstrations held by the Black Panthers, *this campaign was both legal and successful* (quoted in Karif 2005: 122, my emphasis).

However, the retreat from the promise to become a mass Mizrahi movement stirred disappointment and criticism toward the Rainbow. Sami Shalom Chetrit, who was one of the Rainbow's founders but left the organization at an early stage, laments the fact that the Rainbow did not use the Land and Housing campaign as a leverage for mass mobilization of Mizrahim. This mobilization, he argues, could have generated a collective Mizrahi consciousness to continue the struggle against the domination of Ashkenazi elites. According to Chetrit, the Rainbow did not achieve this goal primarily because of the way it had conducted the Land and Housing campaign: "The Rainbow organized its campaign in the housing issue like a lobby in the Knesset and not as a social movement organization that wished to expand and spread its values and ideas among the masses" (Chetrit 2005: 147). Even Moshe Karif, the main Rainbow spokesperson during the Land and Housing campaign, had serious reservations about the fact that the Rainbow decided to use the litigation route alone with rarely having any demonstrations, rallies, and the like (Karif 2005: 178). Hence,

> Even the important victory in the Land and Housing campaign, which meant to stop the privatization process in these two areas, did not give the movement a wakeup call from its sound sleep. The upshot was a triumph by a smart legal group and not by a movement with strong connections to the Mizrahi masses ... only mass action ... could lead to collective consciousness (Chetrit 2005: 149–50).

How did the Rainbow achieve the "victory" in the Land and Housing campaign? How did the universalism/particularism dilemma affect the legal and parliamentary "triumph" in this campaign? This paper suggests that the Rainbow used its own version of the ethno-republican discourse in the debates that the Land and Housing campaign stirred in the public sphere. The Rainbow's version of the ethno-republican discourse also helped it to solve, or at least alleviate, some of the tensions between Israeli (primarily Jewish) universalism and Mizrahi particularism. The Rainbow's version of the ethno-republican discourse highlighted the contribution of the Mizrahim to the Zionist project or, in other words, the Zionist virtue of the Mizrahim. According to the Rainbow, this virtue entitles the Mizrahim to an equal share of the state resources, similar to that of the Ashkenazim. The Zionist virtue of the Mizrahim also enabled the Rainbow to reconcile Mizrahi goals (particularism) with the aspiration for (Jewish) equality in Israeli society (qualified universalism).

The Rainbow knew that it must articulate its demands in a way that would resonate with important segments of the Israeli public. The activists of the Rainbow were aware of the fact that despite the gradual importance of the liberal discourse in Israel's political culture, the most fundamental principle that determines the allocation of goods in Israeli society is one's contribution to the Zionist common good (see Yuchtman-Ya'ar and Peres 2000). The Rainbow activists realized that in order to win public support for their campaign, they would have to reframe their demands.

The Zionist virtue of the Mizrahim became then the focal point of the public reframing of the Rainbow's claims in the Land and Housing campaign. In the public sphere, the Rainbow members emphasized the contribution of the Mizrahim to the Zionist project and even presented them as "halutzim" (pioneers in Hebrew) just as the Ashkenazi farmers portrayed themselves. In September 2002, a few days after the HCJ ruled in favor of the Rainbow's petition in the land issue, Vicki Shiran said to the *Jerusalem Post*,

> The kibbutzim [i.e. the farmers] contended that they were entitled to reap the profits from the lands, because they were the halutzim. They had struggled and died for the land. But by recognizing the principle of just distribution, the court, although it didn't say so specifically, was also realizing that the Mizrahi immigrants, who settled in the development towns on the borders and in the Negev, and in the crowded, poor, and dangerous neighborhoods in the cities, were also halutzim. *They, too, are part of the Zionist ethos* (Gibson 2002, my emphasis).

By petitioning to the HCJ, Shiran and the Rainbow wished to upgrade the contribution of the Mizrahim to the Zionist enterprise from merely quantitative to a qualitative one.[16] The aspiration to be a part of the "Zionist ethos" means that the contribution of the Mizrahim cannot be reduced merely to numbers. The idea is that now (and henceforth) the Mizrahim's contribution to the Zionist project would be valued as qualitative and therefore as equal to that of the Ashkenazim.

However, there was not only a symbolic but also a material component to the Rainbow's quest. The cultural recognition that the contribution of the

Mizrahim was indeed equal to that of the Ashkenazim was very important. But, how would the Mizrahim know that their contribution is really equal to that of the Ashkenazim? Only if the state rewards the Mizrahi pioneers with the same currency as the Ashkenazi pioneers. Shlomo Vazana, one of the Rainbow's main spokespersons during this campaign, said that the Land and Housing campaign

> ... penetrates into the heart of the Zionist ethos dominated by the kib-butzim and moshavim [i.e. the farmers]. 'They deserve it, they are the salt of the earth who contributed to the country and defended it even at the cost of losing their own lives,' but what about those who came in the 1950s [i.e. the Mizrahim]? They were scattered all across Israel's borders, which means that they were fulfilling a state function. If the way the state compensates people for their contribution is by giving free land and housing then let it give some to those who came in the 1950s and their offspring as well (quoted in Yonah 2005: 196).

For Vazana, then, Israeli society must recognize the contribution of the Mizrahim to the Zionist project, but, more importantly, this recognition should be accompanied with economic benefits. Just as the Ashkenazi farmers have gained economically throughout the years from the special status given to them by the Zionist ideology, the Mizrahim should enjoy the same dividends as their Ashkenazi brethren because they too sacrificed to maintain the Zionist project. Dr. Yossi Dahan, another prominent Rainbow member, expressed similar views to those of Vazana: "the Mizrahi immi-grants who settled the frontier were as much pioneers as the mythic Zionist farmers and they contributed to the well-being of Israel just as much as the [Ashkenazi] farmers did" (ibid). With this notion, Dahan is asking to put the Mizrahim on an equal footing with the Ashkenazim. Yagil Levy (2003) goes further to argue that the Land and Housing campaign was no other than an effort to exchange the virtuous contribution of the Mizrahim to the Zionist project for tangible economic capital, i.e. land and/or housing (350–51).

This Rainbow narrative, which highlighted the Zionist virtue of the Mizrahim, increasingly took root in the Israeli public sphere. Despite one failed attempt to delegitimize the Mizrahi Democratic Rainbow as another dissident Mizrahi movement (see Galili 2002), the Rainbow's claims in the Land and Housing campaign were well received by the media. Coverage of this campaign by leading newspapers, such as the *Haaretz* and *Globes*, increased steadily until the HCJ ruling in 2002 (see the appendix). Renowned op-ed columnists, such as Avirama Golan from *Haaretz*, favored the Rainbow's cause to equate the role of the Mizrahim in building the State of Israel with that of the Ashkenazim. She even defined the HCJ ruling in the land issue as a "new chapter in the history of Zionism" (Golan 2002). The strategic decision to use the Zionist virtue of the Mizrahim in this campaign paid off for the Rainbow.

However, the decision to use the Mizrahi contribution to the Zionist project aroused a flood of criticism towards the Rainbow. Rainbow members in the past and the present as well as various commentators argued that the Rainbow belied the great promise it had purported to bring to the Israeli civil society. By focusing on the Zionist virtue of the Mizrahim, the critics argued, the Rainbow contributed to the transformation of the public discussion on land and housing allocation to an intra-Jewish debate, thereby hindering the possible opportunity to open up the case of the continuous discrimination of the Palestinian-Arab citizens in land and housing. Two of these critics were Nabi Bashir (the only Arab member of the Rainbow ever) and Dani Ben Simchon, both of whom left the Rainbow in 1998 after the Rainbow failed, in their eyes, to adopt an activist stance that would include some of the goals shared by the Palestinian-Arab citizens of Israel. They contended that the Land and Housing campaign achieved particular Jewish goals, but not universal ones. That is, Israel's lands and housing might be divided equally between Ashkenazi and Mizrahi Jews as a result of the Rainbow's activism, but the Palestinian-Arab citizens would continue to be excluded from the public debate on those issues. In an article he published after the HCJ ruling in August 2002, Dani Ben Simchon expressed his disappointment with the Rainbow's activism:

> If the Rainbow really had a universal ideology as it proclaimed, it should have understood that Arabs and Mizrahi Jews have more in common than not. The struggle against the privatization of lands is a righteous one, but it should have included the Arabs whose relationship to the land is central to their identity. If the Rainbow really believed in universalism, it should have cooperated with the Arab community, thus enabling the creation of a new and unique movement. Such a movement – based on an alliance between Mizrahi Jews, Palestinians, and people from other neighboring Arab countries surrounding Israel, from which Mizrahi Jews had come to Israel – could have led the fight against injustice in the entire Middle East (2002: 30).

Some Rainbow activists themselves were also uncomfortable with using the Zionist virtue of the Mizrahim. Yossi Yonah admitted that, "Other members and I had serious problems with their [i.e. other Rainbow members] demand for just allocation of lands on the basis of the Zionist virtue, and not on the basis of the universal virtues of equality and justice" (Galili 2002). Yonah and Itzik Saporta, two of the Rainbow's senior members, acknowledged that using the Zionist virtue of the Mizrahim in the Land and Housing campaign actually "drove the Palestinian-Arab minority beyond the borders of the Israeli political community" (2003: 161).

However, using the Zionist virtue of the Mizrahim was the way the Rainbow found to explain to the Israeli public why a Mizrahi organization demanded equal allocation of land and housing. Had the Rainbow relied on Mizrahi grievances alone, it might have been castigated as sectarian movement that pursues the narrow interests of its group without paying adequate attention to the needs of Israeli society by and large. Had the Rainbow based its demands solely on the universal values of equality and social justice, there would not have been any meaning to it being a "Mizrahi" organization. The latter strategy would probably have gained some support in the HCJ, but not so much in the public sphere. The Rainbow used the Zionist virtue of the Mizrahim principally because, "The Rainbow places its Mizrahi identity politics within the cultural-political context of Israeli Jewishness as a necessary and sufficient basis for Israeli citizenship" (Amor 2002: 268). In short, using the Zionist virtue of the Mizrahim was the best way available for the Rainbow to resolve the universalism/particularism dilemma.

Concluding Remarks

This article has analyzed the effect of citizenship structure on ethnic mobilization in Israel. The essay has focused on the Mizrahi Democratic Rainbow, a social movement organization of second- and third-generation Mizrahim (Jews from Arab and Muslim countries), and its activism in the Land and Housing campaign, the Rainbow's most successful campaign in its entire history. From its inception, the identity of the Rainbow was based on two contradictory principles: universalism and particularism. This article argues that the Rainbow's activism was shaped to a large extent by the tensions between universalism and particularism. In order to resolve these tensions, the Rainbow used the republican civic discourse, which suggests that a citizen's civic virtue is determined by his/her contribution to the common good of society. This republican principle allowed the Rainbow to make demands on behalf of the Mizrahim (ethnic particularism) by invoking their contribution to the Zionist project (Jewish nationalism). However, this strategy excluded the Palestinian-Arab citizens from any meaningful participation in the public debate, thereby qualifying the universal ethos of the Rainbow.

The analysis in this article illustrates the perspective that individual actors do not exist in a vacuum, where they can pursue their preferences uninhibitedly. Even if the Rainbow was sincere in its attempt to bring about a radical change for the benefit of the entire Israeli society, its activism was constrained by the Israeli citizenship structure. Nevertheless, the Rainbow's activism definitely opened up a distinct chapter in the Mizrahi struggle for equality and social justice in Israel.

Appendix

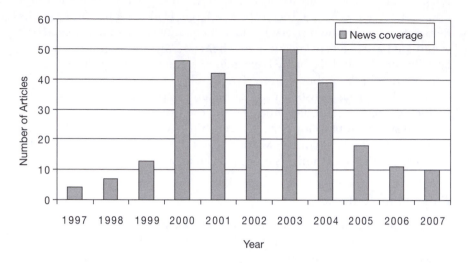

Figure 6.1 News coverage of the Mizrahi Democratic Rainbow in Globes, 1997–2007.

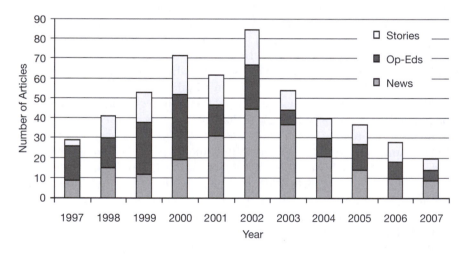

Figure 6.2 Media exposure of the Mizrahi Democratic Rainbow in Haaretz, 1997–2007.

Notes

1 Politics Department and the Schusterman Center for Israel Studies at Brandeis University. The article is based on parts of my master's thesis – entitled "The Mizrahi Democratic Rainbow: Between Theory and Practice" – which was submitted to Tel Aviv University. I am grateful to Nina Weiner and the ISEF Foundation for their generous support. I would like to thank the editors of this volume for

their helpful comments on previous drafts of this article. Needless to say, all the faults of the article are mine.

2 Disclaimer: I was an active member of the Mizrahi Democratic Rainbow from 2002 to 2006. It is important to note that I did not use any information or documents that might have been disclosed to me in confidence during my years in the organization for the preparation of this article. I used only statements, documents, and data that were open and accessible to the general public.

3 The term "Mizrahim" stands for Oriental in Hebrew, and is widely accepted as an umbrella term for all the Jews (and their descendants) that came to Israel from Middle Eastern, North-African, or Asian countries. Similarly to feminist or "race" awareness, "Mizrahi" also denotes a form of political consciousness that stands as an alternative to the Ashkenazi cultural and socioeconomic hegemony.

4 All translations from the Hebrew are mine.

5 This article does not deal with whether or not the Land and Housing campaign was, in fact, successful. The success of this campaign is taken as a given in order to probe into the strategy used by the Rainbow in this campaign.

6 This section relies in part on Shafir and Peled's discussion of Mizrahi peripheral position in Israeli society. See Shafir and Peled 2002: 74–95.

7 The leftist stance of the Israeli Black Panthers stood in stark contrast to the political behavior of the broader Mizrahi community. The majority of the Mizrahim tend to support right-wing political parties and aggressive policies toward the Arabs. This fact can explain why the Black Panthers did not succeed as a political party. However, as Yoav Peled has already shown, these hawkish attitudes toward Arabs and the peace process are a product of specific structural conditions and historical circumstances (see Peled 1990).

8 For elaboration on the concept of ethno-republicanism, see Peled 1992.

9 The Israel Land Council – which comprises 22 people, 12 represent government ministries and 10 represent the Jewish National Fund (JNF), and chaired by Israel's Minister of Housing and Construction – determines the policy for the ILA.

10 Clause 2a of this decision stipulates that "the status and use of agricultural land will not be changed by the authorities for another status or use unless in exceptional instances."

11 The Israeli Supreme Court also sits as the High Court of Justice. This function is unique to the Israeli system because as the High Court of Justice, the Supreme Court acts as a court of first and last instance. The High Court of Justice exercises judicial review over the other branches of government. As a High Court of Justice, the Supreme Court hears over a thousand petitions each year. Often these cases are high-profile ones challenging acts of top government officials. The Supreme Court, sitting as the High Court of Justice, is empowered, among others, to instruct state and local authorities and their officers, and other bodies and individuals statutorily performing public duties, to act or to refrain from acting in said discharge. For more details, see www.mfa.gov.il/MFA/Government/Branches%20of%20Government/Judicial/The%20Judiciary-%20The%20Court%20System

12 An entitlement for public housing in Israel is based on three conditions: (1) The family has at least three children; (2) the couple scored a high score (at least 1400 points) according to certain entitlement stipulations; and (3) the couple work as much as they can, but their monthly income is still very low. People who served in the army have an advantage in getting public housing. This is yet another expression of the ethno-republican discourse, which discriminates mainly against Palestinian-Arab citizens.

13 For an elaborated discussion on this issue, see Barzilai 2003.

14 Nonetheless, in 2002, the Rainbow had to cope with a defamatory campaign that

included the slogan: "The Mizrahi Democratic Rainbow for the [Palestinian] Right of Return." This slogan implied that the Rainbow's activism in the land issue is no other than an attempt to implement a radical leftist ideology (Galili 2002).

15 Despite the fact that *Globes* is a business newspaper (parallels in many respects to the *Financial Times*) and its editorial board obviously supports market-based economy, this newspaper was quite sympathetic (for its own reasons) to the Rainbow cause in the Land and Housing campaign.

16 The Land petition was not the first time Vicki Shiran had attempted to upgrade the contribution of the Mizrahim to the Zionist enterprise. In 1981, Vicki Shiran submitted (with Professor Shimon Shetreet) a petition to the High Court of Justice to bring the Israel Broadcasting Authority to include the narrative of the Mizrahim in the anniversary TV series, *The Pillar of Fire*, which chronologically reviews the Zionist enterprise from its early days until the founding of the State of Israel in 1948.

References

Court Rulings

HCJ 244/00 *New Discourse Association – "The Mizrahi Democratic Rainbow" v. Minister of National Infrastructure*, P.D. 56(6) [Hebrew].

From the Web (all retrieved on July 2, 2009)

www.ha-keshet.org.il/articles/lands/horaat/atirat2_haforum.htm [Hebrew]
www.ha-keshet.org.il/english/land_struggles.htm
www.ha-keshet.org.il/files/about.html [Hebrew]
www.kkl.org.il/kkl/english/main_subject/about_kkl/a_amana.htm
www.knesset.gov.il/laws/special/eng/basic13_eng.htm
www.mmi.gov.il/Envelope/indexeng.asp?page=/static/eng/f_general.html
www.mmi.gov.il/MoatzaWeb/InterHachById.asp?HachId=1 [Hebrew]
www.mmi.gov.il/MoatzaWeb/InterHachById.asp?HachId=343. [Hebrew]

Books and Articles

Amor, M. (2002), "Israeli Citizenship: from Multiculturalism to Interculturalism," in Y. Shenhav et al. (eds), *Mizrahim in Israel: A Critical Observation into Israel's Ethnicity*, Van Leer Jerusalem Institute and Hakibbutz Hameuchad Publishing House, Tel-Aviv [Hebrew].

Archer, M. S. (2003), *Structure, Agency and the Internal Conversation*, Cambridge University Press, New York, NY.

Avidan, G. (1998), "Buzaglo Test for Privatization," *Globes*, June 10 [Hebrew], retrieved on July 10, 2009 from: www.globes.co.il/serve/globes/docviewasp?did=68509&fid=2

Barzilai, G. (2003), *Communities and Law: Politics and Cultures of Legal Identities*, University of Michigan Press, Ann Arbor, MI.

Ben Amos, A. (1995), "Pluralism Impossible? Ashkenazi and Sephardic Jews in Israel's

History Curriculum," in David Chen (ed.) *Education Towards the 21st Century,* Tel Aviv University Press, Tel Aviv [Hebrew].

Ben Simchon, D. (2002), "The Mizrahi Democratic Rainbow: Universality Ltd.," *Etgar,* 8, pp. 24–25, 30 [Hebrew].

Chetrit, S. S. (2003), *The Mizrahi Struggle in Israel,* Am Oved and Ofakim Library, Tel Aviv [Hebrew].

Chetrit, S. S. (2005), "The New Mizrahim: The Radical Mizrahi Discourse and The Mizrahi Democratic Rainbow," in G. Abutbul, P. Motzafi-Haller and L. L. Grinberg (eds), *Mizrahi Voices: Towards a New Mizrahi Discourse on the Israeli Society,* Masada, Jerusalem [Hebrew].

Cohen, Y. (1998), "Socioeconomic Gaps among Jews, 1975–1995," *Israeli Sociology,* vol. 1, no. 1, pp. 115–134 [Hebrew].

Cohen, Y. and Haberfeld, Y. (1998), "Second Generation Jewish Immigrants in Israel: Have the Ethnic Gaps in Schooling and Earnings Declined?" *Ethnic and Racial Studies,* vol. 21, May 3, pp. 507–28.

Cohen, Y. and Haberfeld, Y. (2004), "Second Generation Jewish Immigrants in Israel: Have the Ethnic Gaps in Schooling and Earnings Declined?" in M. Semyonov and N. Lewin-Epstein (eds), *Stratification in Israel: Class, Ethnicity, and Gender* (Studies of Israeli Society, Volume 10), New Brunswick, NJ, Transaction Publishers.

Elmelech, Y. and Lewin-Epstein N. (1998), "Migration and Housing in Israel: Another Look at Ethnic Inequality," *Megamot,* vol. 39, no. 3, pp. 243–69 [Hebrew].

Galili, L. (2002), "A New Campaign by the Kibbutzim: 'The Mizrahi Democratic Rainbow for the Right of Return'," *Haaretz,* March 2 [Hebrew], retrieved on July 21, 2009.

Gan-Mor, G. (2008), *Real Estate or Rights: Housing Rights and Government Policy in Israel,* Association for Civil Rights in Israel, Jerusalem. Can be retrieved here: www.acri.org.il/pdf/DiurEng.pdf

Gibson, E. P. (2002), "To Struggle by Other Means," *Jerusalem Post,* September 13, retrieved on July 21, 2009.

Golan, A. (2002), "The Seven Justices Turned a Page in the History of Zionism," *Haaretz,* August 30 [Hebrew], retrieved on July 21, 2009.

Herzog, H. (1985), "Social Construction of Reality in Ethnic Terms: The Case of Political Ethnicity in Israel," *International Review of Modern Sociology,* vol. 15, no. 1–2, pp. 45–61.

Karif, M. (2005), *The Mizrahi (Hamizrahit): The Story of The Mizrahi Democratic Rainbow Coalition (Hakeshet Hademokratit Hamizrahit),* Globes Library, Tel Aviv [Hebrew].

Levy, Y. (2003). *Another Army for Israel: Materialist Militarism in Israel,* Yedi'ot Aharonot, Tel Aviv [Hebrew].

Lewin-Epstein, N. and Semyonov, M. (2004), "Migration, Ethnicity, and Inequality: Homeownership in Israel," in M. Semyonov and N. Lewin-Epstein (eds), *Stratification in Israel: Class, Ethnicity, and Gender* (Studies of Israeli Society, Volume 10), New Brunswick, NJ, Transaction Publishers.

Lewin-Epstein N., Elmelech, Y. and Semyonov M. (1997), "Ethnic Inequality in Homeownership and the Value of Housing: The Case of Immigrants in Israel," *Social Forces,* vol. 75, June 4, pp. 1439–62.

Loss, Y. (2002), "The Rainbow Campaign to Change the Literature Curriculum," retrieved on July 2, 2009 from: www.ha-keshet.org.il/articles/education/maavak_loss .html [Hebrew].

Peled, Y. (1990), "Labor Market Segmentation and Ethnic Conflict: The Social Basis of Right-Wing Politics in Israel," in A. Arian and M. Shamir (eds), *The Elections in Israel – 1988*, Westview, Boulder, CO.

Peled, Y. (1992), "Ethnic Democracy and the Legal Construction of Citizenship: Arab Citizens of the Jewish State," *American Political Science Review*, vol. 86, June 2, pp. 432–443.

Peled, Y. (1998), "Towards a Redefinition of Jewish Nationalism in Israel? The Enigma of Shas," *Ethnic and Racial Studies*, vol. 21, July 4, pp. 703–27.

Peres Y. and Shemer, S. (1984), "The Communal Factor in the Tenth Knesset Elections," *Megamot*, vol. 28.

—. (1984), "The Ethnic Factor in the Tenth Knesset Elections," *Megamot*, vol. 28, [Hebrew] pp. 316–331.

Regev, M. and Seroussi, E. (2004), *Popular Music and National Culture in Israel*, University of California Press, Berkeley and Los Angeles, CA.

Semyonov M. and Lewin-Epstein, N. (2004), "The Impact of Parental Transfers on Living Standard of Married Children," in M. Semyonov and N. Lewin-Epstein (eds), *Stratification in Israel: Class, Ethnicity, and Gender* (Studies of Israeli Society, Volume 10), New Brunswick, NJ, Transaction Publishers.

Shafir, G. (1990), "The Meeting of Eastern Europe and Yemen: 'Idealist Workers' and 'Natural Workers' in Early Zionist Settlement in Palestine," *Ethnic and Racial Studies*, vol. 13, April 2, pp. 172–197.

Shafir, G. and Peled, Y. (2002), *Being Israeli: The Dynamics of Multiple Citizenship*, Cambridge University Press, New York, NY.

Shohat, E. (1988), "Sephardim in Israel: Zionism from the Standpoint of its Jewish Victims," *Social Text* 19/20, pp. 1–35.

Shohat, E. (1989), *Israeli Cinema: East/West and the Politics of Representation*, University of Texas Press, Austin, TX.

Swirski, S. (2000), *Eligibility for Matriculation Certificates by Locality, 1997–1999*, Adva Center, Tel Aviv [Hebrew].

Urian, D. (2001), "Mizrahi and Ashkenazi in the Israeli Theatre," *Middle Eastern Literatures*, vol. 4, January 1, pp. 19–36.

Yiftachel, O. and Kedar, S. (2003), "On Power and Land: The Israeli Land Regime," in Y. Shenhav (ed.), *Space, Land, Home*, Van Leer Institute in Jerusalem and Hakibbutz Hameuchad Publishing House, Tel Aviv [Hebrew].

Yiftachel O. (2006), *Ethnocracy: Land and Identity Politics in Israel/Palestine*, University of Pennsylvania Press, Philadelphia, PA.

Yonah, Y. (2005), *In Virtue of Difference: The Multicultural Project in Israel*, Van Leer Institute in Jerusalem and Hakibbutz Hameuchad Publishing House, Tel Aviv [Hebrew].

Yonah, Y. and Saporta, I. (2003), "Land and Housing Policy: The Limits of Citizenship Discourse," in Y. Shenhav (ed.), *Space, Land, Home*, Van Leer Institute in Jerusalem and Hakibbutz Hameuchad Publishing House, Tel Aviv [Hebrew].

Yonah, Y. and Shenhav, Y. (2005), *What is Multiculturalism? On the Poverty of the Multicultural Discourse in Israel*, Babel, Tel Aviv [Hebrew].

Yuchtman-Ya'ar, E. and Peres, Y. (2000), *Between Consent and Dissent: Democracy and Peace in the Israeli Mind*, Rowman & Littlefield, Lanham, MD.

7   Fundamentalist citizenships[1]

The Haredi challenge

*Nurit Stadler, Edna Lomsky-Feder
and Eyal Ben-Ari*

Introduction

This paper examines how members of the Haredi fundamentalists group
challenge and negotiate issues of citizenships in Israel. Using concepts from
the study of fundamentalism, we demonstrate how Haredi fundamentalists,
allegedly perceived as hostile or indifferent to the secular state, participate
and contribute to the Israeli collective good and crucial issues of citizenship.
These new notions of participation are translated into concrete strategies by
which Haredi fundamentalists integrate themselves into mainstream Israel.
We argue that a new definition of fundamentalist citizenship and inclusion
has emerged, one that is more pragmatic in its relations with the state and
civil society, yet at the same time maintains high standards of Haredi piety
and religiosity.

   To examine these new forms of fundamentalist citizenship we analyze
three sites of Haredi attitudes and activities. We first explore the ambivalent Haredi attitudes towards military participation and militarism in
Israel. The military in Israel represents the ultimate site for participation,
contribution and sacrifice to the state. Yet while nowadays most Haredim
express militaristic views and support right wing politics they still reject military participation and the attempts to enlist Haredi members into the IDF
(Israel Defense Forces). The second site is the Haredi organization, ZAKA
that emerged as a reaction to escalation of terror attacks in Israel during
the 1990s. ZAKA is an organization of volunteers assisting terror victims and
other deaths. Finally, we analyze *Yad Sara*, an aid organization initiated by
Haredi members as a response to the weakening of the welfare state and lack
of aid for the poor and elderly in Israel. We show how new meanings and
approaches towards citizenship are created in each site and how fundamentalism is changing its nature through these relations.

   What is the context of these transformations within the Haredi world?
Since the mid-1980s Israel has witnessed two broad, interrelated transformations that undermined the nation-state's monopoly over various material
and non-material resources. The first comprises changes in the nature
of conflicts and the reaction of the state and the military towards security
threats. The combination of the first Palestinian Uprising (1987–1992), the

Second Uprising (2000–present) and the Second Lebanon War (Summer 2006) has brought about changes. Palestinian assaults and Hezbollah attacks have targeted civilians as well as soldiers, and Jewish as well as Arab citizens. Accordingly, basic concepts of war and the military have been undermined: for example, the differentiation between front and rear and the very boundaries of the Israeli collective. As a result, concepts at base of the Israeli republican discourse on social hierarchies previously based on contribution through military service and participation in war have been increasingly questioned (Levy 2003, 2007; Levy et al. 2007; Peled 2007). The second broad sweep of change is the result of emerging neo-liberalist policies that have weakened the state, undermined state-mandated arrangements for supplying social and health services, and brought forth new forms of citizen participation (Ben-Eliezer 1999; Peled and Ophir 2001; Ram 2007; Shafir and Peled 2002).

These two trends – in accepted concepts of security and state, and a weakened state role in the economic sphere and social services – have eroded social rights associated with citizenship. This erosion is part of a global move found in many industrial societies (Isin and Turner 2007; Joppke 2007). Peled (2007) contends that we are witness to the development of a new type of society he terms a "post-civil society." Exploring the Israeli case, he emphasizes that marginal groups – in this case Palestinians and peripheral Jewish groups – are for the most part harmed by the changed role of the state.

In this article we explore one aspect of this process that has opened up space for groups operating in civil society to oppose, complement or support the state. The Haredim in Israel are a case study that shows how fundamentalist groups enter this new space of participation and contribution. We argue that Haredim in Israel challenge the accepted concepts of citizenship, create new practices, and at the same time fuse them with fundamentalist piety and devoted life styles. In this context, we analyzed the Haredi challenges to citizenship not only as part of global changes in concepts of the state, but also as related to a transformation of the fundamentalist identity and ways of perceiving sacredness while participating in state-related arenas.

Fundamentalist movements and the nation-state

Fundamentalist groups around the world construct their unique identity through an active work of scripturalism: a selective retrieval of doctrines, religious symbols, and beliefs. The sacred texts, the Torah, the Qur'an, the Bible, are all accepted in the minds of fundamentalists, as being of a divine origin (Almond, Appleby and Sivan 2003: 96). As these groups define their identity they redefine symbols and meanings that are selected from an imagined sacred past and utilized by fundamentalists as a response to what are perceived as testing, troubling times (Antoun 2001). Thus fundamentalists are actively involved in the process of choosing and picking specific elements from their sacred texts and implementing them as grounds for plans, life visions and fantasies. In the fundamentalist imagery the scriptures are thus used to establish and sanction a particular interpretation or view and empower a particular authority (Asad 2003: 11).

Sociologists that have explored different aspects of fundamentalism argued that such groups comprise educated, text-based, intellectual, elite men who are accepted in their communities as virtuosos (Antoun 2001: 3; Riesebrodt 1993 (1990): 9). As such, these men transmit ideas to the new generations in special institutions, and it is their duty to ensure piety as a defense against the outer world. Power and status are reproduced by these valorized devotees who are constantly performing and defending the sanctity of the group. Trained and impressed with the stamp of proper desire, selfhood, masculinity, morality and knowledge, the pious fundamentalist is disciplined to aspire to transcendental qualities that safeguard him from the corrupt world, and by extension safeguard the entire community (Stadler 2009). The nature of scripturalism reinforces the importance of founding new educational institutions such as religious seminars, yeshivot, *madrasas*, churches, theological schools, or Bible schools. To construct a specific model of piety in modernity, new socialization methods are used. Thus in the case of Haredi culture in Israel the yeshiva hall, exactly like the *madrasa*, is a key element of the fundamentalist project in that it serves to maintain a cadre of experts invigorating a moral climate (Heilman 1995: 78).

Scholars dealing with fundamentalist movements and the state contend that because members of fundamentalist groups are convinced of the conspiratorial nature of secularists, they adopt a reactive set of strategies claiming to fight back against the influences of such ideas or preserving their separateness from secular society and the liberal state (Ammerman 1987; Sahliyeh 1995: 135; Sivan 1995: 12). However, at the same time, as Marty and Appleby (1995: 1–2) point out, certain fundamentalist groups do find themselves participating in a common discourse about modernization, political structures, and economic planning. Along these lines, relations between fundamentalists and the state have usually been analyzed through a religio-political discourse emphasizing resistance to ideologies represented by modern states or the creation of a selective and pragmatic politics of participation.

Two forms of relationship of fundamentalists with the modern state are emphasized in the scholarly literature. The first kind has involved resistance to the modern secular state and thus characterized by an ideology of "chosen people" or "holy warriors." These notions are coupled with a call to keep all members of the group away from the corruption, lust and profligacy represented by the modern world. Within this conception a cadre of elected members strives to fully devote themselves to a righteous lifestyle and sacred morality. The radical Sikhs in India and the pious Shiites movements in Lebanon exemplify this kind of attitude towards secular reality (Sahliyeh 1995: 147–8). The second form of the relationship between fundamentalism and the state centers on how when fundamentalists participate in politics, they usually strive to influence state policies and are necessarily involved in compromises and strategic accommodation with state ideologies, practices and obligations (Harding 2000: 12). This kind of pragmatic fundamentalist politics is stressed by Harding in her analysis of Jerry Falwell's Evangelist movement in the United States, and the political religiosity of the *Comunione e Liberazione* in the political realm of the Italian state (Almond et al. 2003). In this analysis politics is used by fundamentalists as a practical tool in order to gain resources and protect interests such as private religious education, religious services and all other particular interests of the community.

However, as we show in this paper, these two pragmatic forms of relations are nowadays changing. To explain this transformation in the fundamentalist reaction towards the state and citizenship we draw on a body of literature explaining how contemporary feminism led to the emergence of an innovative model linking fundamentalists to authority. Feminist scholars have argued that gender consciousness has been a pivotal factor in transforming the nature of fundamentalist movements from within. For instance, in examining Bible-believing women, Brasher (1988: 18) contends that such individuals are powerful agents whose involvement in congregations leads to the development of new positions of authority and the exercise of power. Mahmood (2005) makes a similar argument about the participation of women in mosques belonging to Muslim fundamentalist groups in Egypt since the 1980s. She shows how these women have read and interpreted canonical sources to reconstruct their religiosity and lifestyles thereby reshaping the very nature of female fundamentalism. Likewise, Deeb (2006), in her study of a fundamentalist Shi'i community in Beirut demonstrates how public piety is cast as the women's *jihad* bearing on their lives and lifestyles. We use this argument to explain how Haredim have challenged citizenship nationalism, and the state while creatively using aspects of participation, piety and contribution.

The research on the political and civic participation of Haredim in Israel continues to be based on prevailing assumptions found in the scholarly field. On the one hand, scholars have emphasized the withdrawal of the community from wider society while also stressing their growing pragmatism while negotiating with the state and civil society (Kimmerling 2004; Shafir and Peled 2002). In addition, scholarly discussions on forms of citizenship in Israel are almost completely based on the formulation of Shafir and Peled's analysis of the "incorporation regime" of Israeli society as composed of three discourses of citizenship: the ethno-national, republican and liberal ones. Within this theoretical lens Haredim award religious justification for the ethno-national discourse and as a group are excluded and exclude themselves from the republican discourse. Within this analysis Haredim rarely appear, and one expression of their relative irrelevance is their absence from the volume edited by Peled and Ofir (2001) on the transformation of Israel from a mobilized to a civil society. When Haredim are discussed in scholarly work, their participation in state institutions is interpreted as a combination of closure and instrumental integration developed over time into a pragmatic fundamentalism. Moreover, the activities of Haredim in civil society are seen as resulting from the weakening of the Israeli nation-state, the strengthening of the liberal discourse, and their specific retraction into the ethno-national discourse (Shafir and Peled 2002).

In contrast to this kind of analysis of Haredi fundamentalism in Israel, we suggest a different theoretical approach, stressing the development of a new set of relations between fundamentalism and citizenship. We show that diverging strategies, of opposition and cooperation, can be used by the same fundamentalist group to react to different aspects of citizenship, politics and the modern state. Furthermore, the mixture of these strategies has led to the emergence of a novel fundamentalist public discourse and practice of citizenship that is particular to Israeli society. We demonstrate that Haredi fundamentalism in Israel, quiescent and passive in its nature has challenged ideas of citizenship by fusing Jewish theology of death and ideas about voluntarism and aid. Thus, current Haredi fundamentalists combine religious ideals such as "contribution," "participation" and "sacrifice" with similar ideas promoted by Israeli republican citizenship discourse to create new concepts and conducts. In the context of the exclusion of a variety of collectivities from the Israeli citizenship, such as Palestinian groups, the Haredi community is succeeding in including themselves in many realms of contribution thanks to their organizational abilities and collective dedication.

Methods

To analyze and explain the new concepts of Haredi citizenship created in Israel we drew on ethnographic research on three Haredi realms. Our findings about new Haredi attitudes to the military are based on two sources. The first includes in-depth interviews carried out by the first author with about 42 students at leading *Yeshivot* which were intended to elicit the voices of a new generation among the community. The second source is various texts, audio cassettes, DVDs and video films produced within the community that refer to the army. The analysis of the latter was done to understand the official viewpoint of the community leaders promulgated in public arenas. As we shall see, it is the tension between the two sets of voices which is central to attitudes towards national military service.

Between June 2002 and August we conducted twenty interviews with members of ZAKA entailing questions about organizational aspects, religious justifications for volunteering, and experiences in terror attacks and other assignments. In addition, we held numerous informal conversations with a host of other volunteers and were invited to visit their offices and depots and to attend some social events. In order to understand the context in which ZAKA was established, analyses of newspapers, web pages, and television reports were also systematically collected and analyzed (including internal Haredi media and the media belonging to wider Israeli society). These latter resources were especially important since we wanted a rough gauge of the degree to which ZAKA has been accepted by mainstream Jewish Israeli society. Finally, in order to verify the self-depictions given us by interviewees and in order to look at ZAKA critically, we also talked to some police officials, members of Jewish Burial societies, and journalists.

Research on *Yad Sara* is different from that of the two other sites. Here we focused our analysis on newspapers, material published in the organization's web pages, and television reports on volunteers. While we did not carry out any direct interviews with members of this organization, the hundreds of media reports about it provide a very rich database on which to found our contentions. As we have not conducted interviews with Yad Sarah members, data about volunteers' interpretations is missing but would contend that this level of analysis is less important because participation in Yad Sara is not controversial as in ZAKA and the military, does not pose much tension between Haredi members and the state and as such there is little gap between the formal discourse and religious practices. However this organization is crucial to the study of fundamentalism and citizenship.

Before presenting our findings let us briefly present an overview of Haredi fundamentalism in contemporary Israel.

Fundamentalism in Israel

The term "fundamentalism" in the modern Jewish Israeli context actually covers a number of movements whose historical development and distinctiveness make them different from each other. Three groups appear in the relevant scholarly literature: The ultranationalist Gush Emunim ("Bloc of the faithful"); the Lubavitch-Hasidic or Habad movement; and the Haredi community (Aran 1993; Friedman 1994; Heilman 1994, 1995; Ravitzky 1994; Soloveitchik 1994). Although containing a number of internal variations, here we focus on broad changes in the Haredi world. In Israel, the *Haredi* community now comprises between six and ten percent of the Jewish population (Dahan 1998; Berman 2000). The two largest Haredi concentrations are in Mea Shearim (Jerusalem) and Bnei Brak. Because the absorption capacity of such neighborhoods is limited and the cost of housing relatively high, over the past two decade Haredi quarters have been built in development towns and specially designed towns and suburbs (Shilhav 1998: 6). In these urban enclaves members are provided with all the services necessary for everyday community life: *yeshivot*, synagogues, kosher shops, ritual baths, or book stores. Moreover, they are involved at all levels of managing, planning, and maintaining municipal services (Shilhav 1991, 1998: 7).

Haredi life emphasizes an obligation to learn the *Torah* (the body of Jewish law and lore), an anti-Zionist stand, and a sense of collective trauma resulting from the choice of the majority of Jewish society to leave the folds of traditional life in favor of other Jewish religious or secular options (Friedman 1993: 177). Although unified by the adherence to a strictest version of

Halakha (Jewish law) Haredi members are not monolithic but divided into communities that struggle over power, authority and resources (Heilman 1983; 1992). Caplan (2007) explained that today the Haredi community is generally divided between Ashkenazi Haredim, of European or American descent, and Sepharedic Haredim of Asian or North African descent. This division is marked by separate political parties and educational systems, which protect and reproduce the ethno-cultural division.

Largely, Haredi fundamentalism is predicated on the *Yeshiva* as the exclusive site where the authentic version of Judaism may be learned and where one can actualize the Haredi life-style. In Israel, this community is thus made up of a plethora of *Yeshivot*, and all men and their families are asked to belong to a specific *Yeshiva* and live according to its worldviews. Thus, the *yeshiva* is a "total institution" that covers the entire breadth of the life-cycle of the individual, and is a place of prayer and study, a framework for socializing and leisure, and a community center providing material aid, housing and psychiatric support. The *yeshiva* scholar is asked to withdraw from all worldly practices and to totally devote himself to intellectual and spiritual activities. He is considered a virtuoso of texts and, as such, interprets sacred codes governing everyday behaviors. *Torah* study is a goal to be sought all day long, and interrupting this duty, for any purpose, is defined as a sin. For this reason, national service (particularly the army) or economic dealings or other state duties are considered profanations of the study of the *Torah* and therefore violations of central community taboos (Stadler 2002, 2004, 2009).

In maintaining separate communities in the midst of the modern state, Haredim are in constant conflict with surrounding society on many issues. In Israel the tension with the state and civil society has grown because Haredim do not participate in the labor market, do not serve in the army and are dependent on the largess of the state for survival (Stadler and Ben-Ari 2003). At the same time, however, they have attained impressive success in terms of budgets allocated to them, widening their educational system, the number of institutions catering to their needs and their cultural and political influence (Sivan and Caplan 2003). Shafir and Peled (2002) maintain that Haredim were awarded these rights because of the historical necessity of Israel as a state to receive a religious sanction for its ethno-national boundaries as a Jewish-Israeli collective. Yet the Haredi non-participation in the central arenas characterizing citizenship in nation-states (the labor market and military service) has "spoiled" the delicate balance between civic duties and rights (Isin and Turner 2007).

The criticism against Haredim over their increasing rights over duties has been intensified since the 1977 elections in which Haredi numbers have translated into considerable party power in Israel's coalitional politics (beyond their actual electoral weight). Since then, growing involvement in politics has also been related to the need for resources given the economic conditions of the community. Haredi families are characterized by young age at marriage and a high birthrate (the average number of children in a Haredi home is 7.7 in contrast to 2.6 in the general Israeli population). Berman (2000: 913–4) argues that in Israel the proportion of Haredi men (aged 25–54) who do not participate in the labor market because they attend *yeshiva* full-time rose from 41 percent in 1980 to 60 percent by 1996. Scholars argue that these levels are unprecedented among Jews in other orthodox streams, and far exceed *yeshiva* attendance abroad where young men seldom attend past the age of 25. In these conditions, most members maintain a modest lifestyle, live in poor crowded housing, and are highly dependent on state support (Berman 2000).

Since the 1990s the Haredi community in Israel is undergoing major shifts. Its defining features as Torah dedication, male-based asceticism, and separatism have been recently challenged by members of the community. As a result, Haredim have changed their views on politics, religion, economics, medicine, aid, gender and the family (Caplan 2007). For example, the challenge mounted by Haredi students on yeshiva asceticism and isolation has produced changed attitudes to work and the labor market (Stadler 2002, Lupo 2003). Another example is the internal debate on the status of women as housewives and providers that has led to change in the community with regard to gender and education (El-Or 1994; Caplan 2007). These transformations have been explained by scholars using different paradigms. Some have argued that the change is an outcome of the increased interactions with the wider, non-Haredi, public. Thus, Haredi members have gradually accepted elements of Israeli attitudes and minimized tensions between the state and civil society (Caplan 2007). Others claimed that the economic crisis is most crucial to the *yeshiva* world (Lupo 2003:12). Although the ideal of religious poverty is strong, the current deterioration in living standards is affecting even the most devout members. The economic straits are leading to greater participation of Haredim outside the community. In this article, we analyze different spheres of citizen participation and argue that both explanations work in a different way in each sphere of participation. In each one of these arenas Haredi members express distinctive relations with the state, and civil society.

Haredim and the Army: Militarism without Military Participation

The different attitudes towards the army reflect a complicated view of the relationship between citizenship, fundamentalism and the modern state. The army is seen by most Jewish Israeli citizens as the most important sphere for participation in state institutions. Yet Haredi attitudes to the participation in the Israeli army have changed over the years and today in the official Haredi writings is considered a threat to the community and the yeshiva norms and lifestyle (Stadler and Ben-Ari 2003).

Let us begin with a short history of Haredi exemption from the IDF. The battles for Jerusalem in 1948 saw the emergence of the first discussions about the lack of participation in, and support for, the war on the part of the Haredi community (see Frankel 1994: 249). Later, for a short period between 1956 and the 1960s, some members undertook military service in units meant for Haredi boys who did not see themselves as scholars and who thought they could succeed in a "religious" unit of the army. However, as the society of scholars became the norm in the Haredi world (especially since the seventies), individuals who chose to serve in the army were viewed negatively and perceived as abandoning the right Haredi way (Heilman and Friedman 1991). Towards the end of the 1990s another attempt was made to integrate some Haredi men into exclusive units. This attempt has met with rather limited success: only a very small number of men have been recruited (Hakak 2003). Nowadays, although some Haredim serve, especially in positions related to religious services such as Kashrut, death customs, and Jewish rituals, most Haredi men and all women are exempted from military service.

In contrast to other religious groups in Israel, especially the Zionist religious streams that have accepted military service as part of the religious devotion, Haredi leaders determined that in order to revive and reinforce Haredi culture in Israel they must keep members in the yeshiva away from the army. The ideal of Haredi masculinity and piety was to be attained only through a life of abstinence, ritual and profound study, rather than by becoming soldiers defending the secular state and its merits. The exemption from military service granted to Haredi members has thus become one of the most controversial religious issues in Israel. In a society with a strong militarist ethos, outsiders see the Haredi community's avoidance of army service as an exclusionary, anti-Zionist stance. Large parts of the Israeli public vigorously oppose this exemption, reject its theological justifications, and protest against its expansion and institutionalization. The central criticism against Haredi men is not only that they do not invest three years of conscription in military service, but that they do not risk their lives, as other Israeli men, for the country. Significant groups among the Israeli public have demanded that Haredim pay the price of blood through military service. Inclusion in political life and receipt of state aid should depend, this line of thinking goes, on Haredi participation in the military (Ilan 2000). Their stance stands in sharp contrast to how members of the National-Religious camp take on military service. This camp awards theological meaning to the Israeli state and the military and over the past two decades many of its male members have taken a leading role in the army's combat arms and among its commanders (Cohen 1997; 1999). The very existence of this model linking religious belief, the state and the responsibilities of citizenship has intensified criticisms against the exclusionary Haredi ideology. Indeed, the political and theological representatives of the community, loyal to the basic separatist ideology of fundamentalism, have resisted all initiatives through the years to alter this agreement with the state. Whereas participation in voluntary aid organizations as we discuss later, are first steps toward a theological framing of activities related to citizenship and social participation, attitudes to military service highlight a persistent attempt to preserve the religious separateness of Haredim from secular state activities in order to maintain the exclusive cultural values and Haredi life-style.

During the 1990s, widespread resentment about non-participation in the military resulted in the establishment of the Tal Committee to consider Haredi exemptions from the army. This committee encountered resistance within the community and apprehensions on the part of the military (Ilan 2000; Drori 2005). Several political parties represent opposition to the official position about military exemptions and this opposition culminated in 2003 when the Shinui party gained 15 seats in the Israeli parliament and became the third-largest party in the Knesset. Shinui's key agenda targeted what it considered as the state's preferential treatment of the Haredi sector and yeshiva institutions. Accordingly, they strove to diminish state support for the Haredi educational system, decrease stipends for yeshiva students and abolish military exemptions. Yet, the yeshiva world has grown, from an estimated 35,000 during the 1980s to more than 70,000 at present (see Schiffer 1998: 11; Caplan 2007). Accordingly, the committee recommended that Haredi students decide at the age of 24 whether to remain in the yeshiva or obtain employment after a short period of military or civic service. But these recommendations were immediately seen by most Haredi authorities as threatening the community's very existence. Thus, after publication of the recommendations, most Haredi authorities called upon yeshiva students to devote themselves to sacred duties alone and disregard the recurring appeals of the state. Street posters ('*pashkevils*') in Haredi neighborhoods reminded yeshiva students that community ideals opposed state demands. After the publication of the report, one street poster dramatically declared:

> The loud cry of the boys' souls, seduced to extermination in the army, rises up to heaven. Unfortunate parents cry and mourn the souls of their trapped beloved sons. From heaven we are called upon to act with all our strength for the sake of the souls of Israel, so that they will not be destroyed in the army.

The official instruction to yeshiva students was clearly stated that: Haredi men are obliged to God alone, not to the state or its agents (see Stadler 2009). As of this time, the committee's initiative has met with rather limited success and only a handful of Haredi men have actually been recruited to the IDF (Hakak 2003). During the late 1990s the *Nachal Haredi* unit was established by the IDF as an option for ultra-Orthodox men wishing to serve and maintain their strict religious lifestyle (Drori 2005). *Nachal Haredi* is a combat unit numbering a few hundred men, based on an exhausting course of training, and assigned active operational duties. Yet because it is specifically designated as Haredi it enjoys special conditions designed to serve the religious needs of soldiers, such as special time periods for prayer and Talmud study. Moreover, not only is the command structure in religious hands (modern orthodox individuals are commanders), but teachers and religious "supervisors" are brought in from the outside to oversee ongoing observance and indoctrination (Drori 2005). As stated however, only a few hundred men out of tens of thousands of *yeshiva* students have actually chosen to serve in this framework.

From the perspective of the military the importance of these soldiers is rather marginal and the significance of the unit is symbolic or emblematic. By establishing and maintaining this unit, the IDF signals that it is a "People's Army," in that the inclusion of Haredi soldiers expresses the fact that it encompasses all major groups in Israeli society while taking into account their special needs (Lomsky-Feder and Ben-Ari 1999). The Haredi community well understands this importance and that is precisely the reason why so many of its leaders oppose the existence of this special military unit and continue to call upon yeshiva students to devote themselves to sacred duties alone and resist recurring appeals by state authorities. Texts written by Haredi rabbis include excerpts about military issues defining yeshiva students as other-worldly soldiers – the spiritual warriors – of the people of Israel, responsible for the protection and enhancement of spiritual aspects of the Jewish people (Stadler and Ben-Ari 2003).

In interviews, however, younger Haredim often acknowledge the centrality of army service for full citizenship, loyalty and protecting the Jewish state. Thus, the Haredi explanation of war as resulting from abandonment of Torah studies and the ideology against military participation do not erode Haredi support for intensive military activity in the occupied territories and the general Haredi approval of the army's actions during the "Intifadas." Yet they also highlight the ideal of yeshiva life and support enclave culture. The yeshiva ideal of studying was frequently explained as the only way to preserve Judaism and Haredi lifestyle. For example one student expressed his fear of preferring military service over yeshiva dedication as follows:

> [I]n the long term this matter can harm *Haredi* education very very much … Not only because you can't decide … who will deserve to study in the *yeshiva* and who isn't deserving enough and we'll send him off to the army. A situation can arise where, for instance, some criteria for admission will exist and they'll say to you, "No, you're suitable for the *yeshiva*" and then he'll say to himself, "I'm not bad enough to go to the army so maybe I'll flunk the next test on purpose so they won't take me". This is illogical and impractical … all in all the *Yeshiva* is a very demanding institution; everyone who doesn't succeed in his studies will know he has the alternative of leaving everything behind and going to the army.

This excerpt reflects the fear of losing Haredi students to the army and at the same times yeshiva students' interest in army service and militarism. However, while accepting the tenets of yeshiva-based religiosity many expressed discomfort at being required to lead entirely disciplined lives, without any alternatives or personal choice in the matter. As one interviewee said:

> [The Haredi authorities] presume to build a society with very unrealistic values; it is suitable for a specific handful, a handful of ascetics that enter a monastery and also decide not to marry ... But to take a society, a collective, without distinction, to say that everybody should study ... that abstinence is part of this ideal; this is simply not realistic; this is not what is written in the scriptures, and it is not suitable for human nature.

The debate about army service, perhaps the most hegemonic sphere of state participation, reflects obstacles and difficulties to Haredi men. Yeshiva students have expressed a wish to participate in army service and Israeli wars but the taboo on enlistment is still difficult for members. Interviewees explained that their leaders fail to correctly interpret their wish to participate in the army, seeing it as a way to shirk yeshiva life. Accordingly, for many, participation in the army is wishful thinking that does not turn into social action. However, we believe that the debate on military participation has influenced other forms of participation not bounded by prohibitions. As we presently explain, Haredim invent new forms of participation suited to their norms and at the same time represent such participation as related to their being citizens of the state of Israel.

ZAKA Voluntarism: Haredim and the Management of Death

The most crucial challenge to citizenship posed by a Haredi group emanated from the escalation of terrorist attacks in Israel. It is in this light that ZAKA, the Haredi male organization that identifies victims of terrorist attacks and assembles dismembered body parts, should be seen. ZAKA is an organization of more than 900 volunteers recruited almost exclusively from Haredim. The organization was established in 1995 following a spate of violent attacks throughout the country. ZAKA began to specialize in identifying and collecting body parts following terrorist attacks and then in bringing the dead to a proper Jewish burial. Accordingly, handling victims was, from the first, linked to a religious act seen as especially significant in the Jewish theology of death, burial and salvation. In recent years, the organization has broadened its scope to include medical aid and support for victims and their families, handling deaths not incurred by terror attacks, and rescue and recovery of missing persons (Stadler 2006, 2009).

Numerous op-ed pieces and news reports have portrayed ZAKA in very positive terms and its volunteers gain legitimacy from the public to work in the public sphere, treat victims of attacks and assist with what is usually the exclusive work of state institutions. Newspaper articles have portrayed ZAKA volunteers as the "good Haredim," helping for the first time to deal with problems facing the state in times of conflict and the suffering of loss.

This aid was seen positively because it contrasts sharply with the absence of Haredi members in the IDF and its missions. Thus numerous articles in the popular press appearing after attacks, have portrayed ZAKA volunteers as carrying out sacred work and as performing the Jewish religious important commandments of respect for the dead (Stadler 2006).

The image of ZAKA volunteers stands in contrast to stereotypical portrayals of ultra-Orthodox people as dependent on state support and lacking willingness to contribute to wider society. Moreover, ZAKA has been given public recognition through various awards bestowed by politicians. Thus, for example, its founder was invited to light one of the ceremonial fires in the country's central Independence Day ritual. The ceremony's organizing committee wrote about its decision to choose him to participate in the ceremony:

> Eight years ago after suicide attacks by Arabs, he established ZAKA that trains its volunteers in three areas: first aid, finding missing persons and identification [of bodies] in sites of disaster while maintaining respect for the dead (*Maariv*, 28 April, 2003).

In the framework of the relations between fundamentalism and citizenship, we argue that ZAKA is a unique phenomenon. For the first time Haredim participate voluntarily in the Israeli public sphere by treating the victims of terrorist violence, a consequence of the attack against the very existence of the Israeli state. In contrast to the more established rescue and recovery state forces such as the police, army or ambulance services, ZAKA volunteers not only specialized in handling the results of terrorist incidents according to Jewish theology, but creatively developed new modes of organizational practices and relations with the state. It is important to note that at first the Haredi Rabbis viewed the work of the organization as heresy and sin. In their critic they argued that crossing community boundaries, working with non-Haredi organizations and acting in public were perceived as endangering Haredi values and the enclave lifestyle. However, as the second Intifada intensified, more Haredi members volunteered, and what seemed at the time to be a temporary and marginal association became an established organization (Stadler, Ben-Ari and Mesterman 2005). Moreover, against the Rabbis oppositions, more and more Haredi men volunteered and showed intense commitment to the organization.

When we asked volunteers about their work in ZAKA, Haredi members explained the participation in ZAKA as a central religious duty based on traditional Jewish theology. However, they invent new interpretations of death and use them to help victims as well as to justify their civic contribution. During interviews volunteers explain that recomposing the body after an explosion becomes the most generous act of devotion (Stadler 2006). For example, one man described saving one soul as the most rewarding otherworldly act he could undertake:

That is why I would say that it is much more sacred to be in *ZAKA*. Your place in heaven is much higher. If you have saved someone else's life you deserve the world – like we say "He who saves a soul is one with Israel" ... You can go to [The Israeli Institute of Forensic Science] and see how we honor the dead ... every piece of flesh is collected.

ZAKA volunteers argue that after terrorist attacks they are exclusively responsible for the task of re-gathering of organs and corpses. In interviews volunteers explain how imperative this task is by invoking religious symbols and justifications and highlight the importance of performing it in the public sphere (Stadler 2006). One central element related to participation in ZAKA is the emphasis on religious and nationalistic ideals of sacrifice and thus in order to fulfill Haredi virtues male members that join the organization act voluntarily in public, are ready to work at any time, and frequently renounce their primary religious obligation to the yeshiva and the Haredi male norm to dedicate all time to Talmudic studies. Along the lines of the republican discourse of citizenship, in this kind of contribution there is a special element of devotion to the good of the collective that is suitable only for an elite group. In return for their contribution they enjoy primarily symbolic rewards (Levy 2007).

ZAKA and similar Haredi aid volunteers (such as Hatsolah) exemplify organizations that challenge republican concepts. The Haredim do not justify participation in terms of the hegemonic ideology emphasizing (in its Israeli guise) the achievement of citizenship through military service. They even resist the idea of contribution through state institutions and ask to participate on their own fundamentalist terms and within their own organizations. In this way, some contemporary Haredi groups have introduced concepts such as sacrifice in particular sites as bases for membership in the collective. Through such organizations as ZAKA, Haredi members have created new modes of contribution that widen the state's definition of citizenship while conforming to their own form of the fundamentalist worldview. ZAKA volunteers challenge citizenship by creating a new organization that is exclusively male and specializes in the management of death in public. By doing so, volunteers reshape their own fundamentalism by giving new meanings to ideas about contribution, sacrifice and nationalism.

In contrast to this arena which is characterized as an elite male one and whose power derives from providing a service that has been defined as the responsibility of the religious sector, we now move on to *Yad Sarah* which is very different in nature. Yad Sarah is involved with aid and medical assistance yet it is free of the heroic ethos and provides services that are not only within the purview of religious Jews in Israel.

Yad Sarah: Medical Services and the decline of the welfare state

Yad Sarah was established by Haredim in response to the weakening of the welfare state in Israel and gaps created in provisions for the poor and the elderly. While the organization is only one of a dozen or more ultra-Orthodox charitable trusts – ranging from medical referral organizations to soup kitchens – serving the entire population, it is by far the largest and most well known in Israel. Similar to ZAKA, the organization extends beyond the boundaries of the Haredi community and claims to provide aid to all Israelis by justifying its actions on the basis of Jewish theology. However, unlike ZAKA, joining the organization is not exclusive to ultra-Orthodox individuals or to men. Thus, the organization offers an opportunity for Haredi women to participate in the civic space as well as non-Haredi volunteers to join together with Haredi people to fulfill Jewish practices of aid.

Yad Sarah, was founded in 1970 in Jerusalem by Uri Lupolianski, a Haredi educational figure (who has now become the city's mayor). Yad Sarah is officially named after his mother who perished in the Holocaust but the name combines the Hebrew *Yad* meaning memorial with a biblically based name not uncommon among secular Israelis. Yet the organization's link to the Holocaust is a universal moral one, and contrasts with the emphasis in the Israeli state's effort at commemoration and memory which underscore nationalist ideas (Segev 1991).

The organization has 103 branches throughout the country (in both Jewish and Arab towns). According to volunteers these branches are run by more than 6,000 volunteers who are not all Haredim. One website (www.israaid. org.il/member_page.asp?id=18) explains the main tasks of the organization:

> The organization provides a spectrum of free or nominal cost services designed to make life easier for sick, disabled and elderly people and their families. Today, only 26 years after it was founded, Yad Sarah ... saves the Israeli economy about $300 million a year in hospitalization and medical costs. Yad Sarah's annual operating budget is financed almost completely by donations, over 70 percent of which are raised within Israel. No government assistance is received.

In websites and media reports, volunteers explain that the growth of Yad Sarah is related to the decrease in state support for the needy. In many reports it is argued that one out of two Israeli families has been helped by it and the organization provides medical and social services to more than 380,000 elderly persons per year (Pietrokovski and Zini 2006). In its website, Yad Sarah's mission is described as keeping the ill and the elderly in their homes and out of institutions for as long as possible. Moreover, the organization claims to provide services to all Israeli citizens (including non-Jews) and especially:

[L]ending of medical and rehabilitative equipment on a short-term basis free of charge to anyone who needs it … In addition, *Yad Sarah* provides a wide range of other services, including transportation and day care centers for the disabled, drop-in centers and minimum-charge dental clinics for the elderly, personal computerized emergency alarms monitored 24 hours a day and guidance centers which help disabled people choose the devices most suited to their needs. The organization also provides equipment and services for new mothers, infants, recently discharged hospital patients and others in need. (www.yadsarah.org).

Like ZAKA, the work of volunteers in Yad Sarah is explained as centering on the basic problems facing humanity – disease, hunger, isolation – but with particularly Jewish religious meanings. Volunteers are called to participate in aiding the Israeli public as part of their religious tasks and aspirations. In this respect volunteers are asked to fuse together their citizenry duties with the Haredi fundamentalist piety. This notion is explained in the following report in *The Jewish World* that has framed the story of Yad Sarah in the following terms:

> The growth of Yad Sarah shows how one person, translating the most sublime values of Jewish life into deeds, can capture the imagination of thousands, galvanize them into action, tap their deepest resources of love and goodness – and make a difference (www.aish.com/jewishissues/ jerusalem).

Jewish concepts are presented as the most important as motivation for serving the general Israeli public. The organization's founder explained the social tasks of Yad Sarah in religious terms:

> From the start, our guiding principle has been to help everyone who needs help. Judaism teaches us to respect and care for every human being, created in the image of God. But the Jewish concept of *chesed* goes beyond that: We should actively *seek out* ways to help (www.aish.com/ jewishissues/jerusalem).

The idea of the volunteers doing holy work is expressed in many publications, not only those written within the organization. For example, *The Jewish News Weekly* (May 30, 2003) positioned the activities of the organization in wider terms of communal values:

> One of the most fundamental ideas of a vibrant Jewish community involves the idea of voluntarism on all levels. It is the spirit of the dedicated volunteer that has bound the Jewish community together through the centuries … In Jerusalem, the Yad Sarah organization, which

supplies every level of service to people with special needs, represents one of the shining examples of voluntarism.

Such sentiments are echoed by people outside of the Haredi camp. Thus, for example, the Minister for Senior Affairs called the actions of the organization "holy work" (February 19, 2007, www.yadsarah.org). Much more common are such comments as the one by a secular journalist who observed that the movement is "the only nice part of *Haredi* experience" (*Yedioth Ahronoth*, February 28, 1992). Indeed, the state's acknowledgement of the organization's achievement consisted of awarding it the Israel Prize, the country's highest civilian honor. Framing the movement's activities for external audiences is marked by a pronounced lack of emphasis on specifically Jewish values of voluntarism, help and compassion:

> Discussing the volunteers, Lupolianski said there were many older Israelis who wished to launch a new career that involved community service upon their retirement and there were many practical reasons for that desire. The retiree gets satisfaction out of giving to others and a sense of being productive, as well as social contacts and the joy of contributing to the greater society (*Jewish News Weekly*, May 30, 2003).

The Jewish World (www.aish.com/jewishissues/jerusalem) quoted him in this regard:

> I've gone to Arab villages to help set up *Yad Sarah* branches, and I've served in the IDF. So I'm sensitive to the different worlds ... Some secular Jews think that religious people don't care enough about them. But I believe the opposite is true. If a Jew eats bread on Passover, he may not understand how that could affect me. But from my perspective, all Jews are one family, responsible one for another. So every Jew affects me.

In these publications Lupolianski not only justifies his knowledge of both "societies" (the ultra-Orthodox and the secular) in terms of having done military service but he elides notions of national membership – Jewish belonging – with ideas about citizenship – Arab citizens of Israel as part of the collective.

Going on to another aspect of the organization, it is significant that it often claims to act in coalition with private corporate interests or state entities. To provide only a small fraction of examples, in Israel's southern Negev it joined business people to supply medical equipment (*Yedioth Ahronoth*, May 22, 2000), it teamed up with a large realtor to purchase vehicles to distribute medical equipment (*Yedioth Ahronoth*, August 3, 2005), it held a fair to solicit contributions in a shopping mall in the center of Tel Aviv (*Yedioth Ahronoth*, February 10, 1989), or worked with the Israeli Industrial Association to supply heating equipment for the elderly (*Yedioth Ahronoth*, January 20, 1993).

Working with state authorities, *Yad Sarah* volunteers helped in distributing gas masks and sealing rooms (*Yedioth Ahronoth,* March 18, 2003) or helped the Jerusalem municipality to remove snow after a storm (*Yedioth Ahronoth,* January 10, 2003).

Yad Sarah has also worked to become a global movement, arguing that it has universal missions. It has developed aid programs or instructional courses in such places such as Angola, Cameroon, Jordan, South Korea, or China (*Yedioth Ahronoth,* April 26, 1998; July 7, 2006). And as if to underscore its membership in an all-Israeli coalition along with the IDF, the Prime Minister's Office, El-Al Airlines, and business firms, *Yad Sarah* sent emergency aid to survivors of the flooding in New Orleans (*Yedioth Ahronoth,* September 7, 2005). Finally, in 2005 it was recognized by the United Nations as the first Jewish-Israeli movement to be granted observer status (*Yedioth Ahronoth* January 16, 2005).

Analyzing the activities and discourse of Yad Sarah we see how Haredim have developed a new perception of contribution to the society that circumvents the state, reinforces the boundaries of the Jewish collectivity, and tries to blur the many distinctions based on citizenship in Israel. While the weakening of the state has allowed various groups in society to separate and retreat into enclaves, this very process has paradoxically allowed such groups as the ultra-Orthodox community to join into the larger collective through initiating and supporting Yad Sarah.

The advent of Haredi organizations such as Yad Sarah thus represents a second feature of the fundamentalist challenge to notions of citizenship. Yad Sarah represents the communal equivalent of private business-related corporate responsibility since the state is less and less able and willing to grant aid to its weakened citizens. In other words, while different organizations in Israeli civil society – business firms or youth movements – take on what they see as a conscientious giving to the collective, from the point of view of the Haredi community, this same kind of activity is interpreted in religious terms. Voluntarism and help are justified through recourse to religious texts and orientations; however, and at the same time, the very act of giving is often formulated according to the obligations of citizenship and the needs of wider publics in Israel.

Voluntary fundamentalist organizations hence mobilize resources – people, time, attention, ideas, or funds – on a religious basis stressing mutuality within the community. And again, as in ZAKA, by contributing voluntarily and reproducing Jewish symbols, Haredim strive to fit the liberal worldview of voluntary commitment and contribution as well as their own religious aspirations. While ZAKA bases its challenge on a religious monopoly over handling death, Yad Sarah uses concepts of Jewish compassion to mobilize and encourage people to voluntarily work for civil society and contribute to individuals not provided for by the Israeli state.

Inclusive Fundamentalism and the Challenge of Citizenship

Students of the sociology of religion have emphasized that relations of fundamentalist groups with politics have been expressed through two main prisms: a rejection of the state and citizenship expressed through hostility and resistance or an instrumental approach towards pragmatic politics leading to accommodation according to the particular interests of the group. By contrast, we have suggested in this article that Haredim have created new definitions and patterns of civic contribution that can be fulfilled by Haredi members.

Alongside receding into enclaves and awarding wider Jewish-Israeli society with a religious legitimation for the ethno-national discourse, Haredi members are now trying to actively seek a wider recognition through civic action. While continuing to be pragmatic in regard to state institutions, it is in the sphere of civil society that Haredim make their unique contribution to the state and society. However, we contend that the very same fundamentalist group may attach a variety of religious meanings in reacting to various issues centered on citizenship. We discussed these different realms of participation in three Haredi sites: Military service, ZAKA and Yad Sarah. We argue that within new modes of participation, Haredim have widened the boundaries of the discourse on citizenship by anchoring it within a theologically justified discourse. Rather than formulating their actions in terms of separation or instrumental integration into wider society and the state, we offer the concept of "inclusive fundamentalism" to explain Haredi citizenship. This form of inclusive fundamentalism is based on a religiously inspired worldview and involves wider notions of actively belonging and engaging of its members.

In this form of participation Haredi attitudes towards the military highlight the tense relations of Haredim with the state, especially contradiction between obligations to the secular state as citizens and basic fundamentalist values. ZAKA should thus be seen as a response to the escalation of terrorist attacks and the limits of state institutions such as the police and the army in providing aid and helping victims after they occur. Yad Sarah can be analyzed as a reaction to the changing economic pressures and the weakening of the welfare state in providing assistance in health and welfare. In the case of ZAKA and Yad Sarah, Haredi members do not only use the institutions of the state and civic society for their own limited instrumental ends but attempt to gain recognition through active participation in the wider civic sphere. Thus one should distinguish between the military where participation is still conceptualized in pragmatic terms, and the involvement in ZAKA and Yad Sarah where it is actualized and developed. In this context, acknowledgement by secular "others" sought in the different spheres is based on different principles: ZAKA is based on providing an exclusive religious service, the handling of death, that the state cannot give, while Yad Sarah is founded on a universal aid service that is oriented to all sectors of Israeli society, and as such has been institutionalized and accepted very fast. Yet in both organizations justification for action derives from the notions of the moral Jewish theology and the Jewish textual tradition. The very activity in civic society is awarded theological meaning and textual justification. Moreover, because both organizations have also come to operate on the global scene, they have, interestingly, bypassed the state.

In this paper we suggest the utility of the term "inclusive fundamentalism" to characterize these changing relations of fundamentalists with the state. We have argued that by resisting the army, Haredim, like other fundamentalist groups, challenge the republican ideology of the state, and in its Israeli guise dispute the norm of realizing citizenship through military service. However, new aid organizations such as ZAKA and Yad Sarah are a form of creative participation representing a new model of citizenry roles and notions of the nation state. Haredim created new models suiting both the ideology of the secular state and the norms of a fundamentalist group. The withdrawal of the state from many aspects of citizenry life has brought about the development of new concepts centered on citizenship and the formation of new forms of citizenship that are flexible, and take place within ethno-national boundaries. While changes in civil participation are usually explained as the outcome of global forces and especially the effect of the neo-liberal regime, we have offered a complementary analysis of challenges based on fundamentalist worldviews and practices to existing notions of citizenship.

Note

1 This paper is derived from our "Fundamentalism's Challenges to Citizenship: The Haredim in Israel" published in *Citizenship Studies*, 12(3): 215–31, 2008. Nurit Stadler acknowledges the generosity of the Israeli Science Foundation (Grant no. 382/07) in providing a grant during which the paper was completed.

References

Almond, G., Appleby, R. S., and Sivan, E. (2003). *Strong religion: The rise of fundamentalism around the world*. Chicago, IL: The University of Chicago Press.

Ammerman, N. (1987). *Bible believers: Fundamentalism in the modern world*. New Brunswick, NJ and London: Rutgers University Press.

Antoun, R.T. (2001). *Understanding fundamentalism: Christian, Islamic and Jewish movements*. Oxford and New York: Altamira Press.

Aran, G. (1993). Return to the scriptures in modern Israel. *Bibliotheque de l'ecole des hautes etudes sciences religieuses*, XCIX, 101–31.

Asad, T. (2003). *Formation of the secular: Christianity, Islam, modernity*. Stanford: Stanford University Press.

Ben-Eliezer, U. (1999). Civil society in Israeli society: Politics and identity in new social movements. *Israeli Sociology*, 2 (1), 51–98. (Hebrew).

Berman, E. (2000). Sect, subsidy and sacrifice: An economist's view of ultra-Orthodox Jews. *Quarterly Journal of Economics*, CXV (3), 905–53.

Brasher, B. (1998). *Godly women: Fundamentalism and female power.* New Brunswick, NJ: Rutgers University Press.

Caplan, K. (1997). God's voice: Audiotaped sermons in Israeli *Haredi* society. *Modern Judaism,* 17, 253–79.

Caplan, K. (2007). *Internal popular discourse in Israeli Haredi society.* Jerusalem: The Zalman Shazar Center for Jewish History. (Hebrew).

Cohen, S. (1997). *The scroll or the sword? Dilemmas of religion and military service in Israel.* Amsterdam: Harwood Academic.

Cohen, S. (1999). From integration to segregation: The role of religion in the IDF. *Armed Forces and Society,* 35 (3), 387–405.

Dahan, M. (1998). *The Haredi population and the local authority.* Jerusalem: The Jerusalem Institute for Israel Studies. (Hebrew).

Deeb, L. (2006). *An enchanted modern: Gender and public piety in Shii Lebanon.* Princeton: Princeton University Press.

Drori, Z. (2005). *Between faith and military service: The Haredi Nahal battalion.* Jerusalem: The Floersheimer Institute for Policy Studies. (Hebrew).

El-Or, T. (1994). *Educated and ignorant: On ultra-Orthodox Jewish women and their world.* Boulder: Lynne Rienner Publishers.

Frankel, Y. (1994). The Haredi and religious Jewish communities during the siege on Jerusalem. *Hazionut,* 18, 249–80. (Hebrew).

Friedman, M.,(1991). *The Ultra-Orthodox Community.* Jerusalem: The Jerusalem Institute for Israel Studies. (Hebrew).

Friedman, M. (1993). The *Hardim* and the Israeli society. In J. Peters and K. Kyle, eds. *Whither Israel: The domestic challenges.* London: Chatham House and I.B. Tauris, 177–201.

Friedman, M., (1994). Habad as messianic fundamentalism: From local particularism to universal Jewish mission. In M. E. Marty and R. S. Appleby, eds, *Accounting for fundamentalisms: The dynamic character of movements.* Chicago: Chicago University Press, 328–57.

Hakak, Y. (2003). *Yeshiva learning and military training: An encounter between two cultural models.* Jerusalem: The Floersheimer Institute for Policy Studies. (Hebrew).

Harding, S. (2000). *The book of Jerry Falwell.* Princeton: Princeton University Press.

Heilman, S. C. (1983). *The people of the book: Drama, fellowship and religion.* Chicago: Chicago University Press.

Heilman, S. C. (1992). *Defenders of the faith: Inside ultra-Orthodox Jewry.* New York: Schocken Books.

Heilman, S. C. (1994). Quiescent and active fundamentalisms: The Jewish cases. In M. E. Marty and R. S. Appleby, eds. *Accounting for fundamentalisms: The dynamic character of movements.* Chicago: Chicago University Press, 96–173.

Heilman, S. C. (1995). The vision from the madrasa and bet medrash: Some parallels between Islam and Judaism. In M. E. Marty and R. S. Appleby, eds. *Fundamentalism comprehended.* Chicago: The University of Chicago Press, 71–95.

Heilman, S. C., and Friedman, M. (1991). *The Haredim in Israel.* New York: The American Jewish Committee.

Ilan, S. (2000). *Haredim ba'am.* Jerusalem: Keter. (Hebrew).

Isin, E., and Turner, B. S. (2007). Investigating citizenship: An agenda for citizenship studies. *Citizenship Studies,* 11 (1), 5–17.

Joppke, C. (2007). Transformation of citizenship: Status, rights, identity. *Citizenship Studies,* 11 (1), 37–48.

Kimmerling, B. (2004). *Immigrants, settlers, natives.* Tel Aviv: Am-Oved. (Hebrew).

Levy, Y. (2003). Social convertibility and militarism: evaluations of the development of military-society relations in Israel in the early 2000s. *Journal of Political and Military Sociology,* 31 (1), 71–96.

Levy, Y. (2007). Soldiers as laborers: a theoretical model. *Theory and Society,* 36 (2), 187–208.

Levy, Y., Lomsky-Feder, E., and Harel, N. (2007). From "obligatory militarism" to "contractual militarism" – the changing face of militarism in Israel. *Israel Studies,* 12 (1), 127–48.

Lomsky-Feder, E., and Ben-Ari, E. (1999). From 'the people in uniform' to 'different uniforms for the people': Professionalism, diversity and the Israeli defense forces. In J. Soetres and J. Van Der Meulen, eds, *Managing diversity in the armed forces.* Tilburg: Tilburg University Press, 157–86.

Lupo, J. (2003). *A shift in Haredi society: Vocational training and academic studies.* Jerusalem: The Floersheimer Institute for Policy Studies. (Hebrew).

Mahmood, S. (2005). *Politics of piety: The Islamic revival and the feminist subject.* Princeton: Princeton University Press.

Marty, M. E. and Appleby, R. S. (1995). Introduction. In M. E. Marty and R. S. Appleby, eds, *Fundamentalisms comprehended.* Chicago: University of Chicago Press, 1–10.

Peled, Y. (2007). Toward a post-citizenship society? A report from the front. *Citizenship Studies,* 11 (1), 95–104.

Peled, Y., and Ophir, A., eds (2001). *Israel: From mobilized to civil society?* Jerusalem and Tel Aviv: Van Leer Institute and Hakibbutz Hameuchad. (Hebrew).

Pietrokovski, J., and Zini, A. (2006). The *Yad Sarah* geriatric dental clinic: A different model. *Gerodontology,* 23 (4), 237–41.

Ram, U. (2007). *The globalization of Israel: McWorld in Tel Aviv; Jihad in Jerusalem.* London: Routledge.

Ravitzky, A. (1994). The contemporary Lubavitch Hasidic movement: Between conservatism and messianism. In M. E. Marty and R. S. Appleby, eds, *Accounting for fundamentalisms: The dynamic character of movements.* Chicago: Chicago University Press, 303–27.

Riesebrodt, M., (1993, 1990). *Pious passion: The emergence of modern fundamentalism in the United States and Iran.* Translated by Don Reneau (From German). Berkeley: University of California Press.

Sahliyeh, E. (1995). Religious fundamentalisms compared: Palestinian Islamists, militant Lebanese Shi'ites and radical Sikhs. In M. E. Marty and R. S. Appleby, eds, *Fundamentalism comprehended.* Chicago: University of Chicago Press, 135–54.

Segev, T. (1991). *The seventh million: The Israelis and the Holocaust.* Jerusalem: Maxwell-Macmillian and Keter.

Shafir, G., and Peled, Y. (2002). *Being Israeli: The dynamic of multiple citizenship.* Cambridge: Cambridge University Press.

Schiffer, Varda (1998). *The Haredi Education System, Allocation, Regulation and Control.* Jerusalem: the Floersheimer Institute for Policy Studies (Hebrew).

Shilhav, Y. (1991). *A town in the city: Geography of separation and integration.* Jerusalem: The Jerusalem Institute for Israel Studies. (Hebrew).

Shilhav, Y. (1998). *Ultra-Orthodoxy in urban governance.* Jerusalem: The Floersheimer Institute for Policy Studies. (Hebrew).

Sivan, E. (1995). The enclave culture. In M. E. Marty and R. S. Appleby, eds, *Fundamentalism comprehended.* Chicago: University of Chicago Press, 11–68.

Sivan, E., and Caplan, K., eds (2003). *Israeli Haredim: Integration without assimilation?* Jerusalem and Tel-Aviv: Van Leer Institute and Hakibutz Hameuchad. (Hebrew).

Soloveitchik, H. (1994). Migration, acculturation, and the new role of texts in the *Haredi* world. In M. E. Marty and R. S. Appleby, eds. *Accounting for fundamentalisms: The dynamic character of movements.* Chicago: Chicago University Press, 197–235.

Stadler, N. (2002). Is profane work an obstacle to salvation? The case of ultra-Orthodox (Haredi) Jews in contemporary Israel. *Sociology of Religion,* 63 (4), 455–74.

Stadler, N. (2004). Taboos, dreams and desires: Haredi fantasies on militarism and the military. *Israeli Sociology,* 6 (1), 69–90. (Hebrew).

Stadler, N., 2006. Terror, corpse symbolism and taboo violation: the 'Haredi disaster victim identification team in Israel' (ZAKA). *The Journal of the Royal Anthropological Institute,* 12 (4), 837–58.

Stadler, N. (2007). Playing with sacred/corporeal identities: Yeshiva students' fantasies of the military participation. *Jewish Social Studies: History, Culture, Society,* 13 (2), 155–78.

Stadler, N. (2009). *Yeshiva fundamentalism: Piety, gender, and resistance in the ultra-Orthodox world.* New York University Press, New York.

Stadler, N., and Ben-Ari, E., (2003). Other-worldly soldiers? Ultra-Orthodox views of military service in contemporary Israel. *Israel Affairs,* 9 (4), 17–48.

Stadler, N., Ben-Ari, E., and Mesterman, E. (2005). Terror, aid and organization: The *Haredi* disaster victim identification teams ("ZAKA") in Israel. *The Anthropological Quarterly,* 78 (3), 619–51.

Stadler, N., and Ben-Ari, E., (2003). Other-worldly soldiers? Ultra-Orthodox views of military service in contemporary Israel. *Israel affairs,* 9 (4), 17–48.

Stadler, N., Ben-Ari, E., and Mesterman, E., (2005). Terror, aid and organization: the *Haredi* disaster victim identification teams ("ZAKA") in Israel. *The Anthropological Quarterly,* 78 (3), 619–51.

8 NGOization of the Israeli feminist movement

Depoliticizing or redefining political spaces?

Hanna Herzog

How have the expansion and institutionalization of non-governmental organizations (NGOs), known as the NGOization of the civil society (Lang 1997), affected the women's movement? Since the 1990s this has been a recurrent question among feminist writers. To what extent and in what way have the strengthening of neoliberal trends, privatization, and the retreat of the welfare state that results in NGOization of the feminist movement affected women's political organizations and messages? In Israel, as in the rest of the world, the neoliberal structuring of civil society is perceived in public and academic discourse as a process of rupture and depoliticization of social movements, including feminism (Ben Eliezer 2003; Yishai 2008); hence the claim that the women's movement is being weakened as a socio-political force. The present article seeks to examine whether this argument is consistent with the situation in the Israeli women's movement of the early twenty-first century.

Most of the research focuses on the link between neoliberalism and NGOization and its impact on the women's movement. My major argument is that focusing only on neoliberalism ignores other social perspectives, known mostly as "post" theories. These theories have evolved simultaneously and played an important role in shaping the women's movement. My paper claims that the intersection between a neoliberal regime and various "post" perspectives has become fertile ground for the growth of alternative feminist knowledge and for creating challenging alliances of women.

Logics of Late (Second) Modernity – Theoretical Remarks

In the latter part of the twentieth century, an intense public and academic discourse developed about the characteristics of contemporary society (known variously as "late modernity," "second modernity," "post-modern" society and liquid modernity) and concerning the direction in which this society was moving. It is beyond the scope of this article to discuss this issue in detail. I shall, however, point out some of the logical theories providing the motivating force in this era which have particular relevance for an analysis of the women's movement.

Among those principles upon which the "second modernity"[1] is based and which constitute the moving force behind it is, first and foremost, the institution of neoliberalism which advocates free international markets and cross-boundary movement of capital and labor. Globalization is one of the off-shoots of this neoliberal order together with the retreat of the state in regard to public involvement and public sector employment, as well as privatization of previously public-owned enterprises and the transfer of a share of countries' economic wealth to the top economic percentiles of the population.

The neoliberal principle at the heart of which lies the ideal of individualization suggests that the process of NGOization can be explained through the privatization of responsibility, the privatization of mobilizing capital resources and by increasing reliance on global capital. Alongside this, second modernity encompasses notions which have come to be referred to with the prefix "post."

Here I am in accord with Beck, Giddens and Lash (1994) and Bauman (2000) who define it as a development within modernity that includes different schools of thought that define themselves or are defined by others as "post" – modernism, colonialism, Marxism, feminism, and so forth. None of them can be seen as a monolithic theory; all of them are composed of diverse and often opposing positions.

The element common to all of them is that they challenge the modern, "classical" social order. This is the order that looked at the world through the privileged prism of the male – western, white, bourgeois, heterosexual. Post-modern discourse has subverted the meta-narratives and has heralded the end of ideology and the end of history; critical kinds of discourse like feminism and post-colonialism which have called into question the basic categories of academic and public discourse have engendered a critical discourse based upon multiplicity and variance. Each of these discourses in its own way has cast a look at "the other" and has proposed alternative ways of perceiving society from the perspective of the margins, from the standpoint of one that has been labeled "other" or has had his voice silenced. Added to this was the increasing individualization which produced a claim that there are many social spheres that cannot be encompassed in the old generalized identity categories such as class, ethnicity, and gender. These principles constitute the basis for the increasing legitimacy accorded to multiple identities and to the division into sub-politics. In this manner neoliberalism melds with "post" ideas; but while neoliberalism places the market at its center, "post" theory seeks new ways of defining the social order and social identities.

This paper claims that the process of NGOization, though it divided the women's movement into many small organizations, simultaneously expanded the challenging political discourse of the women's organizations, diversified their strategies, and developed options for civil participation on the part of many women's groups that were previously excluded from the dominant feminist discourse.

What is the Women's Movement?

Before presenting my empirical case study some theoretical reflection is required on the way the leading term – women's movement – is used by me. While the term social movement is widely used, its definition is extensively debated (Della Porta 2006; Goodwin and Jasper 2006; Tilly and Wood 2009). This is so too with regard to the women's movements. Any discussion of the women's movement is inevitably influenced by the dominance of its American incarnation, which has become the symbol of the second wave of feminism that engulfed Western countries in the 1960s and 1970s. The characteristics of the US women's movement generally match the definition of a social movement as proposed by Tilly (1984: 306); that is, a mass movement that seeks to speak on behalf of a public lacking formal representation, which demands a change in the distribution of social power. This demand, directed at the state, is presented through public demonstrations and protests. At its core, the American women's movement consisted of intellectuals who assumed the existence of an audience whose needs were to be advanced actively and who functioned outside the formal political system. The movement calling for a non-elitist, decentralized organization succeeded in enlisting the masses, and established an overarching organization – the National Organization of Women (NOW) – that spoke on behalf of an apparently shared identity category: women. In this sense, the movement in the United States came close to the "old" conceptualization of a social movement, and of resource mobilization theory, which emphasizes the ability to recruit resources, enlist supporters, and adopt effective strategies that influence politics.

From this perspective, a split in the ranks, dependency on the state or economic forces, and/or organizational weakness are all a reflection of the waning – and perhaps the disappearance – of feminism as a social movement. But comparative historical research conducted within and between various Western societies suggests that women conducted their protests in different ways during the 1960s period of the women's movement (Gelb 1989; Lovenduski and Randall 1993; Nash 2002; Threlfall 1996; West and Blumberg 1990). In England, for example, there was no umbrella organization; rather, the movement functioned via multiple, small, non-hierarchical organized groups involved in consciousness-raising, lifestyle change, and the advancement of specific political demands. These groups addressed the state elite, and used lobbying as a major political tool. Thus, in spite of their antipathy toward the state and its institutions, they maintained ties with the Labour Party and the labor unions (Gelb 1989). Drawing upon the Italian feminist movement, Melucci (1996) did not emphasize the organizational aspect or the nature of the connection with formal political systems but rather the social solidarity that transcends organizational boundaries and constructs a collective identity by questioning the dominant codes. Organizations are connected because they share a cultural challenge and participate in the search for new forms of political-cultural. For Melucci, the women's movement is an example of a "new social movement" character-ized by "submerged networks" that exist outside of political organizations (cf. Ben-Eliezer 2003; Keane 1988). Similarly, Eyerman and Jamison (1991), argue that social movements are constituted by a "cognitive praxis," that is the forms of knowledge and identity which are articulated in their historical project. As such, social movements involve both transformation of everyday knowledge into professional knowledge and providing new contexts for the interpretation of professional knowledge (ibid. 52).

In keeping with this theoretical perspective, a movement is defined, first and foremost, by its desire to challenge and alter a dominant discourse and/or to lay a firm foundation for alternative cultural codes. The methods of protest and ways of organizing can take different forms. Accordingly, the degree of cohesiveness required for the success of the women's move-ment, or the possibility that a movement can exist despite division, becomes secondary to the question of whether the cumulative result of the actions of the women's organizations in the civil arena is the accretion of know-ledge and of alternative cultural and organizational patterns to those of the dominant order.

The Women's Movement and the Cost of NGOization

The women's movement at the turn of the twenty-first century exists con-currently with the acceleration of neoliberalization and the reinforcement of systems of power that perpetuate the unequal distribution of wealth, resources, and personal security; such a distribution reinforces social exclu-sion and polarization in society in general and among women in particular. The institutionalization of NGO-organizing and its introduction into fem-inist activism are connected to the transition from a discourse of women's needs to a human-rights discourse. Rights legislation is intertwined with the neoliberal idea, which is grounded in concepts of civil rights and the eco-nomic freedom of the liberal market. According to the neoliberal approach, rights guarantee the freedom of "homo economicus" – in particular, prop-erty owners – to act to advance their own interests. The individual rights approach transfers state responsibility to the individual, and so permits – indeed justifies – the withdrawal of the state from its obligations in the domains of welfare as well as social and economic justice. NGO practices reaffirm the principles of neoliberal discourse, but, in doing so, threaten to turn the civic sphere into an apolitical arena.

Among the criticisms leveled at the NGOization of feminism is the claim that the transition from a broad, grass-roots movement to one dominated by a plethora of isolated, small-scale, specific-goal-oriented organizations has impoverished the women's movement (Jad 2009). Thus, instead of a grand feminist agenda based on a culture of resistance that condemns patriarchalism and seeks emancipation, equality, and construction of a democratic culture, an apolitical organizational structure has emerged based on small organizations, each of which focuses on one issue and develops pragmatic strategies based on hierarchical relations among paid professionals (Lang 1997), very often remote from the grassroots level (Nagar 2006). A significant number of these organizations maintains close ties with the state in return for financial support, or may be forced to seek support from trusts or other funding bodies (Sadoun 2006); the latter are often foreign/global organizations that are not sensitive enough to local needs and sociopolitical context. Very often the donors dictate their agenda as a condition for support (Alvarez 1999; Taylor 1992),[2] in part by selecting certain feminist organizations over others. In order to meet funders' demands, the women's organizations must adopt ways of acting, a lexicon, and organizational practices that are not all that different from those of business firms. There is a growing collaboration between businesses and NGOs which is manifested in a new field of "corporate social responsibility," in which corporate-sponsored and corporate-oriented NGOs work together in a way that responds to business and employer concerns. Shamir (2004) indicates that this hybrid phenomenon, called by him MaNGO (Market Non-Governmental Organizations), helps to shape the notion of responsibility in ways that diffuse its radical transformative potential. Increasingly working through the market, women's NGOs contribute to blurring the boundaries between them and for-profit organizations.

Women's NGOs find themselves vying with one another for the same funding resources, thereby engendering competition instead of cooperation. This competition is exacerbated by sponsored women's organizations, by unions, parties and, in some countries, by religious political authorities that develop non-governmental women's organizations that are working against feminist organizations. In South America, state governments often defer to feminists as "gender experts," thus by subcontracting NGOs the government jeopardizes the autonomy of the women's organizations (AWID 2008).

According to this view, NGOization has weakened feminism as a social actor and a political force. In Silliman's words:

> NGOs have usurped the political space that was occupied by social movements, and in this way contained grassroots mobilization (1999: 46).

Quite rightly, the criticism of NGOization raises questions about the future of the feminist movement in general even as it illuminates phenomena specific to Israel. Indeed, the demands of a neoliberal world, coupled with NGO fragmentation, might well have led to reproduction of the dominant order and a weakening of the influence of women's organizations as an organized collective.

However, further examination reveals contradictory trends and inconsistencies that exist within the NGOization of feminism (Lind 2005). My major claim is that the restructuring of women's organizations has not resulted in depoliticizing of the women's movement but has rather channeled it to new political practices. As my paper will show, observation of the expanding areas of women's activities and their content indicates that at the cultural level, the organizations challenge the dominant discourse and offer an alternative counter-culture. Moreover, at the practical level, the organizations develop new options for women, including political choices. While women's organizations are less involved in formal politics tracks they do enter new spheres of activity, and develop alternative venues for social change.

The Israeli Case – Background Notes

State, economy, and civil society are interconnected in various and complex ways (Diani and Della Porta 1999; Markovitz 1998; Tarrow 1998). The implications of this position are that a sociopolitical study from a historical perspective is needed to examine the nature of the emerging ties between civil society and the political and economic spheres. An examination of the NGOization of the women's movement in various societies indeed indicates different types of influence (Alvarez 1998; Jad 2004, 2009; Lind 2005; Morena 2006; Nagar 2006; Sloat 2005), and a dynamic relationship between women's movements and economic and political forces.

Israel is a good testing ground for examining the contingent relations between neoliberalism and various "post" perspectives and the women's movement. Since the mid-1980s Israel has undergone a rapid change from a socialist-oriented society into a neoliberal economy, that has been followed by a withdrawal of the state from welfare policy, increasing social inequality (Filc and Ram 2004), and a proliferation of social organizations in the civil sphere.[3] In 1981 the *Amutot* (Nonprofit Societies) Law was legislated. The law required every organization to register and to meet a number of criteria. While in 1982 there were 12,000 NGOs, the number reached 27,000 in the year 2000 (Jaffe 2002).

At the same time the inherent contradictions in Israeli discourse remained. A democratic and Jewish state that simultaneously engages in liberal discourse and a republican discourse of civil society (Peled 1992), it is a society of immigrants that brings together Jewish cultures from various diasporas, but 18% of its citizens are Palestinians. The country lives in the shadow of a protracted conflict focused on the issue of the territories occupied by the State of Israel, and an ongoing armed conflict that traps women in a national and gendered dominant discourse (Herzog 1998). Since the 1990s, the society in Israel has experienced historical and political changes that have laid the foundations for various "post" ideas (Ram 2005b). The accomplishment of the formative stage of the settlement project and nation-building, the decline of the Labor elite which was the founder and the leader of this project until the 1970s, the Oslo peace process and the integration of Israel into the global market together paved the way for the establishment of new elites and social groups, and have facilitated the entry of new ideas into the social and public agenda (Ram 2005a). These ideas were introduced by native-born generational units, who construed a shared experience of native citizenship from the particular location in which they were born, and the open or closed social options that the institutionalized arrangements offer them (Herzog 2003). The fragmentation caused by the logic of NGOization was supported by the division caused by competing "post" perspectives. However, it became a springboard for new definitions of politics and constituting new mechanisms of political actions.

NGOization of the Israeli Women's Movement

While the history of the Israeli women's movement has yet to be written, there are several partial surveys (Herzog 2008; Safran 2006; Shalvi 2006; Swirski 1991) and many studies on various chapters of its history (Bernstein 1987; Berkovitch 1997; Dahan-Kalev 2001; Fogiel-Bijaoui 1992; Herzog 2002; Izraeli 1981; Shilo, Kark and Hasan-Rokem 2001). These surveys show that the characteristic that shaped the women's movement from its inception was fragmentation, although the motivating force was to create a comprehensive, organized movement which could speak for the category of women, and could have an impact on the political center.

Established in 1984 as an independent extra-parliamentary body, the Israel Women's Network (IWN), more than any other feminist organization, exemplifies this perception. The stated goal of the IWN was to advance the status of women through legislation, lobbying of Knesset members, and education and research aimed at raising public consciousness. Most of its founders were middle-class, Ashkenazi[4] academics who had participated in preparing the report of the Committee of Inquiry into the Status of Women (1975–1978). In time, they would also be the founders of gender studies programs in the universities. As opposed to radical feminist groups, IWN was an elected, hierarchically organized body headed for many years by its founder, Alice Shalvi. While members of the organization's executive served on a voluntary basis, the IWN employed a staff that included a legal office, spokesperson, and lobbyists. Female politicians and activists from a broad spectrum of political groups were active in the organization.

From the beginning, the IWN was involved in educating the public, in part by engaging in ongoing critiques of the media and the stereotypical representation of women and women's issues. Concurrently, it developed frameworks for training women for leadership roles in politics, and maintained international ties that advanced the exchange of information and knowledge. In the legislative sphere, the IWN's initiatives enabled it to develop strong connections with government bodies while leveling criticism where necessary (Shalvi 2006).

By the mid-1980s, its legislative proposals, media presence, and record of appeals to the High Court of Justice enabled the IWN to exert a powerful influence on the public agenda as the leading feminist body in the country.

Indeed, a significant number of the women elected to the Knesset in 1992, representing a range of political views, were active IWN members. It was during their tenure that the Government Authority for the Advancement of the Status of Women and the Knesset Committee of the same name were established. These actions on the part of Knesset members symbolized the achievements of the feminist movement and the initial attempts at mainstreaming feminist thought.

The substance of the IWN's activities, and the identities of its leading members, as well as the ongoing connection with government and establishment bodies, led to the organization's developing an elitist reputation as a stronghold of the secular Ashkenazi bourgeoisie.[5] While the criticism of middle-class, heterosexual feminism can be traced to the beginnings of the Israeli feminist movement (Safran 2006), it intensified during the late 1980s, and primarily in the 1990s, with the emergence of lesbian organizations (Shadmi 2007) and of Mizrahi[6] feminism (Dahan-Kalev 2001; Shiran 1991). Israeli society has gradually moved from a monocultural regime built by the Ashkenazi elite during the 1950s, based on a clear dominant national melting-pot identity, into a segmented, multicultural society (Kimmerling 2001). However, these cultural changes have not necessarily led to equality between the various segments of the society. The segmented structural inequality in Israeli society as a whole is reflected among women as well. The systematic subordination of Mizrahi women by Ashkenazi women has recurred in interactions between the two groups working jointly on feminist activities. Ethnic conflict within the feminist movement was the catalyst that led to heightened awareness of Mizrahi identity, and recognition of the needs of underprivileged working-class women who were mainly Mizrahi in origin, ultimately causing Mizrahi women to define themselves as a separate group (Dahan-Kalev 2001). Women took an active part in the politics of identity that emerged in the 1990s. It led to the appearance of feminist organizations of Palestinian women, Bedouin women, religious women, and so on.

In counterpoint to the internal debate regarding the unequal status of women in Israeli society, an additional feminist sphere of activity emerged during the late 1980s that focused attention on the connection between gender inequality and war. A feminist discourse has developed within the peace movement (Helman and Rapoport 1997; Svirsky 2004). Women were among the leaders of the movement, but they established separate women's organizations for peace (Chazan 1991; Hermann 2002; Sharoni 1995). These organizations could not avoid internal tensions and conflicts on the background of ethnic, national and sexual identities (Safran 2005; Shadmi 2007). The feminist peace movement, despite being split into many voices, has some common basis. It draws a connection between protracted occupation and oppression in its various aspects: national, gender, class, ethnic, and religious (Emmett 1996; Sa'ar 2004; Swirski and Safir 1991). Over time, perspectives of intersectionality emerged in research (Sachs, Sa'ar and Aharoni 2007;

Shalhoub-Kevorkian 2004) and social practices (Aharoni and Deeb 2004). The gendering of the discourse on peace and security is perhaps the most fruitful area of innovative and challenging thinking and organizational patterns to emerge in Israel.[7]

The fragmentation that characterized feminist discourse in Israel from its inception was reinforced by the NGO Law in 1981. The schism in feminist discourse grew stronger from the mid-1990s onward, with numerous positions put forward by various organizations, many of them established as non-governmental organizations.

Given these tensions, organizational changes, and the absence of prominent actors in the field, it is appropriate to ask at the dawn of the new century: Is there still a women's movement in Israel?

A Submerged Counter-Culture

From its inception, the women's movement in Israel was built upon loosely coupled, submerged organizational networks. Very often, women were involved simultaneously in more than one organization. Though always fragmented, the movement maintained an active presence in the public sphere through a continuous redefining of the social issues, problems, and concerns that needed to be addressed. In 2009 around 70 women's NGOs with a feminist orientation operated in Israel. Many of them are aimed at solving women's everyday problems, others attempt to influence the public agenda and the political sphere by pointing out the multidimensional nature of gender, class, ethnic, and national oppression, and persist in exposing exclusionary gender mechanisms and the politicization of both the public and private domains. Refusing to content itself with proposing alternative definitions of social "problems," the various women's organizations consistently sought to propose new, and occasionally unconventional, solutions.

The strength of a feminist movement in which there is sustained, continuous growth of new organizations derives not only from the mobilization of support from existing communities but also from the creation of new ones by drawing upon knowledge from new sources, locations, and points of view. An analysis of women's organizations in Israel demonstrates that there are a number of critical operating principles that together create a profile of alternative discourse. These include: engaging in a critique of the dominant view and exposing mechanisms of cultural dominance; challenging binary thinking and politicization; redefining dominant categories; and challenging hierarchical perceptions of power and politics (Herzog 2006). While not all organizations act in accordance with all these principles, they do serve as reference points to one degree or another. And though organizations' activities overlap, parallel, and sometimes contradict and compete with one another, together they create a collective mosaic of a vibrant movement.

The premise of feminist political and academic discourse is that women's location in the social order offers a special perspective from which to reveal mechanisms of oppression and inequality. This different point of view creates an alternative understanding of society. It challenges the abstract, universal, neutral perception of "man" that supposedly represents all persons, while ignoring differences of sex, class, race, and so forth. Further, this view postulates that civic discourse requires social equality (Fraser 1997) and the recognition of women as agents for social change. In the Israeli case, "man" is identified as a Jewish, Ashkenazi, bourgeois, secular male. Challenging the prevailing assumptions calls for proposing alternative images not only of "man" and "woman" but of different women. Women are not a monolithic group and do not all share the same standpoint (Haraway 1988). Societal inequalities among women generate situated knowledge, distinctive accounts of nature and social relationships that derive from women's experience of being oppressed by other women as well.

As a result of its basic operating premise that the way the world is perceived and the social order constructed must be continuously challenged, the feminist movement has been involved not only as a critic of the existing order but as a producer of new knowledge. Such knowledge grows out of everyday, grassroots experience. In addition, a complex set of dialogic and critical relations exists between women in different professional domains – researchers, artists, educators, legislators, journalists, and so forth – and women from diverse national, ethnic, and class situations. In this manner, the feminist movement has created a multi-channel dialogue between producers of knowledge in different spheres who have not always been in agreement; indeed, on occasion, this dialogue has involved considerable exchanges of mutual criticism (Dahan-Kalev 2001). The power of such knowledge has been reinforced when used as the basis for creating new publics and constructing alternative social-political agendas; likewise, it has undergone a continuous process of renewal and change.

The NGOization of the women's movement intensified this cognitive praxis. New initiatives aiming to create "other" knowledge in the realm of policy emerged, such as the gender perspective promulgated by the Adva Center,[8] the IWN Research Center and Isha L'Isha.[9] They deal with the state budget, international trade agreements, health services, trafficking in women and so on; they offer a feminist approach to the discourse of peace and war; they develop frameworks such as shelters for battered women, hotlines for women in distress, rape crisis centers, and centers for women facing the threat of "honor killings."[10] These organizations not only provide assistance and welfare but also create alternative knowledge about and for women who seek their services. What these projects have in common is uncovering the connection between the personal and the political/economic. Thus for example, the gendering of the discourse on peace and war exposes the political context of the oppression of women in society and the family, and the vicious cycle of violence in which men are trapped as well (Aharoni and Deeb 2004; Sa'ar 2007). Among the characteristics of women's

organizational frameworks is an awareness of the connection between gender inequality and class, ethnic, and national oppression.

Since the 1990s numerous feminist NGOs emerged combining politics
of identity and instrumental politics. They cover a wide range of locations
and topics. For example, *Ahoti*, the Mizrahi feminist movement established
in 1999 by activists whose goal was to establish a unique movement that
could provide a voice for oppressed women, who were unable to express
themselves. Though initiated by Mizrahi women, they address women in
the peripheries of Israel, *Mizrach El-Hashalom*, the Mizrahi peace organization; the Palestinian women's groups *Al-Fanar, Al-Suwar, Al-Kayan*; women's
peace organizations such as the *Women's Peace Network*, and *Women in Black*;
and women's organizations that propose alternatives to the centrality of the
military and militarism in Israeli society, among them *New Profile – Movement
for the Civilization of Israeli Society*; *Women Refuse –* a movement of Jewish and
Palestinian women in Israel who refuse to be enemies or cooperate in actions
that strengthen the war and the occupation; and *Machsom Watch –* a women's
group that primarily bears witness to abuses at Israeli checkpoints. Others
have taken an active role in urging the ratification by Israel's cabinet of UN
Security Council Resolution 1325, which mandates the inclusion of women
in the peace process (Aharoni and Deeb, 2004). The above organizations
bring a gender perspective to the understanding of general social processes,
not only those that relate to the "narrow" interests of women.

Concurrently, extensive activity has been taking place among NGOs working in the economic sphere, in the areas of women's empowerment and the
promotion of economic initiatives among middle-class and unemployed
women from the geographic and social periphery (Dahan-Kalev, Yanay
and Berkovitch 2005; Sa'ar 2007) . In addition, women's organizations that
oppose the binary distinction underlying conventional definitions of sexuality have contributed to the development of a multidimensional discourse in
the public sphere, with the result that lesbian, homosexual, and transsexual
organizations are evolving in different directions.

These are but a few examples pointing to the existence of other views of
society and definitions of the social order, some of them compatible and others competing. These approaches challenge the existing order yet are also
self-critical. The result is competition between – but also dialogue among
– the women's organizations. These differences expand the boundaries of
discourse and create new publics that are conscious of their problems as
women.

Yet to challenge the gendered structure of society is to constantly grapple
with the following paradox: True, redressing gender injustice involves the
dismantling of gender categories, but engaging in identity politics as part of
this process often reproduces given social categories (Fraser 1997: 11–39).
One way to resolve this contradiction is to subvert the social meaning of
these categories. A prominent example of this process is the politicization of
motherhood undertaken by both the political left (Azmon 1997) and right

(El-Or and Aran 1995). In contrast with the apolitical nature of motherhood when situated solely in the private sphere, women are using motherhood in the political realm to question the binary conception of private versus public. According to this alternative perspective, it is possible to be a mother, and thereby speak from the private sphere, and simultaneously have the legitimacy to speak – from this space – in the political arena.

Politicization of the family is another sphere of activity in which women's organizations are involved. While retaining its centrality in both the Jewish and Palestinian cultures in Israel, the concept of family is undergoing a process of reinterpretation. The *New Family* organization is seeking legal recognition for different forms of family arrangements in Israel that lie outside the conservative conception of the family as applied by both Jews and non-Jews; for example, various types of civil marriages, homosexual partnerships, single-parent families (headed by male homosexuals as well), common-law partnerships, mixed marriages (between persons of different religions or nationalities), families of foreign workers, and so forth. In attempting to expand the definition of family, this organization is also challenging dominant gender arrangements.

Similarly, the debate around dual custody is creating new definitions of family and parenting (Hacker 2003). Equal Parenthood, an organization that argues on behalf of equal rights and obligations of parents who are separated, believes that parents must be allowed to share the burden and responsibility of raising, educating, and meeting the needs of their children. Meanwhile, New Masculinity is engaged in re-examining the definition of masculinity. While these and other organizations use existing identity categories applied in dominant gender arrangements, they reverse and subvert their meaning. Moreover, they are challenging the status quo in the relationship between religion and state in Israel as well as the authority accorded by the state to religious bodies that discriminate against women.

The Politics of Doing

The propensity for fragmentation has led NGOization to be a persistent part of the women's movement. Identification of the political sphere as male, and the many difficulties placed in the path of women who seek to enter it, have made volunteerism a means of entry into the public arena for women (Herzog 1999). Women who engage in politics tend to explain their motivation as follows: "It's a way to get things done" (ibid. 89). Similarly, the decision not to continue political activity in formal frameworks is attributed to "being unable to achieve concrete results" and the belief that "women are business-like and less political" (ibid. 196). Thus women easily embrace the logic of non-governmental organizations (Lind 2005); those NGOs involved in issues that touch women's lives make it possible for them to participate in public activity and to give expression to the practical aspects of their worldview. NGO politics are politics channeled toward action and the advancement of concrete, well-defined goals. While not all the NGOs concerned with women's issues adopt a feminist perspective, the majority do attempt to deal with women's problems. And, not infrequently, such work leads to the participants developing critical thinking and new understandings.

Paradoxically enough, neoliberal policy, which is not particularly favorable to women, is prodding them to develop survival strategies. Often, this leads to the emergence of more militant strategies and more radical demands, at times precisely in those organizations that have not won the support of foundations or the state (Lind 2000).

As indicated earlier, NGOization has the potential to depoliticize the women's movement and co-opt women to serve the needs of the state and/ or funding agencies. Institutionalization, development of specialized small teams, and the need to manage ongoing negotiations with contributors and/or government bodies combine to change the organizational culture of women's organizations, turning them into quasi-business organizations. This process can, however, empower women and lead to new opportunities; thus Pearson (1998), in her discussion of women working in capitalist markets, proposed viewing a variety of consequences of salaried work, and not only the aspects of exploitation and oppression. For example, workplaces can also serve as sites where women can develop political consciousness and where they can organize to protect their interests as workers and as women (see discussion in Berkovitch 2002). A similar argument can be made concerning work in NGOs. Even if a woman assumes a defined role in an NGO, such involvement has political potential, especially in the case of the numerous NGOs whose goals were defined initially in terms of social change.

Examples of this in the Israeli context can be seen in the way various organizations enlisted in the common protest even when the protest was not directly connected to the contents dealt with by those organizations. Thus it was when women from a variety of associations participated in the demonstrations over President Katzav's indictment for rape and sexual harassment of women who worked for him, in signing petitions protesting the exclusion of women from professional-academic conferences,[11] and in their demonstration of support for freedom of expression when women from the New Profile movement were taken for questioning by the police on suspicion of encouraging the evasion of military service. It is important to stress that in all three of these examples not all the organizations that expressed support for these matters were directly concerned with these issues. For example, in the demonstration protesting the police questioning of New Profile activists, there were organizations that do not normally get involved in activities like those of the anti-military organizations, such as the Movement for Economic Empowerment of Women, The Center for Women's Integration into the Workplace, the Ahoti movement, and the Tmura Center which offers legal counseling for victims of sexual assault.[12] Ad hoc coalitions of this nature gradually become transformed into a strategy for advancing a common feminist discourse while retaining the unique character of each organization.

The growth of women's NGOs has opened up a new occupational sphere for a wide range of women from various social strata. The critical thinking that characterizes some NGOs, and the search for alternative ways of conceptualizing goals, have created new areas of "women's expertise," for example as management consultants and advisors to women's organizations, mediators, coaches, mentors, and so forth. These specializations not only provide employment for women and expand their involvement in the workforce but they enable them to become agents of social change through their daily practice. What's more, voluntary activities in many women's NGOs challenge the dominant order. For example, many women – including those from Arab Bedouin communities and poor neighborhoods, low-salaried women, and the like – are involved in different forms of social action as part of organizations that operate in geographical and social peripheries (Dahan-Kalev, Yanay and Berkovitch 2005). Such involvement enables them to acquire experience in expressing their needs, engaging in negotiations with government and/or funding bodies, administering budgets, planning and being partners in projects – all skills that can be useful if women enter the paid labor market.

Undoubtedly, the NGOization of the women's movement has changed the nature of politics as practiced by women. By virtue of their involvement, women have become agents of micro-politics. To a large extent, such politics mirror the fragmentation resulting from postmodern conditions; situations of multiculturalism; and multiple identities. The nature of this participation, as well as the daily decisions made by individuals and collectives, mean that such activities have political implications, even if they are not accompanied by traditional forms of political organization and consciousness (Mann 1994).

Conclusion – Redefining Politics and Political Spaces

Early feminism sought to integrate the theory and practice of social change based on gender as a social category equivalent to "class," "race," "ethnicity," or "nationality." However, while the critical stance toward the existing order leads feminism to create women as a category, the reflexive posture of feminism leads it in exactly the opposite direction. The same logic of critical thought directed at social forces that silence women has been reapplied to assess the women leading feminist and women's groups. The continuous examination of concepts, and repeated questioning of the degree to which these embrace the social experiences of the majority of women, has led to an emphasis on differences and to the determination that there is no one common denominator that embraces all women. Deconstruction into groups and subgroups has given rise to fragmentation, extending virtually to the individual level.

Since the end of the 1980s and, even more so, the turn of the twenty-first century, feminist discourse has been characterized by diversity and fragmentation, intersecting on the cultural level with neoliberal logic. Neoliberalism, whereby the economy, social welfare, and everyday life are privatized, has tremendous impact on women's lives; it imposes structural constraints, and in most cases exacerbates their social inequality. The NGOization of civil society, including women's organizations, has channeled women's activities in the direction of new entrepreneurship and private initiative as a tool for surviving but at the same time for negotiation with the dominant order.

According to neoliberalism, society is dominated by the marketplace, and politics – to a large extent – emerges from and acts within the market. From this perspective, women's organizations have become part of the competition. While subscribing to the market rules they are exploited by the state as volunteers or low-paid labor and their organizations are under continuous threat of depoliticization due to their dependency on external funding. However, this study suggests looking at the other side of the coin. Entering "the marketplace" yields new political opportunities for women. By so doing, they have created new markets and new consumers. NGOization has become a venue for women's inclusion in civil society, and a means for them to expand its social goals and substance. The proliferation of organizations and voices that have accompanied the entry of women into the public arena constitute the dilemma of the feminist movement: How is it possible to exert an influence without becoming marked by division and competition? This dilemma, defined as the "dilemmas of difference" (Di Stefano 1990), has given rise to a social field that is creative in both its thinking and its organizational patterns.

Various researchers (Fraser 1997; Phillips 1993; Young 1994) have pointed to ways in which feminist discourse is attempting to overcome this difficulty, which brings us back to the discussion of the concepts of citizenship and civil society. Belonging to a public (in our case a public of women) – and certainly one with political demands – cannot be taken for granted. Collectives, as argued by Iris Young in her paper "Gender as Seriality" (1994), are not defined categories but processes produced through a series of social relations. The political mobilization of identity is dependent upon time and place. Accordingly, political organizing and the coalescing of political attitudes are viewed as social relations, with dialogue serving as a central instrument of political work (Stoetzler and Yuval-Davis, 2002). The metaphor I would propose in this regard is that of a round-the-world journey in which we are constantly refreshing our understanding of the world by stopping at assorted locations, periodically connecting with different "others," and surveying our surroundings. During the course of this journey, subjectivities composed of multiple-situated identities are not only involved in trying to understand themselves and others but, in so doing, they are constructing an epistemic community whose members have an awareness of the right of human existence, the need to be liberated from every type of oppression, the ethics of solidarity, and moral commitment (Assiter 1996; Warnke 1995).

In terms of political praxis, there is no way to arrive at a sole category of identification or to agree on a single political agenda – nor is there a need to do so. The numerous spheres of activity, as well as the fluid, changing boundaries of a mobilized collective, demand that we search for new ways of organizing and types of actions that create connections, are flexible, and keep changing. Such a process takes place both at different discourse levels and in daily practices. In this approach, politics can be likened to quilting. This is an alternative view of power, suggesting dispersion as opposed to centralization, and dismissing the model of power as hierarchical, prioritized, and determinative of what is or is not political and therefore what is or is not important (Herzog 2002). What we are speaking of here is a form of micro-politics based on women's daily praxis in various social sites, the aggregate of which creates an alternative network of ideas.

Politics, from a feminist perspective, is

> the means by which human beings regulated, attempt to regulate and challenge, with a view to changing unequal power relations (Bhavnani 1993: 44).

The overview of women's activity in civil society as propounded in this article indicates that a multitude of women's voices are being heard in the political arena, in the broadest sense of the term. The ongoing feminist debate is advancing many new topics on the public agenda. Some feminist achievements are due to action by one-issue organizations, while others are the result of cooperation, ad hoc coalitions, and partial adoption of goals shared with institutional organizations. Still other accomplishments are due to the presence of multiple organizations acting in the same arena, in competition with one another. The common denominator, however, is the gendering of social discourse and practices.

Acknowledging contextuality and multiplicity in the definition of gender categories allows for flexibility in defining identity and goals as part of a renewed and ongoing examination of the situations in which organizing takes place. The reflexivity and critical stance implicit in this process enable the continued growth of new organizations, while the rejection of binary thinking opens up options for innovative organizational arrangements as well as social messages that are not limited to notions of "either/or." Such a stance has the potential to create a counter-culture of tolerance (Yanay and Lifshitz-Oren 2003) in which the recognition of difference – coupled with a willingness to view relations not only in terms of competition and/ or zero-sum models of power – allows for temporary stability in coalitions and epistemic communities, even when cooperation is partial, temporary, or strained.

The women's movement at the turn of the twenty-first century is a kaleidoscope of opinions, goals, and frameworks. It is a movement that seeks to change the public agenda through daily practices that permeate many different areas of life. This is not a revolution but rather a process of small-scale micro-political changes. To use De Certeau's (1984) metaphor, these new ideas and practices proliferate within technocratic structures much like microbes penetrating the cell of an organism, taking possession of its individuality and imposing on it a different modus vivendi. In doing so, they engage women from new publics and expand the boundaries of political discourse, infusing it with new meanings. Since society and politics in Israel remain subjugated to dominant knowledge regimes, it is premature to celebrate the achievements of the women's movement. Yet at the same time, we should not dismiss the potential inherent in the deep inroads made by the movement via its everyday actions in the field.

Notes

1 For the purposes of this article I prefer this term which signifies the transformation from one pattern of modernity to another.
2 See Nitza Berkovitch's (2002) extended discussion on the contradictory influences of globalization on women.
3 For the range and numbers of civil society organizations see for example www. ynet.co.il/home/0,7340,L-3551,00.html
4 Jews of European or American (as opposed to North African) extraction.
5 This, despite the fact that Alice Shalvi is a religious feminist.
6 Jews of North African extraction or those hailing from Arab countries.
7 This important issue is worthy of separate discussion, but is unfortunately beyond the scope of this paper.
8 The Adva Center is a non-partisan, action-oriented Israeli policy analysis center. It was founded in 1991 by activists from three social movements: the movement for equality for Mizrahi Jews, the feminist movement, and the movement for equal rights for Arab citizens.
9 Isha L'Isha, established in 1983, is a multicultural grassroots feminist organization and is one of the leading voices of women's rights in the country, devoted to achieving equality for all women and promoting peaceful co-existence between Arab and Jewish women.
10 On honor killing in Israel see Hasan 2002.
11 Thus, for example, in 2009 the Association for the Study of Labor Relations changed the participants in the annual conference of the association after various women's organizations protested that in a conference dealing with the effects of the economic crisis on unemployment, no woman researchers were included nor were representatives of women's organizations dealing with negatively affected groups.
12 www.ynet.co.il/articles/0,7340,L-3708336,00.html, accessed May 2, 2009.

References

Aharoni, Sarai, and Rula Deeb. (2004). *Where Are All the Women? UN Security Council Resolution 1325: Gender Perspectives of the Israeli-Palestinian Conflict*. Haifa: Isha L-Isha – Haifa Feminist Center / Kayan – Feminist Organization.
Alvarez, Sonia E. (1998). "Latin American Feminisms 'Go Global': Trends of the 1990s and Challenges for the New Millennium." In Evelina Dagnino, Sonia E. Alvarez,

and Arturo Escobar (eds), *Cultures of Politics/Politics of Cultures: Re-Visioning Latin American Social Movements*, pp. 293–324. Boulder, Colo.: Westview.

—. (1999). "Advocating feminism: The Latin American Feminist NGO 'Boom'." *International Feminist Journal of Politics* 1: 181–209.

Assiter, Alison. (1996). "Feminist Epistemology and Value." *Feminist Theory* 1: 329–45.

AWID (Association for Women's Rights in Development). (2008). "The NGOization of women's movements and its implications for feminist organizing".

Azmon, Yael. (1997). "War, Mothers, and Girls with Braids: Involvement of Mothers' Peace Movements in the National Discourse in Israel." *Israel Social Science Review* 12: 109–28.

Bauman, Zygmunt. (2000). *Liquid Modernity*. Cambridge, UK, Malden, MA: Polity Press; Blackwell.

Beck, Ulrich, Anthony Giddens, and Scott Lash. (1994). *Reflexive Modernization: Politics, Tradition and Aesthetics in the Modern Social Order*. Stanford, Calif.: Stanford University Press.

Ben-Eliezer, Uri.(2003). "New Associations or New Politics? The Significance of Israeli-Style Post-materialism." *Hagar: International Social Science Review* 4: 5–34.

Berkovitch, Nitza. (1997). "Motherhood as a National Mission: The Construction of Womanhood in the Legal Discourse in Israel." *Women Studies International Forum* 20: 605–19.

—. (2002). "Apocalypse Now?! On Globalization, Discontent and Other Problems." *Israeli Sociology* 4: 465–91.

Bernstein, Deborah S. (1987). "The Women's Workers Movement in Pre-State Israel." *Signs: Journal of Women in Culture and Society* 12: 454–70.

Bhavnani, Kum-Kum. (1993). "Talking Racism and the Editing of Women's Studies." In Diane Richardson and Victoria Robinson (eds), *Introducing Women's Studies*, pp. 27–53. London: MacMillan.

Chazan, Naomi. (1991). "Israeli Women and Peace Activism." In B. Swirski and M.P. Safir (eds), *Calling the Equality Bluff: Women in Israel*, pp. 152–61. New York: Pergamon Press.

Dahan-Kalev, Henriette (2001). "Tensions in Israeli Feminism: The Mizrahi Ashkenazi Rift." *Women's Studies International Forum* 24: 1–16.

Dahan-Kalev, Henriette, Nitza Yanay, and Nitza Berkovitch (eds) (2005). *Women of the South: Space, Periphery, Gender*. Tel Aviv: Xargol.

De Certeau, Michel (1984). *The Practice of Everyday Life*. Berkeley: University of California Press.

Della Porta, Donatella. (2006). *Globalization from Below: Transnational Activists and Protest Networks*. Minneapolis: University of Minnesota Press.

Diani, Mario, and Donatella Della Porta. (1999). *Social Movements: An Introduction*. Oxford; Malden, Mass.: Blackwell.

Di Stefano, Christine. (1990). "Dilemmas of Difference: Feminism, Modernity, and Postmodernism." In L. J. Nicholson (ed.), *Feminism/Postmodernism*, pp. 63–82. New York: Routledge.

El-Or, Tamar, and Gideon Aran. (1995). "Giving Birth to Settlement Maternal Thinking and Political Action of Jewish Women on the West Bank." *Gender and Society* 9: 60–78.

Emmett, Ayala. (1996). *Our Sisters' Promised Land: Women, Politics, and Israeli-Palestinian Coexistence*. Ann Arbor: The University of Michigan Press.

Eyerman, Ron, and Andrew Jamison. (1991). *Social Movements: A Cognitive Approach.* University Park, Pa: Pennsylvania State University Press.

Filc, Dani, and Uri Ram (eds.). (2004). *The Power of Property: Israeli Society in the Global Age.* Jerusalem, Tel-Aviv: The Van Leer Jerusalem Institute and Hakibbutz Hameuchad Publishing House (Hebrew).

Fogiel-Bijaoui, Sylvie. (1992). "The Struggle for Women's Suffrage in Israel: 1917–1926." In D. S. Bernstein (ed.), *Pioneers and Homemakers: Jewish Women in Prestate Israeli Society,* pp. 275–302. Albany, NY: SUNY Press.

Fraser, Nancy. (1997). *Justice Interruptus: Critical Reflections on the "Postsocialist" Condition.* New York and London: Routledge.

Gelb, Joyce. (1989). *Feminism and Politics: A Comparative Perspective.* Berkeley, Los Angeles, London: University of California Press.

Goodwin, Jeff, and James M. Jasper. (2006). *Social Movements: Critical Concepts in Sociology.* Milton Park, Abingdon, Oxon; New York: Routledge.

Hacker, Daphna. (2003). "'Motherhood', 'Fatherhood', and Law: A Sociological Analysis of the Field that Shapes Custody and Visitation Arrangements." *Sociology and Anthropology.*

Haraway, Donna. (1988). "Situated Knowledges: The Science Question in Feminism and the Privilege of Partial Perspective." *Feminist Studies* 14: 575–99.

Hasan, Manar. (2002). "The Politics of Honor: Patriarchy, the State and the Murder of Women in the Name of the Family Honor." *The Journal of Israeli History* 21: 1–37.

Helman, Sara, and Tamar Rapoport. (1997). "Women in Black: Challenging Israel's Gender and Socio-Political Orders." *British Journal of Sociology* 48: 682–700.

Hermann, Tamar. (2002). "The Sour Taste of Success: The Israeli Peace Movement, 1967–1998." In B. Gidron, S. Katz, and Y. Hasenfeld (eds), *Mobilizing for Peace: Conflict Resolution in Northern Ireland, Israel/Palestine and South Africa,* pp. 94–129. New York: Oxford University Press.

Herzog, Hanna. (1998). "Homefront and Battlefront and the Status of Jewish and Palestinian Women in Israel." *Israeli Studies* 3: 61–84.

—. (1999). *Gendering Politics – Women in Israel.* Ann Arbor: The University of Michigan Press.

—. (2002). "Redefining Political Spaces: A Gender Perspective on the Yishuv Historiography." *The Journal of Israeli History* 21: 1–25.

—. (2003). "Postzionist Discourse and the Return of the Social Actor: Sub-Politics, Fragmented Identities and Generational Analysis." *Israel Studies Forum: An Interdisciplinary Journal* 19: 104–14.

—. (2006). "Between the Turf and the Gravel – Women, Politics, and Civil Society." *Democratic Culture* 10: 191–214 (Hebrew).

—. (2008). "Re/visioning the women's movement in Israel." *Citizenship Studies,* 12 (3): 265–82.

Izraeli, Dafna N. (1981). "The Zionist Women's Movement in Palestine, 1911–1927: A Sociological Analysis." *Signs: Journal of Women in Culture and Society* 7: 87–114.

Jad, Islah (2004). "The NGO-isation of Arab Women's Movements." *IDS Bulletin* 35: 34–42.

—. (2009). "The Demobilization of Women's Movements: The Case of Palestine", *Posting to the Women's United Nations Report Network (WUNRN) listserv on January 14 2009.*

Jaffe, Eliezer D. (2002). "Giving Wisely: The Internet Directory of Israeli Nonprofit and Philanthropic Organizations." http://givingwisely.org.il/Copyright.htm.

Keane, John. (1988). *Civil Society and the State: New European Perspectives*. London; New York: Verso.

Kimmerling, Baruch. (2001). *The Invention and Decline of Israeliness: State, Society, and the Military*. Berkeley: University of California Press.

Lang, Sabine (1997). "The NGOization of Feminism." In Cora Kaplan, Debra Keates Marion, and Joan W. Scott (eds), *Transitions, Environments, Translations: Feminisms in International Politics*, pp. 101–17. New York: Routledge.

Lind, Amy. (2000). "Negotiating Boundaries: Women's Organizations and the Politics of Restructuring in Ecuador." In Marianne H. Marchand and Anne Sisson Runyan (eds), *Gender and Global Restructuring*, pp. 161–75. New York: Routledge.

—. (2005). *Gendered Paradoxes: Women's Movements, State Restructuring, and Global Development in Ecuador*. University Park, Pa.: Pennsylvania State University Press.

Lovenduski, Joni, and Vicky Randall. (1993). *Contemporary Feminist Politics: Women and Power in Britain*. Oxford: Oxford University Press.

Mann, Patricia S. (1994). *Micro-politics: Agency in a Postfeminist Era*. Minneapolis: University of Minnesota Press.

Markovitz, Irving Leonard. (1998). "Uncivil Society, Capitalism and the State in Africa." *The Journal of Commonwealth and Comparative Politics* 36: 21–53.

Melucci, Alberto. (1996). *Challenging Codes: Collective Action in the Information Age*. Cambridge; New York: Cambridge University Press.

Morena, Edouard. (2006). "Funding and the Future of the Global Justice Movement." *Development and Society* 49: 29–33.

Nagar, Richa. (2006). "Playing with Fire Feminist Thought and Activism through Seven Lives in India." Minneapolis, MN: University of Minnesota Press.

Nash, Kate. (2002). "A Movement Moves … Is There a Women's Movement in England Today?" *European Journal of Women's Studies* 9: 311–28.

Pearson, Ruth. (1998). "'Nimble Fingers' Revisited: Reflections on Women and Third World Industrialization in the Late Twentieth Century." In Cecile Jackson (ed.), *Feminist Visions of Development: Gender Analysis of Policy*, pp. 171–88. London: Pinter.

Peled, Yoav. (1992). "Ethnic Democracy and the Legal Construction of Citizenship: Arab Citizens of the Jewish State." *American Political Science Review* 86: 432–43.

Phillips, Anne. (1993). *Democracy and Difference*. Cambridge: Polity Press.

Ram, Uri. (2005a). *The Globalization of Israel: McWorld in Tel Aviv, Jihad in Jerusalem*. Tel Aviv: Resling.

—. (2005b). "Post-Zionist Studies of Israel." *Israel Studies Forum: An Interdisciplinary Journal* 20: 22–45.

Sa'ar, Amalia. (2004). "UN Security Council Resolution 1325: Relevance to the Israeli-Palestinian Conflict; an Israeli Viewpoint." In Sarai Aharoni and Rula Deeb (eds), *Where are all the Women? UN Security Council Resolution 1325: Gender Perspectives of the Israeli-Palestinian Conflict*, pp. 59–63. Haifa: Isha L-Isha – Haifa Feminist Center / Kayan – Feminist Organization.

—. (2007). "*A Business of One's Own*", *An Evaluation Research on a Micro-enterprise Project by Economic Empowerment for Women*. Jerusalem: Israel. National Insurance Institute.

Sachs, Dalia, Amalia Sa'ar, and Sarai Aharoni. (2007). "How can I feel for others when I myself am beaten? The impact of the armed conflict on women in Israel." *Sex Roles* 57: 593–606.

Sadoun, Britta. (2006). "Donor Policies and the Financial Autonomy of Development NGOs." *Development and Society* 49: 45–51.

Safran, Hannah. (2005). "Alliance and Denial: Lesbian Protest in Women in Black."

In Chava Frankfort-Nachmias and Erella Shadmi (eds), *Sappho in the Holy Land*, pp. 191–210. Albany: State University of New York.

—. (2006). *Don't Wanna Be Nice Girls: The Struggle for Suffrage and the New Feminism in Israel*. Haifa: Pardes (Hebrew).

Shadmi, Erella. (2007). *Thinking Women: Women and Feminism in a Masculine Society*. Jerusalem: Tzivonim (Hebrew).

Shalhoub-Kevorkian, Nadera. (2004). "Racism, Militarism, and Policing: Police Reactions to Violence against Women in Israel." *Social Identities* 10: 171–93.

Shalvi, Alice. (2006). "Israel Women's Network." In Paula Hyman and Dalia Ofer (eds), *Jewish Women: A Comprehensive Historical Encyclopedia*. Jerusalem: Shalvi Publishing Ltd.

Shamir, Ronen. (2004). "The De-Radicalization of Corporate Social Responsibility." *Critical Sociology* 30: 669–89.

Sharoni, Simona. (1995). *Gender and the Israeli-Palestinian Conflict – The Politics of Women's Resistance*. Syracuse, New York: Syracuse University Press.

Shilo, Margalit, Ruth Kark, and Galit Hasan-Rokem (eds) (2001). *Jewish Women in the Yishuv and Zionism: A Gender Perspective*. Jerusalem: Yad Ben-Zvi Press (Hebrew).

Shiran, Vicki. (1991). "Feminist Identity vs. Oriental Identity." In Barbara Swirski and Marilyn P. Safir (eds), *Calling the Equality Bluff: Women in Israel*, pp. 303–11. New York: Pergamon Press.

Silliman, Jael (1999). "Expanding Civil Society: Shrinking Political Spaces – The Case of Women's Nongovernmental Organizations." *Social Politics* 6: 23–53.

Sloat, Amanda. (2005). "The Rebirth of Civil Society: The Growth of Women's NGOs in Central and Eastern Europe." *European Journal of Women's Studies* 12: 437–52.

Stoetzler, Marcel, and Yuval-Davis, Nira. (2002). "Standpoint Theory, Situated Knowledge and the Situated Imagination." *Feminist Theory* 3: 315–33.

Svirsky, Gila. (2004). "Local Coalitions, Global Partners: The Women's Peace Movement in Israel and Beyond." *Signs: Journal of Women in Culture & Society* 29: 543–50.

Swirski, Barbara (1991). "Israeli Feminism New and Old." In Barbara Swirski and Marilyn P. Safir (eds), *Calling the Equality Bluff*. New York, Oxford: Pergamon Press.

Swirski, Barbara, and Marilyn P. Safir (eds), (1991). *Calling the Equality Bluff – Women in Israel*. New York: Pergamon Press.

Tarrow, Sidney G. (1998). *Power in Movement: Social Movements and Contentious Politics*. Cambridge [England]; New York: Cambridge University Press.

Taylor, Marilyn. (1992). "The Changing Role of the Nonprofit Sector in Britain: Moving Towards the Market." In Benjamin Gidron, Ralph M. Kramer, and Lester M. Salamon (eds), *Government and the Third Sector: Emerging Relationships in Welfare States*, pp. 147–75. San Francisco Cal: Jossey-Bass.

Threlfall, Monica (ed.) (1996). *Mapping the Women's Movement: Feminist Politics and Social Transformation in the North*. New York: Verso.

Tilly, Charles. (1984). "Social Movements and National Politics." In C. Bright and Sandra Harding (eds), *State Making and Social Movements*, pp. 297–317. Ann Arbor: The University of Michigan Press.

Tilly, Charles, and Lesley J. Wood. (2009). *Social Movements, 1768–2008*. Boulder: Paradigm Publishers.

Warnke, Georgia. (1995). "Discourse Ethics and Feminist Dilemmas of Difference." In Johanna Meehan (ed.), *Feminist Read Habermas*, pp. 247–61. New York and London: Routledge.

West, Guida, and Rhoda Lois Blumberg (eds) (1990). *Women and Social Protest.* New York: Oxford University Press.

Yanay, Nitza, and Ruti Lifshitz-Oren. (2003). "Mandatory Reconciliation (Tzav Piyus): The Violent Discourse of Moderation." *Israeli Sociology* 5: 161–91 (Hebrew).

Yishai, Yael. (2008). "Civil Society under Liquidation?" *Civil Society and the Third Sector in Israel* 2: 7–27.

Young, Iris Marion. (1994). "Gender as Seriality: Thinking about Women as a Social Collective." *Signs: Journal of Women in Culture and Society* 19: 713–38.

9 Parading pridefully into the mainstream

Gay and lesbian immersion in the civil core

Amit Kama

Prologue

The present paper is written twenty years after homosexuality was removed from the Israeli legal code. In just two decades homosexual men[1] who mostly lived in the shadowy, obscure, and to be sure, silent margins of Israeli society have emerged into the public stage and are now nearly fully fledged citizens. In spite of not being persecuted, their very existence was fragile and hence no sense of community or minority was consolidated. Consequently, demands for full participation in civil society and civil rights were quite unfeasible, and even unheard of. An abject aggregate of "second-class" citizens[2] who had only their sexual orientation as a common denominator developed into a rather strong, vociferous community who enjoys not only nearly full civic rights but also a distinct visibility in all walks of life. Lesbigays – for the sake of parsimony, this acronym will be used henceforward – conceivably constitute today the strongest minority in Israel. Most of their demands for equality have been met and resolved. Anti-discrimination laws protect their place at the workplace, same-sex couples and families are recognized to a relatively satisfactory extent, anti-defamation laws safeguard their reputation and status, and their presence in the public sphere and various institutions is quite ubiquitous.

Eight years ago I undertook a similar project of delineating the status of gay men (Kama, 2000) and the current paper presents a welcome opportunity to include lesbians and to verify that the trajectory I foresaw has indeed been straight and largely smooth. In the following pages I will integrate parts of my previous paper with recent achievements and developments in order to demonstrate and illustrate what I believe to be the most conspicuous characteristic of Israeli lesbigays, namely a relentless yearning to be assimilated at the very core of mainstream society (Kama, 2002, 2005b).

A caveat is necessary here. For the past decade I have had plenty of opportunities to air and broadcast this tenet, in which I believe and have empirically corroborated in my research. Opposition arose from some of my colleagues and other lesbigay activists who vehemently eschew the liberal ideology and praxis that I in my roles as a researcher, advocate, and activist advance. Regardless of my personal involvement, a radical or queer movement has grown and fermented for a short while. For example, the collective known as *Kvissa Sh'hora* (= Black [i.e. Dirty] Laundry), founded in 2001 and nowadays defunct, was the epitome of challenging and provoking the allegedly acquiescent and complacent lesbigay community at large. Its members called attention to the neglected solidarity with other oppressed groups and above all the continuing occupation of the Palestinians. They also focused on the capitalist co-optation of the lesbigay community manifested, inter alia, in the excessively commercial Pride Parades, etc. As this paper will strive to substantiate, queer ideology and radical opposition have had a negligent impact on the general trajectory and the overall lesbigay objective to have a metaphorical seat by the common table. I do believe that the past twenty years have abundantly and clearly proven the concrete successes and an all-encompassing liberal aspiration of the Israeli lesbigay community to be included within the civil core.

Pre-Pride Era

By and large, two main eras can be demarcated in charting Israeli lesbigay history from a political point of view. The current period beginning on March 22, 1988, when the legal/penal code was changed, and up to that point. The date in itself symbolizes a shift that encompasses wider reifications and consequences than the mere fact of legalizing homosexuality. As this paper will demonstrate, as of 1988 political, cultural, and social processes that concern and involve the lesbigay minority can be regarded as markers of macro phenomena that affect the entire Israeli society and could not be achieved without them. What makes the Israeli case intriguing and unique is the abruptness of the shift between these eras. Within a very short span of time, these pariahs whose civil status had been dubious *de facto* and *de jure*, lesbigays enjoy today nearly equal status and are active actors on the public stage in its most visible manifestations, namely, the media and political institutions (on the national as well as the municipal levels).

A remnant of the British mandate in Palestine, the anti-sodomy law was incorporated into the Israeli legal code after the British rule ended and the State of Israel was founded. It stated that every man who allowed another man to have intercourse with him risked up to ten years of imprisonment. In practice it was rarely enforced, thanks to guidelines written by Israel's Attorney General in the early 1950s, asserting that sexual behavior between two adults in privacy need not be a matter for police prosecution (Harel, 2000; Spivak and Yonai, 1996.) In other words, regardless of not being practically enforced, the law not only positioned homosexuals as criminals *de jure*, but instilled a sense of civil and human worthlessness as well as mirrored omnipresent societal values and norms of conduct.

The inherent risk of legal sanctions reinforced homosexual invisibility and social marginality. Together with general, indeed universal, perceptions of homosexuality as a personal psycho-pathology and social deviance (Epstein, 1988; Garnets and Kimmel, 1993), individuals who practiced homosexuality did not and could not conceive of themselves as worthy human beings, not to say equal citizens. As long as broad socio-political systems excluded homosexuals to the periphery and the scientific discourse medicalized and pathologized (Foucault, 1990[1976]) them; a struggle for civil rights could neither be feasible nor envisioned. Scientifically, culturally, and socially stigmatized perverts constituted a threat to the pristine Sabra (i.e. a Jewish native of Israel). Unlike other 'Western' countries, several unique factors colluded in these practices of repression and oppression in Israel:

1. The Zionist ethos accentuating the hegemonic precedence of a collective and united body of Israelis over personal needs and identities, especially in the face of an enduring sense of immanent threat from Arab neighbors (Horowitz and Lissak, 1977; Katz, Haas and Gurevitch, 1997; Lissak, 1988.) In a climate of opinion where the collective was superior to personal identity, formation of an unorthodox, namely homosexual, identity was seen as an undesired cultivation of a capricious self.
2. Zionism saw "the apotheosis of the masculine" (Hazleton, 1977, p. 94) embodied in the new Jew's strenuously virile ideal (Biale, 1992), thereby precluding and repressing any signs of femininity in the Sabra (Almog, 2000; Gluzman, 2007). Since homosexuality has traditionally been conceived as a sexual inversion (Freud, 1974[1905]), formation of a homosexual identity constituted a dire breach of the strict Zionist gender roles.
3. The legendary indoctrination to self-actualization by bearing as many progeny as was nationally desired – what is today referred to as the "demographic problem" – added another obstacle on the road to self-fulfillment for persons who would perhaps otherwise seek same-sex partners.

It is surely redundant to conclude that during the first four decades of its existence Israeli society, by and large, expressed intolerant attitudes toward 'sexual deviants,' who egotistically broke the nationally cherished and communally nurtured ethos. These individuals – it should be clarified at the outset that the conceptualization of a "lesbigay community" was not imported into Israel until 1979 – might therefore trigger the dissolution of the young country. In this ideological, legal, and social climate, openly homosexual persons were, not surprisingly, excluded from the public sphere. This continued a cyclical route where society would not tolerate outspoken homosexuals, who were thus reluctant to actually materialize what would be termed later on "gay lifestyle" lest the (perceived as well as real) consequences be too dreadful. In short, a vicious circle overruled the formation of a homosexual identity on both collective and individual levels and thus precluded the development of a homosexual movement.

Lesbigays' total symbolic annihilation – that is, the cultivation of invisibility and quantitative elimination of powerless minorities from the symbolic reality, in particular the media (Gerbner and Gross, 1976; Tuchman, 1978) – was ironically emphasized against the backdrop of episodic journalistic reports of indictments of men who committed sodomy with boys or adolescents. For many years it seemed that the only references to "homos" (never using names or photos, thus emphasizing their inhumanity) were in the context of illicit coercion of the younger generation into sexual temptations. Routine coverage included phrases that directly and explicitly reinforced the homosexual-as-child-molester stereotype. For instance, in 1978 *Ha'Aretz* – the most prestigious daily in the country (Kama, 2005a) – published a series of articles on a homosexual brothel in the town of Netanya. A "nest of wasps" was discovered in the home of two men where they and their friends had molested 10- to 16-year-old boys. However, the routine and conventional formula for reporting these cases was quite short (usually less than a hundred words). Generally, then, while lesbians were unequivocally symbolically annihilated; homosexual men were sporadically "allowed" into the public sphere, yet, portrayed as sick, disturbed, and socially and morally decrepit.

The first momentous development in this state of affairs took place in 1975, when the *Society for the Protection of Personal Rights* (colloquially referred to as *HaAguda*, meaning "the association") was founded by a small group of gay men – lesbians did not join the *Aguda* until the early 1980s. A lesbian-feminist organization (*Community of Lesbian Feminists [CLAF]*) was founded in 1987 but has become rather non-operational in the past couple of years[3] – in order to provide a support network, constitute a hub of social activities, and furnish a focus of communal identification for an erstwhile heterogeneous amalgam of disconnected individuals.

An exceptional – in the sense that it did not trigger an immediate chain of events in its wake – event took place in 1979; that is, a full decade after the riots in the New York City Stonewall Inn that have spurred and led to the foundation of the lesbigay civil rights struggle in the United States (Duberman, 1993). The Stonewall riots are regarded today as the symbolic birth of the global lesbigay movement and its call for pride and individual as well as communal 'coming out' (McDarrah and McDarrah, 1994). The first Pride Parade in New York City was conceived to celebrate the first anniversary of the riots. Soon enough, many other American cities held their own Pride Parades and the phenomenon has spread into many big cities around the world ever since. These parades were initially meant to be demonstrations of internal social cohesion and unity in the face of homophobic attitudes and heterosexist practices as well as assertive demands for equal civil rights. Eventually, these political aspirations – in Israel, but probably this is a global common denominator – have yielded to a commercial celebration of consumerism (see a parallel trend in Sender, 2001).

Back to 1979. The *Aguda* tried to organize an international Jewish lesbigay conference. To everyone's chagrin, no hotel in the Holy Land was willing to accommodate such a group. Since all major hotels in Israel must comply with the Chief Rabbinate's kosher regulations, they feared losing their certificate if they hosted such a conference. On Friday, July 20, 1979, some fifty lesbians and gay men (most of whom were American Jews) congregated at the City Hall square in Tel Aviv to protest and picket. The coverage of this historical event was in itself a historical, yet acutely isolated, milestone. Two aspects make the *Yedioth Ahronoth* (the most popular tabloid daily; its circulation is wider than all other Israeli dailies combined (Caspi and Limor, 1999)) story particularly significant in the climate of the period. On the semiotic level a large *en face* photograph of two gay men and two lesbians, constituting a historical precedent in contrast with the faceless anonymity of previous (and, to some extent, future) generations of homosexuals. On the rhetorical level the introduction and hence symbolic construction of a disenfranchised minority. Quoting participants, the reporter advanced the brand new discourse of civil rights: "We live in constant terror lest we'll be fired from our jobs," confessed one gay man, "We demand our rights to live and love, to organize and congregate safely and openly." In other words, this event symbolizes the first introduction of the conceptualization – evidently imported from the United States – of a lesbigay community and its (subordinated) civil status.

In 1971, Uri Avneri, a Knesset – the Israeli parliament – member (MK), initiated the first attempt at amending the Israeli legal code in order to remove the sodomy clause. This first attempt failed. In 1978, five left-wing MKs challenged the Knesset. But, again, pressures from the Orthodox parties proved to be insurmountable. Israeli society by and large (not excluding gay men themselves) was quite indifferent to these efforts. The country's existential predicament invalidated personal issues, such as human and civil rights that were dismissed as petty, at best. Furthermore, changing the law would have meant a controversial confrontation with the explicit Biblical categorization of homosexuality as abomination. However, thanks to momentary favorable circumstance, the law was finally amended on March 22, 1988. Newspapers of March 23 celebrated the amendment on their covers; for instance, *Ma'ariv*, the second largest commercial daily (Caspi and Limor, 1999), wrote: "Sexual Liberalization in Israel. Consenting homosexual relations between adults are no longer punishable." It should be noted that neither lesbigay individuals nor organizational efforts were behind any of these initiatives and endeavors (Yonai, 1998). In other words, the most crucial event in the history of the Israeli lesbigay community was planned and carried out by sympathetic heterosexuals.

The decriminalization of homosexuality proved to be a vital, even necessary, incentive in the self-empowerment of the lesbigay community, consequently establishing a platform for political awareness and involvement. Indeed, shortly thereafter, a political caucus, *Otzma* (power), was founded within the *Aguda*. *Otzma*'s agenda, according to *Al HaMishmar* – the now defunct official daily publication of *Mapam*, the United Workers Party (Caspi and Limor, 1999), was to promote legislation in order to give equal rights to same-sex couples, to enable lesbigays to adopt children, etc. (October 14, 1988). Six months later, newspapers reported the first conference organized by *Otzma*, in which several MKs participated. One of these, MK Rubi Rivlin (of the right-wing *Likud*), declared that "homosexuals are deviants but not evil. I will not fight for homosexuality, but I will fight for everyone who wishes to live like that, and is consequently harmed" (*Yedioth Ahronoth*, March 12, 1989). Henceforward, *Otzma* worked as a political lobby and initiated another decisive development on the lesbigay emancipatory voyage; that is, the addition of sexual orientation to the Law of Equal Rights at the Workplace in 1992.

According to this legal amendment, an employee should not be discriminated against on the basis of her/his sexual orientation in any aspect of his/her employment (Gross, A. M., 2001). The first gay man who enjoyed the benefits of this amendment was Jonathan Danilowitz, an *El Al* (Israel national airline) employee who requested free tickets for his partner (as is done with heterosexual couples, regardless of their marital status). After losing at the first two judicial levels, *El Al* appealed to the Supreme Court, where it lost again. Accepting the media's role as a sort of barometer of public opinion and prevalent attitudes, we can deduct from the newspapers' enthusiasm at the Supreme Court decision that lesbigays were at this moment accepted and embraced into mainstream society. For example, *Yedioth Ahronoth*'s headlines of December 1, 1994 read: "Same-sex couples should not be discriminated against." *Al HaMishmar* labeled the decision "the most significant human achievement of the Israeli legal system." In a report summing up 1994, the paper elaborated on the importance of the decision: "The authorities have acknowledged the right to love [...] It turned out that sordid reality can be changed. The old world of oppression, racism and prejudices can be demolished" (December 30, 1994). I concur and thus will now begin unfolding the main characteristics of a new era.

Era of Immersion

The transition from a state of nearly total symbolic annihilation and self-denial to the recent condition of self-fulfillment and active presence in the public sphere was certainly neither instantaneous nor smooth. I suggest a somewhat arbitrary date – March 22, 1988 – because of its symbolic significance for both lesbigay individuals and the entire social and political constructions. Only from the present perspective is it possible to actually delineate the historical process. The amendment of the penal code permeated into personal and collective consciousness, but slowly and gradually. For instance, for roughly thirteen years after its foundation, the *Aguda*'s impact on both the public sphere and lesbigay individuals was quite negligible. Its leading activists were to a large extent shy of publicly disclosing their identities while their peers dreaded joining the organization. Indeed, even while fighting for adding the sexual orientation clause to the law of equal rights at the workplace, aliases were used in order to evade public disclosure of activists' identities.

After fifteen years of right-wing cum fundamentalist government coalitions, the political climate took a twist in 1992 when Israeli voters caused a crucial shift in the political constellation. The new government coalition was composed of the left-wing Labor and *Meretz* parties. Promptly afterward, a newly elected MK, Ya'el Dayan (Labor), formed a sub-committee for the prevention of discrimination on the basis of sexual orientation. On February 2, 1993, it had its first meeting, which soon proved to be the second crucial turning point in the history of the Israeli lesbigay community. Eleven MKs from various and opposing parties, a psychologist, a rabbi, and some sixty lesbigays were enveloped by dozens of fascinated journalists representing almost every local and international news agency. It would be impossible to reproduce the impressive and unforgettable wave of unflinching support and sympathy that stirred the public sphere in the next days. The Israel Broadcasting Authority allocated an exceptional segment of more than four minutes of its prime-time news, *Mabat*, to cover the event: "The assembled demanded that the state acknowledge their special needs [...] A miracle occurred at the Knesset. Lesbians and homosexuals are out in the House."

The printed press, too, was inundated with photographs and bold headlines during the following days. For the first time in media coverage of lesbigays, personal names and details, and *en face* photographs were explicit; thus constituting a decisive moment in the lesbigay political endeavors by assigning them with humanity. The routine journalistic practice of anonymity (e.g. covered faces, blurred voice, use of aliases, and/or omission of any personal data) of the past era was abruptly renounced. The era of nameless and faceless; that is, non-individual, criminals and marginal outsiders, had ended. Lesbigays are now individuals who have names and recognizable identities. *Yedioth Ahronoth*'s headline read: "Out of the closet, and into the Knesset." Its front-page photograph was captioned: "Proud[4] in the Knesset. Some hundred homosexuals and lesbians (calling themselves proud) disclosed the discrimination against them." *Ma'ariv* wrote: "They knew that an army of journalists and photographers would wait in the Knesset, they were embarrassed, but came to the homosexual assembly feeling that they must come out of the closet. That they must publicly proclaim their sexual orientation, and stand up for their rights." *Hadashot* – a short-lived tabloid in the style of the *New York Post* (Caspi and Limor, 1999) – quoted Prof. Uzi Even: "I did not come to ask for mercy or pity. Let us merge into society."

What Prof. Even did come to demand was the abolition of the discriminatory policy of the Israel Defense Forces (IDF), listing homosexual soldiers as mentally disturbed, automatically assigning them to psychiatric examination, and barring them from so-called "sensitive" positions. The impact of this step soon reverberated in the local and international media. The convergence of several factors made Even's tale a particularly newsworthy item: (1) The simultaneous controversy over military discrimination in the US widely covered by local media; (2) the IDF's status as one of Israel's most revered and pivotal social and cultural institutions (Levy, 2007). Moreover, the IDF constitutes a locus of shared values and positive identification, and serves as a central agent of establishing and reproducing manhood (Kaplan, 2002; Sion, 1997); (3) Even's professional status and personal authority were conducive to the shattering of the effeminate components of the sissy stereotype (Dyer, 1993; Sedgwick, 1993); and, (4) the explicit demand to share in the burden of the military service with the rest of society. Thanks to this impetus, cabinet ministers intervened and, after three months of negotiations between military officers and gay activists, the IDF policy was amended. As of June 1993, soldiers of both sexes[5] can be recruited, placed and advanced regardless of their sexual orientation. Nonetheless, since 1996 there is no mention of sexual orientation in the military codebook, which means that the army – at least, *de jure* – does not take this attribute into any consideration (Gross, 2002).

The effects of these events cannot be overestimated, for they sparked and ignited a rather swift chain-reaction in every aspect of the public domain. Legal, judicial, and political gains have been fostering lesbigay equality, decreasing their formally constructed marginality, and advancing anti-discriminatory measures. The collaboration between a progressively empowered and politically conscious lesbigay community and its institutions and a few dedicated MKs paved the way for far-reaching political gains that enabled a fuller integration of lesbigays into Israeli society. This statement invites a short interval in the present review in order to shed light on the inclusive nature of Israeli lesbigay strategies.

Nowhere is the uniqueness of the Israeli lesbigay community more obvious than in the adoption of American ideological frameworks and tactics for political struggles, while forsaking the ideological and practical leaning towards cultural, social, economic, and geographical segregation often found among American lesbigays (Gamson, 1995; Gross, 1997). There is probably nothing further from the Israeli reality than the "golden ghettoes" (Dario, 1992), in which many overseas lesbigays tend to congregate within segregated enclaves. Geographical assimilation (Blank, 2003; Misgav, 2008) serves as a valid manifestation of the immersion trajectory that fully characterizes the Israeli lesbigay struggle for citizenship. Another example is military service. The American campaign to lift the ban from lesbigays in the military took place simultaneously as local endeavors to change the IDF policy. The latter fought for inclusion into the principal secondary socialization agent. This struggle expressed a need to feel and be part of this great crucible. This was a fight for civil obligation, not personal benefits. Indeed, all legal, judicial, cultural, and social achievements in Israel were but manifestations of activists' assimilationist ideology, or, as Gamson (1995) put it, "inclusionary goals" (p. 395).

In the next sections I will try to corroborate this assertion with some recent and indicative examples from various fields of activity that will explain the current circumstances. Israeli society in general and lesbigays complement each other in the sense that both aim at co-optation and assimilation. This reciprocal interaction is grounded in the "domestication" of opposition carried out by the hegemony, which faces no real resistance. The overall lenient situation and tolerant climate of opinion towards lesbigays is feasible precisely because the lesbigay community professes an entrenchment within the dominant ethos and by and large neither challenges nor contests it. Acceptance of the so-called "gay lifestyle" by the majority is viable since it does not call for fundamental alterations in any social, political, judicial, or even moral systems. On the contrary, the following illustrations will unfold an unrelenting struggle to be embraced by existing institutions and mores while adhering to their basic tenets, albeit by flexing their contours of jurisdiction.

Another aspect that may shed light on the relative ease with which these processes could have been materialized is Israel's size. Being a socially and geographically small country, Israel exhibits a very tight web of interpersonal relationships. Israelis are likely to enact various roles with the same persons in different contexts (Cooper, 1985); therefore one is always, at least potentially, situated in a social context where s/he is known by other/s. In other words, the anonymity sought by lesbigays in other countries (Weston, 1995) cannot be achieved here. As a result, being "out" to some is, as a matter of fact, being "out" to all. That is, compartmentalization of the knowledge that one is lesbian/gay is unfeasible in this social structure. Consequently, the dark nebula encompassing the evil image of an abstract homosexual is, in some instances, crystallized into a concrete, known and loved human being. Accordingly, Israeli society offers less homophobic management of lesbigays, and thus rather easily accommodates their demands. But in spite of the overall lenient atmosphere and an inclusionary inclination, homophobia has certainly not become extinct, what with the terror attack at the *Aguda*'s center in downtown Tel Aviv on August 1, 2009, murdering two and injuring fifteen young lesbigays.[6]

Formal Institutions

Following the footsteps of the *Aguda*, a plethora of organizations have been founded around Israel. Some of these NGOs are geographically oriented (e.g. *Jerusalem Open House for Pride and Tolerance* [JOH], *Gay Galilee*), some accommodate particular populations (e.g. *Israeli Gay Youth, Havruta: Religious homosexuals in Israel, Tehila: Support group for parents of lesbigays, Bat-Kol: Religious Lesbian Organization*, and others), a few target society at large (e.g. *Hoshen: An education center of the GLBT community in Israel, Political Council for GLBT Rights in Israel, Adamleadam*, and others), and finally there are party caucuses (e.g. *The Ge'e Center of the Labor Party* and *Ge'ut*). In short, since 1987 when the second organization, namely CLAF, was established, a few organizations have been flourishing and thriving while most others were short-lived and by now defunct. The chief reason for this phenomenon lies in the fact that nearly all lesbigay organizations and movements were the fruits of labor of a very small number of dedicated activists, whose energies and motivation were sooner or later exhausted and burned out.

Ge'ut merits a distinct discussion for it clearly validates the main thesis of this paper. Although it has fundamentally changed – essentially invalid[7] at the time being – since its inception in 1996, *Ge'ut* proved to have deeply impacted the political arena within the lesbigay community as well as outside its demarcation. The founding fathers, who were already members of the *Meretz* party, petitioned the party leaders and executive forums in order to attain a full statutory position among other party bodies. After its approval, *Ge'ut* became the first lesbigay statutory caucus operating within a national political party in Israel. Consequently, its head automatically joins *Meretz* governing and legislative councils as a full member. *Ge'ut*'s endeavors have been quite impressive. Firstly, lesbigay issues were integrated into the party platform and national election campaigns. In the last two national election rounds several other parties – *Shinui* (Ram and Yadgar, 2008), *Labor, Green Party, Ale Yarok* (Green Leaf) – have incorporated a lesbigay segment into their platforms, as well. In other words, the lesbigay community has become a lucrative voting bloc whose political attention and involvement are keenly sought after.

Second, and perhaps most importantly, *Ge'ut* successfully promoted several gay and lesbian candidates who won seats at the Knesset, the Tel Aviv city council, and the Jerusalem city council. As was the case with platforms, other parties have also allocated energies in order to enlist gay men (not quite surprisingly, no women were involved) to their lists of candidates.[8] However, aside from the three *Meretz* persons, no other gay men or lesbians were elected, so far. Being thus involved within the apparatuses of an established party undeniably paved the road for lesbigay activists to enjoy the benefits of being in relatively powerful positions from which they can affect policies and generate concrete changes, such as allocation of funds to various NGOs, the routinization of Pride Parade in Tel Aviv, the founding of *Beit Dror* (a halfway, emergency home for lesbigay adolescents), and the like.

This institutional trajectory has been contested every now and then, to not much success. For example, in irregular intervals some individuals have been attempting to found a lesbigay party. The last attempt took place in mid-2007 and enjoyed a brief flurry of media attention. According to the nascent leaders, it is time for the lesbigay community to coalesce and fight for its own sake independently of established parties. So far, the idea has never progressed beyond what I would hesitantly call provocative exclamations. Whether the inability to actually found a party and run for office is grounded in personal matters or apathy or disinterest on the part of the community at large cannot be resolved here. What I do find remarkable in this context is the empirical fact that working within "the System" has indeed yielded fruits on both the symbolic and material levels. To verify this last statement the next illustration may be valuable.

The GLBT Municipal Center in Tel Aviv, officially opened in June 2008 in the very center of the city, is a community center managed, operated, and funded wholly by the city hall. Its director and manager are city hall employees. It offers a range of activities for lesbigays and houses the offices of several independent NGOs. *Beit Dror* is equivalent in the sense that it is also run and funded by the Tel Aviv city hall. The largest accommodation in the country for the community is the fruit of endeavors by the gay city council member, Etai Pinkas, whose incorporation within "the Establishment" enabled this project to be designed and completed. Furthermore, the fact that activists as well as lesbigay "laypersons" do indeed participate in these projects and instill life into them attests to an overall inclination to welcome and be embraced by a mainstream institution.

The *Jerusalem Open House* represents entirely different ideology and practices. An independent organization intended to create a tolerant and pluralistic city where sexual and other minorities can live equally and openly, JOH runs a community center in downtown Jerusalem and organizes an annual Pride Parade. This event is definitely the most contested and disputed initiative in the history of Israeli lesbigays. It annually ignites a detrimental chain of events that sweeps over the country and, probably for the first time, succeeds in uniting conflicting segments of the Israeli population. Religious and Orthodox collaborate with allegedly liberal secular Jews. The most striking off-shoot was probably a summit convention of delegates of three religions in 2005 when Moslem, Jewish, and Christian clerics met to issue a decree against the parade.[9] While growing opposition led by the Jerusalem mayor himself escalates, the JOH nevertheless requests that the Jerusalem city hall fund the parade and assist in its realization. Due to brevity constraints, I will not delve into this affair that involves petitions to the Supreme Court, but it may demonstrate the deep-rooted need – even if extremely ambivalent and contested – to be embraced by "the Establishment". JOH fights yearly for visibility in a locale which does not tolerate it and actually operates against the attitudes of the majority of the population. In this sense, JOH acts in a non- or anti-consensual, possibly even subversive, manner. Yet, simultaneously, it demands that the city hall recognizes the parade's importance and help it. In other words, JOH wishes to be supported by the institutional system and at the same time severs an allegorical "umbilical cord" by refusing to accept the prevalent climate of opinion that abhors the idea of a Pride Parade in the "Holy City."

In this context, it is astonishing to see the vast disparity between Jerusalem and Tel Aviv. Unlike the former annual pandemonium and violent clashes, the latter constitutes yet another illustration of the majority of Israeli lesbigays' strategies of immersion. Gay Pride events have been celebrated in Tel Aviv since 1993. These happenings not only enjoy the auspices and financial subsidies of municipal bodies, but make every effort to diminish divisions between the lesbigay community and the rest of society. The 1994 *Gaystronomic Festival*, for instance, was a food fair hosted by the best restaurateurs in Tel Aviv, catering to some 5,000 women, men, and children of all walks of life. After about five years of repeated requests by the *Aguda*, the Tel Aviv city hall agreed to be the producer and financial contributor of an annual parade, in which tens of thousands of people march along the streets lined with rainbow flags (the international symbol of the lesbigay community). In some respects, particularly the official hanging of the flags around the city for several days in late June during the past decade, the coveted immersion within the mainstream seems to have materialized.

Media representation

In recent decades, as part of various minorities' awakenings and struggles for equality, media visibility has become a chief interest of disenfranchised groups. Media scholars have correspondingly begun to look into the social and political reverberations of minority participation in the public sphere (Cf. Gross, L., 2001; Greenberg and Brand, 1994; Greenberg, Mastro and Brand, 2002; Lemish, 2000; Weimann, 2000). Three main developmental stages – ordinarily they are sequential, however in many cases one can be found to exist alongside the other/s depending on the genre, medium, etc. – have been delineated: (1) Quantitative symbolic annihilation of minority members. That is to say that they do not take part in the public discourses, at least comparatively to their proportion in society and certainly not on a regular basis; (2) qualitative symbolic annihilation, which means that there are some representations but these are based on stereotypes grounded on negative prejudices and folkloristic images; and (3) equal integration of actors whose stigma or minority status is largely irrelevant to their media role. In other words, we can speak of invisibility versus caricatured and stereotypical visibility versus fair representation and decent portrayal.

In the Israeli lesbigay case, quantitative and qualitative symbolic annihilation was prevalent until roughly 1993. In the past 15 years the paths of media representation of gay men and lesbian women have dramatically split. Whereas the latter have not moved beyond the quantitative annihilation stage, the former have largely entered the third stage of media integration. Gay men are now represented in a rich array of images; from a stereotypically flamboyant hairdresser in a commercial spot to a "straight-acting" chef who hosts a cooking show, from the international correspondent on Channel 10 to judges on the Israeli version of *American Idol*, and so on. Indeed, as of 1993, coverage of gay men and relevant issues by various genres and media has become rather routine. It is practically continuous and rather sympathetic. Gay men – fictional characters and real individuals – now constitute a vital part of the public discourse. The pervasiveness and commonness of this phenomenon can be illustrated with four randomly chosen cases that may elucidate the entire trend.

Running to the Flat (*Ratzim Ladira*) is a reality television game show similar to *The Amazing Race*, in which teams of two people compete against each other. The second season, which aired on prime-time on Channel 2 – the most popular TV channel – in 2005, featured a gay couple, Rami and Ronen. The winning "royal couple"[10] enjoyed outstanding enthusiasm and admiration as well as high ratings (28%, which comprise some 1.5 million viewers, watched the final episode [ibid]). The couple, both exhibiting well-built and groomed musculature, admitted that were they 'sissy boys' or effeminate they would have not been able to win (*Yedioth Ahronoth*, October 21, 2005). Yet, their very participation in the game attests to the unproblematic – at least, from the point of view of the producers and the audience – integration of gay men within the national mediascape. Nevertheless, their appearance and behavior ignited mayhem within the lesbigay community due to what some critics called their emulation and imitation of the heterosexual norms, thereby invalidating all other types of homosexuals.[11]

Another text can illustrate the ease with which gay characters are immersed within the mediascape. *Yossi & Jagger* is a romantic drama (directed by gay filmmaker Eytan Fox, 2002) about 'forbidden love' between two army officers, who try to find some solace from the daily routine of war. Yossi commands a troop of soldiers. In secrecy, he leads a passionate relationship with his second-in-command officer, Lior, who is nicknamed Jagger for his rock-star-like handsomeness (Wikipedia). The film was screened around the country for many weeks and also on prime-time TV to sympathetic responses and also won several prizes from, among others, the Israeli Television Academy (2003).

Like in the previous example, a mere handful of lesbigay critics resisted and challenged the huge economic, artistic, and popular success, which the movie has attained among both lesbigay and heterosexual audiences. These hard-to-satisfy critics denounced *Yossi & Jagger* because it, *inter alia*, reinforced the prevalent struggles to promote the visibility of gay men who are "like everybody else," and thus dare find a place within "the heterosexual national consensus" (Yosef, 2005, p. 285). These images bolster "the 'normalcy' of the community's members and their 'good citizenship' [... and do] not question the hegemonic position of those institutions or their privilege of deciding who would be or who was a proper national subject. [...] The struggle for visibility, then, raises critical questions, such as whose visibility, in whose eyes, and at what price" (ibid.). These vehement critiques, however, do not diminish the fact that gay men have indeed become part and parcel of "everybody."

A third example for the routinized inclusion of gay-related issues within the national media is a news item on the front page section of *Ha'Aretz* entitled "Gay internet sites dry up the bars" (July 8, 2008). The reporter explains a current phenomenon of closing down of commercial venues in Tel Aviv catering to the lesbigay crowd by offering two reasons: The "bourgeoisification" (sic.) of lesbigay couples who tend to go out less and the boom of "matchmaking" sites that render these bars – that constituted the hub of lesbigay life for many decades (Hooker, 1965) – obsolete. The editorial decision to publish an analysis of ostensibly intra-communal affairs in the hard news section of this prestigious daily substantiates the complementary trends of co-optation by media organizations and lesbigays' willingness to be immersed.

But, on the very same page, a large-print headline reads: "More and more gay men in Israel and the Western world prefer to have casual unprotected sex. This may be one of the reasons for the sharp increase in AIDS cases in the past year." This lengthy article unabashedly conveys that gay men are to be blamed for their illicit and surely irrational practices and consequently for spreading HIV. In other words, its rhetoric reiterates the image of the homosexual as dangerous to himself and society at large (Klin, 2008). As I explained earlier, qualitative symbolic annihilation can and does occur parallel to integrative attempts.

Contemporary lesbigay actors on the public stage are quite frequently members of mainstream Israeli society. Many offer a rather coherent image of wholesomeness, at least in respect to their civil and social conventional "duties." They are more often than not individuals who have settled into a heterosexual-like pattern of familism, thereby conveying a message of integration and consensual "normalcy." The following is an emblematic expression. In his weekly column in *Ha'Aretz Friday Magazine*, Avner Bernheimer refers to his life-partner as "my husband." Appropriating this term into a same-sex relationship in the mainstream publication that caused no public turmoil or negative repercussions signifies not only lesbigays' immersion but also the wider social acceptance – perhaps even by a welcoming embrace – on the part of Israeli society.

To sum up, gay men's visibility in all media and genres is manifold and varied. Stereotypical personifications of comic relief reside side by side with non-formulaic 'salt of the earth' characters hence exhibiting a full range of types. It would nonetheless be quite premature to welcome a new age of complete integration in the context of mediated texts. The yellow road of sensationalism, of which I wrote in 2000, is still applicable in 2008. Media practitioners' voyeuristic fascination with what was, until not long ago, beyond their grasp because lesbigays' lives took place behind closed closet doors, probably constitutes an impetus for their intensive coverage.

Sphericule media

In recent years national public spheres have been giving way to cultural productions of relatively homogeneous groups that converse within their own rather autonomous sphericules (Gitlin, 1998). Sphericule discourses form a primary countermeasure against hegemonic forces that prompt national media to marginalize and render some groups voiceless and invisible (Cunningham, 2001). Political mobilization, setting an independent agenda, self-empowerment, and annulling prevalent stereotypes are paramount among the means utilized to achieve a coveted social change via these "small" media (Kesheshian, 2000; Squires, 2000). In principle and by definition, means of production and ownership are in the hands of minority members, whose personal experiences and extensive contacts within the community are invaluable resources (Dahlgren, 1993). Consequently, sphericule media are characterized by staff, who are rarely paid professionals, but are motivated by commitment for their community's welfare (Riggins, 1992).

The vital and profound political and social changes delineated above have had enormous repercussions, not only in forming a communal identity, but also in triggering a sphericule discourse that called for a platform for expression. Already in 1982, the *Aguda* began publishing a journal, *Nativ Nossaf* (Another Path), published irregularly until 1994. Since the late 1980s, several men (except for two women who briefly published *Ga'ava* [Pride]) have published commercial monthly magazines, among them: *Maga'im* (Contacts) from 1988 to 1994 and *Ha'Zman Ha'Varod* (Pink Times), founded in 1996 and the only surviving magazine. CLAF published *Claf Hazak* (Strong Card) – later renamed *Pandora* – until 2005.

The Israeli lesbigay sphericule media merit a separate discussion (Kama, 2007), but for the purposes of the present paper one publication deserves special attention for it illustrates the trend of immersion within mainstream political, social, and cultural institutions and is its *par excellence* manifestation. *HaZman HaVarod* was founded by Ya'ir Qedar, a radical gay activist, who single-handedly edited and published the monthly magazine until he sold it to the *Aguda* in 1999. Under the new auspices it soon became rather conservative (Kanyas, 2008). In the early 2000s *HaZman HaVarod* was purchased by Schocken group, a national media conglomerate, who appointed a heterosexual woman as its chief editor. In 2008 the Schocken publishers changed its name to *Ha'ir BeVarod* (The City in Pink) in order to be in line with its other local magazines. This is not so surprising bearing in mind that the Tel Aviv municipality subsidized *HaZman HaVarod* in the late 1990s. Furthermore, *Ha'aretz*, which is also published by the Schocken group, used to distribute the paper to its subscribers to celebrate Gay Pride every June for several years. On the other hand, this phenomenon is in striking discrepancy with the situation elsewhere, in particular the United States. Gross and Woods (1999) delineate the historical developments of the American lesbigay press. One attribute of the American history stands in a decided conflict with the *HaZman HaVarod* account. While North American authorities have taken detrimental actions against some of the lesbigay publications (Jackson, 1999), the Israeli establishment never infringed on any lesbigay channel of communication. There has never been any attempt to censor a publication or interfere in any way with this sphericule. On the contrary, one of the most powerful and mainstream media organizations straightforwardly co-opted the magazine, which today is the only medium of sphericule discourse aside from several internet sites.[12] It seems that the latter means of communication – thanks to their multifold functions, such as news reports, chats, and, above all, meeting sexual partners – have made the printed medium redundant and to a large extent demoted it into a superfluous status.

Family

On the personal level, immersion within mainstream society is manifested in two complementary trends: Marriage and having children (whether bio-logical or adopted). Lesbigays tend more than ever before to first join a partner and then become parents. This development is mirrored in adam-ant struggles to be officially and formally acknowledged by the state, and vice versa: The political efforts for full recognition of same-sex couples and their (biological or adopted) off-spring mirror a prevalent and still growing tendency in the social reality. In recent years, political struggles have shifted their focus from the lesbigay individual (e.g. abolition of the sodomy statute, addition of anti-discrimination provisions at the workplace, and the like) to the family (including couples). The latter has become the sole target of social change and signifies the veritable aspiration to fully join mainstream society that is considered to be still very familistic. Indeed, ours is a society that attaches an exceptionally high degree of importance and value to the family unit. Demographic data illustrate this statement especially in compar-ison with other post-industrial societies. It is accepted among sociologists (Fogiel-Bijaoui, 2002; Kulik, 2004) that familism has persevered because religious laws regarding marital status have been institutionalized and also because the family institute is considered both a "national asset" and a basis for the normative collective identity. The normative family model is quite predominant, although processes of post-modernism have yielded new mod-els (e.g. same-sex parents) that are nowadays gaining a foothold.

Lesbigays have not lagged behind the all-encompassing apotheosis of the family. During the pre-pride era, homosexual identity and 'lifestyle' were not feasible options for one's formation of self, therefore many individuals chose – this verb might be an ironic euphemism – to marry an opposite-sex partner while the very idea of a same-sex family was inconceivable. The above delineated processes of the immersion era marked a watershed in this context. As of the late 1990s – subsequent to the success of the Danilowitz precedent, to be more precise – there have been quite a few litigation cases that boldly demanded that same-sex couples and their children should be treated and considered by the state authorities like heterosexual ones. These highly visible cases naturally indicate eagerness in the social reality where growing numbers of lesbigay individuals choose – in the fullest sense of the word – to partner and become parents. Due to brevity constraints, only a handful of noteworthy cases will be now presented. At any rate, the following illustrations are not supposed to depict the highly extensive and quite intense deliberations within academic circles and on both mass and sphericule media, but only to exemplify the centrality of the family in contemporary lesbigay community.

In 2000 the Supreme Court acknowledged the right of two lesbians (Ruth and Nicole Brener-Kadish) to be registered as mothers for each other's children. The decision was contested by the State but was reaffirmed in January 2005 when the Supreme Court stated that although it does not wish to acknowledge the status of the same-sex family unit, it does accept the couple's right to mutually adopt their spouse's children. In February 2006 another lesbian couple (Tal and Avital Yaros-Hakak) were the first same-sex couple to actually adopt each other's children. To date, several dozen other lesbian couples were granted the same adoption right (Goldstein and Spilman, 2005). On February 10, 2008, the Attorney General released his approval for same-sex couples to also adopt non-biological children.

The Supreme Court intervened in another attempt to bolster same-sex couples' rights to be formally recognized and thus implicitly to be accepted by and immersed into the mainstream social fabric. On November 21, 2006, it ruled in favor of five gay couples who were wedded in Toronto, Canada and instructed the Ministry of Interior to register them in the Population Register as married (Yakir and Berman, 2008). Although no exact figures are available, it would be reasonable to estimate that several dozen lesbigays now possess identity cards that confirm their marital status.[13]

In the context of legal petitions, two related cases highlight the centrality of the family unit from another angle. In November 2004, the Nazareth Regional Court ruled that same-sex couples are entitled to enjoy the full inheritance benefits applicable so far exclusively to heterosexual couples, notwithstanding the legal language that states that only "a man and a woman" who conduct domestic partnership (i.e. not a married couple) are entitled to such rights. That is to say that kinship should denote same-sex partners even when the law explicitly refers to heterosexual couples. Incidentally, at the same time the Tel Aviv Family Court ruled that it does have the authority to validate a domestic partnership contract between two men. It declared that the legal term "family" is to be assessed according to the nature of the relationship regardless of gender.

Familism is indeed a prevalent and desired objective manifested in diverse layers of social life. Bat-Kol can serve as another illustration. The organization was founded by ten lesbians in 2005 "to allow women to fulfill both their religious and lesbian identity; to make it possible for women to live in loving relationships, to raise children without deception, but nevertheless stay committed to their religion."[14] Today Bat-Kol has grown and includes roughly a hundred women, most of whom have established a same-sex family and raise children. This attests once again to the primacy and dominance of the institution of family that characterizes not only religious lesbians but all walks of life of the lesbigay community. One final illustration is the recent plan to establish a kindergarten at the lesbigay Municipal Center in Tel Aviv to be targeted at the growing segment of same-sex families. But, above all, the spearhead of this phenomenon is best manifested in the arena of legal and judicial struggles of the past decade and a half.

The centrality of issues concerning the recognition of couples and families constitutes a forthright site of contested and heated discussions among both lay persons – lesbigay or not – and academics. Critical questions revolve around several themes, among which two bear major political consequences: Do lesbigays really want or need to emulate the heterosexual institutions of marriage and family? To what extent will these institutions and the entire social fabric disintegrate? Regardless of the opinions about the issues of couplehood and parenthood *per se* and/or the court decisions in these cases, these voices corroborate that the immersion trend is very much a fact that cannot be denied or overlooked. To support this general conclusion, I conducted a simple breakdown of a database compiled of all published academic papers (including master's theses and doctoral dissertations) and books written in Hebrew by Israeli scholars about lesbigay issues in this country since 1979 to the present. Of ninety-three items, nineteen (20%) focus on various aspects of couplehood, marriage, and/or parenthood. In other words, one-fifth of all research conducted in Israel in the past three decades has been motivated by questions related to same-sex families.

Conclusion: Struggling to Overcome Exclusion

The various incidents and cases delineated so far are indices of a 'grand-narrative' of the fundamental trajectory of immersion or mainstreaming of the vast majority of lesbigay individuals and organizations in Israel in the past dozen years. Normative citizenship is deemed proper and fought for by lesbigays who have been traditionally relegated to a liminal position. They have been negotiating with legal, judicial, and other societal institutions in order to secure a set of rights and entitlements (e.g. marriage and adoption) and obligations (e.g. military service) within the given system. These efforts will ultimately position them on a par with non-lesbigay citizens and thus will mend exclusionary practices of the past. In other words, citizenship is perceived as the solution for this minority group to enjoy the full benefits the state allocates to its "loyal" and "respected" citizens. So far, it seems that the state has indeed – albeit painfully piecemeal and obdurately – acknowledged lesbigays' rights and conceded to grant them their share of the national symbolic and material goods.

This does not inevitably imply that all Israeli homosexual men and women maintain and subscribe to this trend[15], yet the overall narrative is in fact quite self-evident. In response to heteronormative – that is, according to Foucault, an all-encompassing ideology that perceives heterosexuality to be the only option for proper human conduct (Spargo, 1999) – pressures and processes of subordination and negation, they express a yearning to be included within the "normal" social fabric not marked as "Other." This is conceivably a counter-reaction to coercive exclusionary practices. Living on the invisible and muted edge of "proper" society harms one's sense of human worthiness. Therefore, becoming one with the socially constructed and culturally received center is the yearned-for objective of those who were abject pariahs until not very long ago. Life within the cultural, social, and political consensus safeguards one's ontological security and is thus perceived as priceless. This ideology of full integration is achieved via minimizing the differences between minority and majority members.

In sum, Israeli lesbigays wish to abandon the social periphery, where they were conceptualized as second-rate citizens, at best. A great need to belong refutes life in the social fringes. Being situated in the consensual social center is perceived to be not only respectful, but seems to alleviate the prices one pays when situated in the social, cultural, and legal borderland, where one is a nomad wandering between territories in none of which she or he feels at home or accepted as worthy of a home. Consequently, immersion within the center – namely, the coveted home – yields palpable benefits, be they civic, monetary, or symbolic.

Notes

1 The anti-sodomy law did not refer to lesbians or sexual practices between women; therefore some of my assessments do not include women.
2 It should be noted that this paper refers only to Jewish citizens.
3 A popular explanation for the demise of CLAF as well as more radical-oriented groups where lesbians constituted the major force (e.g. *Kvissa Sh'hora*) points to the burgeoning, not to say overwhelming, trend of motherhood. That is to say that many lesbians are nowadays more concerned with their domestic responsibilities and familial tasks and thus allocate fewer resources toward the public sphere. At the same time, this trend probably facilitated the founding of *Bat-Kol* (see further on).
4 Proud translates into the Hebrew word *gĕ-ĕ*, which, due to its alliteration, sometimes denotes "gay."
5 This is the first time lesbians are mentioned in an Israeli official document.
6 Due to conciseness constraints, homophobia and its manifestations cannot be adequately reported here (for further information, see Pizmony-Levy, Kama, Shilo and Lavee, 2008).
7 Some of its gay leaders have joined the Labor party in the mid-2000s. No formal party caucus is currently active.
8 It should be stressed that I refer only to individuals whose lesbigay identity is publicly acknowledged. No doubt there have always been lesbigay candidates and/or representatives on both national and municipal levels whose homosexual orientation was not disclosed in the public sphere.
9 See, for example, online. Available at www.nytimes.com/2005/03/31/international/worldspecial/31gay.html (accessed 8 August 2010).
10 Online. Available at www.nrg.co.il/online/5/ART/995/634.html [in Hebrew] (accessed 7 July 2008).
11 Online. Available at www.gogay.co.il/content/article.asp?id=3591 [in Hebrew] (accessed 8 August 2010).
12 Other media – a few radio programs and one short-lived TV show – operated briefly throughout the 1990s (Kama, 2007).
13 It should be clear that the civil law does not recognize a marriage not conducted

by an Orthodox rabbi according to the Halachic law. In other words, same-sex couples must be wedded outside the country and be registered only *post factum*.

14 This excerpt is quoted from *Bat-Kol*'s official site (Online. Available at: www.bat-kol.org/?page_id=51 accessed 8 August 2010).

15 Gross (2002), for example, writes that this approach "is problematic because it makes equal treatment conditional on one's achieving the goal of being 'like everybody else,' and thus tickets of admission are granted only to homosexuals who can closely fit themselves to the model of standard masculinity" (p. 176).

References

Almog, O. (2000) *The Sabra: the Creation of the New Jew*, trans. H. Watzman, Berkeley: University of California Press.

Biale, D. (1992) *Eros and the Jews: From Biblical Israel to Contemporary America*, New York: Basic Books.

Blank, Y. (2003) 'No homeland for homos: globalization, spatial disintegration, and the lesbigay ghetto', *Te'orya U'Bikoret*, 23: 83–111. [in Hebrew]

Caspi, D. and Limor, Y. (1999) *The In/Outsiders: The Media in Israel*, Cresskill, NJ: Hampton Press.

Cooper, R. L. (1985) 'Language and social stratification among the Jewish population in Israel', in J. A. Fishman (ed.) *Reading in the Sociology of Jewish Languages*, Leiden: E. J. Brill.

Cunningham, S. (2001) 'Media as "Public Sphericules" for Diasporic Communities', *International Journal of Cultural Studies*, 4(3): 131–47.

Dahlgren, P. (1993) 'Introduction', in P. Dahlgren and C. Sparks (eds.) *Communication and Citizenship: Journalism and the Public Sphere*, London: Routledge.

Dario (1992) 'Contradictions and miseries of the gay ghetto', in S. Likosky (ed.) *Coming Out: An Anthology of International Gay and Lesbian Writings*, New York: Pantheon Books.

Duberman, M. B. (1993) *Stonewall*, New York: Dutton.

Dyer, R. (1993) *The Matter of Images: Essays on Representations*, London & New York: Routledge.

Epstein, S. (1988) 'Moral contagion and the medicalization of gay identity: AIDS in historical perspective', *Research in Law, Deviance and Social Control*, 9: 36–47.

Fogiel-Bijaoui, S. (2002) 'Familism, postmodernity and the state: the case of Israel', *The Journal of Israeli History*, 21: 38–62.

Foucault, M. (1990[1976]) *The History of Sexuality, Vol. I: An Introduction*, trans. R. Hurley, Harmondsworth: Penguin.

Freud, S. (1974[1905]) 'Three essays on the theory of sexuality', in J. Starchey (ed.) *The Standard Edition of the Complete Psychological Works of Sigmund Freud*, London: Hogarth.

Gamson, J. (1995) 'Must identity movements self-destruct? a queer dilemma', *Social Problems*, 42(3): 390–407.

Garnets, L. D. and Kimmel, D. C. (eds) (1993) *Psychological Perspectives on Lesbian and Gay Male Experiences*, New York: Columbia University Press.

Gerbner, G. and Gross, L. (1976) 'Living with television: the violence profile', *Journal of Communication*, 26(2): 173–99.

Gitlin, T. (1998) 'Public Sphere or Public Sphericules?', in T. Liebes and J. Curran (eds) *Media, Ritual and Identity*, pp. 168–74. London: Routledge.

Gluzman, M. (2007) *The Zionist Body: Nationalism, Gender and Sexuality in the New Hebrew Literature*, Tel Aviv: HaKibbutz HaMeuchad. [in Hebrew]

Goldstein, O. and Spilman, V. (2005) 'Only one mother? regarding the ruling in the case of Yaros-Hakak *vs.* the State Attorney', *He'Arat Din*, B(2): 92–111. [in Hebrew]

Greenberg, B. S., Mastro, D. and Brand, J. E. (2002) 'Minorities and the mass media: television into the 21st century', in J. Bryant and D. Zillmann (eds) *Media Effects: Advances in Theory and Research*, 2nd edn, Mahwah, NJ: Lawrence Erlbaum.

Greenberg, B. S. and Brand, J. E. (1994) 'Minorities and the mass media: 1970s to 1990s', in J. Bryant & D. Zillmann (eds) *Media Effects: Advances in Theory and Research*, Hillsdale, NJ: Lawrence Erlbaum Associates.

Gross, A. (2002) 'Sexuality, masculinity, army, and citizenship: comparative perspectives on lesbigay military service', in D. Barak-Erez (ed.) *Military, Society, and the Law*, Tel Aviv: Ramot [in Hebrew]

Gross, A. M. (2001) 'Challenges to compulsory heterosexuality: recognition and non-recognition of same-sex couples in Israeli law', in R. Wintemute and M. Andenaes (eds) *Legal Recognition of Same-Sex Partnerships: A Study of National, European and International Law*, Oxford: Hart.

Gross, L. (2001) 'The paradoxical politics of media representation', *Critical Studies in Media Communication*, 18(1): 114–19.

Gross, L. (1997) 'From South Beach to SoBe', in S. J. Drucker and G. Gumpert (eds) *Voices in the Street: Explorations in Gender, Media, and Public Space*, Cresskill, NJ: Hampton Press.

Gross, L. and Woods, J. D. (1999) 'In our own voices: the lesbian and gay press', in L. Gross and J. D. Woods (eds) *The Columbia Reader on Lesbians and Gay Men in Media, Society, and Politics*, New York: Columbia University Press.

Harel, A. (2000) 'The rise and fall of the Israeli gay legal revolution', *Columbia Human Rights Law Review*, 31(2): 443–71.

Hazleton, L. (1977) *Israeli Women: The Reality Behind the Myths*, New York: Simon & Schuster.

Hooker, E. (1965) 'Male homosexuals and their "worlds"', in J. Marmor (ed.) *Sexual Inversion: The Multiple Roots of Homosexuality*, New York & London: Basic Books.

Horowitz, D. & Lissak, M. (1977) *The Origins of the Israeli Polity*, Tel Aviv: Am Oved. [In Hebrew].

Jackson, E. (1999) 'Flaunting it! a decade of gay journalism from *The Body Politic*', in L. Gross & J. D. Woods (eds) *The Columbia Reader on Lesbians and Gay Men in Media, Society, and Politics*, New York: Columbia University Press.

Kama, A. (2007) 'Israeli gay men's consumption of lesbigay media: "I'm not alone in this business"', in K. G. Barnhurst (ed.) *Media Queered: Visibility and its Discontents*. New York: Peter Lang.

Kama, A. (2005a) *"One Human Mass, One Israeli Nation": Groups' Identities Formation in Letters-to-the-*Ha'Aretz*-Editor*, Tel Aviv: Tel Aviv University Press [in Hebrew].

Kama, A. (2005b) 'An unrelenting mental press: Israeli gay men's ontological duality and its discontent', *The Journal of Men's Studies*, 13(2): 169–84.

Kama, A. (2002) 'The quest for inclusion: Jewish-Israeli gay men's perceptions of gays in the media', *Feminist Media Studies*, 2(2): 195–212.

Kama, A. (2000) 'From *terra incognita* to *terra firma*: the logbook of the voyage of gay men's community into the Israeli public sphere', *Journal of Homosexuality*, 38(4): 133–62.

Kanyas, Y. (2008) '"My pride is not his pride": discourse of oppression, threat, and intimacy in the Israeli gay and lesbian press', unpublished thesis, The Hebrew University in Jerusalem. [in Hebrew]

Kaplan, D. (2002) *Brothers and Others in Arms: The Making of Love and War in Israeli Combat Units*, New York: Harrington Park Press.

Katz, E., Haas, H. and Gurevitch, M. (1997) '20 years of television in Israel: are there long-run effects on values, social connectedness, and cultural practices?', *Journal of Communication*, 47(2): 3–20.

Kesheshian, F. (2000) 'Acculturation, communication, and the US mass media: the experience of an Iranian immigrant', *The Howard Journal of Communication*, 11: 93–106.

Klin, A. (2008) 'Between myths and science: The AIDS narrative in the Israeli press (1981–2007) as a cultural construction of a disease', *Media Frames*, 2: 50–85. [in Hebrew].

Kulik, L. (2004) 'Transmission of attitudes regarding family life from parents to adolescents in Israel', *Families in Society*, 85(3): 345–54.

Lemish, D. (2000) 'The whore and the other: Israeli images of female immigrants from the former USSR', *Gender and Society*, 14(2): 333–49.

Levy. Y. (2007) 'The right to fight: a conceptual framework for the analysis of recruitment policy toward gays and lesbians', *Armed Forces & Society*, 33(2): 186–202.

Lissak, M. (1988) 'Various schools of perceiving the Jewish settlement', in N. Graetz (ed.), *Perspectives on Culture and Society in Israel*, Tel Aviv: The Open University. [In Hebrew].

McDarrah, F. W. and McDarrah, T. S. (1994) *Gay Pride: Photographs from Stonewall to Today*, Chicago: A Cappella Books.

Misgav, C. (2008) 'The urban space as viewed by gays and lesbians in Tel-Aviv-Jaffa' unpublished thesis, Israel Institute of Technology.

Pizmony-Levy, O, Kama, A., Shilo, G. and Lavee, S. (2008) 'Do my teachers care I'm gay?: Israeli lesbigay school students' experiences at their schools', *Journal of Gay and Lesbian Youth*, 5(2): 33–61.

Ram, H. and Yadgar, Y. (2008) '"New" racism and "old" racism: the case of *Shinui* party', in Y. Shenhav and Y. Yonah (eds), *Racism in Israel*, Jerusalem: Van Leer Institute. [In Hebrew].

Riggins, S. H. (1992) 'The promise and limits of ethnic minority media', in S. H. Riggins (ed.) *Ethnic Minority Media: An International Perspective*, Newsbury Park, CA: Sage.

Sedgwick, E. K. (1993) 'How to bring your kids up gay: the war on effeminate boys', in M. Warner (ed.) *Fear of a Queer Planet*, Minneapolis, MN: University of Minnesota.

Sender, K. (2001) 'Gay readers, consumers, and a dominant gay habitus: 25 Years of the *Advocate* magazine', *Journal of Communication*, 51(1): 73–99.

Sion, L. (1997) *Images of Manhood among Combat Soldiers: Military Service in the Israeli Infantry as a Rite of Initiation from Youthhood to Adulthood*, Jerusalem: The Hebrew University. [In Hebrew]

Spargo, T. (1999) *Foucault and Queer Theory*. Cambridge: Icon Books.

Spivak, D. and Yonai, Y. (1996) 'Law and homosexuals in Israel: myth and reality', *Tat Tarbut*, 2: 39–41. [In Hebrew]

Squires, C. R. (2000) 'Black talk radio: defining community needs and identity', *The Harvard International Journal of Press/Politics*, 5(2): 73–95.

Tuchman, G. (1978) 'Introduction: the symbolic annihilation of women by the mass media', in G. Tuchman, A. K. Daniels and J. Bennett (eds), *Hearth and Home: Images of Women in the Mass Media*, New York: Oxford University Press.

Weimann, G. (2000) *Communicating Unreality: Modern Media and the Reconstruction of Reality*, Thousand Oaks, CA: Sage.

Weston, K. (1995) 'Get thee to a big city: sexual imaginary and the great gay migration', *GLQ*, 2: 253–77.

Yakir, D. and Berman, Y. (2008) 'Same-sex marriages: is it really necessary? is it really desirable?', *Ma'asei Mishpat*, A: 160–77. [in Hebrew]

Yonai, Y. (1998) 'The law concerning homosexual orientation in Israel: between history and sociology', *Mishpat & Mimshal*, 4(2): 531–86 [In Hebrew].

Yosef, R. (2005) 'The national closet: gay Israel in *Yossi and Jagger*', *GLQ*, 11(2): 283–300.

10 Inward turns
Citizenship, solidarity and exclusion

Guy Ben-Porat

The Israeli-Palestinian peace process in the early 1990s offered a glimpse of hope also to the relations between Israel and its Arab citizens. The peace process, once accomplished, could change the security framework within which the minority was perceived and provide an opportunity of equality for the minority. Thus, a liberal framework of citizenship could end all discriminations and inequalities and allow the integration of Arab citizens. The developments since 1993, and especially since 2000, demonstrate not only the fragility of the peace process but also the limited possibility of a liberal citizenship in Israel. As the developments indicate, the rejection of the Jewish majority of a liberal state "of all its citizens" is matched by new voices of Arab-Palestinian citizens who demand recognition as a national minority.

The Israeli-Palestinian negotiations, between Israel and the PLO, defined as their goal (somewhat vaguely and without specifying borders) a two-state solution that would supposedly end Israeli occupation of the West Bank and Gaza. But, what underscored Israeli policymakers' strategy was also a "demographic trade-off" in which territorial compromise would not only end the occupation but also guarantee the status of a Jewish state. This "demographic engineering" (McGarry, 1998) intends to redraw borders in order to ensure a Jewish majority within Israel so it will be able to maintain its Jewish identity. The use of this trade-off in Israeli political discourse, however, has negative implications for the status of Palestinian citizens whose aspiration for equality are to be denied. The use of the slogan "we are here, they are there" in election campaigns to describe the goal of the peace process indicated that the Jewish majority has no intention of negotiating the status of the Palestinian minority.

Arab citizens seem to either give up on the hope for equality based on a liberal model of citizenship or reject it as insufficient. Between December 2006 and May 2007 several "future vision documents" composed by Arab intellectuals and public figures were published, demanding what they described as the transformation of Israel from an ethnic to a democratic state (Jamal, 2008). The documents provide a harsh critique of the Zionist ideology and the State of Israel in relation to the Palestinian nation, citizens of Israel and Palestinians in the territories, and call upon the State of Israel to adopt principles of corrective and distributive justice vis-à-vis the Palestinian minority (Jamal, 2008). It is of special significance that the writers of the documents chose to refer to themselves as "Palestinian Citizens of Israel." Consequently, what the documents raise, among other things, are demands by a minority defined not only in terms of individual equality but also in terms of collective rights and recognition that stretch beyond liberal concepts.

The limits of the liberal model of citizenship will be discussed in this paper against the actual developments in the past two decades: the failed peace process, the growing use of demographic arguments and the growing frustrations of the Arab/Palestinian citizens of Israel. Specifically, I will outline three interrelated developments: a turning inward of Israeli Jewish society and a discourse of unity, the continued political marginalization of Palestinian citizens through the use of demographic arguments that underscore the latest partition efforts – the separation fence and the withdrawal from Gaza and the attempts of Palestinian/Arabs to re-assert their struggle in the name of a national minority. Combined, these developments render the liberal model of citizenship impossible and insufficient.

Minorities and the State

Many states in the contemporary world face the challenges of national minorities demanding to change "the rules of the game." Nationalist claims, as Keating demonstrates, have to be understood in context as they are made in relation "to a particular state form and balance of political and social forces and face a particular array of opportunities and barriers in each case." Therefore, nationalist claims can be, and have been, negotiated, managed and compromised (2001: 23). The saliency of conflicts within states has led to a scholarly focus on ethnic identities and to the conclusion that ethnic nationalism or politicized ethnicity is a major ideological legitimator and deligitimator of states, regimes and governments (Rothschild, 1981).

Cultural diversity and ethno-national politics are common to most contemporary states who, contrary to their image of the homogeneity, must contend with a multicultural and at times multinational reality (Connor, 1994; Tully, 2002). The growing reality of multinational and/or multicultural democracies, composed of cultural, linguistic, religious and ethnic minorities who struggle for and against distinctive forms of recognition and accommodation, creates new challenges for the democratic regime (Tully, 2002). The demands of ethnic minorities present an especially acute dilemma for "ethnic states" that provide a national home for a dominant ethnic group "trapped" between commitment to the dominant nation and to democracy (Rouhana, 1998) but also to liberal democracies where dominant majorities are challenged by new demands of immigrant and indigenous groups to change the existing order.

The focus on the characteristics, attitudes and behavior of individuals and groups in the study of ethnic politics often misses the crucial elements of the "playing field" that institutional theory stresses (Thalen and Steinmo, 1992). Thus, it is not only the desires of individuals and ideologies but the context in which those develop and are expressed. An institutional framework – that takes into account the structures of the state's and civic society's institutions and their role in cementing, creating, or attenuating cultural or identity politics – can help us understand the development of ethnic politics (Crawford, 1998). Citizenship, in spite of its claims of equality and universality, often delineates a hierarchy between and within social groups in the state. Consequently, on the one hand, it structures the opportunities afforded by the state to different people, included, excluded and marginalized by the definition of citizenship and, on the other hand, it impacts ethnic identity and its political mobilization (Brass, 1985; Rothschild, 1981: 2).

The inclusion and exclusion patterns and practices are part of the legitimacy strategy of the state. Its legitimacy, when dominated by one nation, depends on its ability to manage differences and contain their politicization. This management is often based on a "hierarchy" of divisions and a compatible strategy of exclusion/inclusion based on different measures of assimilation, co-option, oppression or indifference. As such, divisions can be played off against each other, assimilating one group by demarcation of another. The wider political manifestations are "multiple traditions" of citizenship within a single polity that entails a series of inclusions and exclusions and, thereby, social stratification (Shafir and Peled, 2002: 7). Some selective inclusions can be achieved as the state develops new practices of inclusion and co-opts groups previously left out. But, these exclusions can be re-invoked when the state is challenged by internal conflicts or external pressures and chooses to forge cohesion via the exclusion of some group not central to that particular conflict (Marx, 2002).

It is within this context that majorities and minorities develop their ideologies and political platforms. From the minority perspective their status can be changed either by a liberal model of citizenship that would turn the state into a neutral entity and provide equality for all citizens, regardless of their ethnicity or, by recognition, that would provide it with some autonomy. The majority, on the other hand, would seek to preserve its status and, under some circumstances be willing to sacrifice territory for homogeneity. Accordingly, the idea of partition, if conflict erupts, can be adopted (at times with international support) as a lesser of two evils (Mearshimer and Van-Evara, 1995). A disputed territory, according to the logic of partition, is replaced by a rational division that creates homogeneous communities. But, historically, in most actual cases of partition, successor states were not ethnically "pure," often leaving minorities frustrated by boundaries they perceived as unjust (Berg and Ben-Porat, 2006). The continued existence of minorities within states, on the one hand, and the strengthened majority nationalism expressed in the desire for partition and homogeneity, might strengthen tensions between the majority and minorities. Thus, the expectations of national homogeneity might disappoint the majority, alienate the minority and render the possibility of liberal citizenship evermore unlikely.

As will be presented below, this was the trajectory in Israel where the resolution of an external conflict was underscored by the mobilization of national unity and demographic arguments. While initially, the resolution of the conflict seemed to carry a promise for the minority, suffering from the implications of the conflict, its the logic of a "Jewish state" had adverse effects for the national minority. Specifically, the presence of Israel in the occupied territories of the West Bank and Gaza was presented by policymakers and supporters of peace as a "demographic threat" to the "Jewish State." The logical conclusion they drew was that Israel must withdraw from the territories in order to secure a solid Jewish majority within the state's boundaries. While this strategy was at most partially effective vis-à-vis the Jewish majority, it alienated the Palestinian citizen minority who came to realize that the peace process holds limited promise for a constructive discussion of Israel's citizenship regime and the status of the Palestinian minority.

The Palestinian Citizens of Israel

The Jewish–Arab divide is considered the deepest schism in Israeli society. Arab citizens are a non-dominant, non-assimilating, working-class minority and are considered by the Jewish majority as dissident and enemy-affiliated (Smooha, 1989: 218). For their part, Palestinian citizens, in a recent document, described Israel as an "ethnocratic state" that denies full citizenship to the minority. Since *el-nakba* (literally: tragedy, the term used by Palestinians for the war of 1948), Palestinian Arabs have suffered from "extreme structural discrimination policies, national oppression, military rule that lasted until 1966, land confiscation policy, unequal budget allocation, rights discrimination and threats of transfer" (Future Vision, 2006). The demands for equality and representation, or individual and group rights, challenge some of the basic foundations of the state and encounter widespread resistance from the majority, who are committed to the idea of a Jewish state.

The definition of Israel as a "Jewish State," on the one hand, and its conflict with native Palestinians and the wider Arab world, on the other hand, have significant ramifications for the status of Palestinian Arabs within Israel. The Jewish character of the state, almost a consensus among the Jewish majority, implies that Palestinian Arabs are citizens of a state whose symbols reflect the Jewish majority's culture and are exclusive in nature. Beyond the symbolic issues, the preference of Jews over non-Jews is anchored in laws that deal with immigration, use of state land and semi-governmental institutions, as well as in Israel's basic laws that anchor the Jewish character of the state (Rouhana, 1998). The exclusion of Arabs is justified by an ethno-republican discourse of citizenship (Peled, 1992) in which Jewish ethnicity is mandatory to be part of the community and contributions to the common good determines one's status in that community. Arab citizens are exempt from military service, considered the most significant contribution to the common good, and, therefore, cannot count as "good citizens." Given that many social rights in Israel are tied to the performance of military service, the lower status of Arabs is excused by their non-contribution.

The exemption of Palestinian Arabs from military service is the outcome of the wider conflict and the state's perception of the Palestinian Arabs as a "fifth column." From the end of the war in 1948 until 1966, in spite of their formal citizenship, Palestinian Arabs were placed under military rule that limited their movement. The gradual relaxation of Israeli policies towards Arab citizens has not diminished the social gaps between them and the Jewish majority, nor has it eased their economic, social and political marginalization (Gavison and Abu-Ria, 1999; Lewin-Epstein and Semyonov, 1993; Lustik, 1985). Specifically, Arab citizens suffer from higher rates of poverty, low quality of public services and are underrepresented in the public sector.

The politicization of Palestinian citizens was translated into various struggles designed to achieve individual equality and/or struggles for collective recognition. While individual equality according to some analysts (for example: Smooha, 1992) can be achieved within the Jewish definition of the state, collective claims of recognition (described as "Palestinization") challenge the foundations of the state. The demands, however, seem to interact as the failure to achieve individual equality could be a contributor to the consolidation of a Palestinian identity and collective claims, especially among the younger generation. The solidarity of Palestinian citizens with the Palestinians in the occupied territories was almost always expressed within the confines of the law. The former have consistently advocated a solution of "two states" in which they remain citizens of Israel but demanded widespread reforms, namely, the annulment of its Jewish character that would allow them to integrate or provide them with some form of cultural autonomy (Ghanem, 2000).

The Israeli–Palestinian conflict, on the one hand, influenced the largely negative and suspicious attitudes of Jewish Israelis towards Palestinian citizens and, on the other hand, presented a dilemma for Palestinian citizens, who were torn between their interests as a minority within a Jewish state seeking integration and their commitment to their brethren's plight. Integration, in other words, is held back not only by the Jewish majority's exclusion but also by the Palestinian minority's difficulty integrating into a state that holds Palestinians in the occupied territories under military rule. Accordingly, peace between Israel and the Palestinians, it was believed, could relieve Israel's security problem and, consequently, provide greater acceptance for Arab integration. In addition, it could also solve the Arab citizens' moral dilemma. Indeed, research findings in the mid-1990s, when the peace process was in gear and Rabin's government made important overtures to the Arab population, especially in budget allocations designed to narrow inequalities, revealed "growing integration into Israeli society and politics on the one hand, and a growing distance from Palestinian identity and politics on the other" (Smooha, 1998).

But, as will be elaborated upon below, the hopes that peace would change the relation between the minority and the majority were short-lived. First, the difficulties and eventual collapse of the peace process re-created the security dilemma and possibly worsened it, as terrorism invaded the heart of Israel. Second, the forceful action and reaction of the Israeli military in the territories re-posed Arab identity dilemmas. Third, the gradual shift towards partition with the discourse of demography, internal Jewish unity and a strong commitment to a Jewish state precluded any serious discussion on the status of the Palestinian citizens. And, fourth, the deep internal (Jewish) divisions exposed in the assassination of Prime Minister Yitzhak Rabin led to various reconciliation measures that highlighted the common Jewish identity and further alienated the Palestinian citizens. Thus, with the collapse of the peace process and the eruption of violence, Jewish society has turned "inward," the divide has deepened and the status of Arab citizens has not improved.

The Promise of Peace

The Oslo Agreement between Israel and the PLO, signed in 1993, presented a framework for a peace process based on mutual recognition, co-existence, mutual dignity and security. The core proposal revolved around a partition that would supposedly answer Israel's desire to maintain its Jewish status, as well as the Palestinian demand for independence. Three significant obstacles, however, challenged the possibility of partition. First, since the 1970s, Israel had been building a system of settlements across the West Bank and Gaza, so by 1993 over 100,000 Israelis were living on the land of the supposedly would-be Palestinian state. Second, Palestinians who fled or were deported from Israel in the 1948 war were demanding, for themselves and their progeny, "the right of return" to their original homes from the refugee camps and other places of habitation. And, third, both sides lay uncompromising national and religious claims to the city of Jerusalem.

Partition was to be achieved gradually, through a series of interim agreements involving Israeli withdrawal and established cooperation. The difficult issues mentioned above, which could not be resolved at this stage, were deferred to a later stage, in the hope that the trust and cooperation built up in the interim agreements would facilitate their resolution. The difficulties of the peace process, the rising toll of violence and the growing schisms within Israel that culminated in the assassination of Prime Minister Yitzhak Rabin resulted in two conclusions among the Israeli-Jewish public. The first, which gradually developed in subsequent years, was that Israel must separate itself from the Palestinians with or without an agreement. The second was that Jewish Israelis must put their differences aside and make peace among themselves before making peace with the Palestinians. Essentially, both conclusions were about drawing boundaries and making peace from within, based on a national unity. Both strategies, however, have also had important implications for the status of the Palestinian citizens of Israel.

The Inward Turn of Israeli Society

The hopes placed on the peace process for the status of Palestinian citizens and Jewish–Arab relations were overly optimistic not only because of the instability of the process but also because of its structure. For the majority of Jewish Israelis, the peace process with the Palestinians was intended to end the occupation and the conflict that, since the Intifada of 1987, had became a burden for Israel. The slogan "we are here and they are there," used by the left to convey the need for peace, is indicative of the significance of a Jewish state for the entire spectrum of the Jewish population in Israel and of the purpose of peace for securing the future of a Jewish state. It is not accidental, therefore, that the relations between the Jewish majority and the Palestinian minority in Israel were not mentioned in the agreement and were hardly discussed, as the peace process within Israel was framed as a solution to a "demographic problem" that would re-affirm the Jewish state.

The Jewish public in Israel, however, was deeply divided in the 1990s over the Palestinian question and the future of the occupied territories. The highly charged debate over the Oslo agreements in Israel included acts of civil disobedience and political violence. The assassination of Prime Minister Rabin by a right-wing religious fanatic exposed the depth of the political division in Israel. Jewish unity, therefore, was far from a reality and was to become a political project in itself, a pre-condition for the peace process. The initial reaction to the assassination of Rabin was widespread resentment against the extreme right and the rise of support for the Labor Party. This support, however, was short-lived, as after another cycle of violence between Israelis and Palestinians in 1996 the left–right divide regained its significance and the Labor party was defeated in the elections by the anti-Oslo Likud. Many in the pro-peace camp came to the conclusion that resolving the internal, Jewish division was either more important than peace with the Palestinians, or a pre-condition to peace. Rabin's assassination triggered reconciliation initiatives and the formation of civil society institutions, often funded or supervised by the state, promoting encounters between religious and secular, and right and left. This can be described as a centripetal-centrifugal process where, on the one hand, common security and identity concerns underscored the initiatives to foster dialogue and understanding across Jewish divides but, on the other hand, with little if any concern for Jewish–Arab relations.

The rifts between right and left, secular and religious were to be ameliorated by a common denominator all sides found easier to agree upon – Jewish identity. A 1999 study (Levy et al. 1999) found that Jews in Israel wanted the state to have a Jewish character, even though they could not agree on what that term meant, but revealed "worrisome findings" on the deterioration of relations between different groups in Jewish-Israeli society.

The feeling of internal Israeli unity and that of general Jewish unity has eroded. In addition, a gradual decrease in Jewish identity among the non-religious (especially Ashkenazim and the educated) is evident and a general confusion regarding the meaning of the concept "Jewish" and the definition of the character and contents of the Jewish state. But, in spite of the above, there is no doubt that adherence to a personal Jewish identity and the quest for the crystallization of a common Jewish identity characterize the great majority of Jews in Israel. (Levy et al., 1999)

The conclusions of the research are manifested in the concerns and program of Tzav Pius, a private initiative of reconciliation, dialogue and unity. The logo of Tzav Pius imitates an army logo and its name rhymes with the Hebrew term for a conscription order, thus making "a symbolic and emotional connection between a call for arms, national duty, unity and state and between forgiveness, reconciliation, and agreement" (Yanay and Lifschitz-Oron, 2003). Its activities include encounters between religious and secular Jews in various settings where the sides come to know each other or engage in joint studies of Jewish texts. Tzav Pius also works in religious and secular schools (both systems are under state control) to promote understanding and break down stereotypes. In its brochures, beneath the army-like logo, appears the statement "We have no other country" and below, "Let's solve it together." Participants in meetings organized by Tzav Pius expressed anxiety over what they perceived as a breakdown of Jewish society and searched for a common ground against extremism using unifying concepts such as "Jewish roots," "Jewish heritage," common experiences such as army service and a common past, especially the Holocaust experience (Yanay and Lifschitz-Oron, 2003). Arabs, therefore, are not simply absent from the programs and discussions of Tzav Pius, but are external to its raison d'être. Indeed, it is their very absence that enables reconciliation and their presence that supposedly prevents it. This democratic anomaly was revealed again in another initiative of reconciliation known as the "Kinneret Declaration."

The declaration signed in October 2001 by 56 Israelis – secular, traditional, religious, left and right – received much attention and replicated the exclusion strategy described above. It was wider in scope and a more ambitious project, attempting to rewrite Israel's declaration of independence into a covenant between these groups:

In establishing the State of Israel, the founders of the state performed an extraordinary historic deed. This deed has not ended; it is at its height. The return to Zion and the effort to found a Jewish-democratic sovereign entity in the land of Israel face great challenges in the twenty-first century. We, who have joined together in this agreement, see ourselves as responsible for carrying on this deed. We see the State of Israel as our shared home. In accepting this agreement upon ourselves, we pledge to undertake all that can and must be done to guarantee the existence, strength, and moral character of this home.

The declaration was an initiative supported by the Rabin Center, dedicated to the memory of Rabin, and by the Avichai Foundation (also a sponsor of Tzav Pius) who formed the "Forum for National Responsibility." This forum, an initiative of Israel Harel, a former chair of the Settlers Council (representing the Jewish settlers of the West Bank and Gaza), was intended to be a political body independent of political parties and without active politicians. The participants described themselves as united in a feeling that something must be done. "A historical window of opportunity," "the shock of the intifada," "the minute when something must be done," "because we are one people" and "because it is a critical component of national security," were among the explanations for their willingness to commit to this project (Levi-Barzilai, 2002). Indeed, participants in the initiative described the urgency and crisis that required (Jewish) society to close its ranks and pull together:

> From day to day the feeling of crumbling apart is getting stronger, the result of several factors: a dramatic increase in socio-economic gaps; a political system based on sectoral interests and the ignoring of the common interest; a multicultural ideology that respects every sector but ignores the necessity to maintain a common cultural identity. When adding all of this to the daily threat to personal security, it is easy to understand the feeling of collision (Sheleg, 2002).

The declaration affirmed Israel's commitment to its democratic as well as its Jewish character but Arab citizens, a large minority of 20%, were not represented but were to be addressed at a "later stage." Yael Tamir, one of the founders of Peace Now, a former minister in Barak's government and a philosopher renowned for her work on liberal nationalism (and since 2006 the Minister of Education) explained that the absence of Arabs was necessary:

> "I understood that if we begin with Jews and Arabs, the break up – not between us and the Arabs, but between me and the right wing people, among us – would come quickly. We agreed that right after the Kinneret Declaration we would turn to a dialogue with the Arabs" (Levi-Barzilai, 2002).

The declaration, however, left limited room for an open dialogue with the Arab population. It opens with the statement that Israel is the national home of the Jewish people and declares that it is a democratic state, without acknowledging any democratic deficits in regard to its non-Jewish citizens. The two civic initiatives are indicative of the inward turn of Jewish-Israeli society and its desire for secure boundaries and homogeneity. This desire underscored, on the one hand, the support for the fence separating Israel from the (non-citizen) Palestinians and ensuring a demographic majority that would protect the Jewish state and, on the other hand, the popular demand for a (Jewish) national unity government.

National Unity and Political Exclusion

The Palestinian minority, despite having the right to vote and run for office, has been consistently marginalized in Israeli politics. Arab politicians who joined Zionist parties usually played minor roles within the parties and were not appointed to ministerial positions. Arab independent parties, on the other hand, were automatically relegated to the opposition and considered illegitimate for being part of the coalition. This marginality changed briefly during the peace process but returned after it collapsed. Rabin's government (1992–1995) was an important exception when Arab parties were not officially part of the coalition but supported it from the outside. The willingness of the government to rely on the support of the Arab parties and its attempt to make peace with the Palestinians offered some hope for the future of the Arab citizens. These hopes, as described above, were cut short by two interrelated developments. First, the assassination of Rabin underscored the inward turn of Israeli Jewish society, which sought reconciliation and unity and, intentionally or not, excluded Arab citizens. Second, and more important, the debate over the peace process was gradually framed as an "internal" Jewish debate regarding the (Jewish) common good, namely the future borders of the state. The right wing's argument that a Jewish majority was necessary for territorial compromise was eventually accepted by the center-left so that a Jewish (right-left) coalition was preferred and Arab parties returned to exclusion.

Rabin's willingness to rely on non-Jewish votes was used by the right-wing opposition to de-legitimate the government and its decisions. In the elections of 1996, after Rabin's assassination, supporters of Netanyahu, the Likud's candidate, used a popular slogan "Netanyahu is good for the Jews." The message was clear, de-legitimizing reliance on Arab support of the Labor Party and the political participation of Arab parties. The power of this message became more evident some three years later when the Labor Party under Ehud Barak returned to power in 1999. Barak, winning by a landslide, with the help of about 96% of the Arab vote (365,000 votes) declared his intention to form a broad coalition. The broad coalition envisioned, it was shortly revealed, was a Jewish coalition designed to grant widespread (Jewish) legitimacy for future negotiations. Consequently, the Arab parties were not invited to the coalition talks and were largely ignored throughout Barak's term. Their frustrations exploded a year later after the violent collapse of Camp David. A series of demonstrations that followed violent events in the West Bank and Gaza resulted in the death of 13 demonstrators, Arab citizens, killed by the Israeli police.

National unity governments in Israel are often the reaction to perceived political crises that justify "breaking" the rule of coalitions that govern with a slim majority. The term itself connotes the inherent dilemma of Israeli politics, as nation and state do not conflate, so national unity means Jewish unity. Unity governments that included the Labor and Likud parties were formed in 1967, before the war, and in 1984, during an economic crisis. The collapse of the peace process, combined with a fear that the growing internal divisions were undermining Israel's security, made the conditions ripe in 2001 for a broader national unity government. After the failure of Camp David and Barak's declaration that there was "no partner" with whom to negotiate, Israelis were generally skeptical about the possibility of peace with the Palestinians (Arian and Shamir, 2002) so the major divisive issue was off the table. Then, the terrorist campaign of suicide bombers after Camp David gave prominence to security concerns that overrode all other issues. Finally, as was discussed above, the growing support for "national unity" expressed the desire for the reconciliation of Israel's "internal" divisions and for a concentration on deflecting the external threat.

During the last months of his government and after the breakdown of the peace process, Ehud Barak made some attempts to form a unity government in order to avoid elections that did not materialize. Ariel Sharon, the Likud candidate, who won the election by a landslide, followed his declared intentions during the election campaign and formed a unity government with the Labor Party that lasted less than two years, but enjoyed widespread public support. After the breakdown of the government and another land-slide victory, Sharon attempted again to form a unity government. In a survey conducted for Israeli Radio two weeks before the elections, 74% of the respondents expressed a desire to see a national unity government after the elections (http://bet.iba.org.il/32448.htm). In a speech, after formally being appointed by the president to form the government, Sharon explained that the government was facing economic and security challenges that called for unity and compromise:

> We will have to make crucial decisions that will require widespread agreements across the nation. Nobody can stand aside. In order to face the challenges and realize our hopes we must walk together. Everybody who desires peace must join the government or bear responsibility for his refusal. He who says "no" to unity betrays the wish of the Israeli public … No party should be disqualified. All Zionist parties will be invited to join the government. (*Maariv*, February 9, 2003)

"National unity" was presented as the required response to external dangers and, accordingly, a "responsible" act expected from political parties. Public figures and senior businesspeople concerned with "stability" appealed to the Labor Party, which had declared in the election campaign that it would not join a national unity government (a declaration that according to some analysts had a negative impact on the campaign), to join the government.

But, the differences between the parties prevented the formation of the national unity government. Despite public pressure and desires, a national unity government was not formed, as differences between parties could not be overcome. The pressures for national unity, however, had three significant implications. First, there was a demand for Jewish parties to "act responsibly," or, be punished at the ballot box – as the downfall of the Labor and the left-wing Meretz parties demonstrated. Second, all Jewish parties (including the extreme right-wing parties) were perceived as potential coalition members. And, third, Arab parties, by definition, were not part of a national unity government and, therefore, further marginalized. The implications of national unity governments for the political orientations of the Arab minority are yet to be studied.

Security and Demography

The concept of a fence between Israel and the Palestinians was not new to the political discourse in Israel. Israeli liberals have often used demography and the threat of a bi-national state, or the need to preserve the Jewish State from a possible Arab majority, as the rationale to end the occupation. From the time of Oslo, especially when the process was undermined by violence, the fence was raised as a fallback position, a security measure Israel could or should use unilaterally, if the Palestinians failed to cooperate. The concept of the fence gained momentum when the peace process collapsed into violence, and local initiatives along the frontier created security barriers between Israel and the territories that have gradually made separation a local reality and a national possibility (Ben-Porat and Mizrahi, 2005). Separation received the initial political momentum when the Labor Party in the 1996 campaign, losing its support due to stepped-up terrorist attacks, adopted the slogan "we are here, they are there, a fence in between." This strategy emphasized the need to achieve security by ending the occupation, unilaterally (if necessary) drawing the future borders and securing a demographic Jewish majority. The fence strategy failed to win the election, but the idea was embedded in the political discourse and re-emerged four years later.

Ironically, it was the Likud government and Prime Minister Sharon who had previously opposed the fence that, six years later, made it into a reality. The new Likud government had to face the fact that despite the large number of members of terrorist organizations, including leaders, killed or captured by Israeli military initiatives, suicide bombings continued and worsened. Consequently, the concept of a fence gained momentum and public support that the government could no longer ignore. Surveys held in 2002 sent a clear message to the government, as they indicated that a majority of Israelis (83%) supported unilateral disengagement, even at the price of evacuating some of the settlements and believed that the fence could prevent or significantly reduce terrorism (Tami Steinmetz Center for Peace Research, 2002). The fence was not only a security measure but also a demographic measure advocated by Israeli doves to convince fellow (Jewish) Israelis. Uzi Dayan, a retired major general and the head of the "Forum for National Responsibility," a dovish movement that includes many former generals, described the fence as a security measure with long-term significance for the preservation of Israel as a Jewish and democratic state, a measure against the "demographic threat."

> A decisive Jewish majority must be preserved only through democratic and moral means, otherwise it will not be a Jewish state ... the state of Israel should decide on its borders in the next few years, according to two considerations: security and demography: security, so that all the citizens of Israel live in safety, and demography, so that the nature of this state will continue to be Jewish and democratic. (Dayan, 2002)

Partition, therefore, underscored the new consensus among Jewish Israelis and tied together issues of security and demography. The shift of the peace process away from the concept of cooperation, first to partition and then to unilateral partition, had important implications not only for Israeli-Palestinian relations but also for the relations within Israel between Jewish Israelis and Palestinian citizens of Israel. The significance of the demographic discourse – "we are here, they are there" – employed by both the right and the left was not simply a temporary exclusion of Palestinian citizens but rather a hierarchical move that placed the Jewish character of the state outside the debate and, consequently, the status of Palestinian citizens. This geographic or demographic discourse about setting boundaries, as the next section will demonstrate, was supplemented by a discourse about national (Jewish) unity.

National Unity, the Fence and the Gaza Withdrawal

The withdrawal from Gaza in the summer of 2005 was a logical continuation of the fence strategy. The demographic concerns that underscored the campaign for the fence were raised again to justify a unilateral withdrawal from the densely populated Gaza Strip. Like the fence, this idea was also the result of the growing belief that "there is no partner" on the other side and that, consequently, Israel should re-deploy its forces according to its own interests. Moreover, like the fence, this initiative was supported by many on the left, but also by the center and moderate right, who either believed that the price of holding on to Gaza was too high, or that the withdrawal in Gaza would allow Sharon to retain important parts of the West Bank. Overall, like the fence, the unilateral move focused on an Israeli interest/need and had little concern for Palestinian interests/needs.

The "we are here, they are there" approach underscored the withdrawal from Gaza, as the supporters of the plan explained the threat to the Jewish majority if Israel retained control of the heavily populated Gaza Strip. The demographic rationale was supplemented by a security argument that the disengagement from Gaza and the removal of settlements would free large numbers of troops that could be deployed elsewhere. Thus, the disengagement plan was presented to the public not as a peace plan but as a unilateral move based on Israeli interests. The plan brought together a coalition between the Likud and the Labor parties, but moved the right-wing and religious parties to the opposition. While the polls indicated public support for the plan, the opposition of the settlers and especially of right-wing extremists brought back memories of the months prior to Rabin's assassination. But, while settlers and their supporters actively opposed the police and army during the evacuation of settlements, violence was limited. The Israeli public that followed the media coverage of the withdrawal witnessed, on the one hand, settlers confronting soldiers and policemen with hard words but, on the other hand, embraces of brotherhood between the sides.

The disengagement, backed by demographic and security arguments, was not only an internal Israeli affair that excluded the Palestinians but also largely an internal Jewish affair. The unilateral nature of the plan left limited room for cooperation with the Palestinians or for a renewal of substantive peace talks. Internally, the continuous use of demography, Jewish unity and the future of the Jewish state could hardly make this plan attractive to the Arab citizens of Israel. Arab parties, critical of the unilateral plan because of its unilateral nature, chose to abstain when the plan was brought to the parliament for approval. Similarly, the fence was supported by 76% of Jewish Israelis but only 10% of Palestinian citizens (Smooha, 2006).

Arab Citizens' Re-defined Struggle

The inward turn of Jewish society and the political and social exclusion of Arabs have made the possibility of liberal equality remote and contributed to a change in the Arab citizens struggle for equality. Arab elites began to address critically the model of a "Jewish and democratic state" and the exclusion it entails and have begun to address themselves as a "national minority," often in comparison to other national minorities (Rekhes, 2009). The events of October 2000, following the collapse of the Camp David negotiations and the break-up of the second Intifada, were the watershed event that marked the future. A series of demonstrations in Israel that followed violent events in the West Bank and Gaza escalated to open violence and resulted in the deaths of thirteen demonstrators – Arab citizens, killed by the Israeli police. An inquiry commission established after the events found fault in the police actions and, more important, deeper structural issues:

> The events, their exceptional character and their adverse consequences were the result of structural factors that caused an explosive situation among the Arab public in Israel. The state and the elected governments consistently failed to seriously engage with the difficult problems of a

large Arab minority within a Jewish state. The government's treatment of the Arab sector was generally of neglect and discrimination. At the same time, not enough was done to enforce the law in the Arab sector … as a result of this and of other causes, the Arab sector suffered deep distress evident, among other things, in high levels of poverty, unemployment, shortage of land, problems in the education system and serious deficiencies in infrastructure. All those created ongoing discontent, heightened towards October 2000.

The majority of the recommendations of the committee for ending discrimination were not implemented, probably because from the Jewish majority perspective the events were the result of Arab unaccepted violent behavior. The call of Jewish right-wing activists to punish Arab citizens by boycotting their businesses has added to the alienation and distrust between the sides. It was at this period when Arab NGOs (see Jamal, in this volume) were formed and Arab political parties adopted more radical positions regarding their future status in Israel. In the 2001 elections, following the events, the majority of Arabs boycotted the elections as only 18% showed up in the polls and demands for separate Arab representative institutions has risen (Rekhes, 2009). Between December 2006 and May 2007 the different demands crystallized into several "future vision documents" composed by Arab intellectuals and public figures, demanding, what they described as the transformation of Israel from an ethnic to a democratic state (Jamal, 2008).

The documents provide a harsh critique of the Zionist Movement and the State of Israel in relation to the Palestinian nation, citizens of Israel and Palestinians in the territories, and call upon the State of Israel to adopt principles of corrective and distributive justice vis-à-vis the Palestinian minority (Jamal, 2008). More importantly, it stated a clear identity position. Arab citizens, argued the document were not just a national minority but also an indigenous minority wronged by the state (Rekhes, 2009). In the words of the document:

> We Are the Palestinian Arabs in Israel, the indigenous peoples, the residents of the State of Israel, and an integral part of the Palestinian People and the Arab and Muslim.

This assertion of nationality included the symbolic and historical demands such as the commemoration of the Nakbah (the disaster, as they referred to the war of 1948 and its consequences) and concrete demands for equality and representation:

> The State should recognize the Palestinian Arabs in Israel as an indigenous national group (and as a minority within the international conventions) that has the right within their citizenship to choose its representative directly and be responsible for their religious, educational

and cultural affairs. This group should be given the chance to create its own national institutions relating to all living aspects and stop dividing between the different religious sects within the Palestinian Arabs in Israel ... The relations between the Palestinians and the Jews in Israel should be based on the attainment of equal human and citizen rights ... The two groups should have mutual relations based on the consensual democratic system (an extended coalition, between the elites of the two groups, equal proportional representation, mutual rights to veto and self administration of exclusive issues). (p. 9)

State of the Division

The turning inward of Israeli Jewish society was matched by the growing frustrations of the Palestinian minority. Not only had the peace process had little if any positive influence, but since October 2000 the two sides had also seemed to be drifting farther apart. While Palestinian citizens have made some gains through the Supreme Court, which has handed down several decisions against discrimination, their overall marginality has not significantly changed. The violent events in October 2000 led many Jewish Israelis to avoid visiting Arab towns and villages either because of (unjustified) growing fear or in retaliation for the Palestinian actions. The fears are mutual: while Jews fear a Palestinian rebellion inside Israel, Palestinian citizens are concerned about their political status, the severe infringement of their citizens' rights and the violence inflicted on them by the state (Smooha, 2006). Interestingly, the events are interpreted by Palestinian citizens as a result of their continued exclusion and discrimination but by Jews as "national and religious-based opposition to the state of Israel" (Sagiv-Shifter and Shamir, 2001).

The fears were translated again into demographic concerns and growing intolerance. A leading politician, Benjamin Netanyahu, stated in 2003, "We have a demographic problem – but it is not focused on the Palestinian Arabs but rather on the Israeli Arabs ... if they integrate well and reach 35–40%, the Jewish state will cease to exist and become a bi-national state." A survey conducted after these words found that 71% of Jews agreed that Arabs constituted a demographic threat and 41% felt that Netanyahu's words were appropriate (Smooha, 2006). Tolerance towards Palestinian citizens also eroded, as Jews surveyed expressed growing resistance to Palestinian citizen inclusion and growing support for security measures against them. A majority of Jews also opposed Palestinian citizens' participation in democratic decisions over the future borders of the state (Sagiv-Shifter and Shamir, 2001). This trend was exacerbated in the 2009 elections when the right-wing party Israel Beitenu and its leader Avigdor Lieberman used anti-Arab rhetoric and legislation proposals as part of their campaign. The party became the third largest in the Israeli parliament and Lieberman was nominated Foreign Minister. One of the first laws the party declared it would promote was a "statement of loyalty" demanded of all Israeli citizens. Needless to say, the demand of the suggested loyalty oath to affirm Israel as a Jewish state was aimed at the Arab minority.

According to Smooha (2006), the majority of Palestinian citizens accept the right of Israel to exist as a Jewish and democratic state but oppose Zionism, which they perceive as a form of discrimination and exclusion. The distinction between a Jewish state and a Zionist state is questionable and should therefore be translated into questions that pertain to individual equality and recognition of minority rights. The "future vision" document, written by Palestinian scholars for the "National Committee for the Heads of the Arab Local Authorities in Israel" outlines a program based not only on individual rights but also on the recognition of the Palestinians as a national minority and wider institutional changes regarding the Jewish character of the state. A recent survey (Rekhes, 2007) finds that a minority of Palestinians has read the document but a majority agrees with its ideas. In the Hebrew media, the document received widespread and mostly negative attention. The questions of equality, through individual or group rights, and of the future institutional arrangements of majority-minority relations, are yet to be seriously discussed.

Conclusion

The hope for liberal equality for the Arab citizens of Israel in the 1990s was short-lived at most as the Jewish majority never had the intention to change the Jewish identity of the state. At most, Arab citizens could hope that the end of the Israeli-Palestinian conflict would end their perception as a "security threat" and allow for more mobilization and less discrimination. However, not only has the collapse of the peace process brought back the old dilemmas of loyalties and suspicions but the dynamics of the process itself have accentuated the dilemmas of identity and belonging. The goal of a Jewish state with secure boundaries and an assured demography became a consensus among major parts of Jewish Israelis, and became a major argument for a two-state solution. But, intentionally or not, this goal and the rhetoric involved have continued the marginalization of the Arab minority within Israel.

While in itself partition and a two-state solution could be an important beginning for positive internal change, three important, interrelated factors discussed above have prevented these changes. First, the instability of the peace process has led to growing emphasis on Jewish unity and, consequently, the exclusion of the Palestinian minority. Second, more and more emphasis was placed on demographic arguments and measures that alienated the Palestinian minority from the peace process. And, consequently, third, the political and social marginalization of the Palestinian minority has not changed, and since 2000 may have even worsened.

The equality demands of Palestinian citizens stretch across the three components of the Marshallian paradigm: individual freedoms, participation and social equality (Marshall, 1950; Turner, 2001). The full inclusion of Palestinian citizens, therefore, would have to engage not only with individual freedoms and equalities and with economic deprivation but also with the collective status of the minority and the re-definition of citizenship so it would allow both equality and recognition. The unwillingness of the Jewish majority to allow for full liberal equality, on the one hand, and the demands of the Arab citizens to be recognized as a national minority, on the other hand, render the liberal model of citizenship unlikely for the near future.

References

Arian, A. and Shamir, M. (2002) *The Elections in Israel 2001* (Jerusalem: Israel Democracy Institute).

Ben-Porat, G. and Mizrahi, S. (2005) "Political Culture, Alternative Politics and Foreign Policy: The Case of Israel" *Policy Science* 38: 177–94.

Berg, E. and Ben-Porat, G. (2008) "Partition vs. Power-Sharing" *Nations and Nationalism* 14 (1): 29–37.

Brass, P. (1985) *Ethnic Groups and the State* (London and Sydney: Croom Helm).

Connor, W. (1994) *Ethnonationalism, the Quest for Understanding* (Princeton: Princeton University Press)

Crawford, B. (1998) "The Causes of Cultural Conflict: An Institutional Approach" in Crawford and Lipschutz (eds.), *The Myth of Ethnic Conflict* (Berkeley: UC Berkeley International and Area Studies Press).

Dayan, U. (2002). Speech at Herzliya Conference, http://www1.idc.ac.il/ips/content/2002transcripts.asp (Accessed August 21, 2005).

Future Vision of the Palestinian Arabs in Israel, (2006), The National Committee for the Heads of the Arab Local Authorities in Israel www.mossawacenter.org/files/files/File/Reports/2006/Future%20Vision%20(English).pdf

Gavison, R. and Abu-Ria, I. (1999) *The Jewish-Arab Cleavage in Israel: Characteristics and Challenges* (Jerusalem: Institute of Democracy) (Hebrew).

Ghanem, A. (2000) "The Palestinian Minority in Israel: The 'Challenge' of the Jewish State and its Implications" *Third World Quarterly*, 21 (1): 87–104.

Jamal, A. (2008) "The Political Ethos of Palestinian Citizens of Israel: Critical Reading in the Future Vision Documents", *Israel Studies Forum.* 23 (2): 3–28.

Keating, M. (2001) *Nations Against the State: The New Politics of Nationalism in Quebec, Catalonia and Scotland* (London: Palgrave).

Levi-Barzilai, V. (2002) "In Tiberias We Defined the Jewish State", *Haaretz* 4.1.02 (Hebrew).

Levi, S., Levinson, H. and Katz, E. 1999. *Jews Israelis: Portrait.* Jerusalem: Israeli Democracy Institute (Hebrew).

Lewin-Epstein, N. and Semyonov, M. (1993) *The Arab Minority in Israel's Economy,* (Boulder, Co: Westview Press).

Lustik, I. (1985) *Arabs in a Jewish State,* (Haifa: Mifras) (Hebrew).

Marshall, T. H. (1950) *Citizenship and Social class, and Other Essays* (Cambridge: Cambridge University Press).

Marx, A. (2002) "The Nation-State and Its Exclusions", *Political Science Quarterly* 117 (1): 103–26.

McGarry, J. (1998) "'Demographic engineering': the state-directed movement of ethnic groups as a technique of conflict regulation" *Ethnic and Racial Studies*, 24 (4): 613–37.

Mearshimer, J. and Van-Evara, S. (1995) "When Peace Means War", *The New Republic*, December 18, 1995.

Peled, Yoav (1992). "Ethnic Democracy and the Legal Construction of Citizenship: Arab Citizenship of the Jewish State." *American Political Science Review*. 86 (2): 432–43.

Rekhes, E. (2007) "Opinion Survey of the Arab Population in Israel" Dayan Center at Tel-Aviv University www.dayan.org/kapjac/arab_survey_2007.pdf

— (2009) "The Arab Minority in Israel and the Seventeenth Knesset Elections: The Beginning of a New Era?" in Arian, A. and M. Shamir *The Elections in Israel 2006* (New Brunswick, NJ: Transaction Publishers).

Rothschild, J. (1981) *Ethnopolitics, A Conceptual Framework* (New York: Columbia University Press).

Rouhana, N. (1998) "Israel and its Arab citizens: Predicaments in the relationship between ethnic states and ethnonational minorities", *Third World Quarterly* 19 (2): 277–96.

Sagiv-Shifter, T. and Shamir, M. (2002) "Israel as a laboratory for the study of political tolerance" Cohen Institute for Public Opinion Research, October 2002.

Shafir, G. and Peled, Y. (2002) *Being Israeli* (Cambridge: Cambridge University Press).

Sheleg, Y. (2002) "On the critics of the Kinneret Declaration" *Haaretz* 22.1.2002.

Smooha, S. (2006) *Index of Arab-Jewish Relations in Israel 2004* (Haifa University: Jewish-Arab Center).

—(1998) *Autonomy for the Arabs in Israel?* (Raanana, Israel: Research Center for Arab Society) (Hebrew).

—(1992) *Arabs and Jews in Israel* Vol.2 (Boulder, CA and London: Westview Press).

—(1989) *Arabs and Jews in Israel* Vol. 1, (Boulder, CA and London: Westview Press).

Tami Steinmetz Center for Peace Research (2002) *Peace Index 2002*, Tami Steinmetz Center for Peace Research, www.tau.ac.il:80/peace

Thalen, K. and Steinmo, S. (1992) "Institutionalism in Comparative Politics" in S. Steinmo, K. Thelen and F. Longstreth (eds), *Structuring Politics* (Cambridge: Cambridge University Press).

Tully, J. (2002) "Introduction" in A. G. Gagnon, and J. Tully (eds), *Multinational Democracies* (UK: Cambridge University Press).

Turner, B.S. (2001) "The Erosion of Citizenship", *British Journal of Sociology* (2)52: 189–209.

Yanay, N. and R. Lifshitz-Oron, "Mandatory Reconciliation (tzav Piyus): the Violent Discourse of Moderation", *Israeli Sociology* 5(1), 2003, 161–91 (Hebrew).

11 Civic associations, empowerment and democratization

Arab civil society in Israel

Amal Jamal

This paper argues that minority groups, especially homeland minorities, utilize all means to empower their citizenship and influence the political order in which they live. Civic associationalism forms one of the major modes of minority collective action, seeking to empower society and democratize the state. Civic associations are established voluntarily and are based on the understanding that citizens are better engage in associating and communicating in order to determine their future, despite the fact that they cannot guarantee a clear correspondence between intentions and results. Civic associations are motivated by various social, economic and political needs and interests and seek interacting and transforming their political surroundings in order to correspond with their needs and interests. Civic associations seek enriching public life and answering material and symbolic needs of their society, challenging any state bias. When there is a lack of one given agreed collective design, minority civic associations become gradually loaded with goals and ideals that strive to influence their social and political surrounding. Hence, despite the fact that civil society should not be conflated with political society, in the case of minority civic association it is the challenging of the hegemonic political order that provides the raison d'être of minority civil society.

In order to demonstrate these assertions this paper examines Arab civic associations and the ways they have become a major vehicle of development, empowerment and democratization in Israel. It is argued that these associations seek to play a political role by empowering Arab citizenship and challenging the dominant political, material and symbolic power structure. Although Arab civil society operates within the confines of state law and is separate from political society, it contends state policies towards Arab society, challenges the hegemonic symbolic order and demands democratization of the state. The gradual expansion of civic associations led to the establishment of a new realm of political action that interacts and communicates with Arab political society and with the state. As a result, Arab civil society plays a major political role by the mere fact that it seeks to develop, empower and democratize its society and state. However, since collective endeavors do not always succeed and many times lead to unintended results, it is claimed that Arab civic association manage to empower and develop, but remain short of democratizing the Israeli state. The latter seeks ways to overcome civic engagement and maintain the hegemonic ethnic ideology of the state.

The paper is not limited to state–Arab civil society relations. It sheds some light on the complex relationship between civil society institutions and Arab society, which it seeks to mobilize and advocate. The paper demonstrates the hesitant position taken by Arab civic associations vis-à-vis basic social problems in Arab society. As a result, the impact of Arab civic associations, including feminist associations, on empowering weak segments of Arab society and democratizing it is rather limited. Arab civic associations did not manage to promote liberal values and support the basic rights of underprivileged social groups, such as women, children and the elderly. These groups may have received some support from various Arab civic associations, but their fundamental situation as underprivileged groups did not fundamentally change.

This paper also points out several of the sources of weakness of Arab civil society, such as its fragmentation, personalization, sectarianism and the close affinity between civic associations and political parties. The paper pinpoints the implications of these phenomena on the empowerment, development and democratization policies of civil society.

Debating Civil Society and its Ambivalent Role

Examinations of the history of the idea of civil society have demonstrated that it is not a theoretical specification of a substantive model, embodying a set of institutions that stand in opposition or complete separation from the state. In his contribution to the understanding of the history of the concept of civil society Sunil Khilnani makes clear that "[i]n its original sense, [civil society] allowed no distinction between 'state' and 'society' or between political and civil society: it simply meant a community, a collection of human beings united within a legitimate political order, and was variously rendered as 'society' or 'community'" (Khilnani, 2001: 17). He demonstrates that it was the German tradition instigated by Hegel that bifurcated the concept, leading to the understanding that state and civil society are "redescriptions of one another" (ibid.: 17). Recent depictions of civil society, such as that of Cohen and Arato have pointed out that the "structures of socialization, association and organized forms of communication of the lifeworld to the extent that these are institutionalized or are in the process of being institutionalized", as the main reference of civil society (Cohen and Arato, 1996: x). The institutionalization of these structures of socialization, association and communication constitute the realm of the state as much as they are constituted by it.

Such an understanding focuses attention at the interaction between civil society and political society, without falling into either conflating them or establishing a chasm between them. Civil society interacts with political society, seeking to constitute the political order and the substantiation of citizenship in such a way that promotes equal civility as the shared common ground of all citizens and communities in the state (Vertovec, 1999; Delanty, 2000; Enjolras, 2008). Although this understanding does not come to completely abolish the relative autonomy of state institutions, it does not submit to the understanding that views civil society and the state, as rivals. Civil society encompasses the idea that politics is open for free competitive human action that seeks interactions, seeking common purposes. It does not assume a pre-given social design or is committed to a specific political form, but is open for numerous social interactions without a pre-given specific substantive end-state. The concept of civil society does not ignore the tendency of political actors to identify the state with one specific model of collective life (Dunn, 2001). However, it is about the lack of ability of any of these actors to freeze politics and identify social interactions with a specific model of end-state. Civil society is about the self-constitution of society through self-mobilization that takes place in a sphere of associations, social movements and forms of public communication, which may accept some organizing principles and is based on conceptual maps, but avoids seeking submission of social groups to pre-given models of the state or enter into lethal confrontation that frustrates the basic trust necessary for politics to exist. Civil society is not the result but is actually about the reducing of the role of power and money in determining the form of collective life. It is about the maintaining of an open autonomous sphere of civic interaction where identity and politics are freely debated, seeking influence in the political realm. But it is not committed to pre-given rigid identitarian solidarities that abolish civility or to transcendental beliefs that abolish free and open-ended social communication. In other words, civil society is about the empowerment of the citizen and the setting of limitations on state power and money in order to guarantee political contestation, mobilization and communication, as the basic manifestation of civil society itself.

This dynamic and open-ended view of civil society prevents conflating the mere rise of civil institutions and their mere activity with liberalization and democratization. It is the influence of civil institutions and their free contestation over possible models of the state that turn them into genuine civil society. When these institutions are cut of determining the characteristics and the dominant principles of the political order and are limited to the generation of identitarian solidarities, the promotion of undebatable belief systems or the supplying of basic material needs, civil society is emptied of its substantial meaning.

On the other hand, a thorough examination of the contribution and impact of civil society institutions has to seriously consider the structural circumstances under which they operate and the intentions and policies of state institutions towards them. When examining civil society institutions one should not conflate the influence that civil society associations could have on development and empowerment with their impact on the democratization of the state. As we shall see, civil society associations can contribute to development and empowerment and be either non-democratic or act democratically, but not manage to democratize the state.

The democratization wave in South America (Habib, 2005; O'Donnell and Schmitter, 1986; Schneider, 1995) and Eastern Europe (Linz and Stepan, 1996; Pelcynski, 1998; Havel, 1985) have led scholars to believe that there is a positive relationship between the rise of civil society associations and empowerment and democratization. Many scholars believed that democratization processes are deeply influenced by the rise of vibrant civil society, which set new challenges to authoritarian political regimes (Huntington, 1991; Cohen and Arato, 1992). In most studies on democratization the role of civil society is considered crucial and necessary (Burnell and Calvert, 2004; Mendelson and Glenn, 2002). However, contrary to such established views of civil society in the literature in most of the 1980s, many scholars raise doubts regarding the causal relationship between the number of civil society institutions and the chances for social development, political empowerment and democratization (Mercer, 2002; Clarke, 1998; Haynes, 1996; Hulme and Edwards, 1997; Edwards, 1999; Wiktorowicz, 2000). Many scholars have concluded that the emergence of civil society may be a necessary condition for development, empowerment and especially democratization, but it is not always sufficient. It has become doubtful that the rise in the number of civil institutions necessarily leads to major changes in the basic principles of the political order dominant at a time (Foley and Edwards, 1996). It has become clear that one has to differentiate between the developmental and empowering role of civil society and its democratization impact. Civil associations may provide fundamental basic resources to widening segments of society and empower some of its member groups, but may not be able to transform the political regime and lead to democratization.

Based on the ambivalent role that civil society institutions played in different contexts, Quintan Wiktorowicz states that "Rather than assume that civil society enables democracy or serves as a mechanism of empowerment, it is important to understand the political context that shapes and limits its potential as an engine of political change" (Wiktorowicz, 2000: 46). The structural opportunities in which civil society organizations operate are crucial to their contribution to empowerment, development, and political change (Tarrow, 1996). The state has a major effect on the ability of civil society institutions to influence their surrounding social and political reality. Evidence from various countries shows that the role of civil society in challenging state authority rises when the political regime begins transforming (Wada, 2005). On the other hand, the experience of the Weimar republic demonstrates that civil society can have a destructive potential, where civil society associations could be used by radical political forces to undermine democracy (ibid). In nineteenth-century America and contrary to the Tocquevillian view, civil society associations tended to be sectarian and exclusive, leading to major tension and internal strife (Whittington, 1998).

Similar fears of the negative use of civil society institutions is raised by Foley and Edwards in regard to the radical and nondemocratic Islamic movements that may use civic associations to promote a nondemocratic theocratic political change (Foley and Edwards, 1996).

Notwithstanding the dangers of negative use of civil society, most scholars agree to the positive potential of civil society institutions. Civil society institutions, as Linz and Stepan have demonstrated can contribute to the rise of counter-hegemonic projects that set limits on authoritarian regimes (Linz and Stepan, 1996). These institutions construct an autonomous sphere of social interaction that meets basic needs of ordinary people, despite the fact that the mere existence of civil society institutions does not inherently imply democratization. It is a well-known phenomenon that civil institutions may be rich and active but do not have a strong impact on policy and decision making in the state.

The examination of civil society institutions in their political context integrates the policies and intentions of the political regime into the analysis. One should be aware that political regimes can utilize civil society institutions for their purposes, establishing a façade of democratic rule, while limiting the contribution of civil society to fulfilling tasks that are ignored or neglected by the state. Civic associations could be a part and parcel of neo-liberal process in which the state withdraws from taking a welfare role and gives this responsibility to civil society institutions supported by external resources, which willingly and unwillingly play the role (Foley and Edwards, 1996). Although such a situation could lead to empowering civil society institutions, enabling them to exert pressure on the political regime; nevertheless, civil society institutions end up fulfilling a task that is usually the responsibility of the state. Such a process leads to the neo-liberalization of civil society itself, drawing it closer to competitive behavior patterns known from the market.

Debating Arab Civil Society in Israel

The rise of civil society network in Israel is still an under-examined phenomenon, despite its growing impact on the public agenda. Several scholars, such as Shany Payes, Oded Haklai and Dan Rabonowitz have addressed the phenomenon (Payes, 2003; Haklai, 2004, 2008; Rabinowitz, 2001). Payes' has been the most comprehensive so far. She focused on the expansion of the Arab NGO sector and pointed out the relationship between Arab civic associations and the Israeli state. She claims "[a]lthough the importance of [Palestinian Israeli civic associations] are rarely acknowledged in scholarly literature, these organizations have in fact played a significant political role in the campaign of the Arab minority for civil equality in Israel (Payes, 2003: 82). She claims that "[Palestinian Israeli civic associations'] contribution has manifested itself in the creation of avenues for participation in public life by groups that have traditionally been under-represented. First and foremost, they have empowered the Arab minority *vis-a-vis* the state and the Jewish majority. NGOs have also contributed to the process of empowerment by enhancing the professional ability of Arabs to oppose discriminatory state policies" (ibid.: 84). She follows Korten showing that Arab civic associations in Israel have been shifting from welfare through development to building political consciousness and mobility (ibid.: 83; Korten, 1990). Although these statements, made by Payes in 2003, are still partially valid today they have not established the necessary differentiation between the ability of civic associations to empower and develop and their ability to promote political change and democratization. The mere existence of civic associations is not inherently equal to democratization, empowerment or development. They are a necessary but not sufficient condition.

Despite its wide scope, one of the limitations of Payes' study is that it is predominantly focused on the confrontational relationship between Arab civic associations and the state and pays little attention to the developmental role played by the former, especially the Islamist associations. Payes' claim is true that in the last two decades there has been a constant rise in the number of Arab civil society institutions, with some major fluctuations in several historical junctions. Payes deals with the causes behind the rise in the number of Arab civic associations, but does not provide a comprehensive explanatory model to the rise of these civil society institutions.

This paper continues Payes' endeavor and delves deeper into the direct as well as indirect causes of the rise in Arab civic associations in Israel. The paper complements Payes' claim that the rise in the number of these institutions and their intensive involvement in public social affairs generate social capital (Putnam, 2000) that strives for political influence and social change (Jamal, 2006a). Arab civil society institutions assist in the empowerment and the development of Arab society. They provide services in different fields, such as education, health, communication, welfare, religious services and planning. They also advocate and lobby for the rights of the Arab citizens inside Israel and internationally. Arab civil society institutions also provide information necessary for political mobilization, identity formation and cultural preservation.

Nonetheless, the vibrant activity of Arab civil institutions and their search for means and methods to empower Arab citizens and substantiate their citizenship and influence the dominant principles of the political order, leading to the democratization of the Israeli state have not managed to transform the hegemonic Israeli political order. These efforts were also short of liberalizing Arab society itself.

In some aspects, this paper follows Hakali's cautious position, who claimed that "the impact of the mobilization of [Arab civic associations in Israel] on structural reforms [of the state] is debatable" (Haklai, 2004: 165). On the other hand, this paper differs from Haklai's conceptualization of Arab civic activism as "ethnic civil society." His latter elaboration of this concept does not provide the justifications for such a use and led to the reduction of civic activity to identitarian solidarity. Haklai has contributed very much to our understanding of Arab civic associations in Israel. However, he is rather biased when claiming that Arab civic associations should not be viewed as promoting universal civil values, but rather as "a mode of *ethnic mobilization*, targeting the *empowerment of an ethnic community*" (ibid.: 157). His concep-tualization of ethnic civil society is rather limited. Haklai claims that "the term is coined in reference to ethnicity based organizations that seek to span parochialism in the ethnic community while focusing primarily on collect-ive community interests. Ethnic civil society activists hold state values and practices of uniethnic favouritism responsible for the minority's subordinate position. They mobilize to challenge the institutional order that they believe entrenches unequal inter-ethnic relations and to strengthen the ethnic com-munity vis-a-vis other communities and the state" (Haklai, 2008: 3). Such an understanding is based on three major misconceptions that ought to be briefly made clear. The first is that Arab civic associations are not purely Arab and in many cases employ Jewish activists who share the same values and seek to promote civic culture and genuine democratization of the Israeli state. Arab civic associations are open to any civil activist who shares universal civic values and is willing to join. Their criteria of recruitment were never ethnic. Many of them have not only Jewish employees, but also inter-national employees and volunteers. Second, Haklai does not take seriously enough the fact that Arab civic associations are genuine when demanding equal citizenship and thereby promoting universal liberal values, exactly like many other homeland minorities in the world (Keane, 1998b). His concept of ethnic civil society entails an understatement that Arab civic associations manipulate liberal values for ethnic purposes. It is true that such a poss-ibility could be the case for some of the Arab civic associations, especially anti-liberal religious ones. However, Hakali's generalizing conceptualization goes beyond that, reducing all Arab civic efforts into merely identitarian and even deceitful collective endeavors. Major efforts of Arab civil society, as manifested in the recently published 'future vision documents" (Jamal, 2008) seek to re-envision the Israeli state and promote shared civility that respects ethnic identities, but does not submit the whole political order to rigid identitarian politics and ethno-national exclusive constitutional order, such as is the case in Israel (Jamal, 2007a). Many of the Arab civic associa-tions seek liberalization within Arab society itself, paying a heavy price in terms of social prestige and reputation, such as the case of feminist NGOs.[1] Furthermore, by limiting his treatment of Arab civic associations to ethnic boundaries Haklai makes this NGO network responsible for not achieving its goals instead of viewing the state as not being responsive to demands of a significant part of its citizenry.

Arab civic experience in Israel has particular characteristics, stemming from the combination of historical, cultural and political circumstances in which Arab civic associations operate. Rabinowitz has already shed some light on this topic, especially on the civic associations affiliated with the

Islamic movement and the way these civic associations utilize developmental resources in order to promote a non-liberal model of society (Rabinowitz, 2001). However, one cannot limit the activities and goals of Arab civic associations to this level only. A large number of Arab civic associations seek to promote civil equality in Israel and demand the liberalization and democrat-ization of the Israeli state in order to meet demands of not only Arab citizens, but also Jewish citizens based on universal liberal values. The language of human rights, liberal multiculturalism and recognition characterizes the discourses and praxis of most Arab civic associations in Israel. However, the extent to which they manage to create change remains debatable, since the democratization of the state depends on state willingness to democratize and incorporate excluded groups – Arab and Jewish – in the determining of the substantive dimension of the dominant political order based on shared principles and by democratic means.

Activating Arab Citizenship and the Politics of Contention in Israel

In the first three decades of state history, Arab demands for equality were predominantly based on distributive justice and individual liberal philo-sophy, according to which the state should integrate its Arab citizens as equal participants in society and state.[2] Dominant political movements in the Arab minority, especially the Communist party, believed for a long period of time that it is possible to establish a common Arab-Jewish Israeli identity, subsiding Zionism as the dominant ideology of the state (Kaufman, 1997). Based on such a dominant political vision, most of Arab society sought to promote its interests from within the formal political system, namely the representative system manifested in the Knesset. Accommodating the system and seeking to influence it from within was viewed as the best strat-egy in the given circumstances. The fact that such a strategy served the interest of the Communist party, the dominant political force authentic-ally representing the interests of the Arab minority, made it even more solid. The Communist party challenged every voice that countered such a strategy and sought to co-opt any political force that developed separately such as the "Abna'a Al-Balad Movement" (Sons of the Village/land), estab-lished in 1972. That was the goal behind the establishment of the Front for Peace and Equality in the Knesset elections in 1977. The Communist party integrated Arab national intellectuals and leaders that were active in the Nazareth area as well as broadened its representative base to include politicians who were not Communist, but strengthened the party (Rekhess, 1993). This accommodative pattern of political conduct was followed by all Arab parties that were established since 1984. The Progressive List for Peace, established as a Jewish-Arab list, adopted a similar policy of influen-cing the official political system by entering the Knesset, despite its strong nationalist rhetoric. The same goal was sought by the Democratic Arab

Party, established as pure Arab party by a veteran of the Zionist Labor Party in 1984.

The accommodative political strategy of Arab parties was adopted for good reasons. The experience of the 1948 war and the disintegration of Palestinian society, leading to the dispersal of the majority of Palestinians living in the areas that became the state of Israel, played a vital role in the minds of the remaining Arab population. The Palestinians who remained within Israel have suspected that their stay is temporary and that any "wrong" behavior will lead to the state expelling them. Furthermore, the enforcement of the Military Government over areas inhabited by Arabs helped to control them and eliminate any attempt for alternative patterns of collective conduct (Cohen, 2010). Manufacturing consent among Arab citizens has been one of the main goals of the ideological and disciplinary apparatuses of the Israeli state (Jamal, 2009). The educational and communicative systems as well as the policing and internal intelligence agencies have long tried to nourish an Arab collective consciousness that submits to the ideological and ethnic character of the state. Since 1948, hundreds of school books were introduced to educate the Arab community based on visions that were manufactured by Jewish educators and academics (Mari, 1978; Al-Haj, 1995; Bar-Tal and Teichman, 2005). Furthermore, the Israeli state introduced new media institutions in Arabic in order to set the agenda of the Arab delegitimizing any Arab opposition to state policies (Wolfsfeld et al., 2000). The Police and General Security Service have been very active in Arab towns intimid-ating dissenters and encouraging either traditional clan leaders or others to cooperate in blocking any opposition to the well-sophisticated control system the police and the security services established since 1948 (Lustick, 1980). The Israeli methods of control have undergone many changes but remained persistent in seeking consent and in aiming to tame any Arab resentment of Israeli policies, be it civil or political (Or Commission Report, 2003; Rabinowitz, 1997).

Despite the material and ideological hegemony of the state and despite the fact that the Arab minority never abandoned formal politics, this society managed to develop new conceptual horizons leading to the emergence of an oppositional consciousness (Jamal, 2007c). This is manifested in the moral and political justifications Arabs utilize to challenge Israeli discrimin-atory policies (Jamal, 2006c). The Arab opposition to submit to the Israeli control mechanism started as early as in the 1950s. However, it did not become apparent until the mid-1970s. Since then we witnessed the rise of a new political leadership that took the lead and introduced new patterns of political behavior (Jamal, 2006a). Arab politicians have challenged Israeli policies and introduced new demands seeking to achieve full equal, act-ive and effective citizenship, including full representation in existing state institutions and establishing special organizations in domains neglected by the state.

In the last two decades, Arab intellectuals and politicians are reframing their struggle for equality in Israel by emphasizing the obligation of the state to recognize them as an indigenous national minority (Jamal, 2005). They are demanding an official recognition as an indigenous people entitled to collective rights that should be translated into self-government. The demand for collective rights does not replace the demand for full citizenship equality, but rather complements it. Collective rights are increasingly viewed as a precondition to guaranteeing individual equality (ibid). The demand is for self-government in several aspects of Arab life including education, communication, planning, control over resources, social welfare and development (Haifa Document, 2007; Future Vision, 2007). Arab citizens increasingly demand affective representation and full participation in defining the policies and priorities of the state including determining the future of the land resources owned by the state, which were confiscated from Arabs since 1948 and are devoted since then for almost exclusive Jewish use only.

One of the manifestations of this oppositional consciousness is the growing number of Arabs disillusioned with Israeli democracy (Jamal, 2007b). Although the majority of the Arab population still takes part in the elections to the Knesset and despite the fact that the three major Arab parties advocate participation, we witness a constant change in the position of Arab citizens vis-à-vis elections to the Knesset. Since the late 1980s, there has been a constant drop in the number of people participating in elections (Jamal, 2002). The widespread abstention of the Arab population in the 2001 prime ministerial elections, and the drop in the number of Arab voters in the 2003, 2006 and 2009 Knesset elections have sharpened the debate between those who still hold some trust in parliamentary politics, and those who call for a boycott on ideological principles. Amendments to the election laws, introduced by the Knesset in May 2002, aiming at putting limits on Arab Knesset members and later on their persecution strengthened the claim that participating in the Israeli elections only legitimates the state and its ideology without accruing benefits to the Arab population (Jamal, 2007c). Whereas Arab parties convince people that participation in the elections and having representatives in the Knesset gives the Arab population a chance to raise its voice in the Jewish public, critics of parliamentary politics call on the population to act outside the parliamentary framework through participation in social movements, the work of civic associations, and international lobbying. The 2009 elections have demonstrated that the vast majority of Arab eligible voters either grant their votes to Arab parties, or boycott the elections.

This latter trend has been a central ideological component of the Abna'a al-Balad movement since the 1970s. In the mid-1990s, part of the Islamic Movement, led by Sheikh Ra'ed Salah, also adopted this position. Salah called for a boycott of Knesset elections, and for Arabs to operate in separate spaces in which they are not committed to the procedural rules of the parliamentary system set by the Jewish majority (Rubin-Peled, 2001). Several Arab academics adopted this idea, viewing an imbalance between the benefit the Arab community secures by being represented in the Knesset, and the price the community pays by legitimating the Zionist character of the political system. They emphasize the fact that political parties are prohibited from running for the Knesset under a platform that rejects the notion of a Jewish state, or advocates for change to that state identity, something that limits the ability of Arab parties to use legitimate democratic means to challenge the hegemony of the Jewish majority over state institutions.

Another manifestation of the oppositional consciousness is the growing number of civil society institutions that act on local, regional and national bases and present a new model of political activity. The mid-1970s have marked the initial process of establishing civic associations in order to address a pressing collective need. Arab civic associations began advocating community interests and sought to provide services to the Arab community in areas neglected by the state. One of the first civic associations was the "Committee for the Defense of Arab lands," which was established in order to lobby against the Israeli policy of land confiscation. During this period the "Arab Student Union" was established and as well as the "Union for Arab High Schools Students." These civic associations were hyper-political and sought to represent the basic rights of the Arab community in Israel. This wave of establishing civil society institutions was promoted by the Communist party and was used by it to promote its own political interests vis-à-vis the Israeli authorities that viewed the party as illegitimate opposition albeit legal (Bashir, 2006).

The number of Arab civic associations began to rise constantly from the early 1980s. Although not all registered civic associations are active, the number of those registered reached around 2,609 in 2006 out of which around 1,517 civic associations are still active at the start of 2011.

Table 11.1 Civic associations.

Year	Accumulated number of civic associations	Number of civic associations registered each year
1974	2	2
1976	4	2
1978	5	1
1980	10	5
1981	15	5
1982	32	17
1983	81	49
1984	132	51
1985	174	42
1986	219	45

Year	Accumulated number of civic associations	Number of civic associations registered each year
1987	281	62
1988	363	82
1989	452	89
1990	536	84
1991	634	98
1992	702	68
1993	830	128
1994	953	123
1995	1090	137
1996	1218	128
1997	1334	116
1998	1441	107
1999	1570	129
2000	1712	142
2001	1872	160
2002	1984	112
2003	2121	137
2004	2307	186
2005	2474	167
2006	2609	135

Among the active civic associations, there are 1,385 autonomous service-providing and 132 advocacy civic associations.[3] The wide network of Arab civic associations that operate in different fields forms a counter-public where the interests of the Arab community are represented in such areas as land and urban planning, housing, health services, educational infrastructure, legal rights and services, media and communication, and human rights monitoring.

These civic associations seek to develop and empower Arab society, as well as defend its basic rights vis-à-vis the state. They provide goods and services not adequately or sufficiently offered by the state (Payes, 2003). The activities of the Arab civic associations in various fields have challenged state policies and led to important changes in some fields. Adalah's contribution to the Israeli legal discourse and its impact on state policies in several fields have

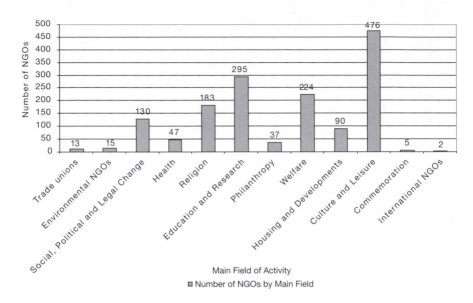

Figure 11.1 Fields of NGO activity.

been significant. The lobbying activities conducted by Mossawa have also influenced, at least slightly, the allocation of resources by governmental institutions. Al-Aqsa Society has had a direct impact on the renovation of important religious and historical Arab sights. These examples and many others illustrate the contribution of Arab civic associations to the welfare of the Arab society in Israel. Although one cannot claim that civic associations have led to revolutionary results, nonetheless one has to recognize the impact of Arab civic associations on the Israeli public sphere and on the development and empowerment of Arab society. Civic associations have certainly assisted in answering some of the needs of the Arab community in a situation where it is discriminated against by state agencies.

Causes Behind the Gradual Expansion of Arab Civic Associations Sector

When it comes to explaining the extensive rise in the number of Arab civic associations in the last two decades it is necessary to look at immediate and direct causes as well as remote and indirect ones. Furthermore, there are internal as well as external, negative and positive causes that have to be considered. Only the combination of all these factors can provide a satisfactory explanation for the quick and constant rise of the number of civic associations active in Arab society.

Table 11.2 The rise of Arab Civic Associations.

Negative Factors

Internal	External
1. Decline of traditional forms of social solidarity and mutual support.	1. Ineffective political participation in the Knesset.
2. The weakness of Arab political parties.	2. Lack of sufficient social and economic services provided by the state.
3. Inefficiency of social services of the Arab municipalities.	3. Segregated Israeli job market and lack of economic opportunities matching capabilities of educated Arabs.

Positive factors

Internal	External
1. The growing of individual autonomy in Arab society.	1. The globalization of the human, minority and indigenous rights' discourse.
2. Growing number of Arab academics and their professional capabilities.	2. The rise of social movements and civil society in other countries of the world.
3. The rising socio-political consciousness of the Arab population and its insistence on equal citizenship rights.	3. The rise of Israeli NGO sector and its vibrant presence in the public arena.
4. The rising social entrepreneurship among young Arab leaders and the success of many Arab civic associations.	4. The availability of external financial resources.

Internal Negative Factors

1. Arab social structure in general and in Israel in particular has been undergoing a massive change. The familial solidarity that characterized Arab society, which provided one of the most important sources of support for the individual, has been eroding in the last few decades. Although one cannot claim that the Arab family does not exert power in the daily life of the average Arab citizen, nevertheless the extended family can no longer be considered as a coherent sociological entity. The Arab family has shrunk to include almost only first blood ties. This major change is neither homogeneous nor universal. Nonetheless, it is leading to the rise of alternative social mechanisms to fill the gap of solidarity and support. Local, regional and national civic associations with clear philanthropic orientation have been playing an important role in providing such a social need. This role has been extended to include civic associations providing alternative educational frameworks, such as the pre-schooling systems established in Arab towns and cities mainly by civic associations affiliated with the Islamic movement, and elementary schools, established by regional or national civic associations to set an alternative educational system to the official one provided and strictly controlled by the state.

2. One of the characteristics of Arab politics in Israel is the inability of Arab political parties to influence the decision-making process in Israel (Jamal, 2007b). One reason behind this is that Arab parties are a recent phenomenon of only the last two decades. Except for the Communist Party, which is a Jewish-Arab party despite the fact that since the mid-1960s it has been dominated by Arabs, the first pure Arab party, the Democratic Arab Party, was established in Israel in 1988. The United Arab List and the National Democratic assembly entered the Knesset elections only in 1996. This late access to the political arena has resulted in an exclusion from main junctures of power in the Israeli political system to minor influence in the political system. Arab parties have not been able to efficiently represent the basic interests and needs of the Arab society. They are not given a chance to influence basic decision-making processes that have direct implications on the Arab population. This reality has not led Arab citizens to abandon the Israeli democracy.

   Despite the declining number of Arab voters for the Knesset, the majority of eligible Arabs still participate in the elections. Most Arab citizens vote for Arab parties, holding the state rather then the parties responsible for their poor economic and political situation. Notwithstanding this pattern of behavior, many Arab leaders began searching in the last decades for alternative methods and mechanisms to influence the Israeli state and lobby for Arab rights. Whereas a minority of people became apathetic, many of those disappointed from the Knesset began establishing professional civic associations that anchor a subject matter central to the welfare and interest of the Arab society. In many cases, the activists establishing the civic associations, or leading them, were affiliated with a particular political party or political movement, such as with the Galilee Society or Al-Aqsa society.

3. Arab municipalities have always been discriminated against in the allocation of governmental resources (Al-Haj and Rosenfeld, 1988; Razin, 2000; Fares, 2002b). To that one should add the inefficiency in running Arab municipalities caused by internal political reasons, mainly familial patronage politics (Jamal, 2006a). As a result, Arab municipalities were never in a position to be able to provide efficient social services to their population. This situation has led many young activists to take the lead and initiate local or regional organizations that assist the poor families, especially towards the opening of the school year or before central holidays. These initiatives were developed and even politicized, mainly by the Islamic movement, which viewed philanthropy as an important pillar in the Islamic faith. Therefore, many of the civic associations, providing basic social services, such as funds for education or financial support for poor families are affiliated with the Islamic movement, thereby forming a basic source of its influence and power among the Arab population.

External Negative Factors

1. As mentioned earlier, Arab parties are excluded from the major junctures of power in the Israeli regime. Arab parties are viewed as illegitimate partners when it comes to forming governmental coalitions in Israel. Even in crisis situations, such as during the Rabin government in the early 1990s that needed the Arab parties to maintain its rule, the Arab parties were not brought into the coalition but were asked to form a minority block in the Knesset that prevented the opposition from having a majority and vote out the government. Since they are in the opposition, Arab parties cannot exert political pressure or lobby efficiently for the basic rights of Arab society. Therefore, Arab leaders, especially those disappointed in formal politics, have been seeking new avenues of influence. Many of them viewed the NGO sector as a good avenue of influence that does not entail commitment to the rules of the game set by the Knesset. Some of the major advocacy and lobbying civic associations, such as Adalah and Mossawa, provide the parties with important informative and political backing. They empower the parties either by providing them with information or by sharing the responsibility for convincing state agencies to change their policies. These two civic associations advocate the case of the Arab society internationally, thereby broadening the pressure on the state to change its policies towards this population.

2. The Israeli state has never viewed Arab citizens in equal terms, enacting policies that translated its dominant ethnic character into the social reality (Jamal, 2007c). Government policies have not only discriminated against Arab citizens but also excluded them from social and economic benefits provided by the state in major fields such as pre-school services, social security, health services, educational youth frameworks, public libraries, and care for the elderly. The lack or deficient provision of such basic services has deepened the need for internal social support. However, the decline of traditional norms and forms of solidarity mentioned earlier made new forms of social support necessary. It was exactly in this unintended collusion between state policies and social transformations that philanthropic and welfare civic associations appeared to be necessary and as a result began to form. In the last few years the municipalities in Israel in general and in Arab society in particular have sought to deliver some of these services, especially in social welfare and sport, but not only through independent social actors, such as civic associations. This development is part of a broader process of privatization that meets the neoliberal philosophy dominant in Israel today. This trend has resulted in the rise of many local civic associations.

3. The Israeli job market has always been segregated on national grounds. "Avoda Ivrit" (Jewish handcraft) has been a basic Zionist value since the initial stages of the movement. The integration of Arabs into the Jewish economy was fraught with social and economic disadvantages in that Arab

workers were generally hired for jobs on the bottom of the employment scale (Lewin-Epstein and Semyonov, 1993). Arabs, who were mostly farmers during the 1950s and 1960s lost their land as a result of a systematic process of land confiscation (Kidar and Yiftachel, 2006). This policy has led to a proletariatization of Arab society, leading to total dependency of Arab labor on the Jewish economy. The lack of a broad employment infrastructure in Arab towns, and the evident preference of Jewish employers for Jewish workers caused income gaps, inequality and clear differences in standard of living for the two communities. Liberalization of the job market in the 1980s and 1990s further highlighted the structural inferiority of the Arab labor force in Israel. The expansion of labor force opportunities in the scientific, academic, and service sectors and the reduction in the number of people employed in manual work, including the agricultural sector, made discrimination against the qualified and professional Arab labor force even more conspicuous. In 1999, 50.5% of the Ashkenazi Jews (descendants of parents from European-American origins), and 23.7% of Mizrahi Jews (descendants of parents from Asian-African origins) were engaged in academic, professional or administrative professions. On the other hand, only 14.7% of the Arab labor force occupied the same fields that year (Adva Institute, 1999). Most Arabs with an academic background are employed in the field of Arab education as teachers and headmasters. In 2002, 65% of the Arab labor force was still engaged as skilled and unskilled workers in the fields of construction, light industry and services (Fares, 2002a). The absence of Arab workers in lucrative fields, like high-tech, informatics, aviation and communication clarifies not only the structural inequality that the Arab labor force is facing, but also explains the need for Arab academics to look for alternative job opportunities. The marginal presence or complete absence of Arab professional workers in most governmental offices and state companies, like the Electric company, Mekorot (administrator of the water economy in Israel), Bezeq (the "national" telephone company), Solel Bone (a construction corporation), Amidar (a public housing company), etc. lead to major frustration among the Arab educated elite. Of the 59,938 workers in the state's services in January 2000, only 2,835 (5%) are Arabs, most of whom worked in either the Ministry of Health or the Ministry of Education (Sikkuy Center, 2000).

This reality has led some Arabs to look for independent jobs, such as in commerce or in the professional market. Many Arab families, able to finance the study of their children, have encouraged them to study medicine, law, or civil engineering. These professions were conceived to be prestigious and independent with a high income. In a later stage, those who graduated from college and did not seek to be independent professionals and were politically conscious saw the NGO sector as a good avenue to combine at least three elements: a decent job, professional autonomy and a sense of contribution to the welfare of Arab society. Therefore, it is important to note in this context that some of the Arab educated elite joined the NGO sector voluntarily and not because of the lack of job opportunities in the Israeli economy. These view the NGO sector as an avenue for protest and contention and thereby challenge the state and its policies.

Internal Positive Factors

1. As mentioned earlier, Arab society has been undergoing major structural changes. The extended family structure has been declining and instead there has been a constant rise in the centrality of the small family cell. Although this process is not homogeneous, it is recognized in all parts and segments of Arab society. An important splinter of this process is individualization. This last process is intensified with the influence of the democratic system in Israel on Arab society. These factors have broadened the autonomy of the Arab individual, mainly men but recently in large cities also women. This individual autonomy has enabled Arab individuals to seek futures beyond their tradition, norms or scope of the family. Among the avenues of individual mobility is the NGO sector, which is usually based on voluntary and individual decisions. The NGO sector is a realm that is beyond the family but does not fall within the confines of the state, thereby enabling a major space for personal freedom and autonomy (Hegel, 1952; Keane, 1998a; Rosenblum and Post, 2002).

2. This process has been aided by a constant rise in the number of Arab academics and other Arab educated elite in Israel. Despite the fact that the number of Arab academics is still low compared with those from Israeli-Jewish society, nevertheless the rising number of academics has acted as social agents with initiative providing answers to pressing needs and fighting harmful policies. The available data on Arab students and academics show a clear growth in their numbers (Al-Haj, 2003). In 1956/7 there were 46 Arab students, which amounted to 0.6% of all students in the Israeli universities that year. In the school year 1979/80 the number went up to 1,634 (3%). In 1998/99 the number of Arab students went up to 7,903, which is 7.1% of all students in Israel. These changes show that there is clear expansion in the number of Arab citizens that attend higher education to get a profession or improve their chances in the job market. The percentage of Arab students that finished their B.A. studies went up in a decade (1988–1998) from 6.7% to 8.7%. The rise in the number of Arab academics and cultural elites has influenced the political awareness of the whole Arab population which was made more aware of its rights.

   This new educated elite has acquired very important social and cultural capital that made it aware of its own disadvantages relative to Jewish-Israeli counterparts or compared with Arab educated elites in the Arab world, where avenues of mobility and promotion are much higher. While seeking avenues of influence, this elite has to face the limits set on its integration in the economic and political fields. The NGO sector became a default solution for some and a free choice for others. Regardless of the reason, given the structural opportunities available for the average Arab academics and the fact that their national commitment cannot be translated into state patriotism, they sought the civic avenue, namely the NGO sector, in which they can combine personal career with a national commitment towards the Arab minority.

3. The success of some of the civic associations reflected a broader social process, among which is the rise of a strata of Arab social entrepreneurs that set new models of political and social thinking and behavior. These social entrepreneurs did not operate in the business world, but nevertheless adopted much of the patterns of thinking and behavior dominant there. They had to be fully aware of the Israeli political scene, of the opportunities within the international NGO sector and have the capabilities to compete over scarce resources provided by the foreign funders. The initial success of these entrepreneurs and their ability to lead their civic associations into social and political prominence led many other Arab activists to follow the lead. The successful civic associations and their leaders became a model to imitate in the local, regional and national level. Many new civic associations were either established by people who were previously employed in the field and decided to go independent or by a particular NGO that sought to expand on one aspect of its activities or encourage the rise of a new avenue of civic activity. In many cases, the entrepreneurs establishing a new NGO were aware of what needs to be done in order to promote and succeed in their project.

External Positive Factors

1. An important factor that influenced the rise of the Arab NGO sector was the rise of similar sectors in other parts of the world. The success of the pressure exerted by civil organizations on the authoritarian regimes of Eastern Europe during the 1970s–80s influenced many political and civil activists as well as scholars to believe that civil society contributes to empowerment (Touraine, 1983; Diamond, 1994; Feldman, 1997). As Tsutsui put it; "linkage to global civil society gives rise to ethnic mobilization because it diffuses models of claim-making based on human rights ideas (Tsutsui, 2004). Civil society was conceived to be not only necessary but also sufficient for democratization. This belief led to the rise of civic associations in many countries all over the world. Among the central groups that viewed civic associations as a good avenue to promote their interests were indigenous and national minorities, which began establishing civic associations to protect their rights. Civic associations were viewed also as agents of empowerment and development and therefore were established by many deprived groups. This belief in civic associations' power to lead to political democratization, empowerment and development influenced Arab leaders in Israel. The rise of NGOs in the Occupied

Palestinian Territories intensified the process. Political or social activists that did not want to join the parties or state agencies began establishing their own civic associations.

2. The international trend was strongly felt within the Jewish sector in Israel. Hundreds if not thousands of civic associations have been established in Israel since the enacting of the civic associations law in 1980. Israeli civic associations were established mainly by Jewish activists and were engaged with matters concerning the Jewish population in Israel. Therefore, they were conceived to be national (Ben-Eliezer, 2001; Yishai, 1997). Although there were attempts to integrate Arabs in some Israeli civic associations and there were many Jewish-Arab civic associations established to promote the relationship between the two communities or provide services needed in both communities, Arab social entrepreneurs were not ready to be on the margins of Israeli civil society the way they are on the margins of the Israeli polity and economy. Arab social entrepreneurs therefore took the Israeli Jewish NGO sector as a model that could be imitated based on the same legal regulations.

3. The final but crucial factor influencing the quick rise in the number of Arab civic associations in Israel is the availability of foreign financial funding. It is hard to evaluate all the money pumped into the Arab civil sector in Israel (Haklai, 2008). Nevertheless, one can speak of several millions of dollars that are distributed to tens of civic associations. The first main source is Western countries, mainly European, American and Canadian. The second source is Arab countries. Most of the money received from Western sources goes to secular civic associations, whereas most of the money received from Arab states goes to religious civic associations belonging to the Islamic movement. Only a small number of Arab civic associations receive money from the state. This heavy dependency of Arab civic associations on foreign donors raises the fears expressed in the literature that ideas are driven by priorities of donors (Hulme and Edwards, 1997). The suspicious reaction of American donors to the publication of the Future Vision Documents, mentioned earlier, is a good example to illustrate the inherent relationship between donors' agenda and policies adopted by civic associations (Jamal, 2008).

Impact and Implications of the Growth in the Arab NGO Sector in Israel

As indicated earlier, the literature on the role and impact of civil society institutions is neither united nor monolithic. Nevertheless, there are several themes that are common to most examinations of civic associations and civil society. These themes sum up the disputes between civic associations' scholars and will form the frame within which the impact of Arab civil society institutions will be addressed, namely democratization, empowerment and development. Such a task is not easy to be summed up briefly. This section will present general ideas supported by selective examples. It is not an over-statement to claim that each of the following cases could become a focus for future independent research projects.

1 Civic associations and democratization

A basic assumption of the liberal literature, especially the Tocquevillian tradition, is that Civic associations bolster civil society by virtue of their participatory and democratic approach (Kaviraj and Khilnani, 2001). A strong and plural civil society is necessary to guard against excesses of state power. Civic associations are viewed as central to the mobilization of pressure for political change. Civil society is considered to be important for checking abuses of state power and for preventing authoritarian forces from taking over a political system. It is also important for encouraging wide citizenship participation and public scrutiny of the state. Civic associations strengthen the institutional arena, giving more opportunity to different social groups to have a voice and to form a watchdog vis-à-vis the state. Furthermore, civic associations can lead to an associational revolution in which one or more civic associations deal with topics of public concern. The process of civic associations networking is very helpful in pluralizing civil society, expanding the number of voices addressing government and establishing a buffer zone between the state and the citizens. Such a zone is important for the autonomy of the individual and her pursuit of the "good life."

There are about 1,517 acting Arab civic associations out of almost 33,000 civic associations in Israel in general, so this amounts to almost 5% of all civic associations in Israel. This is a relatively small number that does not represent the percentage of the Arab population in Israeli society (18%). Nevertheless, the 1,517 existing civic associations mirror a trend that has been taking place mainly in the last two decades.

Civic associations are being established in order to address needs and interests of groups of citizens, thereby increasing the number of voices exerting pressure on the government to meet certain needs. The rising number of Arab civic associations since the early 1990s has marked the intensive pluralization of Arab society. The variety of civic associations in terms of mandate, mission and strategic goals is very high. There are numerous civic associations in the fields of development, empowerment, advocacy and lobbying. There are also a great number of civic associations in the social welfare, educational, legal, housing, public health and religious fields. The multiplicity of civic associations in terms of ideological and political orientation is also very high. The high number of civic associations certainly reflects plurality and diversity, thereby contributing to the internal democratization of Arab society. The diverse number of Arab civic associations contributes to tolerance and to internal dialogue between the different organizations and social groups they represent. Despite their differences, Arab civic associations, managed to introduce new social, political and cultural patterns of behavior which were not carried out by political parties. The number of conferences organized by civic associations and in which activists and the public participate is in far higher proportion then before they were founded. Arab civic associations have opened new spheres of deliberation for the Arab public. These new spaces enable various segments of the Arab public to participate in discussing matters of public interest, be they vis-à-vis the state or internal to Arab society.

Furthermore, the variety of Arab civic associations mirrors the rising attempts to scrutinize state policies and challenge official decisions that harm the Arab population, while replacing state agencies in providing support for the average Arab citizen. The NGO sector is leading to a fundamental associational change that increases the number of voices raised against governmental neglect, forming a buffer zone between the state and Arab citizens. Arab civic associations assist Arab citizens to be aware of misuses of power by the state and provide strategies of resistance.

An example is Adalah's recent success with the Supreme Court, leading to a landmark ruling on February 27, 2006, in which a seven-Justice panel unanimously ruled to cancel a governmental decision establishing "National Priority Areas,"[4] finding that it discriminates against Arab citizens of Israel on the basis of race and national origin. The Court declared that the division of the country into "National Priority Areas" (NPAs) in the field of education should be canceled since the policy lacks clear and consistent criteria in the awarding of very lucrative benefits, and discriminated against Arab citizens of Israel (Decision No. 2288).[5] The Supreme Court gave the Education Ministry a year to change its policy and marked it as unconstitutional, something that could lead to major changes in other fields. The success of Adalah to discredit governmental policy that has been applied in various fields is a clear example of the role and impact that Arab civic associations could have on the democratization of the state.

However, as mentioned in the theoretical introduction, one has to be cautious when it comes to the inherent relationship assumed between civil society institutions and democratization. One has to address the question of why the advocacy and lobbying of civic associations do not always succeed. To clarify this issue and answer the question I relate to five different interrelated topics.

a. When it comes to creating political change leading to democratization, state intentions are very important to evaluate the contribution of civic associations in the context of democratization. The Israeli state, which is an ethnically nationalizing state (Brubaker, 2004), sought ways to dismantle civic associations' demands for more equal allocation policies and bypass requests for integrating more Arabs in decision-making positions. The government policies towards Arab civic associations are best mirrored in the policies adopted to overcome court rulings and bypass its verdicts when these verdicts promote equal rights for Arab citizens, such as in what has become to be known as the Ka'adan case.[6] Furthermore, although Arab civic associations can always address the Supreme Court, the intentions of other state agencies are very important when examining the influence that the NGO sector could have on democratization. The example of the Bill of the "National Jewish Fund Land," mentioned earlier, demonstrates the state's legislative branch attempts to bypass court rulings.. The same could be said about the attempts made to block activities made by the Committee of Internally Displaced Palestinians in Israel, seeking to promote the rights of the internally displaced. Another example of state efforts to block activities of Arab civic associations is manifested in declaring religious and traditional sights, such as mosques and cemeteries, as closed military zones, aiming to prevent efforts made by the Al-Aqsa society to renovate them.[7]

b. Another important issue to address when examining the impact of Arab civic associations on democratization is the influence that the donors have on civic associations' policies. Although Arab civic associations in Israel were not set as a result of an external scheme and are grassroots organizations stemming from genuine needs, this does not mean that they cannot fall into the "trap" of survival, developing "upward" rather than "downward" accountability. The fact that the major financial support of Arab civic associations, with the exception of the Islamic civic associations, comes from Western countries, one has to consider the relationship between the agenda of these sources and governmental policies. The support given to Arab civic associations could free the Israeli government from its responsibility towards Arab society without having to pay the price of losing its tolerant and democratic appeal.

c. In their classical book, *The Civic Culture*, Almond and Verba claimed that "Pluralism, even if not explicitly political pluralism, may indeed be one of the most important foundations of political democracy (Almond and Verba, 1989: 265). Notwithstanding this position, however, the pluralization of society and the rise of diversity could reflect fragmentation and become a ground for destructive competition, especially when the state views internal divisions as a major tool of domination. As could be seen in the case of Arab civic associations, there is a clear split between the secular and the Islamic civic associations. Each of these sectors operates separately. On the other hand, a brief look at the relationship between the civic associations within each sector, shows there is much evidence that many civic associations boycott each other or fiercely compete with each other on personal grounds or based on their party affiliation. Many of the prominent Arab civic associations are affiliated with political parties and this pattern of relationship leads to much tension between them, thereby harming their ability to mobilize commonly to achieve the rights of their constituency. This internal competition between Arab civic associations has a vital constructive dimension, but it also has negative implications. Much energy and resources are invested in waging internal competitions rather than in developing plural civic culture.

d. The personalization of civic associations should be viewed as another important phenomenon harming the democratization role of civic associations. As Hadenius and Uggla have claimed, the "traditional norms, rituals and patterns of authority are part of the reason why a strong and viable civil society is absent in many Third World countries" (1996: 1625). Although one should not expect that social norms and deeply rooted socio-cultural values and behaviors have to be totally transformed in order for civil society to develop, some democratic attributes and communicative norms have to develop in order for civil society to promote tolerance, willingness to compromise and respect for opposing viewpoints (Diamond, 1994: 8).

   When examining Arab civil society in Israel one notices that some traditional norms and patterns of authority still dominate many of the civic associations such as its personalization. The personalization of institutions and leadership roles is by no means unique to Arab society. It has been a familiar feature of the political landscape throughout history, and continues to exist in varying degrees in many parts of the world, including Israel. Overall, however, its significance as a shaper of politics, especially public institutions, began to decline with modernity and the spread of democratic forms of government and the influence of modern media (Deutsch, 1966; Mutz, 1998). Despite the fact that such a process has partially taken place in Arab society, the identification of public institutions, such as parties and civic associations with particular leaders is still common. Personal patterns of leadership in civic associations is also common, where leaders control the decision-making process and enforce their will on the rest of the staff.[8] This pattern of behavior turns many of the civic associations internally undemocratic, characterized by authoritarian or charismatic personalized leadership limiting the contribution of their NGO to the flourishing of civic culture. In such cases, internal debates are suffocated and the gap between discourse and practice becomes apparent. In some cases such a gap leads to the fragmentation of NGOs and their public delegitimation.

e. The patriarchal social structure is another important factor that has to be considered when examining the role of civic associations in democratizing society (Kandiyoti, 1991). This factor is especially important when it comes to the impact of feminist civic associations on women's rights in society. Although there are a number of feminist Arab civic associations seeking to promote women's rights and change traditional social patterns of behavior, the impact of these civic associations on Arab society is marginal. Some women civic associations are traditional, operating according to Islamic law. Others, which are secular, do not dare engage in direct conflict with dominant social and cultural norms. Furthermore, there is much social resistance to efforts made by women civic associations, especially when it comes to women taking central social roles or women having autonomy over their bodies. The waves of Islamization characterizing

Arab society in the last two decades render feminist efforts to liberalize society limited to symbolic fields only (Shalhoub-Kevorkian, 2007).

2 Civic associations and empowerment

Empowerment is viewed as one of the most basic contributions of civic associations. When looking at the literature on civic associations one finds that it is usually assumed that civic associations lead a process of enhancing the capacity of individuals or groups to make choices and to transform those choices into desired actions and outcomes. Central to this process are actions which both build individual and collective rights, and improve the efficiency and fairness of the organizational and institutional contexts which govern the use of these assets (World Bank, 2006; Mercer, 2002). Civic associations are expected to provide their stakeholders with information necessary to socially and geographically widen their possibilities of political participation; to provide information that is lacking in order to uncover discriminatory governmental policies; to deepen the personal and organizational capacity of citizens' engagement in the public sphere; to enhance the representation of interests of the marginalized groups within the wider public arena; to campaign on behalf of marginalized groups, especially in the case of minorities, and seek to influence public policy towards them; and to challenge state power by developing alternative sets of perspectives and policies and to monitor its activities. These roles of civic associations strengthen civil society by increasing the number of intermediary organizations between citizens and state (Fisher, 1998).

When examining Arab civic associations in Israel one finds that most of the expected tasks described in the literature are aspired to. Some of the Arab civic associations enhance the capacity of individuals and groups within Arab society to make better choices by providing them with the necessary information. Many civic associations have developed special capacities to research the field in which they are active. For instance, *Women Against Violence*, a feminist NGO that provides shelter for battered women has conducted a large research on the attitudes of Arab society on women's status and roles (Ghanem, 2005). I'lam has conducted its own research on media consumption culture in Arab society (Jamal, 2006b). Mada has investigated Arab attitudes on various political and social topics (Mada al-Carmel, 2004; Rouhana, 2007). The Galilee Society ran its own social index poll. Mossawa has published extensively on budgetary issues and explicated the areas and methods where Arabs are discriminated against, and on discrimination and racism against Arab citizens (Fares, 2004; Mossawa, 2009).

These civic associations and others have published their own newsletters, brochures, booklets, and other publications. The information provided by Arab civic associations has been very important and necessary for Arab as well as other political parties to exert pressure on the political system to change public policy in certain central fields. One of the best examples is Mossawa's follow-up on the governmental budget and its implications on the Arab society. Another example is the information provided by the Alternative Planning Center on housing and planning policies of the state and their implications on the Arab population. A good example in this regard is the publishing of the plan to expand residential areas in upper Nazareth in order to block the development of the Arab village Ein-Mahel (*Kul al-Arab*, October 25, 2007).

An important example of the empowering role played by Arab civic associations is the extensive educational program developed by the Arab Association for Human Rights (HRA) in Arab schools. HRA runs an educational program in Arab elementary and high schools, in which pupils are exposed to human rights discourse and are made aware of their basic rights as humans and as citizens. The aim of the program is to empower pupils and make them aware of the gaps between their tangible reality and their fundamental human and civil rights. Such a mission reflects the community anchoring and outreach of the HRA, empowering a greater segment of Arab society by teaching them, not only what their rights are, but also how to achieve them. The HRA educates for human values, such as liberty, equality and individual autonomy. Such a task does not only help pupils become aware of their rights vis-à-vis the state, but also to be aware of the repressive norms and values within the traditional Arab society.[9]

Another educational program developed by the Islamic organization Iqra'a, developed special centers to assist school pupils before exams, offering special courses that prepare high school students for university studies, and operates on university campuses to assist students in their studies. Such activities come to empower Arab youth and certainly contribute to what Rabinowitz has described as a special model of civil society developed by the Islamic movement (Rabinowitz, 2001).

Notwithstanding these constructive activities, the internal fragmentation and competition between Arab civic associations weaken its empowering mission. A brief look at the Arab NGO scene in Israel shows the fierce competition over financial resources on the one hand and over public appeal on the other. In many cases one finds that the competition between civic associations on financial resources aligns with party affiliation or ideological grounds. The civic associations affiliated with the Islamic movement and the secular civic associations hardly cooperate (ibid.). The differences between them and secular civic associations are usually limited either to ideological or personal reasons. Islamic civic associations' empowerment and development activities are utilized to nurture the movement's political power and ideology. The Islamic movement, both wings, strive for an ideal society that does not necessarily meet the standards of liberal freedom of equality. This movement is satisfied with the fact that the state is not fulfilling its duties in certain fields, such as in education, enabling the movement to run its own educational system.[10] The deep connection between development and non-liberal traditional ideology clashes with the goals and interests of many secular

NGOs, especially those concerned with human rights and feminist interests.

The competition between secular civic associations, however, over financial support is much stronger, since all of them are supported by the same European or North American foundations. This tension has led according to some activists to "industrial espionage," where certain civic associations either helped in drying other civic associations from financial resources by leaking misinformation about them or by "stealing" ideas and programs and presenting them to donors as originally theirs.[11]

Another example of the fragmentation within the Arab NGO sector is on spatial and geographical background. Arab society is located in three almost completely separate areas, namely the Galilee, the Triangle area and the Negev. The NGO sector is most developed in the Galilee, especially in the three big Arab or mixed cities – Haifa, Nazareth and Shafa'amer. There are serious gaps in number, size and scope of activity of civic associations between the three areas. Almost all the Arab civic associations operating on the national level are located in the Galilee. The exceptions are the Civic associations affiliated with the Islamic movement that is centered in Um Al-Fahem, one of the largest Arab cities in the northern part of the Triangle area. This gap between the number, size and scope of civic associations leads to some tension and competition between the regions and leads to the pluralization of particular places at the neglect of others. The gaps between Galilee and Negev are huge. In fact, most national civic associations that established an office or extended their activities to the Negev area had to close their office or stop their engagement there. An exception is the office and activity of Adalah, which came under regional attack. The Regional Council of the Unrecognized Villages (RCUV) in the Negev has several times accused the civic associations coming from the north of ignoring the authentic needs of the local Bedouin population and operating in forms that promote their interests rather then the interests of the population.[12]

3 Civic associations and development

It is hard to address all themes related to development. Therefore, this part will be limited to two themes only, namely wage gap and poverty, and pre-school education. Both issues demonstrate that Arab society shares many characteristics with societies in the developing world. These characteristics make the contribution of NGO to development central.

Arab society in general is located on the lower economic scale in Israel. According to the National Insurance Institute, comparisons between the average wage data from Arab and Jewish settlements indicate that the average Arab income is 60% that of the average Jewish income (Bendleck, 2002). Recent information about the equality index released by the Adva Center in December 2006, notes the average income of an Arab employee is 72% that of the average urban employee income in Israel (Swirski and Konor-Attias, 2006). It is important to note that the same study puts the average income of a Jewish employee of oriental origin at 100%, while the average income of a Jewish employee of Ashkenazi origin is 139%.

The number of Arab citizens living under the poverty line is far beyond their proportion in society. The number of Palestinian Arab families living in poverty has increased from 47.6% of all Palestinian Arab families (112,300 families) in 2002 to 48.4% of all Palestinian Arab families (119,700 families) in 2003. The overall percentages of poor families in Israel, however, was 18.1% in 2002 and 19.3% in 2003. The percentage of poor Jewish families in 2002 was 13.9%, compared to 14.9% in 2003. This data reflects the big gap between Jewish and Arab families (Fares, 2004).

Development activities provided by civic associations are expected to make an important contribution to the welfare of society. Looking at the Arab NGO scene one notices various types of activities that lend support to different segments of Arab society. Many of the welfare and development activities are conducted by religious civic associations. These civic associations have adopted a special model of operation that meets the needs of Arab society (Rabinowitz, 2001). Religious civic associations provide poor families with basic groceries every holiday. They collect their own resources from society and sometimes abroad in order to provide poor families with the support they need.

Furthermore, religious civic associations have provided Arab families with pre-school education in many towns and cities, a basic service that is not universally provided by the state (Filk and Ram, 2004). For example, I'qra'a, an NGO that specializes in providing support to high school pupils and in preparing them for university studies, has alone established kindergartens in more than 30 Arab towns and cities.[13] This NGO has 21 centers in which after-school activities take place. Such a scope is very impressive when taking into consideration the fact that the financial resources of the NGO are very limited and are usually generated from the Arab public through activities organized by the NGO itself. An important characteristic of Iq'ra'a's activity is that many of them are conducted by volunteers. When compared with secular civic associations, there are no secular civic associations with such a scope of voluntary educational activity. This pattern of conduct mirrors the attempts made by civic associations, especially religious, to find internal solutions to problems that Arab citizens face daily. This pattern of voluntarism mirrors the impact of religious communal values on collective action and civic engagement, but also the lack of correspondence between civic associationalism and social liberalization and democratization.

An important characteristic of the religious civic associations concerned with development activities, especially in education, is that they know how to prioritize social change. Religious civic associations are deeply involved in establishing a society that is religious and at the same time aware of modern needs. For that purpose leaders in the movement declare clearly that despite the unfortunate discriminatory policy of the state, they are satisfied to be given a chance to help their own society to develop and promote education according to Islamic tradition.

When it came to educational development, the state has always discrimi-nated against Arab society. The state not only did not assist in establishing independent and alternative schools when Arab parents sought such an option, but also blocked the way for new initiatives, seeking to keep the whole Arab educational system under its direct surveillance. The experiences of Massar in Nazareth and Hiwar in Haifa with the Education Ministry are good examples of the difficulties that civic associations can face, when they challenge the exclusive control of the state over the Arab educational system. The same could be said about the pre-school systems opened by local civic associations in various localities. In most cases, the state was not willing to extend help to these schooling institutions, leaving the responsibility to the civic associations to come up with solutions for their own needs.

These initiatives, led by the growing network of civic associations, whether secular or religious, are playing a growing role in social service provision, strengthening civil society and establishing what Clarke has called a "virtual parallel state" or what could be called in the case of the Arab society in Israel, "default cultural autonomy" (1998). The withdrawal of the state from social services and the unwillingness to assist in providing educational solutions for pre-school children is enabling the Arab NGO sector to establish spheres of education and other social services autonomous from direct state control.

The Israeli state decided to gradually withdraw its social services leaving thousands of people in need of basic help (Filk and Ram, 2004). The decline of the Israeli welfare state demonstrates the importance of an active and broad NGO sector that provides services for those who fall on the margins of the economic cycle. On the other hand, when looking at the Arab civic associations and its resources one notices the financial shortages of the latter. As pointed out by many NGO scholars, it is doubtful that civic associations can offer sustainable substitution for state spending (Edwards, 1999), an observation that is applicable to Arab civic associations in particular, despite their good intentions. The best evidence is the deterioration in the stand-ards of living of a growing number of Arab families and the rising number of those living under the poverty line. The economic crisis that broke out in late 2008 and early 2009 and has continued for a long time has already shown a tremendous negative impact on global civil society in general and on Arab civil society in particular. Since most resources of Arab civic associations come from abroad, the economic decline in all countries has led to budget cuts that hit first what is conceived to be luxurious altruism.

Conclusions

This paper provides several conclusions. The first and most central is that Arab society in Israel has been undergoing a deep process of civic institu-tionalization, where a large number of active civic associations have been established. This process of association has intensified the engagement of

Arab society in lobbying its interests and advocating its needs in the Israeli public sphere and vis-à-vis the state. The rising number of Arab civic association has led to the rise of a plural Arab civil society that may not agree on one political ideal, but nevertheless acts to improve the status of Arab citizens in Israel and substantiate their citizenship. Arab civic associations act to limit state hegemonic power and seek transforming state identity in order to accommodate the ideal of shared citizenship and democratic culture.

The rise of a growing number of Arab civic associations demonstrate the restructuring of Arab politics from one focused solely on formal tools, such as elections, whereby the political party was the main political agent, to adding informal politics, where civic associations became a new and important mobilizer. This change is especially important since civic associations provided Arab society with services that the political parties did not manage to extract from the state. When looking at the Israeli public agenda one cannot but notice the dominant role played by civic associations in bringing Arab issues to the fore and communicating Arab interests. Arab civic associations have provided services in many fields where the state has failed. They pushed state institutions to change their policies in various fields. Thereby, Arab civil society plays a strong counter-hegemonic role vis-à-vis the state, assisting political parties to improve their role in the political arena, despite the fact that one could not easily claim that Arab civil society managed to democratize the Israeli state. The 2009 elections and the rise of the radical right to power provide an indication as to the chauvinist trends taking place in Israeli society and politics.

Nevertheless, Arab civic associations provide a sphere of autonomy from direct state severe power and provide some legal and cultural buffer zone for underprivileged Arab citizens. Despite the fact that the state is not ready to consider the devolution of its power, other than in local authorities and in welfare services, still the Arab NGO sector, whose sources are mostly foreign, manages to be relatively and by default "autonomous." Arab civic associations run a large number of activities that enrich Arab society and culture and supply material and symbolic needs that otherwise are completely ignored.

Notwithstanding the counter-hegemonic role played by Arab civic associations, one cannot but address the gaps between their impact on democratization versus empowerment and development. As demonstrated above, the Arab NGO sector did not manage to strongly democratize the Israeli state towards Arab society. On the contrary, the more the Arab NGO sector is active, the more the state is becoming ethnically oriented. The Citizenship law and the Jewish National Fund law are two cases that illustrate the willingness of the state to take racial measures in order to avoid providing Palestinian-Arab citizens with equal substantive citizenship rights. One could generalize saying that despite the rising number of Arab civic associations in the last few years and their significant lobbying and advocacy efforts, they did not manage to lead to the substantiation of Arab citizenship in Israel. The Israeli state has taken measures that strengthened its ethnicizing and nationalizing policies, leading to the hollowing out of Arab citizenship (Jamal, 2008; Peled, 2007).

The fact that Arab civic associations do not manage to make a serious impact does not mean that they do not make efforts. The weak impact of Arab civic associations on the political character and cultural-ethnic identity of the Israeli state cannot and should not be blamed on the civic associations. The state has been reluctant to respect any efforts made to change its policies towards Arab society. Arab civic associations did not manage to convince or "force" the Israeli state to change its policies and identity in order to accommodate Arab identity and basic rights as equal Israeli citizens.

When looking at empowerment and development one finds that the situation is better. There is no doubt that Arab civic associations managed, either by their own resources or by extracting resources from the state, to solve many problems in the Arab society. It is enough to look at what has been done concerning the basic rights of the unrecognized village in order to get a feel for the contribution of Arab civic associations to the welfare of Arab citizens. Although Arab civic associations cannot provide their constituency with all solutions and despite their internal fragmentation, personalization, lack of institutionalization and the possibility that they play into the hands of neoliberal forces, their contributions to empowerment and development cannot be ignored. Arab civic associations managed to change minority-state relations, but without being able to steer this change in the wished-for direction, something that leaves a big gap between the intentions and the end results of collective action.

Notes

1 Personal interview with a group of Arab civic activists, April 2008.
2 An exception in this regard has been Al-Ard (the land) movement, which drew its name based on the principle of 'first occupancy' and challenged the state on collective national terms. On Al-Ard see: Jiryis, 1976.
3 By autonomous service-providing civic associations I mean those that are not financed fully by the state or any of its agencies, such as the Israeli Association of Community Centers. For details on this type of civic association see: www.matnasim.org
4 The Israeli government has always adopted a policy that divided the country into different areas that were given different levels of attention from governmental offices. The areas that received the mark A were given priority over other areas in the allocation of official resources. Areas close to borders, especially in the northern border with Lebanon, were given special attention and drew much governmental investments. The priority areas include usually exclusively Jewish residential areas. Arab towns and villages have been systematically excluded from these areas. For more details on this policy see: O. Yiftachel (1998) "Construction of Nation and Space Allocation in the Israeli Ethnocracy: Land and Communal Gaps", *Iyoni Ha-Mishpat* (*Law Review*) 21(3), pp. 637–65 (Hebrew).
5 H.C. 2773/98 and H.C. 11163/03, *The High Follow-up Committee for the Arab Citizens in Israel, et. al. v. the Prime Minister of Israel*. www.adalah.org
6 The Ka'adan case has to do with an Arab family that sought to move and live in

a Jewish town near its original village. Its request was rejected by the Israeli Land Authority. The Israeli High Court changed the decision. On this case see: H. Jabareen (2002) "The Future of Arab Citizenship in Israel: Jewish-Zionist time in a place with no Palestinian memory", in D. Levy and Y. Weiss (eds), *Challenging Ethnic Citizenship* (New York: Berghahn Books), pp. 196–220.

7 Personal interview with Sheikh Kamel Rayan, a prominent leader in the Islamic movement, the southern wing and head of Al-Aqsa Society, Tel Aviv, July 24, 2007.

8 Personal interview with a group of NGO leaders, Baka Al-Garbya, February 24, 2009.

9 Personal interview with Mohammad Zeidan, head of Arab Association for Human Rights, Nazareth, August 19, 2008.

10 Personal interview with Sheikh Kamal Khatib from the Islamic Movement, Kfar Kana, July 31, 2008.

11 Personal interview with group of NGO leaders, Tel Aviv, December 5, 2007.

12 Personal Interview with Atwa Abu Freih, General Director of the Regional Council of the Unrecognized Villages in the Negev, Beer Al-Sabe'a, June 8, 2007.

13 Interview conducted by my assistant, Umayma Diab, with an activist in I'qra'a NGO in Um Al-Fahem, August 13, 2007.

References

Adva Institute (1999) *Moa'sakim Lifi Mishlah Yad, Yabishit Lida, Kvotsat Okhlosia Vi-Mean* (Employment according to trade, continent of origin, group affiliation and gender), www.adva.org/ivrit/pearim/occupation-continents.htm

Al-Haj, M. (2003) "Higher Education among the Arabs in Israel: Formal Policy between Empowerment and Control", *Higher Education Policy*, 16, pp. 351–68.

Al-Haj, M. (1995) *Education Empowerment and Control: The Case of the Arabs in Israel* (Albany: State University of New York Press).

Al-Haj, M. and Rosenfeld, H. (1988) *Arab Local Government in Israel* (Tel Aviv: International Center for Peace).

Almond, G. A. and Verba, S. (1989 [1963]), *The Civic Culture: Political Attitudes and Democracy in Five Nations* (Newbury Park, Ca.: Sage Publications).

Bar-Tal, D. and Teichman, Y. (2005) *Stereotypes and Prejudice in Conflict: Representation of Arabs in Israeli Jewish Society* (Cambridge, UK: Cambridge University Press).

Bashir, N. (2006) *Land Day* (Haifa: Mada Al-Carmel).

Bendleck, J. (2002) "Mimotsaa' Skhar Vi Hakhnasa Lifi Yishov Vi Lifi Mishtanin Kalkaliyem Shonim, 1999–2000" (Average wages and incomes according to settlement and different economic variables, 1999–2000). (Jerusalem: The National Insurance Institute).

Ben-Eliezer, U. (2001) "Why there wasn't and is there a Civil Society in Israel?" in *The Characteristics of Civil Society in Israel* (Beer Sheva'a: Center for Research of Third Sector).

Brubaker, R. (2004) *Ethnicity without Groups* (Cambridge, MA.: Harvard University Press).

Burnell, P. and Calvert, P. (eds.) (2004) *Civil Society in Democratization* (London: Frank Cass).

Clarke, G. (1998) "Non-governmental Organizations and Politics in the Developing World", *Political Studies*, XLVI, pp. 36–52.

Cohen, H. (2010) *Good Arabs: The Israeli Security Agencies and the Israeli Arabs, 1948–1967*, Berkeley: University of California Press.

Cohen, J. and Arato, A. (1992) *Civil Society and Political Theory* (Cambridge, Mass.: MIT Press).

Delanty, G. (2000) *Citizenship in a Global Age: Society, Culture, Politics* (Buckingham, Open University Press).

Deutsch, K. (1966) *Nationalism and Social Communication: An Inquiry into the Foundations of Nationality* (Cambridge, Mass.: MIT Press).

Diamond, L. (1994) "Rethinking Civil Society: Toward Democratic Consolidation", *Journal of Democracy*, 5, pp. 4–18.

Dunn, J. (2001) "The Contemporary Political Significance of John Locke's Concept of Civil Society", in S. Kaviraj and S. Khilnani (eds), *Civil Society: History and Possibilities* (Cambridge: Cambridge University Press), pp. 39–57.

Edwards, M. (1999) "NGO Performance – What Breeds Success? New Evidence From South Asia", *World Development*, 27, pp. 361–74.

Enjolras, B. (2008) "Two Hypotheses about the Emergence of a Post-National European Model of Citizenship", *Citizenship Studies*, 12(5), 495–505.

Fares, A. (2004) *The State Budget and the Palestinian Arab Citizens in Israel*, 25 (Haifa: Mossawa Center).

Fares, A. (2002a) *Characters and Ranking of Arab Local Authorities Based on the Social-Economic Scale* (Haifa: Mossawa Center).

Fares, A. (2002b) *Taktsiv Hamdina Li Shnat 2002 Vi Hilka Shil Haokhlosia Haa'ravit* (The state's budget for the year of 2002 and the share of the Arab population) (Haifa: Mossawa Center).

Feldman, S. (1997) "NGOs and Civil Society: (Un)Stated Contradictions", *Annals of the American Academy of Political and Social Science*, 554, pp. 46–65.

Filk, D. and Ram. U. (eds) (2004) *The Rule of Capital: Israeli Society in the Global Age* (Tel Aviv: Hakibutz Ha-Miuhad).

Fisher, J. (1998) *Non-governments: Civic Associations and the Political Development of the Third World* (West Hartford: Kumarian Press).

Foley, M. and Edwards, B. (1996) "The Paradoxes of Civil Society", *Journal of Democracy*, 7, pp. 38–52.

Future Vision (2007) (Nazareth: The Committee of Heads of Arab Local Authorities in Israel).

Ghanem, H. (2005) *Attitudes Towards the Status of Palestinian Women and their Rights in Israel* (Nazareth: Women Against Violence Association).

Habib, A. (2005) "State-Civil Society Relations in Post-Apartheid South Africa", *Social Research*, 72(3), pp. 671–92.

Hadenius, A. and Uggla, F. (1996) 'Making Civil Society Work, Promoting Democratic Development: What Can States and Donors Do?', *World Development*, 24(10): 1621–39.

Haifa Document (2007) (Haifa: Mada Al-Carmel).

Haklai, O. (2004) "Palestinian Civic Associations in Israel: A Campaign for Civic Equality or 'Ethnic Civil Society'"? *Israel Studies*, 9(3).

Haklai, O. (2008) "Helping the Enemy? Why Transnational Jewish Philanthropic Foundations Donate to Palestinian NGOs in Israel," *Nations and Nationalism* 14(3) (July 2008): 581–99.

Havel, V. (1985) "The Power of the Powerless," in J. Keane (ed.), *The Power of the Powerless* (Armonk: M. E. Sharpe), pp. 78–79.

Haynes, J. (1996) *Democracy and Civil Society in the Third World: Politics and New Political Movements* (Cambridge: Polity Press).

Hegel, G. W. F. (1952) *The Philosophy of Right* (Oxford: Oxford University Press), pp. 266–78.

Hulme, D. and Edwards, M. (eds.) (1997) *Civic Associations, States and Donors: Too Close for Comfort?* (London: Macmillan).

Huntington, S. (1991) *The Third Wave: Democratization in the Late Twentieth Century* (Norman, Okla.: University of Oklahoma Press).

Jamal, A. (2009) "Media Culture as Counter-Hegemonic Strategy: The Communicative Action of the Arab Minority in Israel", *Media, Culture and Society*, 31(4), pp. 1–19.

Jamal, A. (2008) "Future Visions and Current Dilemmas: On the Political Ethos of Palestinian Citizens of Israel", *Israel Studies Forum*, 23(2), pp. 3–28.

Jamal, A. (2007a) "Nationalizing States and the Constitution of 'Hollow Citizenship': Israel and its Palestinian Citizens", *Ethnopolitics*, 6(4), pp. 471–93.

Jamal, A. (2007b) "Political Participation and the Lack of Effective Vote for Arabs in Israel", in S. Hasson and M. Karayanni (eds.), *Arabs in Israel: Barriers to Equality* (Jerusalem: Floersheimer Institute for Policy Studies), pp. 125–40 (Hebrew).

Jamal, A. (2007c) "Strategies of Minority Struggle for Equality in Ethnic States: Arab Politics in Israel", *Citizenship Studies* 11(3), pp. 263–82.

Jamal, A. (2006a) "The Arab Leadership in Israel: Ascendance and Fragmentation", *Journal of Palestine Studies*, 35(2), pp. 6–22.

Jamal, A. (2006b) *The Culture of Media Consumption among National Minorities: The Case of Arab Society in Israel* (Nazareth: I'lam Center).

Jamal, A. (2006c) "The Vision of the 'Political Nation' and the Challenge of 'State of all its Citizens': Explorations in Azmi Bishara's Political Thought", *Alpayeem Journal*, 30, pp. 71–113.

Jamal, A. (2005) "On the Morality of Arab Collective Rights in Israel", *Adalah's Newsletter*, 12, available at www.adalah.org/newsletter/eng/apr05/ar1.pdf.

Jamal, A. (2002) "Abstention as Participation: The paradoxes of Arab politics in Israel, in A. Arian and M. Shamir (eds), *The Elections in Israel—2001* (Jerusalem: Israeli Institute for Democracy), pp. 57–100.

Jiryis, S. (1976) *The Arabs in Israel* (New York: Monthly Review Press).

Kandiyoti, D. (ed.) (1991) *Women, Islam and the State* (Philadelphia: Temple University Press).

Kaufman, I. (1997) *Arab National Communism in the Jewish State* (Gainesville: University of Florida Press).

Kaviraj, S. and Khilnani, S. (eds) (2001) *Civil Society: History and Possibilities* (Cambridge: Cambridge University Press).

Keane, J. (1998a) *Civil Society and the State: New European Perspectives* (London: University of Westminster Press), pp. 1–31.

Keane, J. (1998b) *Civil Society: Old Images, New Visions* (Cambridge: Polity Press).

Khilnani, S. (2001) "The Development of Civil Society", in S. Kaviraj and S. Khilnani (eds), *Civil Society: History and Possibilities* (Cambridge: Cambridge University Press), pp. 11–32.

Kidar, S. and Yiftachel, O. (2006) "Land Regime and Social Relations in Israel", in H. de Soto and F. Cheneval (eds), *Realizing Property Rights* (Zurich: Ruffer and Rub Publishing House).

Korten, D. (1990) *Getting to the 21st Century: Voluntary Action and the Global Agenda* (West Hartford, CT).

Lewin-Epstein, N. and Semyonov, M. (1993) *The Arab Minority in Israel's Economy* (Boulder: Westview).

Linz, J. and Stepan, A. (1996) *Problems of Democratic Transition and Consolidation: Southern Europe, South America, and Post-Communist Europe* (Baltimore, Johns Hopkins University Press).

Lustick, I. (1980) *Arabs in the Jewish State: Israel's Control of a National Minority* (Austin: University of Texas Press).

Mada al-Carmel, (2004) *Palestinians in Israel: Socio-Economic Survey 2004* (Haifa).

Mari, S. (1978) *Arab Education in Israel* (Syracuse: Syracuse University Press).

Mendelson, S. and Glenn, J. (eds.) (2002) *The Power and Limits of Civic Associations: A Critical Look at Building Democracy in Eastern Europe and Eurasia* (New York: Columbia University Press).

Mercer, C. (2002) "Civic Associations, Civil Society and Democratization: A Critical Review of the Literature", *Progress in Development Studies*, 2(1), pp. 5–22.

Mossawa, *Racism Report*, 21.3.09. Available at: www.mossawacenter.org/default.php?lng=1&dp=2&fl=13&pg=2

Mutz, D. (1998) *Impersonal Influence: How Perception of Mass Collectives Affect Political Attitudes* (Cambridge: Cambridge University Press).

O'Donnell, G. and Schmitter, P. (1986) *Transitions from Authoritarian Rule: Tentative Conclusions about Uncertain Democracies* (Baltimore: The Johns Hopkins University Press).

Or Commission Report (2003) (Jerusalem: Ministry of Justice).

Payes, S. (2003) Palestinian Civic Associations in Israel: A Campaign for Civic Equality in a Non-Civic State, *Israel Studies*, 8(1), pp. 60–90.

Pelcynski, Z. A. (1998) "Solidarity and 'The Rebirth of Civil Society'" in Poland, in J. Keane (ed.) *Civil Society and the State: New European Perspectives* (London: Verso), pp. 361–80.

Peled, Y. (2007) 'Citizenship Betrayed: Israel's Emerging Immigration and Citizenship Regime', *Theoretical Inquiries in Law* 8(2): 333–58.

Putnam, R. (2000) *Bowling Alone: The Collapse and Revival of American Community*, New York: Simon & Schuster.

Rabinowitz, D. (2001) "De Tocqueville in Um Al-Fahem", in Yoav Peled and Adi Ofir (eds.) *Israel: From a Military to Civil Society?* (Jerusalem: Van Leer and Hakibutz Ha-Miuhad), pp. 350–60.

Rabinowitz, D. (1997) *Overlooking Nazareth: The Ethnography of Exclusion in Galilee* (Cambridge: Cambridge University Press).

Razin, I. (2000) *Gaps in Budgets' Wealth of the Local Municipalities in Israel 2000* (Jerusalem: Floersheimer Center).

Rekhess, E. (1993) *The Arab Minority in Israel: Between Communism and Arab Nationalism.* Tel Aviv: Hakibbutz Hamiuchad.

Rosenblum, N. and Post, R. (eds) (2002) *Civil Society and Government* (Princeton: Princeton University Press), pp. 1–25.

Rose, R. (1994) 'Postcommunism and the Problem of Trust', *Journal of Democracy*, 5(3): 18–30.

Rouhana, N. (ed.) (2007) *Attitudes of Palestinians in Israel on Key Political and Social Issues: Survey Research Results* (Haifa: Mada al-Carmel).

Rubin-Peled, A. (2001) *Debating Islam in the Jewish State* (New York: State University of New York Press).

Schneider, C. L. (1995) *Shantytown Protest in Pinochet's Chile* (Philadelphia: Temple University Press).

Shalhoub-Kevorkian, N. (ed.) (2007) *Palestinian Feminist Writing: Between Oppression and Resistance* (Haifa: Mada Al-Carmel).

Sikkuy Center (2000) *The Report of "Shiluv" (Integration) Plan* (Jerusalem: Sikkuy).

Swirski, S. and Konor-Attias, E. (2006) *Israel: A Social Report – 2005*. Tel Aviv: Adva Center.

Tarrow, S. (1996) "Making Social Science Work across Space and Time: A Critical Reflection on Robert Putnam's *'Making Democracy Work'*", *American Political Science Review*, 90, pp. 389–97.

Touraine, T. (1983) *Solidarity: The Analysis of a Social Movement: Poland, 1980–1981* (Cambridge: Cambridge University Press).

Tsutsui, K. (2004) "Global Civil Society and Ethnic Social Movement in the World Today", *Sociological Forum*, 19(1), pp. 63–87.

Vertovec, S. (1999) "Minority Associations, Networks and Public Policies: Reassessing the Relationship", *Journal of Ethnic and Migration Studies*, 25(1), pp. 21–42.

Wada, T. (2005) 'Civil Society in Mexico: Popular Protest Amid Economic and Political Liberalization', *International Journal of Sociology and Social Policy*, 25(1/2): 87–117.

Whittington, K. (1998) "Revisiting Tocqueville's America: Society, Politics and Association in Nineteenth Century", *American Behavioral Scientist*, 42, pp. 21–32.

Wiktorowicz, Q. (2000) "Civil Society as Social Control: State Power in Jordan," *Comparative Politics*, 33(1), pp. 43–61.

Wolfsfeld, G., Abraham, A. and Abu-Raya, I. (2000) When Prophesy Always Fails: Israeli Press Coverage of the Arab Minority Land Day Protests, *Political Communication*, 17(2), pp. 115–31.

World Bank (2007) *World Bank–Civil Society Engagement: Review of Fiscal Years 2005 and 2006* (Washington DC: The International Bank for Reconstruction and Development).

Yishai, Y. (1997) *Between the Flag and The Banner: Women in Israeli Politics* (Albany: State University of New York Press).

12 All by myself? The paradox of citizenship among the FSU immigrants in Israel

Michael Philippov and Evgenia Bystrov

Since 1989 a mass migration from the Soviet Union to Israel has been unfolding. At the beginning, when the choice of a host country was available, many migrants in fact preferred to move to one of the Western developed countries such as the United States. However, the US stopped offering automatic refugee status to Soviet Jews in 1989. According to Lazin (2005), in 1989 almost 90 percent of the Soviet Jews wanted to resettle in the United States. After 1989 Israel became the only possible destination for mass Jewish immigration. During the 1990s, some million residents of the former Soviet Union arrived in Israel, increasing its population from five to six million. Most of them were highly educated and secular. The main push and pull factors of the 1990s immigration were socio-economic reasons such as poverty in the FSU and relatively favorable economic perspectives in Israel. Therefore, Israeli researchers recommended not employing the term *aliya* (repatriation) to these immigrants, regarding them instead as economic immigrants per se (Remennick 2007).

The process of integration of the highly skilled FSU immigrants was not easy, because of the problems of unemployment, the erosion of their social status in a small and inflexible Israeli labor market, problems in acquiring relevant language skills, because Hebrew bears no similarity to any European language, and a tendency to social aloofness and a strong desire to keep their "Russian" culture in Israel. In addition, relations with native Israelis were not perfect. Some of the Israelis even regarded newcomers as a threat to the labor market and to their cultural-religious space (Lissak and Leshem 1999; Remennick 2007). Compared to previous waves of Soviet migration to Israel, FSU immigrants of the 1990s have abandoned their cultural baggage gradually and have not immediately become Israelis without any "Russian" components in their identity. The term "integration without assimilation" is an adequate phrase for describing this situation. Although the majority of migrant Russian youngsters of the second generation have learned Hebrew, and become acquainted with new cultural norms and codes, they still prefer their Russian-speaking circle of friends and have not forgotten their Russian roots (Remennick 2007).

Consequently, this partial integration is reflected also in the political culture of the immigrants – attitudes, behavior and perceptions of democracy and citizenship – that remains different from that of native Israelis and is highly influenced by their former Soviet culture. Specifically, as we demonstrate below, FSU immigrants tend to be alienated from political participation, suspicious of political authorities and liberal values. While FSU immigrants often adopt a patriotic attitude, it is coupled with political passivity and perceptions of self-help and, somewhat surprisingly, lower willingness to live in Israel. These contradictions are explained by the practical attitude towards the state and the political culture "imported" from the Soviet Union.

Russian Immigrants' Non-liberal Political Attitudes in Israel

One of the most interesting characteristics of the FSU immigrants is related to their political culture. Horowitz (1996) describes them as absolutely modern people who encounter difficulties adapting to Western political values. Though immigrants' political behavior was partly influenced by the *perestroika* period and by the Israeli experience, a substantial portion of their cultural-political baggage is based on their native political outlook. Most immigrants have rapidly developed a patriotic Zionist vision often adopting a right-wing political orientation. Many of them hold favorable attitudes toward strong leadership, which is in the mind of immigrants the sole institution that has the power to solve problems. This attitude toward strong leadership has been fully recorded in Israel since the 1970s (Gitelman 1977, 1982; Goldstein and Gitelman 2004; Philippov 2008). These studies have also demonstrated a stereotypical understanding of the Arab minority in Israel and a negative, sometimes even antagonistic, attitude toward them. Some studies explain this attitude by reference to a post-Soviet behavioral pattern that is known as the 'Enemy Image' (Fialkova and Yelenevskaya 2007; Philippov 2008; Remennick 2007).

The undemocratic culture and tradition imported from the Soviet Union constitutes an important component of the immigrants' political culture in Israel. The *post-Soviet Man* supports most individual liberties, but expresses quite a number of reservations. For example, 1990s immigrants decisively oppose any deviation from acceptable social norms, and most of them believe that people who harm the country's flag or those who refuse to be recruited to the Israel Defense Forces should not be protected by law (Al-Haj and Leshem 2001).

Interestingly, the situation of the Russian-speaking community in America is rather similar. Though most American-Russians were more successful than the Israeli-Russians in integrating into the local society in the social and economic spheres, Russian immigrants to the US still differ from the native American Jews in their political attitudes. Remennick (2007: 197) addresses this Russian political vision in USA as "living on welfare, but voting Republicans," for 73 percent of the immigrants support war against terror (even at the expense of personal liberties), 77 percent support the death penalty, and 81 percent are opposed to gay marriage. Most of them support strong leadership and vote for the Republican Party.

Civic Passiveness of Russians in Israel and Non-belief in their Ability to Influence

Horowitz (1996) also points to the substantial impact of the Soviet background on immigrants to Israel from the former Soviet Union. The Israeli *Homo Sovieticus* is a person who does not believe in his/her ability to influence politics and simultaneously respects the political symbolism in the state (Horowitz 1996; Horowitz and Leshem 1998). Nevertheless, according to some studies, Israeli socialization has succeeded in changing some of these norms and in creating a new type of Soviet immigrant, much more integrated and involved in the Israeli political arena. Lisitsa (2007), for instance, refers to the fact that the immigrants' turnout rate in elections is equal to the turnout from the rest of Israeli society; therefore, the level of the immigrants' political integration is high. Horowitz (2003) also considers voting patterns among immigrants, observing that the Russian voice has become more significant in the Israeli political sphere and hence immigrants are no longer mere passive citizens in Israel: they are on their way to creating the appropriate patterns of active citizenship.

These conclusions seem to us overly optimistic because electoral behavior is merely a basic civil activity. High turnout rates might be a product of successful political recruitment programs rather than a sign of high-level civil culture. Undoubtedly, immigrants' votes have influenced the Israeli political spectrum and brought new parties into parliament along with new ideas and agendas. But is that enough to declare the end of the era of passive citizenship? To investigate further the immigrants' political vision, we need to undertake a deeper examination of the feelings of electoral power and attitudes regarding the capabilities of ordinary citizens to bring about changes in the state. The power to change must persist not only during the election period but also in everyday life through the availability of simple and immediate options for citizens' activity. Levada (2000) places considerable importance on this kind of definition since the belief of many Russian natives in their political power has not changed their civic passiveness since leaving Russia. Moreover, some of the Russians in the 1990s used passivity and inertia in the election as an excuse for voting for the most radical parties: if nothing matters in any case, let us try to shock the system. The same pattern was evident in Israel during the elections in 1996 and 2006. Immigrants' passivity led to electoral support for radical parties and the immediate reconstruction of the system. In 1996 they chose Israel Be-alia (an ethnic party which promised Russians to take political influence away from veteran Israelis, especially those from Asia and Africa) and in 2006 they voted for Lieberman's party which offered radical changes almost in every sphere in order to resolve all the political, demographic and security problems in Israel (Philippov 2008). Lieberman's radicalism is explicitly expressed in his program of disengagement from the Arab settlements of the 'triangle', an area in Northern Israel populated mostly by Arab citizens of Israel. He proposed to transmit this area to the Palestinian authority. He also demanded that every Israeli citizen should declare his/her loyalty to the state. This "citizenship law" was clearly intended to divide Zionist Jewish from Arab citizens of Israel.

Evidence from places other than the former Soviet Union and Israel also demonstrates that specific civic orientations might open the electoral market for right-wing populist parties that propagate nationalistic, xenophobic, and anti-democratic policies. These are just some of the consequences of Eastern European nations joining the European Union (Welzel et al. 2003). In addition, civic orientations in the new Eastern European member states are significantly below the EU average (Rose 2001; Fuchs and Klingemann 2002).

However, the main consequences of passive citizenship reach far beyond the political sphere. FSU immigrants' low socio-economic status has not changed significantly over the last 20 years. At the end of the first decade of the new millennium, FSU immigrants in Israel were still among the most underprivileged groups in Israeli society. As mentioned earlier, immigrants face problems of social-status decline in comparison with that of their native country, low salaries compared to the rest of the Israelis and low standards of housing (Dubson 2006; Remennick 2007; Lewin-Epstein and Semyonov 2008). It has been reported that

> Russian Jews in Israel became proletarians. The most popular professional occupation is a factory worker and no more an engineer or a teacher. The dreams of the Soviet communists about social conversion of the Russian Jewry came true in Israel ... (Dubson 2007: 301).

Most of the particular problems of FSU immigrants in Israel were never solved by the Israeli government. One of the reasons for this failure is that, by comparison with immigrants from Asia and North Africa, including recent immigrants from Ethiopia, FSU immigrants have not accepted the idea of social contestation as a legitimate and appropriate method of dealing with urgent social challenges. With reference to past experience, one might have expected that Russians would create strong social and political movements aimed at struggling for their rights. Such protest movements as the "Black Panthers" received public attention in 1971 and highlighted the problems of the immigrants from Asia and North Africa. Likewise in 1982 a political movement named *Shas*, which later became a powerful political party, was established in order to promote the needs of those immigrants.[1] Among the Russians, however, the only attempt to represent their social interests occurred in 1996, as we have already mentioned, but contrary to *Shas*, Be-alia the Russian party disappeared from the political arena shortly after its formation. Another political party, which sometimes is attributed to the Russian community, namely Israel Beitenu, rapidly realized that focusing on local and sectorial issues is not a political strategy which would lead in the long run to a sustainable political success. In that case, it might deter the native Israeli voters, who have no interest in solving Russian problems, and also become unattractive for the ex-Soviets who place a general political agenda much higher than their personal affairs (Philippov 2008). Even though Russian parties were formed almost immediately after the Russians arrived, this process was merely an adaptation of the Israeli political system to the new electoral potential. Russian-speaking Israeli politics cannot be regarded as evidence of political activism on the part of the immigrants. After all, voting in general elections for general issues is just a basic civil activity.

Similar political behavior has also been found among Russian immigrants in Germany. The Russian-speaking community has had an image of passivity, and as a group is not seen to be "politically active in any sphere of public life. Throughout the 1990s there were no attempts whatsoever at establishing a political party or social movement ..." (Elias, 2008: 25). These patterns of Russian immigrant political participation might be regarded as rather typical behavior of all post-Soviet citizens.

Citizenship and Political Behavior in the USSR

Every study of political attitudes and behavior of the former Soviet Union (FSU) immigrants in Israel should consider their Soviet and post-Soviet cultural background. According to classical research on political culture, social circumstances play a crucial role in political socialization and in the formation of human beliefs and values (Almond and Verba 1963; Putnam 1993). Soviet and post-Soviet political space created a unique political environment full of contradictions in Western terms. While Soviet political culture contained several well-known basic elements, post-Soviet natives grasped the term "democracy" differently from their Western counterparts. For example, modern Russians see no inconsistency between their country's democratic conduct and a strong centralized government, which always knows what is best for its people (Reisinger et al. 1994; Carnaghan 2001). A typical post-Soviet citizen does not believe in the principles of liberal democracy and gender equality, has a militant vision toward state security conditions, and vehemently hates enemies. Levada (2000, 2001) documents the absence of a democratic tradition to the political culture of the Russian Federation in which the majority of the citizens have been willing to exchange democracy for a "strong government and stable order." Democracy appears to be too complex.

One of the most important components of the undemocratic vision of the Soviet natives is their skeptical and negative attitude towards a civil society and the ability of a citizen to make an impact on state affairs. Almond and Verba (1963) identified several types of civic culture. Thus, they provided a theoretical framework where this sort of behavior might fit. A condition in which citizens in certain societies tend to grant the authorities full legitimacy to act in every domain owing to a feeling of their inability to influence anything is defined as "passive citizenship." A passive citizen is one who in general greatly and uncritically respects the government, but is blind to the citizens' own inability to affect its policy. The perceived distance between the citizen and the government is significant and hierarchical. Passive citizens do not presume to reduce that distance and participate in political life, but instead they continue to generally trust the government.

Dahl (1998) perceived citizen participation as the first sign of democratic process. A situation where all citizens (or several groups of citizens) do not influence politics is clearly undemocratic. Organized groups, political parties, government, religious and economic institutions – all these constitute a civil society and are part of a democratic polity (Skocpol and Fiorina 1999). Political activism may change forms in general. The trend in the US, for instance, is that civil society is constantly "reinventing" itself. In contrast to the erosion of social capital, there is evidence of the growing power of the role played by non-political associations, which construct a part of a civil society. As a result, American civil engagement is still highly active despite the change in individual behavior: participation in voluntary organizations is on a rise while electoral turnout is in decline.

However, the political non-activism of Soviet and post-Soviet society differs from the general trend. The term passive citizenship can, therefore, explain the attitude of the post-Soviet citizens toward the authorities. In the following discussion, we present several examples of interactive relations between the state and people and describe the mechanism whereby this interaction operates.

Firstly, by the 1960s and 1970s researchers had recognized that Soviet Man views state authorities on all levels (state and regional) as very distant bodies from the people. Interestingly, this concept was prevalent in all classes, and even the Soviet intellectual elite held this attitude that politics, with all its institutions and branches, is no place for the ordinary citizen. In a paradoxical manner, the people who protested in the Red Square in 1968 against the Russian invasion to Czechoslovakia insisted on informing the foreign press that they were not dealing in politics! Jewish dissidents often said the same thing in later periods. Examples of passive citizenship were also described in the 1990s. Russian political culture is characterized by the citizens' total alienation from politics. This social characteristic is even valid for politicians who participated in the research. Russian-lawmakers spoke of the regime in the third person merely as bystanders, and blamed the regime for professional incompetence, breaking laws and so forth (Gozman and Shestopal 1996).

Second, the alienation of citizens from politics is an expression of their effort to keep away from the political world that is filled with vagueness, deception, and false propaganda. Indeed, during the Soviet period, citizens expressed a certain kinship to their country (Mirskii 2003), went on protests, were members in voluntary organizations, and participated in elections. But everyday reality did not allow them fully to identify themselves as an integral part of the state. Most Soviet citizens fell into poverty by Western standards, felt unprotected by the rule of law, and did not perceive the state as offering any protection if the need should arise. Moreover, the Soviet state was unsuccessful in getting citizens to believe in state propaganda, because Soviet citizens learned that news was usually inconsistent with reality, the written law was never valid, and leaders' statements were contrary to actual events. Even the enemies of the Soviet Union became "friends" within a week, and the "truth" in the daily newspaper was true only for the day on which it was published and likely to change by the following day. Clearly, when images on television are so far from real life, it is unreasonable to expect the citizen to express loyal attitudes toward the state. On a blue screen there is a world where leaders and politicians live, whereas the world of the common people differs from the world of television (Gozman and Shestopal 1996). Shlapentokh (1989: 3), who examines the weaknesses of the Soviet civil culture, argues that "the distinction between the public and private spheres is of crucial importance for understanding Soviet society and for predicting its evolution."

Third, people in the Soviet Union have always found it useful to keep some distance from the authorities. This distance allowed the Soviet and post-Soviet citizens to develop an autonomous framework with rules and norms that they set for themselves without any intervention by the state. The distance also allowed justifying this sort of behavior. Soviet natives are not interested in assuming responsibility for events because they feel that either way nothing will change the current situation, that politics is immoral, and that the authorities always lie. Every action by the state which is not comforting and gratifying for the citizens produces in them a profound sense of hurt. In such cases individuals do not go out to protest, but neither do they feel that they are part of the state, and therefore its decisions are not binding (at the best). After all, it is clear to everyone that no true democracy existed in either the former Soviet Union or in contemporary Russia. "They" (the authorities) are the ones who hurt the common people by raising the prices, are unable to provide food and keep order in the state, and manage to corrupt it in various ways (Levada 2000). No wonder that in modern Russia a majority of Russian citizens thinks that no connection exists between the government's actions and the citizen's wishes, and neither does the government care for what citizens think (Colton and MacFaul 2001; Hahn 1991).

Citizens learned to cope creatively with state injustice. "Individuals prudently confined their thoughts to their own private circles of relatives and close friends. In this way, face-to-face primary groups became a substitute for civil society rather than an integral part of it. People devised strategies for communicating ideas without stating them directly" (Rose 1994: 22). What is more, citizens further sharpened the perceptual distinction between their private world and the world of the hostile regime, with which it is best not to meddle, cooperate, or argue. If the law is unjust, people do not protest against it; they rather manage with existing conditions, and try to improve their personal situation despite the authorities and against their strange and distant laws (DiFrancesco and Gitelman 1984; Levada 2000). As a result, to the Russian mind, a politician who breaks the law is corrupt, while a regular citizen who does the same is acting in accordance with the traditional creativity of the Russian people.

In the same way, Carnaghan (2001) describes strongly negative attitudes among the Russians toward the state institutions in modern Russia. She suggests that these attitudes originated from Russian character and she offers a non-cultural explanation. Carnaghan claims that Russians tend to use liberal rhetoric while discussing democracy. Furthermore, most of the Russians are ready to vote and obey the law. At the same time, the majority of Russian citizens have little confidence in the authorities. They prefer strong and effective leaders to parliamentary debates. The author concludes that Russians' political attitudes tend to be cynical and that overall people are disappointed with the local political institutions. This, however, does not mean that Russians as a whole support an undemocratic political approach.

Various explanations presented above regarding the nature of passiveness do not alter the consequence: passive citizenship does not enhance a democratic model of society and places passive citizens on its periphery. People who play hide and seek with the state and do not influence politics on a daily basis face difficulties in creating any sustainable inputs. According to the classical model of Easton (1957), a democratic state will not return any serious output to those groups which do not create any significant input inside the political system.

One of the ways to evaluate whether Soviet immigrants in a democratic state are still "soviet" and passive is by analyzing the interaction between the state and the citizens. The discussion about the continuity and survival capacities of the post-Soviet political culture has no geographic limits. Since the *perestroika* period many Soviets emigrated from USSR. Israel was one of the major destinations for the Jews in the early 1990s. Other Western countries that received major parts of this out-migration flow from the FSU were the USA, Canada, Germany, and Australia (Remennick 2007).

We focus on the Israeli case for several reasons. This case is unique and promising in analytical terms: the proportion of the former Soviets in Israel is relatively large comprising a fifth of the local population at the moment of their arrival. Therefore, their potential to produce input and receive output from the state might have been significant. In addition, the comparison between the attitudes of the immigrants and those of the rest of the citizens in Israel might also provide some fruitful insights, given the fact that the political culture of immigrants is substantially marked by their Soviet past. Moreover, in this specific context, migration is an indicative process for analyzing citizenship as such. It is in the process of emigration from an undemocratic state when the attitudes of the new citizens toward the receiving democratic state are revealed, and it is during the phase of the integration in the new society when the immigrants need the state the most.

Current Research

The political culture of former Soviet citizens differs significantly from the political culture of the host public in the receiving countries, to which they arrived after the collapse of the Soviet Union. As we mentioned earlier, FSU immigrants in Israel provide a unique opportunity to study citizenship, because their political culture suits the model of passive citizenship. Even 20 years after the beginning of mass immigration to Israel, we find significant differences in both political attitudes and behavior between the immigrants and the rest of Israelis in the sphere of citizens-and-state relations. In order to deepen our knowledge regarding active and passive citizenship, we must learn how people perceive their competence to bring about a result. Only if we find that the immigrants' perceptions are the same as those of the rest of society, could we argue in favor of progression towards active citizenship.

The current research compares the vision of the citizen's power over government's decisions between the former Soviet Union immigrants who arrived in Israel from 1989 onward and other Israeli Jews. It also examines the degree of alienation between the citizens and the government. Our data originate from a series of national surveys organized by the Guttman Center at the Israel Democracy Institute from 2003–2008.[2]

An attitude towards citizenship includes a specific set of political world views and value orientations. Why focus on various values instead of one overall ideology? Arian (2005) suggests that analyzing discrete values does not expect or require people to develop an integrated belief system. People's interpretation of a multifaceted and changing world can be captured through their attitudes that might be neither connected nor coherent. This approach recommends itself, for values in political situations are often contradictory and complex.

Similarly to other scholars (Levada 1995, 2000, 2001; Gudkov 2004), we believe that post-Soviet culture is not homogeneous but fractured by internal conflicts. Democratic and authoritarian values intermingle with the consciousness of the FSU immigrants in Israel in ways that often seem strange and illogical. Our concern is with those areas where the political attitudes of the FSU immigrants vary from those of the rest of Israeli Jews. We are interested not only in the context in which that variety exists, but also with the scope of the variety.

We expect to find differences between the attitudes of the FSU immigrants and the rest of the Israeli Jews toward citizenship. Our hypothesis is that, after living in Israel for a decade or two, a certain fraction of immigrants still display attitudes of powerlessness, have difficulties in understanding the role of civil society and prefer not to meddle with the state institutions, even when they feel deprived and underprovided. Our goals are to measure the extent of these phenomena and evaluate whether the rise in socio-economic power or undergoing socialization in a democratic society creates more pro-active citizenship. That is, we analyze whether those immigrants who hold middle and high social status in Israeli society demonstrate a more "modern" or "civic" approach to their civil power. We also consider the attitudes of young immigrants. We aim to provide some guidelines that not only sharpen our understanding of the immigrant community but also shed light on processes underlying the concept of citizenship.

Political Identity of Russians in Israel: Patriotism and Sacrifice

One of the major components of citizenship is the level of patriotism, as expressed by willingness to sacrifice one's own life for the sake of the state in case of major security threats. We find that 78 percent of the immigrants are proud to be Israelis compared to 86 percent of the rest of the Israeli Jews (2007). These numbers are extremely high, considering that FSU immigrants arrived in their new home country only one or two decades ago. In addition, only 28 percent of the immigrants support the idea that "personal interests are more important for the citizens, compared to the interest of the state." Among the rest of Israeli Jews 39 percent believe so. In other words, despite all the problems that the newcomers face, only a minority place their narrow interests above the broader aspects of the state agenda.

Likewise, most of the immigrants are ready to fight for the state of Israel and the rate of militancy and patriotism is especially high among the elderly immigrants (see Figure 12.1). Analyzing the unusually high levels of patriotism among the immigrants aged above 40 years, we should mention that the vast majority of them have never served in the Israeli army and are not expected to serve there in future. So immigrant youngsters who are obliged to perform an army duty exhibit only a moderate level of patriotism. This group of immigrants aged 40 and below displayed in 2007 lower levels of patriotism than their Israeli counterparts.

Looking for explanations of these trends, we suggest the following: firstly, older people whose political socialization was completed during their residence in the USSR, who grew up according to the Soviet norms of self-sacrifice and who hold collective memories from the Great Patriotic War, tend to support a militaristic approach. This approach is maintained both among the former Soviets who immigrated to Israel and among those who stayed in Russia: 77 percent of the citizens of Russian Federation are also ready to fight for their country. However, only 43 percent of Spanish citizens and 58 percent of French are ready to fight.[3]

Second, many of these people originate from educated Jewish families and owing to their higher education have been exempted from military duty in the Soviet army. Therefore, they might have developed a rather romantic

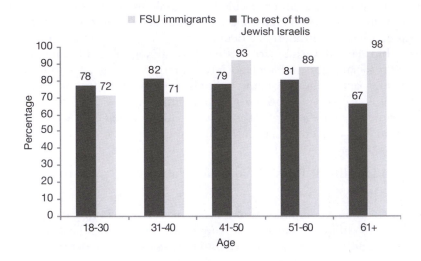

Figure 12.1 Willingness to fight for the state by age (percentage of "strong" and "moderate" willingness, by age groups)

Source: data of Guttman Center at the IDI (2007) processed by the authors.

view of the military, warfare and combat.

Another explanation is based on the integration process of the immigrants. Senior immigrants face several obstructions in their way of entering Israeli society. They experience difficulties acquiring a new language, developing successful careers and finding opportunities in the new society. Hence, developing patriotic sentiments toward the state of destination might function as an important social tool which promotes their subjective feeling of being "at home." This kind of feeling could facilitate their absorption and moderate the drawbacks of daily existence. Such behavior is also commonly described as an "entering ticket" into the host society (Al Haj and Leshem 2001).

Political Ineffectiveness and Political Non-involvement Beyond Elections

About half of the immigrants do not believe in political effectiveness (see Figure 12.2). The immigrants' belief in their ability to influence the government's policy is lower than that of the rest of the Jewish Israelis. These differences are statistically significant (p<0.001) though not large. Overall, one can observe a decline in the percentage of non-believers in political effectiveness as social class rises. In other words, those respondents, who belong to a higher social class, show greater confidence in their power to make things happen. According to Arian, Philippov and Knafelman (2009), only a small percentage of Russians in Israel feel that they influence the local politics. A half of the immigrants feel that "citizens like them" cannot

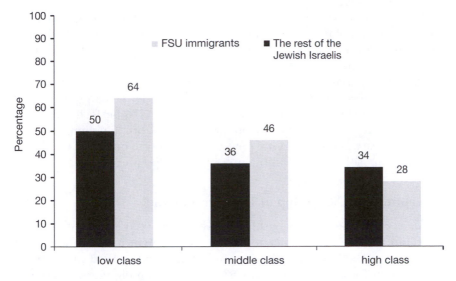

Figure 12.2 "Do not influence the governmental policy in any extent" by social class (percentage, by class)

Source: data of Guttman Center at the IDI (2003–2007) processed by the authors.

change anything, even at their workplace. Immigrants are the most passive and helpless groups compared to the rest of Israeli Jews and even to the Arab minority in Israel.

Interestingly enough, FSU immigrants of higher social class are the most empowered group: they proclaim the highest potency to influence the governmental policy. Nonetheless, the latter group comprised only five percent of the immigrants in 2006 (as opposed to 11 percent among the rest of the Jewish Israelis), while 32 percent defined themselves as middle class (62 percent among the rest of Jewish Israelis) and the vast majority of 63 percent declared belonging to the low class (27 percent among the rest of Jewish Israelis).

Al-Haj and Leshem (2001) claim that Russian immigrants have chosen a rational strategy of creating a Russian ghetto that was intended to increase the social mobility of this group. We argue that it could have also been an unconscious willingness of ex-Soviets to hold to their culture and tradition in order to preserve their sense of affiliation and belongingness. People who went through the stress of immigration were united by their common background. More important, the ghetto evolved owing to the economic circumstances, in which most of the immigrants preferred to live on the Israeli periphery where the real estate prices were relatively low. These findings support the previously mentioned notion that being one of the most underprivileged groups in Israel, immigrants possess only scarce means and do not count in many cases. Consequently, such state of affairs promotes further immigrants' civil passiveness.

However, our next series of findings might cast doubt on immigrants' complete distrust in political effectiveness. In 2006 only 30 percent of immigrants agreed that "the elections do not alter the situation, and, therefore, it is not important for whom to vote" as opposed to 42 percent of other Jews in Israel (p<0.001). Apparently, the alienation from the government and the inability to change things in the state are part of the immigrants' viewpoint most of the time. At the same time, for the majority of them it is perfectly clear that on election days the citizen is the one who decides. So, the immigrants are definitely aware of their electoral power, their ability to influence the parliament's composition and to punish an unpopular politician.

Perceptions of Citizenship of Russians in Israel

The next component of citizenship that we describe is the immigrants' individualism and their reluctance to see the government interfere with their lives. When asked about the governments' obligation to provide income and employment for every citizen, only 53 percent of immigrants agreed with this statement compared to 69 percent of the rest of Israeli Jews (p<0.001). And when asked: "Why are some people poor?" 35 percent of the immigrants answered that "they were not trying hard enough" as opposed to only 18 percent among the rest of Israeli Jews. Though immigrants do not believe in their call, they are less interested in the government's help in finding a job than the rest of the Israeli Jews, and even blame the poor, who do not try hard enough. These findings seem of the highest importance in light of the fact that while immigrants deal with objective problems when entering a new job market, they still refuse to transfer the responsibility for their fate to the state or pose the blame on the government.

Whereas immigrants do not seek assistance from the state, they also do not turn to alternative institutions such as non-governmental organizations. One of the reasons why they focus on individualism as a major driving force is their lack of trust in civil society and misapprehension of this concept, for 46 percent of the immigrants do not see any difference between getting support or services from the state and from a public organization. Among the rest of Jewish Israelis only 18 percent think the same way. Moreover, 52 percent of the immigrants and 39 percent of the rest of the Israeli Jews presume that most of public organizations are corrupt.

Attitudes of distrust toward the state extend further when the citizen tries to exploit the system and benefit from its imperfections. In 2004 teenagers aged 14–17 were questioned as to whether they support two of the following actions: to claim benefits that one is not eligible to receive from the state and to cheat on tax payments. More than a quarter of immigrant teenagers answered that these actions are justifiable: 27 percent said it is acceptable to claim benefits and 28 percent justified cheating on taxes. Among the rest of Jewish Israeli teenagers only 10 percent answered positively to both questions (p<0.001). Such questions were not presented to adults for obvious methodological reasons. We cannot expect to obtain reliable results by phone on these sensitive issues.

An additional example to the extent of distrust toward the state can be illustrated in a straightforward manner by measuring the proportion of people who agree that "in order to be a 'real Israeli' a person should respect laws and institutions of the state." In 2003 the percentage of immigrants who agreed ("strongly agree") to the above statement was 59 percent while the share of the rest of Jewish Israelis was 78 percent (p<0.001).

These results reflect a well-known citizen's niche which Levada (2000) describes as "a convenient and cozy shell" where a person is allowed a certain degree of freedom and flexibility in determining his or her own destiny. One of the strongest ways to decide a person's fate operates through the option to emigrate, as we shall see in the next section.

Emigration – Solving the Problems on a Personal Level

According to the Central Bureau of Statistics (CBS) 970,000 immigrants from the former Soviet Union have arrived in Israel since 1989. But the official number of immigrants who left Israel since then is dubious. CBS summarizes that 48 percent of the emigrants from Israel since 1990 were FSU natives, while during 2003–2004 this proportion was more than 60 percent.[4] Between 1989 and 2005 some 111,000 FSU immigrants left Israel permanently. Yet, this number is problematic; for instance, it does not include immigrants who left Israel but who came back for a visit every year (for example to see their relatives).

The Center for Research and Information of the Knesset does not report the exact numbers of the Russian emigration from Israel. At the same time, Mei-Ami (2006) argues that "the rate of emigration among the FSU immigrants is much higher than among the rest of Israelis. Many of the young and highly educated immigrants left Israel and went to the West. Today many of them go back to Russia" (Mei-Ami 2006: 7).

Our data endorse the observation of the officials; we find that willingness to live in Israel is consistently lower among the immigrants than among other Israeli Jews (see Figure 12.3). After the Second Lebanon War which had a direct and negative impact on the Russian community settled in the Northern Israeli periphery, we observe a decline in the immigrants' willingness to stay in Israel.

What then is the connection between emigration and citizenship? Is it a paradox when somebody who is ready to fight for the state also wants to leave? In terms of the post-Soviet political culture, there is no contradiction whatsoever. Practical and materialistic approaches toward the state have always included a high level of patriotism. Government should not interfere in the personal life of its citizens, yet it must defend them from enemies and give them a strong feeling of personal security and pride. You can love

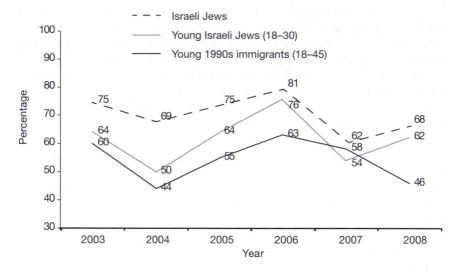

Figure 12.3 Willingness to live in Israel in the long term (percentage of "certainly willing," by year)

Source: data of Guttman Center at the IDI (2003–2008) processed by the authors

your country but if your government cannot defend you from the rockets of Hezbollah, your flexible citizenship position allows you to pack your baggage and go to a state where you can find safer conditions for you and your family. Actually, it is acceptable to leave even without a war when personal efforts to improve living standards have failed to produce the anticipated results.

Concluding Discussion: Practical Approach Toward the State

Our main findings argue that in general FSU immigrants in Israel tend to be more distant from the authorities and the state than the rest of Jewish Israelis. About a half of the Israeli Russians do not feel they have any power to influence the situation in the state on a daily basis. They fulfill their claims to the state only on the day of elections. Based on previous research, we draw a connection between passiveness in daily life and the willingness to "take revenge" by the use of electoral power. As a result, even 20 years after the beginning of mass immigration, voting patterns of the FSU immigrants differ from those of the rest of Jewish Israelis. The immigrants usually prefer radical parties with a revolutionary agenda, which may include crucial changes of the status quo.

White, Rose and McAllister (1997) referred to the post-Soviet citizen as "two persons in one body." One of these persons keeps a distance from the state and acts according to personal norms. The other person generally trusts authorities and presents a high level of pride in the country. Our research supports this terminology arguing that Israeli socialization has not succeeded in changing this dual attitude of the Soviet native toward authorities and citizenship. There still exists a paradoxical combination of high levels of patriotism (especially among the older respondents) and the tendency to withdraw from the state. Contrary to other Israeli Jews, the immigrants are not only ready to fight, but they also support the idea that the interests of the state are equal to or more important than the interests of individual citizens. This combination is probably imported from the post-Soviet framework to Israel without any significant transformation: an average post-Soviet citizen loves his/her country on a symbolic level, as Horowitz (1996) described it in the early 1990s, but still recognizes the importance of not allowing the authorities to become involved in his/her private life. According to this approach, a real patriot of a country could be an individualist who survives without revealing any demands from the state. Therefore, many immigrants are not familiar with the rules of the democratic game of civil society. They do not appear to grasp what makes a difference between the role of the state and non-governmental organizations inside the state.

One of the most important findings of this study is that there exists a relatively high percentage of the FSU immigrants who express very practical or materialistic approaches toward the state. For instance, some youngsters justify claiming illegal benefits from the state and cheating on tax payments and some adults are not certain of their willingness to live in Israel for the long term. The high level of migration out of Israel among FSU immigrants supports the argument that most of them retain a high sense of personal survival and ambitious attitudes where no option of acquiring assistance from the state exists, but there is the option of taking charge of one's own destiny. Most immigrants have no experience of a normative state–citizen relationship within a democratic environment. But all of them know how to increase their distance from the state by simply leaving the country.

In general, we have presented a rather complicated picture of the immigrants' vision of citizenship. It is not surprisingly very similar to the one proposed in existing studies of post-Soviet cultural space. Much has been said about the high level of patriotism, practical and materialistic attitudes as well as the willingness to fight and to sacrifice. However, it is important to stress that we are speaking about a passive practical approach whereby people learn to survive and to seek better conditions. These attitudes are far from being individualistic in a post-modern sense. In this context people are neither ready to speak about their problems nor place them above the general problems of the state. Only a small percentage among the Russians regards the set of unique immigrant problems as something that the government should or could resolve immediately (Philippov 2008). A person who was brought up by a Soviet value system was taught to care more about some abstract issues like the security agenda, state goals, or the Zionist idea than about small-scale personal problems. The state and politicians thrive in a cosmic sphere far removed from the world of the citizens: the citizen is too insignificant to bother them and in any case they can survive without them, if not in Israel then in Canada.

At the same time, the civic passivity of the Russians creates an extremely stable and comfortable position for the Russian-speaking politicians. Without too much effort, they can mobilize their community during elections and hence feel free from any obligations during the period in between the elections. Since the electorate is mostly troubled with geopolitics and global affairs, trying to survive on the Israeli periphery, the Russian politicians are never asked inconvenient questions about what they have actually achieved during their period in office. To illuminate the last point, in 2009 two political parties *Shas* and Lieberman's *Israel Beitenu* that joined the governmental coalition were supported by different ethnic sectors. Most supporters of *Shas* traditionally belong to the Eastern Jewry, whereas *Israel Beitenu* was supposed to represent FSU immigrants. Before signing a coalition agreement, *Shas* demanded from the future prime minister a commitment to grant a lot of social benefits for its supporters. In contrast, *Israel Beitenu* preferred to advance such blurred issues as "defeating the rule of Hamas" and "citizen-ship law" which redefine who is a loyal Israeli citizen and who is not. Contrary to the Eastern Israeli Jewry, which defines itself as a group with a specific list of priorities, FSU immigrants are not really interested in declaring them-selves as a collective that shares common needs and problems. At least, they have not been ready to proclaim it publicly so far.

In our opinion, the case of the FSU immigrants in Israel becomes more comprehensible when we review the theory. To some degree the situation is reminiscent of the Italian case shown by Putnam (1993). The social capital of the Israeli Russians is similar to the traditional social capital of Southern Italy where interpersonal trust is extremely low. Social groups that hold to these values cannot expect to comprise an integral part of the modern polit-ical system where political involvement moderates political processes and establishes the decision making. Bottom-up processes not only benefit the ordinary citizens but also determine how these citizens react to the political system through the feedback mechanisms.

For those Russian immigrants who continue to keep a distance from the state and do not believe in their civic power, the situation cannot change. The second generation of immigrants will gradually integrate in the Israeli society, but unfortunately most of them will be predisposed to the civil mal-adies of the Russian community of Israel.

To sum up, in this article we mainly exposed the phenomenon of pas-siveness among Russians in Israel. It is clear that the connection between social passiveness and the absorption difficulties of the immigrants should be further investigated. Forthcoming research might be both fascinating and challenging. The first challenge is to evaluate the political culture of the second generation of Russians in Israel. To what extent will the youngsters continue to keep the political values that were implanted in their parents by previous Soviet realities? The second challenge is to define the main factors that encourage or rather slow down the political re-socialization of immigrants in Israel: what is the weight of age, seniority and place of residence of the immigrants? All these questions should be considered in the future.

Finally, the current research contributes to a more general discussion about the transition to democracy in Eastern Europe, where cultural inflexibility also makes the democratization process slow and uncertain. Future research among ex-Soviets in the West could significantly enlarge our knowledge about the survival capacities of undemocratic values and help social scientists to create appropriate forecasts regarding the pace and progress of democratization in Eastern Europe and elsewhere.

Notes

1 For discussion on political struggling of the immigrants from Arab countries see S. Smooha, 2008. 'The Mass Immigrations to Israel: A Comparison of the Failure of the Mizrahi Immigrants of the 1950s with the Success of the Russian Immigrants of the 1990s', *Journal of Israeli History* 27(1): 1–27. Y. Peled, 1998. 'Towards a Redefinition of Jewish Nationalism in Israel? The Enigma of Shas', *Ethnic and Racial Studies*, 21(4): 703–727.
2 The interviews were conducted by telephone in Hebrew or Russian between 2003 and 2008. The sample is representative for Israeli society. The sample of adults comprised two groups: immigrants from the former Soviet Union since 1989 (hereinafter "immigrants") (N varies from 130 to 311 in each year) and Jews who were born in Israel or who arrived before 1989 (hereinafter "the rest of Israeli Jews") (N varies from 768 to 1477 in each year). The age of respondents varied between 18 and 90. The data were compiled from seven surveys (2003, 2004, February 2005, March 2005, February 2006, March 2006 and 2007).
3 Authors' calculation based on the WVS data (1999), www.worldvaluessurvey.org
4 Israel Central Bureau of Statistics press release, *Emigration from Israel 2005*, August 14, 2007 www.cbs.gov.il

References

Al-Haj, M. and Leshem, E. (2001) *Immigrants from the Soviet Union in Israel: Ten Years Later*, Haifa: University of Haifa.
Almond, G. A. and Verba, S. (1963) *The Civic Culture: Political Attitudes and Democracy in Five Nations*, N.J.: Princeton.
Arian, A. (2005) *Politics in Israel: The Second Republic*, Washington DC: CQ Press.
Arian, A., Philippov, M. and Knafelman, A. (2009) *The Democracy Index 2009: 20 Years After the Beginning of the Mass Emigration From the Soviet Union to Israel*, Jerusalem: The Israel Democracy Institute.
Carnaghan, E. (2001) 'Thinking about Democracy: Interviews with Russian Citizens', *Slavic Review*, 60(2): 336–66.
Colton, T. J. and McFaul, M. (2001) 'Are Russians Undemocratic?' *Carnegie Endowment Working Papers*, Carnegie Endowment for International Peace 20: 1–24.
Dahl, R. A. (1998) *On Democracy*, New Haven & London: Yale University Press.
DiFrancesco, W. and Gitelman, Z. (1984) "Soviet Political Culture and Covert Participation", *The American Political Science Review*, 78 (3): 603–21.

Dubson, B. (2007) 'Sozialno-proffesionalnaya mobilnost immigrantov' (Socio-professional mobility of the immigrants), in M. Kenigstein (ed.) *'Russkoe' Lizo Izrailya* (A Russian Face of Israel), Jerusalem: Gesharim.

Easton, D. (1957) 'An Approach to the Analysis of Political Systems', *World Politics*, IX: 393–400.

Elias, N. (2008) *Coming Home: Media and Returning Diaspora in Israel and Germany*, New York: SUNY Press.

Fialkova, L. and Yelenevskaya, M. N. (2007) *Soviets in Israel: From Personal Narratives to a Group Portrait*, Detroit: Wayne State University Press.

Fuchs, D. and Klingemann, H. D. (2002) 'Eastward Enlargement and the Identity of Europe', in P. Mair and J. Zielonka (eds) *The Enlarged European Union: Diversity and Adaptation*, London: Frank Cass Publishers.

Gitelman, Z. (1977) 'Soviet Political Culture: Insights from Jewish Emigres', *Soviet Studies*, 29(4): 543–64.

Gitelman, Z. (1982) *Becoming Israeli*, New York: Praeger Publishers.

Goldstein, K. and Gitelman, Z. (2004) 'From 'Russians' to Israelis?', in Arian, A. and M. Shamir (eds), *Elections in Israel 2003*, New York: SUNY Press.

Gozman, L. Y. and Shestopal, E. B. (1996) *Politicheskaya Psikhologiya* (Political Psychology), Rostov na Donu: Fenix.

Gudkov, L. (2004) *Negativnaia Identichnost* (Negative Identity), Moskva: Novoe Literaturnoe Obozrenie.

Hahn., J. W. (1991) 'Continuity and Change in Russian Political Culture', *British Journal of Political Science*, 21 (4): 393–421.

Horowitz, T. (1996) *Bein Shalosh Tarbuyot Politiyot: Haolim miBrit Hamuatzot Lesheavar Beisrael*, (Between the Three Political Cultures: FSU Immigrants in Israel), Jerusalem: Open University Press.

Horowitz, T. (2003) 'The Increasing Political Power of Immigrants from the Soviet Union in Israel: From Passive Citizenship to Active Citizenship', *International Migration*, 41 (1): 45–71.

Horowitz, T. and Leshem, E. (1998) 'The immigrants from the FSU in the Israeli cultural sphere', in M. Sicron and E. Leshem (eds) *Profile of an Immigration Wave: The absorption process of immigrants from the former Soviet Union, 1990–1995.* Jerusalem: Magnes Press.

Lazin, F. (2005) *The Struggle for Soviet Jewry in American Politics: Israel versus the American Jewish Establishment*, Lanham, MD: Lexington Book.

Levada, Y. (1995) 'Homo Sovieticus Five Years Later: 1989–1994', *Russian Social Science Review*, (26): 3–17.

Levada, Y. A. (2000) *Ot Mneniy k Ponimaniu: Sotsiologicheskie Ocherki 1993–2000* (From opinions to understanding: Sociological articles 1993–2000), Moskovskaya shkola politicheskikh issledovanii.

Levada, Y. (2001) 'Soviet Man Ten Years Later, 1989–1999', *Russian Social Science Review*, 41 (1): 4–28.

Lewin-Epstein, N. and Semyonov, M. (2008) 'Baalut al Diyur ve Tnaey haMegurim shel Ohlusiyat Bnei 50 ve Maala be Israel' (Ownership of private housing and the living conditions among the 50+ in Israel), *Bitahon Sotsialy*, 76: 153–74.

Lisitsa, S. (2007) 'Index Integrazii Immigrantov' (Index of Absorption of the Immigrants), in M. Kenigstein (ed.) *'Russkoe' Lizo Izrailya* (A Russian Face of Israel), Jerusalem: Gesharim: 141–64.

Lissak, M., and Leshem, E. (1999) 'Development and consolidation of the Russian community in Israel', in S. Weil (ed.), *Roots and Routes: Ethnicity and Migration in Global Perspective*, Jerusalem: Magnes Press.

Mei-Ami, N. (2006) *Netunim Al Erida Mihaaretz* (Data regarding the Immigration from Israel), Jerusalem: The Center for Research and Information of the Knesset, August 27, 2006.

Mirskii, G. (2003) 'Did Totalitarianism Disappear Together with the Twentieth Century?' *Russian Social Science Review*, 44 (5): 32–58.

Philippov, M. (2008) '1990s Immigrants from the FSU in Israeli Elections 2006: The Fulfillment of the Political Dreams of Post-Soviet Man?', in A. Arian and M. Shamir (eds) *The Elections in Israel 2003*, New York: SUNY Press.

Putnam, R. (1993) *Making Democracy Work: Civic Traditions in Modern Italy*, N.J.: Princeton University Press.

Reisinger, W., Miller A., Hesli V., and Maher, K. (1994) 'Political Values in Russia, Ukraine and Lithuania: Sources and Implications for Democracy', *British Journal of Political Science*, 24: 183–223.

Remennick, L. (2007) *Russian Jews on Three Continents*, New Brunswick, New Jersey: Transaction Publishers.

Rose, R. (1994) 'Postcommunism and the Problem of Trust', *Journal of Democracy*, 5 (3): 18–30.

Rose, R. (2001) 'A Divergent Europe', *Journal of Democracy* 12: 93–106.

Shlapentokh, V. (1989) *Public and Private Life of the Soviet People*, Oxford: Oxford University Press.

Skocpol, T. and Fiorina, M. P. (1999) *Civic Engagement in American Democracy*, Washington DC: Brookings Institution Press.

Welzel, C., Díez-Nicolas, H., Halman, L., Klingemann, H., Pettersson, T. and Rabusic, L. (2003) *Changing Patterns of "Civicness": Citizenship, Identities, and Values in Europe*, Integrated Project Proposal, December 8, 2003.

White, S., Rose, R. and McAllister I. (1997) *How Russia Votes*, N.J.: Chatham House Publishers.

13 The rise and fall of liberal nationalism

Yoav Peled

Introduction

The general elections of 2009 have returned the most right-wing Knesset in Israel's history. The Labor Party, that had founded the state and was led in these elections by Ehud Barak, formerly prime minister and chief of staff of the IDF, elected only thirteen members to the new Knesset, two members short of *Yisrael Beitenu* (Israel Our Home), an extreme right wing party headed by a West Bank settler, Avigdor Lieberman.[1] Lieberman, under investigation for corruption for the past several years, had gained notoriety with his plan to shift Israel's border westward in the central section of the country, heavily populated with Palestinian citizens, in order to deprive its Palestinian inhabitants of their Israeli citizenship. His main slogans in the 2009 elections were "no citizenship without loyalty" (implying that Israel's Palestinian citizens should be denied citizenship rights) and "Lieberman understands Arabic" (which, of course, he doesn't). In the new cabinet formed by Benjamin Netanyahu after the elections, Lieberman serves as foreign minister.

How has Israel's leadership shifted, in less than 20 years, from the duo of Nobel Peace Laureates, Yitzhak Rabin and Shimon Peres, to Benjamin Netanyahu and Avigdor Lieberman? In this chapter I offer an explanation based on an analysis of the citizenship discourse prevailing in Israeli political culture.[2]

Israel's citizenship discourse has consisted of three different layers, superimposed on one another: a republican discourse of community goals and civic virtue, a liberal discourse of civil, political and social rights, and an ethno-nationalist discourse of inclusion and exclusion.[3] Conceptually, since 1967 the differential allocation of entitlements, obligations and domination legitimated by these three discourses has proceeded in a number of stages. First, the liberal idea of citizenship functioned to separate the Jewish and Palestinian citizens of Israel from the non-citizen Palestinians in the occupied territories. Then the ethno-nationalist discourse was invoked to discriminate between Jewish and Palestinian citizens within the State of Israel. Lastly, the republican discourse was used to legitimate the different positions occupied by the major Jewish social groups: *ashkenazim* vs. *mizrachim*, males vs. females, secular vs. religiously orthodox.

Over time, the relations between the three discourses have changed, with the republican discourse dominant in the *yishuv* (pre-statehood Jewish community in Palestine) period and until 1977, the liberal and ethno-nationalist discourses contending for domination between 1977 and 2000, and these two discourses splitting the pie between them since 2000, with the liberal discourse dominant in the economy and the ethno-nationalist one in most other areas of social and political life.

The Ethno-Republican Incorporation Regime

The *yishuv* was an ethno-republican community organized to achieve a common moral purpose – the fulfillment of Zionism. Its pioneering civic virtue encompassed the two bases of legitimation invoked by the Zionist settlers: Jewish historical rights in Palestine and the redemptive activities of the pioneers: physical labor, agricultural settlement and military defense. Being a virtuous member of the *yishuv* meant being a Jew and engaging in those redemptive activities. Thus the foundation was laid for distinguishing between the citizenship not only of Jews and Arabs, but also of different groupings within the Jewish community, based on their presumed contributions to the project of Zionist redemption.

The *ashkenazi* Jewish settlers of the First *aliya* (1882–1903) relied on Palestinian farm workers who were much cheaper to employ than the Jewish immigrants who arrived from Europe in the Second *aliya* (1904–1914), lacking any experience in agricultural work. As a result, the latter adopted a new settlement strategy: the establishment, on nationally owned land, of a separate Jewish economic sector, employing only Jews, under the control of the Labor Zionist movement. This economic sector, with the *kibbutz* as its symbolic center, gradually developed into an economic empire encompassing, at its height, agricultural, industrial, construction, marketing, transportation and financial concerns, as well as a whole network of social service organizations. This conglomerate operated under the aegis of the *Histadrut* umbrella labor organization, and as long as Labor was in power (1933–1977), it enjoyed the support first of Zionist institutions and then of the state as well. At the same time, this economic infrastructure played a crucial role in maintaining the political and cultural hegemony of the Labor Zionist movement, thus ensuring the privileged position of a large segment of *ashkenazim.*

The dominant status of *ashkenazim* in Israeli society is usually attributed to their earlier settlement in the country. In actual fact, however, Jewish immigrants from Yemen arrived in Palestine at the same time as the *ashkenazi* founding fathers, and were expected to replace Palestinian workers in the Jewish-owned plantation colonies. Like their *ashkenazi* counterparts, however, the Yemenites also failed in this attempted "conquest of labor." But whereas the *ashkenazi* workers went on to make history by establishing cooperative and communal settlements, the Yemenites were relegated to the sidelines.

The different historical trajectories of the two groups of Jewish immigrants reflected the superior organizational ability of the *ashkenazim*, which placed them in a better position to procure resources from the World Zionist Organization, through the *Histadrut*. The *ashkenazim* legitimated their demands, however, by drawing a distinction between themselves, as "idealistic," and the Yemenites as "natural" workers. "Idealistic workers" were those who had forfeited the comforts of European urban life and the opportunity of migrating to America, and chose to become agricultural workers in Palestine instead. "Natural workers," on the other hand, were those "capable of performing hard work, living in uncomfortable circumstances … obedient … and above all – content with little" (Druyan 1981, p. 134). "Idealistic workers" were the stuff pioneers were made of, blazing the trail and setting moral standards for the community. "Natural workers," on the other hand, were to be foot soldiers in the Zionist campaign, adding "quantity" to the pioneers' "qualitative" efforts.

This distinction between "quality" and "quantity" proved to be of crucial importance in the 1950s and '60s, when the pioneers, now occupying all dominant positions in the society, had to deal with a massive influx of *mizrachi* immigrants. Thus, as Jews immigrating under the Law of Return, *mizrachim* were granted all civil and political rights. At the same time, however, they were socially marginalized: sent to settle in border areas and in towns deserted by Palestinians in 1948, to beef up the military, and to provide unskilled labor for the country's industrialization drive. The resultant "ethnic gap" between *ashkenazim* and *mizrachim* has persisted, and in some respects even widened, to this day (Cohen 2002, p. 51).

The democratic tradition of the *yishuv*, the vital integrative function of the uniform rule of law, and the keen interest shown by the international community in the new country's affairs, all combined in 1948 to ensure the universal grant of citizenship to all residents of Israel, Jews and Palestinians alike. Thus, the 160,000 Palestinians who had remained in the territory of the State of Israel at the conclusion of the 1948 Arab–Israeli war were granted Israeli citizenship, or were allowed to apply for it under certain conditions. Until 1966, however, they were ruled through a military administration "which imposed severe restrictions on their freedom of movement and economic opportunities, and placed them under surveillance and military law" (Medding 1990, p. 25). The military administration was opposed by some Jewish Israelis, either because it violated the Palestinians' citizenship rights or because it was seen as an electoral instrument in the hands of the ruling party, *Mapai*, which repeatedly garnered the lion's share of the Palestinian vote. In response to this opposition, many of the restrictive regulations of the military administration had been gradually relaxed, beginning in the late 1950s. Its final abolition, however, came only in December 1966, following the development of labor shortages in the (Jewish) labor market due to the country's rapid industrialization.

Since the abolition of the military administration, Palestinian citizens have enjoyed political rights on an individual, liberal basis. They have been excluded, however, from political citizenship in the republican sense; that is, from participating in attending to the common good of society. In 1985 an amendment to *Basic Law: The Knesset* provided for the possibility of barring political parties that challenged Israel's definition as a Jewish state from participating in Knesset elections. A similar provision was made for parties challenging Israel's democratic character or inciting to racism, reinforcing the Palestinian citizens' liberal rights. (So far only extreme right-wing Jewish political parties have been actually barred under this amendment.) The state has also consistently refused to recognize the Palestinian citizens as a national minority deserving of any kind of collective rights (Jamal, 2007).

As to social rights, these have been tied in Israel, in truly republican manner, to the performance of military service. Since most Palestinian citizens are not called up (by administrative practice, rather than by law), this exemption has been used to justify the abridgement of their social rights. Moreover, the institution of an alternative form of national service for the Palestinian citizens (which has been done in the case of religious Jewish women) has not been attempted until very recently. Since it was instituted, this civil service has been fiercely opposed by practically the entire Palestinian intellectual, religious, and political leadership, because they see it as undermining Palestinian national identity. However, according to an extensive attitude survey conducted in the citizen-Palestinian population, around 70% of the respondents, including young people eligible for the civil service, expressed support for that service (Smooha 2008: 19).

As the struggle over land is the crux of the frontier situation, most Palestinian-owned land within the State of Israel has been expropriated and turned over to national (Jewish) ownership. This has eliminated much of the Palestinians' subsistence agriculture and redirected the rest towards cash crop production for the Jewish market. No significant Palestinian industry or modern financial or commercial sectors are in existence and, consequently, half of the Palestinian labor force needs to seek employment in the Jewish sector. Thus, while the expansion of the Israeli economy has raised the overall standard of living of most Palestinian citizens, it has also widened the gap between them and Israeli Jews. To illustrate, in 2003–2004 45% of Palestinian families, as against 15% of Jewish families, were below the official poverty line, *after* taxes and transfer payments; a Palestinian elementary school student received 1.51 weekly hours of instruction from the state, as against 1.87 hours for a Jewish student; in Palestinian cities there was one professional medical clinic per 29,500 residents, whereas in Jewish cities there was one per 15,500 residents (Sikkuy, 2003–2004, p. 55).

The Palestinian population in the occupied West Bank and the besieged Gaza Strip has lived under military occupation since 1967 and possesses no effective civil, political, or social rights. Palestinian residents of the occupied territories are neither citizens nor members of Israeli society. For about 35 years they functioned as Israel's metics: a cheap and flexible labor force and captive consumers and tax payers. Since 1993, and especially since 2000, they have been excluded from the Israeli labor market as well.

Since 1967, about two-thirds of the land in the West Bank has been declared "state land," and much of it has been allocated for Jewish settlement. Most of the water resources in that area have also been diverted to Jewish use, either in the West Bank itself or in Israel (Selby, 2003). According to the World Bank:

> Forty years of occupation in WBG [West Bank and Gaza] has [sic] left a heavily distorted economy in a state that is almost completely dependent on the Israeli economy ... The size of the average industrial enterprise is about four workers, no larger than it was in 1927 ... It was hoped that with limited autonomy arising from the Oslo Accords of September 1993, the Palestinian private sector would take off ... Unfortunately, this did not materialize and the economy has suffered even more since Oslo (World Bank 2007, p. i).

On the other hand, generous state subsidies have nourished the Jewish settlement project in the West Bank. The settlers have appropriated Labor Zionism's pioneering ethos and applied it, mostly under a religious garb, in the newly conquered territories. Their efforts have been facilitated by the provision of "state" (that is, formerly Palestinian-owned) land at below-market prices and substantial loans at very favorable terms. Jewish settlers in the occupied territories have also enjoyed the protection of Israeli civil law, while the Palestinian residents have been subjected to arbitrary and oppressive military rule. Moreover, Israeli law enforcement authorities in the occupied territories have been extremely lenient toward crimes committed by Jewish settlers against their Palestinian neighbors.

According to B'Tselem, an Israeli human rights organization, between December 1987 and March 2001 Israeli civilians killed 119 Palestinians in the Occupied Territories. In some cases, the police did not investigate the killings at all, and nearly one-half of the cases that were investigated were closed for failure to locate a suspect or obtain sufficient evidence. In most cases where the defendants were convicted, they were found guilty of manslaughter or negligent homicide, and were given light sentences. In the vast majority of the murder convictions the sentences actually served were considerably shorter than those meted out by the court.

> "The failure of the law-enforcement system and the contempt for human life are particularly conspicuous when a comparison is made with the handling of cases in which Palestinians killed Israeli civilians. This comparison reveals flagrant discrimination" (B'Tselem 2001, pp. 42–43).

The privileged position of the settlers is understandable in view of their "qualitative" contribution to the Zionist project – historical continuity and pioneering commitment – as well as their demographic presence in the occupied territories. More puzzling is the fact that the ultra-orthodox, anti-, or at least non-Zionist communities have been granted privileges beyond any proportion to their numbers or electoral strength. Unlike religious Zionists, the ultra-orthodox do not serve in the military, nor do they perform any other pioneering activity. Their privileged position stems, then, exclusively from their service as living symbols of Jewish historical continuity in the Land of Israel.

Claiming to speak in the name of a worldwide Jewish *nation*, both internally and externally, the Zionist movement required at least the tacit approval of those universally recognized as the Jewish spokesmen – the orthodox rabbis. But, with the exception of a small orthodox-Zionist faction, until after the Second World War most rabbis remained anti-Zionist. The Zionists' need to cater to the orthodox dictated, firstly, the choice of *Eretz Yisrael* as the movement's target territory (which was in dispute until Herzl's death in 1904), and then the use of a whole array of religious Jewish symbols and other cultural constructs. While different tendencies in Zionism have tried, in varying degrees, to endow these traditional themes with secular national meanings, they could never be purged of their original religious content.

Even more significant than the cultural subservience of secular Zionism to Judaism has been the active promotion of religious institutions, some of them openly anti-Zionist, and the concessions made to orthodox Jewish parties in several major areas of legislation and public policy. These include the recognition and financing of autonomous orthodox educational systems; the virtual monopoly given to rabbinic courts (and to religious courts of the non-Jewish communities) in matters of personal status; exemptions from military service granted to orthodox women and *yeshiva* students; and the use of religious criteria for determining who is a Jew for the purpose of state law.

The near-monopoly enjoyed by religious courts over matters of personal status has endowed that law with a pronounced pro-male bias. This is manifested in marriage, divorce and alimony laws that discriminate against women, in an intrusive and restrictive (though not prohibitive) abortion law, and in an unquestioned adoption of the traditional patriarchal model of the family as normative.

The effects of official, public religiosity mesh with militarism and with Jewish demographic anxieties to confine women to their traditional role as mothers and homemakers. As a frontier society, Jewish society in Israel has valued military service as the highest form of civic virtue, and has also been greatly concerned with the demographic balance between Jews and Palestinians. This has led not only to almost frantic efforts to induce Jews, or anyone with one Jewish grandparent, to immigrate to Israel, but also to powerful ideological efforts to encourage fertility among Jewish women.

This emphasis on maternity as women's prime contribution to the common good of society has had devastating effects on women's struggle for equality.

Liberalization and Its Discontents

The differentiated citizenship structure described so far resulted from, facilitated, and depended upon a highly intrusive but formally democratic state, engaged in intensive mobilization and control of societal resources. Over the years, however, the country's economic development, funded to a very large extent by unilateral transfers, had weakened the state's and the *Histadrut*'s control over the economy in favor of private business interests. This sectoral shift manifested itself in policy changes that began as early as the late 1960s, in the field of arms production, and were gradually intensified over the following two decades, enhanced by the 1979 peace treaty with Egypt. Under the Labor government of 1992–1996, drastic neo-liberal reforms were instituted in key areas of the economy and society.

The economic, social and political values reflected in these reforms were rooted in the liberal discourse of citizenship, rather than in the ethno-republican discourse of pioneering civic virtue. The social group responsible for, and benefiting from, these changes was mostly upper-middle class *ashkenazim*, who were interested in jumping on the bandwagon of economic globalization. But the international opportunities open to Israeli businesses were limited because of the Arab–Israeli conflict. The Arab boycott and general considerations of economic and political expediency made cooperation with Israel risky for many foreign companies. For 20 years the occupied Palestinian territories provided a partial substitute for the international market and a clandestine trade outlet to the Arab world. But the economic benefits of the occupation – a cheap and reliable labor supply and a captive market – were sharply reduced by the first *intifada* (1988–1993). By the late 1980s the economic costs of the occupation had come to overshadow its benefits.

For these reasons, settling the conflict – decolonizing portions of the occupied territories through accommodation with the PLO – became an economic necessity for the Israeli business community. Its support for the peace process was thus motivated by two principal considerations: reducing the size of the state and weakening the *Histadrut*, and integrating into the international economy. After the Oslo Accords, many foreign markets, in the Middle East and beyond, had indeed opened up to Israeli capital, while direct foreign investment in the Israeli economy skyrocketed, leading to unprecedented economic prosperity.

The turn toward peace did not occur, however, due to "pull" factors only. There was an important "push" factor involved in it as well, namely the first *intifada*. The *intifada* strained the resources of the state, both materially and morally, while the state's mobilizational capacity was being undermined by economic and social liberalization. Israel lost about 2%–2.5% of its gross domestic product (about one billion US dollars) in 1988–89 due to the *intifada*. After 1989 the Israeli economy adjusted itself successfully to the new situation and entered a period of economic growth due, primarily, to massive immigration from the former Soviet Union.

The political effects of the *intifada* were longer lasting. The uprising resurrected the Green Line (pre-1967 border) in the consciousness of most Israelis. This highlighted the failure of the efforts, led since 1977 by Likud governments, to establish the inseparability of the West Bank and Gaza from Israel as a hegemonic notion in Israeli political culture (Lustick 1993). As personal security for Jews deteriorated on both sides of the Green Line, the argument that holding on to the occupied territories was essential for Israel's security also lost much of its force.

Morally, the brutally oppressive methods used by Israel's security forces to try and suppress the first *intifada* (that were mild in comparison with the methods to be used in the second *intifada*), forced the Israeli public to face, in a way it never had to do before, the discrepancy between the two systems of rule prevailing on both sides of the Green Line. This resulted in growing support for withdrawal from the occupied territories, and even in the appearance of a small movement of primarily reserve soldiers refusing to take part in policing them.

Ethno-Nationalist Opposition to Liberalization

Both liberalization in general and the peace process in particular generated powerful opposing forces in Israeli society. Jewish settlers in the occupied territories and their supporters openly and violently opposed the decolonization of the Palestinian territories. No less important was the opposition to liberalization as a whole among large segments of the Jewish public, for both economic and cultural reasons.

Economically, liberalization resulted in rapidly increasing income inequality. While initially the loss of economic income by the lower socio-economic strata was mitigated by transfer payments, social services came under a great deal of political pressure. As a result, education and healthcare had deteriorated significantly for those who could not afford to privately supplement the declining services provided by the state. The opposition to economic liberalization was articulated not in economic terms, however, but in cultural and political ones, due to three factors:

1 Economic policy had not been at issue between the major political parties at least since the mid-1980s. The first successful liberalization program was launched in 1985, by a national unity government in which Labor and Likud were equal partners. (The fault line regarding economic policy fell *within* the Labor party, between its parliamentary and *Histadrut* wings.) With no major political, social or intellectual force in society offering an alternative economic analysis, the opposition to neo-liberal economics

could be expressed only in moral terms. This meant, almost inevitably, that it would be expressed in terms of the ethno-nationalist discourse.

2 *Mizrachim* have not formed a peripheral, but rather a semi-peripheral, group in Israeli society, located between the *ashkenazi* Jews on top, and the Palestinians, both citizens and non-citizens, at the bottom. Being in this intermediary position, *mizrachim* have naturally sought to ally themselves with the Jewish state and with the *ashkenazim* who control it, rather than with the Palestinians, with whom they share many economic and cultural characteristics. Generally speaking, *mizrachim* have therefore conceptualized their marginalization in cultural, rather than class or ethnic terms, and have asserted their Jewishness, the one quality they share with the *ashkenazim*, as the basis for their claims of social and economic equality.

3 Culturally, liberalization entailed, first and foremost, secularization. All of the elements of the religious status quo that had traditionally prevailed in Israel – the monopoly of Rabbinic courts in matters of family law, observance of the Sabbath and of *kashrut* (Jewish dietary law) in the public sphere, and the exemption of *yeshiva* students from military service – had been challenged by liberal, secular Jews. These challengers had found important allies in the liberal Supreme Court and in the one million immigrants from the former USSR, many of whom were not Jewish by the orthodox religious definition. In addition, women's rights, tolerance for diverse sexual lifestyles, cultural Americanization and the growing political assertiveness of Israel's Palestinian citizens have all contributed to the anxiety of the more traditional elements in society, comprised largely of lower-class *mizrachim*.

Shas, a political party founded in 1984, with the onset of economic liberalization, has successfully mobilized lower-class *mizrachim* with a message of Jewish solidarity and the restoration of traditional Jewish values. It accompanied this message with rhetoric of social justice and with an impressive array of social service institutions of its own. It presented no alternative economic vision, however, and has consistently voted, after some bargaining, for every neo-liberal economic measure enacted by the government.

For its first fifteen years, SHAS assumed a relatively moderate position with regard to the Israeli-Palestinian conflict, and sought to have constructive relations with Israel's Palestinian citizens. This attitude reflected the political preferences of much of the party elite, but was almost diametrically opposed to the views of its voters. Since 1999, with the Oslo process reaching its moment of truth at Camp David and then collapsing, the party's attitude towards the Palestinians, both citizens and non-citizens, has become aligned with that of its voters (Peled 2001; Chetrit, 2004).

The Decline of Political Liberalism

The outbreak of the second *intifada* in September 2000, following the failure of the Camp David summit in July, and Ariel Sharon's highly militarized visit to the Temple Mount/Haram-al-Sharif, highlighted the role played by the Israeli military in shaping the country's policy toward the Arabs. In the first three weeks of the uprising the Israeli army shot one million bullets at largely unarmed Palestinian demonstrators. As a result, the kill ratio at the beginning of the *intifada* was 75 dead Palestinians to four dead Israelis. (The desire to even out this ratio was a major reason behind the Palestinians' decision to renew suicide bombings in March 2001.) According to journalist Ben Kaspit, who first reported these numbers, this violent reaction was not authorized by the government but reflected, rather, the policy of the military high command itself (Kaspit, 2002).

At the same time, the national police acted in essentially the same manner toward Israel's Palestinian *citizens*. As a result, thirteen Palestinian demonstrators were killed by police inside the borders of the State of Israel. (One Jewish motorist was also killed, by citizen Palestinian demonstrators, during the same period.) The Or Commission, appointed to investigate these events, concluded that the police had acted as an independent agent, shooting unarmed demonstrators with rubber-coated bullets and live ammunition, in contravention of the law and of its own internal guidelines. This illegal behavior was not authorized by the government, which was either unable or unwilling to stop it (Peled, 2005).

Until Likud's return to power in 2001, as a direct result of these events, the project of dismantling the welfare state had been stymied by path dependency, lack of resolve on the part of political elites, and concern over the possibility of massive popular discontent. While the Gini coefficient for overall inequality rose from 0.498 in 1993 to 0.528 in 2002 (with a particularly sharp increase of 0.019 between 2001 and 2002), inequality of *disposable* income (which reflects taxes and transfer payments, in addition to economic income) was much more moderate, rising from 0.339 in 1993 to 0.350 in 2001 and 0.357 in 2002.[4] The percentage of families whose economic income was lower than the poverty line (50% of the median income) remained stable throughout this period at around 34%, up from 28% in 1980 (Swirski and Konnor Attias, 2003; Arian et al., 2003; Shalev, 2003).

The burst of the hi-tech bubble, the global economic slowdown and, most importantly, the breakdown of the Oslo process, plunged the Israeli economy into deep recession. Per capita GDP decreased by 3.2% in 2001, 2.8% in 2002, and 0.5% in 2003. The recession, coupled with a sharp increase in military spending due to the *intifada*, was used to justify six rounds of budget cuts, budget realignments and structural economic changes between September 2001 and September 2003. In overall monetary terms, the state budget was cut by nearly 20%. The cumulative effects of these budget cuts and structural changes harmed the interests of workers and, increasingly,

of the middle class (Swirski and Konnor Attias, 2007). The levels of employment, wages, unionization, social services and transfer payments declined,
while the security of retirement plans was eroded.

The new economic policy was greatly beneficial, however, to the upper
layers of the business community. It has granted them lower labor costs,
greater labor market "flexibility," and lower taxes. As a result, the profits of
the top 25 companies traded on the Tel Aviv Stock Exchange tripled between
2002 and 2003, and those of the major banks have increased by 350 percent.
In 2003, the salaries of these banks' top executives were 50 times higher
than those of their tellers, and 100 times higher than the minimum wage
(Kaplan 2004). With such an economic bonanza provided by the state, it is
unsurprising that Israel's top capitalists have preferred not to rock the boat
and remained silent on the issues of peace and non-economic liberalization.

The first few years of the new millennium marked the erosion not only of
social citizenship rights, but also of the civil and political rights of Israel's
Palestinian citizens. In July 2003 the Knesset enacted the Citizenship and
Entry into Israel Law (Temporary Order) that prohibited the granting of
residency or citizenship in Israel to Palestinians from the occupied territories, even those who are married to Israeli citizens or have Israeli citizens
for parents or children. The duration of the law was to be for one year, but
it has been extended repeatedly since then.

Prior to the enactment of this law, "foreign" (i.e. non-Jewish, non-Israeli)
spouses of Israeli citizens had to go through a graduated process of naturalization lasting four-and-a-half years, from the time the Israeli spouse applied
for family unification to the time the foreign spouse could be granted
Israeli citizenship. During this time the foreign spouse was examined on
a yearly basis to ensure that he or she did not pose a criminal or security
risk to the country (and, of course, that the marriage was a legitimate one).
This arrangement is still in force for non-Palestinian foreign spouses of
Israeli citizens.[5]

The new citizenship law established, for the first time, an explicit, if only
consequential, distinction between the citizenship rights of Jewish and
Palestinian citizens, because only Palestinian citizens are likely to marry
non-citizen Palestinians from the occupied territories. The state did not deny
that the new law infringed the rights of its Palestinian citizens to equality
and to family unification, but justified this infringement as a security measure, designed to prevent Palestinian terrorists from entering the country.
This argument, however, rested on shaky empirical grounds, as very few
Palestinians who had entered Israel through family unification have ever
been alleged to be involved with hostile activities. Still, when the constitu-
tionality of the law was challenged in the High Court of Justice, the Court
upheld it by a 6:5 majority (HCJ 7052/03; Peled 2007a).

Opponents of the law, and even some of the High Court justices, attributed its enactment to demographic, rather than security considerations.
And, indeed, talk of the demographic danger posed by the Palestinian

citizens had become much more salient since the outbreak of the second *intifada* in 2000. Another manifestation of this heightened demographic fear was the appointment of Avigdor Lieberman, the promoter of a plan to deprive 200,000 Palestinian citizens of their citizenship by moving Israel's eastern border westward in the mid-section of the country, as Deputy Prime Minister (Peled 2007a; 2007b). Verbal attacks on Palestinian members of the Knesset, as disloyal to the state, have also intensified, culminating in the accusation that the most intellectually prominent among them, Dr. Azmi Bishara, had collaborated with Hizballah during Israel's failed campaign in Lebanon in the summer of 2006. In the wake of this still informal accusation, Bishara opted to leave the country, rather than face a long stay in prison while the allegations against him are being examined in court.

Conclusion

In the two-and-a-half decades since the economic turnaround of 1985, Israeli society has gone through two profound transformations: 1) from a corporatist, relatively egalitarian society in conflict with its Arab neighbors to a more liberal, highly inegalitarian society seeking accommodation with them; and 2) to an even more harshly inegalitarian society engaged in an open-ended war with the Palestinians. The republican discourse of citizenship, that had legitimated the corporatist socio-economic regime and served as the basis of Jewish solidarity, has lost its position of prominence. The two other discourses of citizenship have each become prominent in one area of social life – the liberal discourse in the economy, and the ethno-nationalist discourse in politics. This duality has resulted in declining political stability, with six national elections and seven Prime Ministers (including Yitzhak Rabin, who was assassinated in 1995) since the signing of the Oslo Accords in 1993.

Until Ariel Sharon's accession in 2001, it was widely believed that Israel had to choose between economic liberalization and accommodation with the Palestinians, on the one hand, and continuing occupation and a welfare state, on the other. Sharon tried to cut that Gordian knot and pursue economic liberalization and war simultaneously. The price he was willing to pay was the withdrawal of Israel's military forces and Jewish settlements from the Gaza Strip and parts of the West Bank. His idea, however, was not to relinquish control of the Palestinian territories and population, but to make that control more cost effective. Sharon's scheme would have backfired with him at the helm too, because it failed to address the basic contradiction of a self-defined democracy ruling over a large population deprived of all citizenship rights. His exit from the political arena in 2006, due to a stroke, expedited the arrival of the moment of truth.

Ehud Olmert, who succeeded Sharon as prime minister, promised to pursue Sharon's "disengagement" plan, then shifted, rhetorically, back to the old idea of a "two-state solution." As it turned out, however, he pursued neither of these strategies, and only led Israel into two highly controversial military operations, in Lebanon in 2006 and in Gaza in 2009, before leaving office under indictment for political corruption. While Olmert's political party, *Kadima*, lost only one Knesset seat in the general elections that ensued, it was unable to form a governing coalition and remains, at the time of writing, the main opposition party.

The accumulated ills of the occupation of the Palestinian territories, coupled with the devastation wrought by neo-liberal economic policy, have caused most Israeli Jews to mistrust political parties that even pretend to hold moderate views on the Israeli–Palestinian conflict. While the booming economy (that withstood the current global crisis) and the country's high international standing, due to the global "war on terror" (Klein 2007), cause 80% of Israeli Jews to feel good about their present state of affairs, a deep crisis of legitimation is revealed when their level of trust in the society's major institutions is examined. On the eve of Israel's 61st anniversary, in 2009, only the military enjoyed the high level of trust – 91% – it has traditionally enjoyed, with all other institutions faring markedly worse: the Supreme Court 57%, the mass media 43%, the police 39%, the executive branch 34%, the Knesset 30%, and the political parties 21% (Yaar and Hermann 2009). Interestingly, the three most representative institutions – the executive, the legislature and the political parties – fare worst in terms of public trust among Israeli Jews. This may explain, at least partially, the success of Avigdor Lieberman, widely believed to be a strong man and a straight talker.

Lieberman, who seems to be calling the shots in the Netanyahu administration, has already announced that the two-state solution was dead, that negotiations with the Palestinians, that began (again) in September 2010, would not lead to an agreement, that Syria was not a partner for peace, and that the Obama administration would accept whatever Israel threw its way. He may be right on some of these points, and able to determine the others. With no credible opposition in the Knesset, and with a Jewish public that has tired of liberal ideas, except in the economy, Lieberman may be the face of Israel's future.

Notes

1 Together with its liberal sister party, Meretz, Labor now has sixteen Knesset seats, down from 56 seats in 1992.
2 The following two sections of this chapter are mostly based on Shafir and Peled 2002. For detailed bibliographical references please consult that book.
3 The presence of these three discourses of citizenship in the political culture is not unique to Israel, of course. For a similar argument regarding the US see Smith 1997.
4 The Gini coefficient is a measure of statistical dispersion most prominently used as a measure of inequality of income or wealth distribution. It is defined as a ratio, with values between zero and one: zero corresponds to perfect equality (everyone having exactly the same income) and 1 corresponds to perfect inequality (one person has all the income, while everyone else has zero income).

5 Curiously, while Israeli citizens do not have an explicitly stated right to bring in their "foreign" spouse, child or parent into the country, non-citizen Jews immigrating under the Law of Return, as amended in 1970, do have that right, down to the third generation.

References

Arian, A., Nachmias, D., Navot, D., and Shani, D. (2003) *Democracy in Israel: 2003 Follow Up Report, "Democracy Index" Project* (Jerusalem: The Israel Democracy Institute) (Hebrew).

B'tselem: The Israeli Information Center For Human Rights In The Occupied Territories (2001) *Tacit Consent: Israeli Policy On Law Enforcement Toward Settlers In The Occupied Territories* (Jerusalem) (Hebrew).

Chetrit, S. (2004) *The Mizrahi Struggle in Israel: Between Oppression and Liberation, Identification and Alternative, 1948–2003* (Tel Aviv: Am Oved) (Hebrew).

Cohen, Y. (2002) "From a Country of Refuge to a Country of Choice: Changing Patterns of Immigration to Israel," *Israeli Sociology*, 4:1, pp. 39–60 (Hebrew).

Druyan, N. (1981) *Without a Magic Carpet: Yemenite Settlement in Eretz Israel (1881–1914)* (Jerusalem: Ben-Zvi Institute) (Hebrew).

HCJ 7052/03, *Adallah v. Minister of the Interior* [2006] 2 TakEl 1754.

Jamal, A. (2007) "Nationalizing States and the Constitution of 'Hollow Citizenship': Israel and its Palestinian Citizens," *Ethnopolitics*, 6:4, pp. 471–93.

Kaplan R. (2004) www.hevra.org.il, accessed April 7, 2004 (Hebrew).

Kaspit, B. (2002) "Two Years of the Intifada," *Ma`ariv*, September 6 and 13, pp. 8–11, 32 and 6–10, respectively (Hebrew).

Klein, N. (2007) "Political Chaos Means Israel Is Booming Like It's 1999," *The Guardian*, June 16.

Lustick, I. (1993) *Unsettled State, Disputed Lands: Britain and Ireland, France and Algeria, Israel and the West Bank-Gaza* (Ithaca: Cornell UP).

Medding, P. Y. (1990) *The Founding of Israeli Democracy, 1948–1967* (NY: OUP).

Peled, Y., ed. (2001) *Shas: The Challenge of Israeliness* (Tel Aviv: Yediot Aharonot) (Hebrew).

Peled, Y. (2005) "The Or Commission and Palestinian Citizenship in Israel," *Citizenship Studies*, 9:1, pp. 89–105.

Peled, Y. (2007a) "Citizenship Betrayed: Israel's Emerging Immigration and Citizenship Regime," *Theoretical Inquiries in Law*, 8:2, pp. 333–358.

Peled, Y. (2007b) "Towards a Post-Citizenship Society? A Report from the Front," *Citizenship Studies*, 11:1, pp. 95–104.

Selby, J. (2003) *Water, Power and Politics in the Middle East: The Other Israeli-Palestinian Conflict* (London: IB Tauris).

Shafir, G. and Peled Y. (2002) *Being Israeli: The Dynamics of Multiple Citizenship* (Cambridge: CUP).

Shalev, M. (2003) "Placing Class Politics in Context: Why is Israel's Welfare State so Consensual?" presented at the conference *Changing European Societies – the Role for Social Policy*, Copenhagen, 13–15 November.

Sikkuy, 2003–2004. *Sikkuy Report*, www.sikkuy.org.il/

Smith, R. (1997) *Civic Ideals: Conflicting Visions of Citizenship in US History* (New Haven: Yale UP).

Smooha, Sammy (with Nuhad Ali) (2008) Civil Service for the Arabs in Israel:

Findings of an Attitude Survey Among the Arab Public and Leaders, Fall 2007 (Haifa: Haifa University) (Hebrew).

Swirski, S. and Konnor-Attias, E. (2003) *Social Report – 2003* (Tel Aviv: Adva Center) (Hebrew).

Swirski, S. and Konnor-Attias, E. (2007) *The Shrinking of the Middle Class in Israel: Update to 2005* (Tel Aviv: Adva Center) (Hebrew).

World Bank, 2007. *West Bank And Gaza Investment Climate Assessment: Unlocking The Potential Of The Private Sector* (Report No. 39109 – GZ).

Yaar, Ephraim and Hermann, Tamar, *War and Peace Index April 2009*, Tel Aviv University, Tami Steinmetz Center for Peace Research, www.tau.ac.il:80/peace.

Index